Managing and Leasing Commercial Properties

ALAN A. ALEXANDER, CPM, CSM, CRE

RICHARD F. MUHLEBACH, CPM, CSM, CRE, RPA

WILEY

JOHN WILEY AND SONS

New York • Chichester • Brisbane • Toronto • Singapore

Library of Congress Cataloging-in-Publication Data

Alexander, Alan A.
  Managing and leasing commercial properties.

  Includes bibliographical references.
  1. Real estate management. 2. Commercial buildings—
Management. 3. Commercial leases. 4. Building leases.
I. Muhlebach, Richard F., 1943–   II. Title.
HD1394.A55   1989   333.33′8   89-24961
ISBN 0-471-62415-2

To my loving wife and partner, Jeanne,
whose dedication, love, and support
make endeavors such as this book possible.

A. A. A.

To my parents, Frank and Flora,
who instilled in me the work ethic
to be a property manager.

To my children, Kathy and Eric,
who have shared the life of a property manager.
And especially to my loving wife, Maria,
who, for over 20 years, has always been
with me when I needed her.

R. F. M.

Preface

Managing and Leasing Commercial Properties addresses the number one issue in property management in the 1990s—enhancing value. This book provides practical and successful techniques for a proactive approach to managing, marketing, and leasing commercial properties. This is not a book on the theory of property management; it is a practical, hands-on approach. The reader, whether a property manager, asset manager, portfolio manager, leasing agent, developer, or investor will be able to immediately implement management, marketing, and leasing techniques after reading the relevant chapters. The information is provided in a logical sequence that takes the reader through the process of managing and leasing a commercial property.

A third of Managing and Leasing Commercial Properties is devoted to marketing and leasing. Greater opportunities exist to enhance value by increasing the property's income than by reducing expenses. The chapter on leasing explains how to develop, implement, and administrate an effective leasing program.

Management techniques common to the management of every type of commercial property are discussed in chapters on budgeting, maintenance management, and emergency procedures.

Specific management techniques for shopping centers, office buildings, and industrial properties are discussed in three chapters.

A history of commercial property management and the state of the industry is reviewed in the opening chapter. This is followed by a chapter reviewing the operations of a property management company.

This book was written as a day-by-day, hands-on guide that the real estate manager, whether a property manager, asset manager, or leasing agent, will return to time and again to find answers, proactive management and leasing approaches, and useful forms. In addition, the book offers the philosophy that managing the real estate asset is a profession that involves managing and successfully dealing with people rather than managing brick and mortar, steel, and concrete. Following this approach to managing real estate assets, all transactions must be good for everyone involved for the property to be successful.

ALAN A. ALEXANDER
RICHARD F. MUHLEBACH

San Francisco, CA
Bellevue, WA
October, 1989

Acknowledgments

A special acknowledgment to Karin Grice and Margaret Morris for their invaluable assistance in the preparation of this book.

The authors are grateful for the knowledge and insight they gained through their association with Robert Parks, TRF Pacific; John D. Lusk, The Lusk Company; Alan Levy, Tishman West Management Corp.; Harry Newman, Newman Properties; Stephen Roger, Aldrich Eastman and Waltch, Inc.; William Stites, Ferguson and Burdell; Tom Jackson, Hall-Conway-Jackson; and William Steele, American Building Maintenance.

A special debt of gratitude is owed to the Institute of Real Estate Management, the International Council of Shopping Centers, and the Building Owners and Managers Association for their excellent educational programs and outstanding publications that have played an important role in formulating the management philosophy of both of the authors.

A.A.A.
R.F.M.

About the Authors

ALAN A. ALEXANDER, CPM, CSM, CRE, is president of Alexander Consultants, San Bruno, California, which specializes in the managing, leasing, developing, and consulting of income-producing properties. Currently the firm's projects include office buildings, apartment complexes, and shopping centers. He has provided problem-solving consultation on properties throughout the United States. He is the former senior vice-president of Fox & Carskadon Management Corporation with responsibilities for a portfolio of properties worth in excess of $100 million dollars in four western states. As director of leasing for Fox & Carskadon Financial, Mr. Alexander was responsible for the leasing of all shopping centers owned by the company throughout the United States. Mr. Alexander is on the national faculty of the Institute of Real Estate Management and is a frequent speaker at the International Council of Shopping Center Programs. He has been the moderator and speaker for over 200 seminars on developing and management and leasing of shopping centers and small office buildings for the Northwest Center for Professional Education. He is the author of several articles published in the Journal of Property Management and is a contributing author of the book *Managing the Shopping Center* published by the Institute of Real Estate Management. Mr. Alexander was inducted into the Academy of Authors of the Institute of Real Estate Management in February 1984. He is the past president of the San Francisco Bay Area Chapter of the Institute of Real Estate Management.

RICHARD F. MUHLEBACH, CPM, CSM, CRE, RPA, has over 20 years experience in managing and leasing commercial and residential properties. In his early years in property management, he served as an on-site general manager for a regional mall, an office building, and a major mixed-use

ix

development. In the mid-1970s, he served as project manager for converting a distressed open regional center into a successful enclosed mall. He developed and is currently president of TRF Management Corporation in Bellevue, Washington. He is also vice-president of leasing for TRF Pacific, developers of commercial properties on the West Coast and in Alaska.

His prior responsibilities were vice-president of Tishman West Management Corp. and vice-president of the Lusk Company in California. He is a senior instructor for the Institute of Real Estate Management and an instructor for the International Council of Shopping Centers.

Mr. Muhlebach has written over 30 articles in numerous real estate journals and he is a member of the Institute of Real Estate Management's Academy of Authors. He is a Certified Property Manager, Certified Shopping Center Manager, Counselor of Real Estate, Real Property Administrator, and he taught real estate management at the college level.

Contents

9   Maintenance Management   370

One

Introduction

Property management has evolved during the twentieth century from a role of caretaker to a profession with responsibility for creating or enhancing value in real estate.

At the turn of the century, property management was limited primarily to rent collection and maintenance. The property manager's role did not change significantly until after World War II, when vacancies reached a level of concern to property owners. At that point, the manager's responsibilities were expanded to include renting and leasing.

Historically, property management was not considered a leading position in real estate. That changed in the early 1970s, when REITs (Real Estate Investment Trusts) and syndications became the popular method of purchasing income-producing real estate. These arrangements were very successful, and within a few years the real estate market was glutted with them. In their competition to purchase property, many REITs and syndicators overpaid for properties and miscalculated their income and expense projections. Thousands of properties across the country were foreclosed. Banks and other institutions became owners of scores of problem properties. These lenders looked to property managers for merchandising, leasing, and renting expertise to assist in turning around their distressed properties. Property management was no longer perceived as a secondary position.

The commercial real estate market continued to improve in the mid to late 1970s. This was one of the best times in the history of the shopping center industry. Although the office building market had been soft, by the end of the decade vacancies were down to 1% or 2% in several metropolitan areas. Industrial development, especially high-tech developments, also flourished during the late 1970s. During this period, the property manager's role was focusing on management, operations, and energy conservation.

In the early 1980s, the market picture was different for office buildings than it was for shopping centers. The hot market in commercial real estate was office buildings, which were being built at an astounding rate. During that same period, shopping center development and leasing experienced its most difficult time. Double-digit interest rates, which eventually reached 25%, prevented the small business person from borrowing money to start or expand a business. The recession slowed sales, and the early 1980s saw the greatest number of business failures since the Great Depression.

It was inevitable that the office building boom of the early 1980s would result in the worst office building market in history. By 1983, the office vacancy factor ranged from 15 to 25% in most metropolitan and suburban areas. The office building market improved over the next few years but still experienced a vacancy factor of 10 to 20% in almost all areas of the country.

The shopping center market improved during the mid-1980s. By the late 1980s, most areas of the country were still overbuilt with shopping centers; however, there were several areas, such as southern California, where shopping center development was booming. The industrial and high-tech markets were generally overbuilt during the 1980s.

Entering the 1990s most metropolitan areas are still overbuilt in office buildings. The shopping center market is mixed, with considerably less development activity than occurred during the seventies and eighties. The industrial and high-tech markets are improving but are also overbuilt in most areas.

§ 1.2   NEW BREED OF OWNERS

In the early 1980s, it was virtually impossible for developers to obtain traditional financing for a project. Obtaining 100%, 90%, or even 80% financing at interest rates below 10% was impossible. To continue to operate and build projects, developers either participated in joint ventures with an institution that provided most or all of the funds to develop the project, or they obtained a loan at an interest rate below market and provided the lender with a percentage of the equity or cash flow and appreciation of the property.

Property managers who worked for developers now also reported to the developer's institutional partner. When the office building market was overbuilt in the mid-1980s and rents were 25% below pro forma, many institutional partners became sole owners of buildings. If the developers were unable to contribute their share of the cash call to support the building's deficits, their equity positions were reduced. In many cases, the developer's position was eliminated, although the developer continued to manage and lease the project. This is the primary reason why relatively few foreclosures of medium to large commercial buildings occurred in the mid to late 1980s.

Syndication was again popular in the 1980s, and property managers were again managing property for syndicators. However, the Tax Reform Act of 1986 reduced the tax benefits of owning properties, and many syndicators were unable to continue to obtain funds from investors who were seeking tax benefits. Many syndicators dramatically reduced their real estate purchases.

Pension funds and insurance companies were another major player in commercial real estate during the 1980s. By the late 1980s, these institutions became the major purchasers of medium to large commercial projects. Their objectives in purchasing real estate differed somewhat from the developers' or syndicators' objectives. Pension funds and other institutions are typically long-term investors. They are not fee-driven buyers. Their analysis of the property for purchase, called a due diligence, is typically intense, thorough, and sophisticated. They are purchasing property for its potential yield. Yield has two components—cash flow and the appreciation of the property. Institutional buyers are looking to enhance the value of the property they purchase. Pension funds, through pension fund advisors, and institutions will continue to be the major purchasers of medium to large commercial properties through the 1990s. The challenge for these buyers will be to find institutional-grade quality properties. As the nation enters the 1990s, the demand for quality properties far exceeds the supply.

After the properties are purchased, the institutions assign them to an asset manager. The asset manager is responsible for a portfolio of properties and complements the responsibilities of the property manager. The eight generic functions of asset management are (1) acquisition, (2) selection and supervision of the property management company, (3) performance monitoring/control, (4) retenanting/rehabilitation, (5) peripheral development, (6) refinancing, (7) restructuring ownership, and (8) disposition.[1]

§ 1.3 PROPERTY MANAGERS OF THE 1990s

The goals and objectives of institutional owners, combined with their reliance on the property manager to achieve their goals, have changed

[1] Real Estate Research Corporation, *The Key to Profitable Real Estate Investment: Asset Management* (1985).

the manager's role. Property managers are expected to enhance value. They must understand how their responsibilities effect the property's net operating income and thus its value.

Property management has become more proactive than reactive. The successful manager anticipates problems and opportunities and responds in advance to control the situation.

Management today is complex, and the astute property manager must have a multitude of skills and abilities. A typical week's activity will bring the manager in touch with legal problems, maintenance situations, marketing and leasing activities, human relations problems, construction needs, accounting problems, and a host of other diverse but interrelated activities. Many tenants are sophisticated business people, and the commercial property manager often interacts with some of the top talent in the business community. When tenants decide to open a store in a shopping center or lease space in a high rise, they are making a major financial commitment to the success of their business and that of the building. As a result, it is not uncommon for a prospective tenant to inquire into the capabilities of the building's management and even into the qualifications of a specific manager.

The property manager responsible for the direct management of the property is daily accountable for enhancing the property's value. Most property managers of the 1990s will be working either directly for the institutions as fee managers or employees, or indirectly for institutional owners as employees of a developer who has a joint venture with the institution.

§ 1.4   PROFESSIONAL ORGANIZATIONS

Managing a property is no different from running a business. Both entail accounting, financial analysis, financing, marketing and sales (leasing), public relations, people skills, maintenance, real estate and business law, and handling the unexpected. No one can be an expert in all these areas. Fortunately, the commercial property management industry is served by three professional organizations. These organizations trace their history to the early years of property management. They conduct research, present educational programs, publish periodicals and textbooks, hold local and national meetings, lobby on a local and national level, award professional designations, and serve their members and the real estate industry on a local and national level.

(a) INSTITUTE OF REAL ESTATE MANAGEMENT

The Institute of Real Estate Management (IREM), an affiliate of the National Association of REALTORS®, was founded in 1933. IREM awards the Certified Property Manager (CPM®) designation to managers who have distinguished themselves in experience, education, and ethical conduct. All CPM® members must abide by a code of ethics established by the Institute of Real Estate Management. Those violating the code are subject to revocation of their designation. To qualify for the CPM® designation, a candidate must successfully complete an intense series of IREM courses.[2]

IREM offers the most complete real estate education program in the industry. Its 300 series of courses are week-long programs that provide the foundation for a solid property management education. Each course focuses on a specific property type—apartments, office buildings, shopping centers, or government-assisted housing, providing an in-depth examination of management techniques for that particular property.

IREM's 400 course, Managing Real Estate as an Investment, is designed for property managers involved in fiscal policy decisions for investment real estate. The course also discusses the management plan.

The 500 course, Problem Solving and Decision Making for Property Managers, teaches students to identify problems that affect a property's performance and to formulate viable solutions.

Course 701, Managing the Management Office, teaches the latest techniques in the operation of a successful management office. Course 702, Advanced Management Practices and Techniques, is designed for executives who want to sharpen their management and human relations skills.

IREM publishes a comprehensive line of professional books, monographs, cassette tapes, and a leading property management periodical, *The Journal of Property Management.*

In 1945, the Institute set standards under which certain firms could be recognized as Accredited Management Organizations (AMO). Holders of the AMO designation have met IREM's standards of education, experience, integrity, and fiscal stability.[3]

There are approximately 100 local IREM chapters in the United States. Each conducts monthly meetings, provides miniseminars, and serves the interests of the property management profession.

IREM's national headquarters are located at 430 N. Michigan Avenue, Chicago, IL 60611 (312/661-1930).

(b) INTERNATIONAL COUNCIL OF SHOPPING CENTERS

The International Council of Shopping Centers (ICSC) was formed in 1956 to serve the shopping center industry. ICSC awards two

---

[2] Institute of Real Estate Management, *Your Real Estate Investment Deserves a Certified Property Manager* (1989).

[3] A. Downs, *Principles of Real Estate Management*, p. 18 (1987).

professional designations, CSM (Certified Shopping Center Manager) and CMD (Certified Marketing Director).

The objectives of the CSM program are to:

1. Establish and advance high standards in shopping center management. A CSM must be able to manage all types and sizes of shopping centers, in a wide range of geographical locations.
2. Recognize managers who meet these professional standards.
3. Encourage others to train for careers in shopping center management.
4. Establish and maintain educational standards for the profession.[4]

The first CSM exam was administered in May 1964. It is a written examination that covers operation and construction, leasing, accounting and record keeping, finance, center retailing and merchandising, promotions, community relations, insurance, and law.

The Certified Marketing Director program, formerly the Accredited Shopping Center Promotion Director (ASPD) program, was initiated by ICSC in 1971.

The objectives of the CMD program are to:

1. Establish high professional standards in the marketing activities of shopping centers. A CMD must be able to direct the marketing and promotion efforts of all types and sizes of shopping centers in a wide range of geographical locations.
2. Give industrywide recognition to marketing/promotion directors who achieve professional standing.
3. Establish educational standards for the profession.
4. Encourage others to train for careers in shopping center marketing.[5]

The CMD examination is a multiple-choice written test that covers the marketing plan, product development/center merchandising, retailing/store merchandising, media planning, public relations, and administration.

ICSC offers extensive educational programs at the regional and national level. The University of Shopping Centers is a week-long session offering courses on development, finance, leasing, management, design and construction, and marketing. Idea Exchanges are two- and three-day seminars on specialized topics that are offered throughout the

---

[4] International Council of Shopping Centers, *CSM, CMD Directory* (1987).

[5] International Council of Shopping Centers, *CSM, CMD Directory* (1987).

country. The annual convention, held in May, is a week-long program featuring speakers, a trade show, exhibits, and a leasing mall. At the leasing mall developers, brokers, and retailers meet to make business deals. The Institute also offers several one-week courses on shopping center management, advanced shopping center management, marketing, and promotions. ICSC publishes books, technical reports, legal reports, and other specialized bulletins as well as checklists designed for use in the field.

The International Council of Shopping Centers is located at 665 Fifth Avenue, New York, NY 10022 (202/421-1818).

(c) BUILDING OWNERS AND MANAGERS ASSOCIATION

In 1907, a group of 75 office building managers formed the National Association of Building Owners and Managers, later known as the Building Owners and Managers Association (BOMA). They held their first convention in Chicago in 1908. The program for this inaugural event included such topics as ventilation, economy in electric lighting, varnishes, cleaning problems, and division of costs of services in buildings—topics that are still discussed today. This convention was the first time commercial property managers met nationally to share ideas and exchange information.

In 1920, the association published the industry's first major research report on office building operating expenses, the annual *Experience Exchange Report* (EER). The EER analyzes the income and expenses of more than 3,000 office buildings across the United States and Canada, providing a standard of performance comparison for all office buildings. The report is the leading reference guide for building operation.[6]

BOMA monthly publishes *Skylines*, the only periodical devoted to the office building industry. BOMA International has published several books on office building management and leasing, including *Office Building Lease Manual, Leasing Concepts, Standard Method of Floor Measurements,* and *A Guide to Commercial Property Management.*

Through its educational arm, the Building Owners and Managers Institute International, BOMA provides college-level courses leading to the professional designations of Real Property Administrator (RPA), Systems Maintenance Technician (SMT), and Systems Maintenance Administrator (SMA). The courses are taught locally in the United States and Canada and are also available through home study.

The RPA program consists of seven advanced education courses that cover building design, operation, maintenance, finance and investment, administration, insurance, and legal concepts.

---

[6] BOMA International, *Forging the Future of the Office Building Industry* (n.d.).

Through a separate eight-course curriculum, the SMT and SMA programs provide hands-on courses detailing the operation and maintenance of building systems, building design, energy management, and employee supervision.[7]

BOMA has a chapter in every major metropolitan area and in many smaller cities as well. These chapters hold monthly meetings, lobby on behalf of the industry, and conduct miniseminars. BOMA also holds an annual convention and office building show. BOMA's national headquarters are located at 1201 New York Ave. N.W., Suite 300, Washington, DC 20005 (202/289-7000).

§ 1.5   PROFESSIONAL DESIGNATIONS

The real estate industry is placing greater emphasis on professional designations. Today many institutional decision makers hold professional designations, and they are familiar with the stringent requirements for becoming a CPM®, CSM, or RPA. It is not uncommon for an asset manager to request that the property manager hold one of the aforementioned designations. Similarly, lenders and institutional owners often want to know about the qualifications of the property manager before becoming involved with a management company. They know that the quality of management will make the difference between a property that is operated as a first-class property and one that has chronic problems. They also know the importance of the property manager in enhancing value. An owner will want a CSM or CPM® to manage its mall and an RPA or CPM® to manage its office building or industrial property.

Professional designations offer tremendous benefits to the property manager. The recognition that professional designations bring places the property manager in an elite group of professionals in the real estate community. The educational requirements to obtain the designations give the manager the knowledge and practical skills needed to succeed.

There are also financial benefits to be gained by holding a valued professional designation. The Huntress Real Estate Executive Search Firm in Kansas City did a survey of all its placements and found that when the only difference between candidates was a professional designation, people with designations obtained a starting salary 10% to 15% higher than those without them.

[7] Ibid.

§ 1.6 ABOUT THIS BOOK

Managing and Leasing Commerical Properties discusses property management with a view to enhancing value. The book offers a hands-on approach to the management, operations, and leasing of commercial properties. It addresses the daily problems of the property manager and suggests answers. Where appropriate, the text mentions management and leasing strategies that have not been successful to keep the reader from repeating the mistakes of others.

The introduction reviews the history of property management, how the responsibilities of the commercial property manager have evolved, and what is expected of property managers in the 1990s. Because no single individual can acquire the knowledge to stay at the cutting edge of the industry by him- or herself, this chapter has reviewed the services offered by professional organizations in commercial property management and explained the value of three leading property management designations.

Chapter 2 discusses how to start a commercial property management company, identify its market niche, and administrate the company.

Chapter 3 on income and expense analysis reviews the methods in developing a property's month-to-month cash flow projection.

Chapters 4, 5, and 6 review the three commercial property types—shopping centers, office buildings, and industrial properties—and the responsibilities the property manager will face with each on a daily basis.

Chapter 7 is a step-by-step guide to developing and implementing a marketing and leasing program. All areas of marketing and leasing are discussed: working with the brokerage community, finding tenants, analyzing deals, reviewing the leases for each property type, re-leasing, and lease renewal.

Chapter 8 takes the reader through the steps in conducting a market survey and determining market rates for a building.

Once a lease is executed, the property manager must administer it. Chapter 9 reviews the procedures in administrating the obligations of the tenants and the landlord.

Properties can be maintained in a crisis intervention manner or under a maintenance management program. Chapter 10 outlines a step-by-step method for creating a maintenance management program.

Property managers will handle multiple emergencies, from natural disasters such as earthquakes, hurricanes, and tornadoes, to man-made disasters such as fires, bomb threats, and assaults. Chapter 11 discusses how to establish and implement emergency procedures.

Chapter 12 on reports to owners establishes a reporting format that keeps the property owner aware of the activities of the property, the market conditions, financial forecasts, and potential opportunities and problems.

This book was written to help property managers immediately implement the principles and techniques of effective commercial property management in their daily activities. This is not a book on theory, but a hands-on book that explains state-of-the-art techniques for managing and leasing commercial properties.

§ 1.7   CONCLUSION

Commercial property management is a challenging and rewarding career open to all. There is nothing that a property manager does that cannot be performed equally well by either gender, and age is no barrier at all; the selection factors are ability, knowledge, and judgment—in other words, professionalism. Commercial property management is both satisfying and frustrating. There are many rules and yet there are none. Because we are dealing with many personalities, we need to amend rules, change approaches, and rethink procedures to satisfy the various occupants and users of our properties.

This book hopes to convey two important principles that are important for the successful property manager of the 1990s: one, property managers are hired to enhance the value of a property and, two, property managers do not manage brick and mortar and steel and concrete, they manage people.

This book is not meant to replace the fine educational programs of the Institute of Real Estate Management, The International Council of Shopping Centers, The Building Owners and Managers Association, or other active property management organizations. Rather, it is meant to be a guide to principles and practices that have been successful over the years. It is hoped that this book will provide direct answers to many of the day-to-day problems that property managers face and, more importantly, that it will provide a strong base of understanding of commercial property management and leasing that will guide the property manager to proper decisions well beyond the scope of the book itself.

Two

The Property Management Company

§ 2.1 INTRODUCTION

The principles property managers use to operate a property and enhance its value are the same principles needed to operate a successful property management company or department. The property management company is a service business that seeks to generate profits and enhance the value of the company. The primary responsibilities of the person who heads a property management company are business development, personnel management, and establishing and monitoring policies and procedures. This chapter reviews the concepts used in developing a market, establishing a property management company, and marketing the company.

The products a property management company has to offer are time and expertise. They are provided by the company's personnel and are reflected in its operating expenses. The single largest operating expense, usually ranging from 60% to 75% of the operating budget, is payroll costs. This chapter also discusses staffing, position responsibilities, and personnel issues.

§ 2.2   MARKETS TO SERVE

Every business must develop a market niche to be competitive and successful. In the retailing industry, a small retailer cannot compete with Sears or JC Penney by carrying every product line found in a giant department store. It isn't possible or necessary for the small retailer to carry every product a potential customer needs. It makes more sense to try to be the best in one or a limited product line or specialty. The merchant can develop an area of expertise and offer a depth of merchandise selection and service that even the giants cannot offer. The store becomes knows in its area as the best source for a particular product or service. This philosophy has helped many small businesses succeed in the competitive retailing industry.

Most property management firms are small businesses. These entrepreneurs are competing with each other, with the regional and national full-service brokerage firms, and with developers who have entered the fee management business. The small- to medium-size property management firm can be competitive and successful in the real estate industry by copying the philosophy of the successful small retailer and developing its own market niche. Property management is a specialty within the real estate industry. Within this specialty are subspecialties, such as property types and special services. The property management firm needs to develop an expertise in one or more of these areas. This becomes its market niche.

There are four interrelated criteria to consider in developing a market niche: property type, level of service, geographic area, and property ownership. Each must be analyzed as to the availability of product, the company's interests, the expertise of the staff, the competition, the cost to do business, and the profit potential.

(a)   PROPERTY TYPE

Most property management firms operate in metropolitan areas in which various types of property exist. This allows the firm to specialize in the management and leasing of one or two particular types of property. Firms in rural areas have limited opportunities in any one property type and often must manage a combination of properties.

Most property management firms will specialize in either residential or commercial management. Commercial properties include office buildings, industrial properties, and shopping centers. The subtypes are garden, mid-, and high-rise office buildings; freestanding industrial buildings; multitenant industrial parks; strip, neighborhood, community, and specialty centers; and regional malls. Each subtype requires a distinct expertise, and commercial property management firms must decide in which type they will specialize.

When developing a market niche, the property manager must determine which properties are available for fee management. Most large commercial buildings, such as high-rise office buildings and regional malls, are managed by the owner. Every major developer has an in-house property management division, and many regional and national syndicators have their own property management companies.

When an institution purchases a large commercial property, it frequently looks to a developer with whom it has a relationship to manage its acquisition. When a property is purchased from a developer with guaranteed rents for a period (e.g.,one to three years), the developer retains the management of the property at least through the guarantee period.

The opportunities for most property management companies are in managing small- to medium-size commercial properties of up to 300,000 square feet. It is virtually impossible for smaller firms to acquire the management of large commercial properties. The few opportunities that exist are in smaller communities where it is not cost-effective for the owner to manage the property.

Most commercial property management firms will develop an expertise in one or several subproperty types. In today's competitive market, it is very difficult to cross over to another property type without previous experience. For instance, a firm that specializes in the management of suburban low- and mid-rise office buildings can extend its services to industrial properties or shopping centers, but it is difficult to develop the same level of expertise for all three property types. Likewise, apartment building managers with many years of experience may have a difficult time breaking into commercial property management. On the other hand, a client with whom a position of trust has been built may ask a manager to cross over and manage another type of property.

Institutional owners and other absentee owners look for a company with a specific area of expertise to manage their $5 million to $50 million investment. The owner will look not only at the company's reputation, but at the competence of the manager who will be responsible for the property. Professional designations—the RPA (Real Property Administrator) for office buildings, the CSM (Certified Shopping Center Manager) for shopping centers, and the CPM (Certified Property Manager) for all types of properties—are evidence that a manager is experienced and has received specialized training.

Once the firm has selected a type of property to specialize in, it can select the level of service, the geographical area, and the clientele it wishes to serve.

(b) LEVEL OF SERVICE

The field of property management offers different levels of services, depending upon the expertise of the firm, the needs of the owner and, ultimately, the level of service a company wishes to provide. All owners do not need the same level of service. A property owner who lives a few miles from the property, who knows the area, and has no partners to report to may prefer a basic level of service with a lower management fee. However, an absentee institutional owner who is representing an investment fund or a pension fund may prefer a complete and high level of service.

A company that tries to offer different levels of service will become known as the lowest common denominator of services. The owners and directors of the company must determine what level of service it will provide and develop and market the company to that level.

(c)   GEOGRAPHIC AREA

The third criterion in developing a market niche is targeting which geographic area to serve. The area can range from a limited two-mile downtown radius to an entire state or region. The management company should analyze its existing portfolio, the company's personnel and capabilities, its cost to do business, management opportunities, and competition in determining its areas of service.

The property type will partially dictate the area to serve. A firm specializing in the management of neighborhood and community shopping centers will manage in the suburbs and in several counties. A firm specializing in the management of older mid-rise office buildings will manage in the downtown area.

Next, the size and capabilities of the staff must be considered. A firm with only two property managers does not have the economies of scale to effectively and profitably manage a portfolio of properties located over a wide area. The cost of doing business increases as the properties are farther away from the office and from one another. The cost is measured in direct expenses and travel time.

If there are sufficient opportunities to manage properties in another county or state, the profit potential may justify expanding a management company's geographic area of service. Or a valued client might request that a firm manage one of its properties outside the firm's normal geographic service area, and the company might move into the new area to preserve the relationship with the client. However, managing one large neighborhood shopping center that is an hour's flight from the main office is seldom cost-effective or profitable.

The level of competition is another factor to consider when determining which areas to serve. A company might turn a profit if it can fill a void in a portion of a state that has few professional commercial property management firms. Conversely, venturing into a highly competitive area may prove to be unprofitable and a poor use of the company's most valuable resource—its personnel's time.

(d) PROPERTY OWNERSHIP

A property management company must identify its clients and develop the company to meet their needs. For instance, institutional owners require extensive accounting using their reporting format, while a local owner will probably accept the property management firm's basic reporting format. The experience and abilities of the person assigned to manage the property must match the needs of the owner. A sophisticated owner may not interact well with an entry-level manager.

Analyzing the four criteria mentioned above will enable a company to identify, establish, and market its services. The final result will be a well defined market niche around which the company can be built and promoted.

§ 2.3 STARTING A PROPERTY MANAGEMENT DEPARTMENT OR COMPANY FOR A DEVELOPER

A development company is in an excellent position to create a property management department or company because the developer has an existing portfolio of properties that can be used as a starting point.

In the mid 1980s, almost every metropolitan area was overbuilt or close to it. Commercial development activities slowed, and many developers expanded or started their own property management company or department. In many areas of the country this trend will continue through the 1990s as developers look for ways to create profit centers or just cover their operating expenses.

There are several advantages for a developer to have a property management company, and there are cautions that must be heeded. A property management company can be a separate profit center. The size of the portfolio and the size of the properties will be one of the major determining factors in the profit potential. Managing a portfolio of large commercial properties should be more profitable than managing small- to medium-size properties, but overall profit potential should not be overestimated. Some developers start a management company to cover the development company's overhead only to find that the size of the development company's staff and the salary and benefits of the owner and executives are too much for the profits of a property management company to offset. The profits can, however, cover the developer's payroll or operating expenses for a limited period.

Another advantage in setting up a property management company is the additional service a developer can offer a joint venture partner. Many medium and large commercial properties built in the 1980s were joint ventures with an institution, frequently an insurance company. The joint venture partner will look to the developer partner to manage the property. A developer can attract additional partners by offering professional property management services. The key word is *professional*. A developer's credibility will be tainted and the relationship with the partner jeopardized if the service offered is not state of the art.

A third advantage is the ability to manage the properties when they are sold, with the developer guaranteeing the income stream, specific tenants' rents, or the rent for vacancies or weak tenants for a period, usually between one and three years. The developer needs to be certain that the management of the property doesn't negatively effect the marketing and leasing program.

Developing a property management department or company is similar to starting a property management company. First, a market niche must be identified and developed. The initial market niche for the developer's property management company is the property type it develops. The market niche can easily be expanded, as explained later in the chapter.

The next step in developing the property management company is to determine the staffing needs. Although it is usually best to promote someone internally, a developer may not have a person with property management expertise on staff. The new property management company must start with expertise. Credibility is established not by a company's name or affiliation with an existing company but by the level of service it provides.

An experienced property manager is needed to develop the company. If the initial portfolio of properties is small—less than ten small properties or eight medium-size properties—the director of property management, with the assistance of an administrative assistant, will be responsible for managing them. When the portfolio is more than nine or ten small properties or seven or eight medium-size properties, additional property managers will be needed. Whether the next property manager hired will be an experienced manager, an entry-level manager, or someone promoted from an administrative position within the company will depend on the size of the portfolio, budget constraints, the level of service provided, and the amount of time the director of property management can devote to training.

An adequate support staff is needed to back up the property manager and to handle the accounting responsibilities. Ideally, the property management company will not share clerical and bookkeeping personnel with the developer. When the work of both companies is assigned to one person, the developer's work takes priority. A professional commercial property management company cannot be developed if it is treated as a second-class entity.

If the property management company is handling properties not owned by the developer, these properties must be given first priority. Every property owner wants to believe that his or her property is the only one the company manages. The company should provide services that give this impression.

It is best to have the management company's accounting department separate from the developer's accounting department. At first this may not be possible, but once the property management company needs at least one full-time bookkeeper, that person should report solely to the director of property management. It is possible for the controller of the developer's accounting department to oversee the property management company's accounting department, but the property management company should have its own accounting department as soon as its size justifies the separation.

If the property management company is to be profitable, it must charge market fees for all the properties it manages, including the developer's properties. Many developers will offer a lower management fee as part of the negotiations with a joint venture partner and then wonder why the property management company is not profitable.

It usually takes six to eighteen months before a property management company starts to show a profit. The developer must be able to endure the start-up costs. The size of the portfolio managed and whether or not the fees are at market rates are major factors in determining when the company becomes profitable.

One of the most misunderstood issues in property management is whether the developer's property management company must have a corporate real estate broker's license and a licensed property manager. If the property management company is a separate company from the development company, many states will require that the company must be licensed. If a property management department is established as part of the development company, the developer may need to be licensed only if property management services are provided for properties not owned by the developer in the name of the development company.

A real estate license is required when managing properties for others, and may even be required when managing properties owned by the developer. If the developer is a general or limited partner in a project owned by the partnership, a real estate license probably will be required because the property management department is not managing a property owned by the development company but one owned by the partnership. The best way to avoid this problem is to have a corporate real estate license for the developer's property management company and have all property managers licensed. The real estate laws of the state where the company operates should be checked. There are differences in many states' licensing laws.

§ 2.4   STARTING A FEE MANAGEMENT COMPANY

Starting a fee property management company has challenges that are not faced when starting a management company for a developer. Starting a business without any properties to manage can place financial as well as mental strain on the new entrepreneur.

A start-up fee management company is invariably a very small organization. It is likely to consist of an owner/property manager and a secretary, or possibly two partners, a bookkeeper, and a secretary. The main initial challenge is developing the business and convincing potential clients that the firm has the expertise and depth of management to operate the properties efficiently.

One of the most critical concerns in starting a company is also the most difficult to determine—the aptitude for self-employment. It is possible to be an excellent property manager as an employee but not do well working alone. Once the manager becomes self-employed, the duties expand well beyond day-to-day property management activities. Now there is a company to run as well as properties to manage. This entails business development, employee relations, accounting supervision, governmental reporting, cash flow management, and a host of other responsibilities that have little to do with property management but a great deal to do with business management.

The form of the business structure is also important. Most small management companies start out as proprietorships. While there are many advantages to incorporation, there are also many drawbacks, and it is commonly held that the individual property manager receives limited liability protection through incorporation. Depending on the income level of the owner of the company, there may be some advantages to incorporation from a tax point of view that are not normally available to the individual. Partnerships allow managers to share the load, but they also make one partner liable for the acts of the other.

All of the steps outlined in the previous section, "Starting a Property Management Company for a Developer," are necessary in starting a fee management company. The manager must take the lead in organizing the office. Before the doors of the new company open, policies and procedures, an accounting system, forms, and reporting formats must be in place.

It is critical for the small entrepreneur to decide what type of properties the company will handle because many owners look for experience in a particular property type. The temptation will be strong to be a generalist and take on all types of properties, thereby increasing the potential client base and the management portfolio. However, today's commercial property market is so complex that it is much better to specialize and become recognized in one specific area of property management.

A second important decision concerns the area to be served. A small company cannot effectively cover a large geographic area, but a manager may have to target a larger area just to have sufficient product to support the new business.

Before leaving a lucrative job for the uncertain area of self-employment in fee management, the property manager should analyze past and present contacts to determine if these are likely future clients. Great care must be taken, however, in contacting clients of the present employer as there may be ethical and legal issues involved. If the property manager has been in contact with many property owners and has been active in professional associations and civic activities, there probably are a sufficient number of potential clients to start a company. Since this is a very subjective decision, it is important to be honest in evaluating one's situation. An error in judgment can be very costly to the entrepreneur.

Business development is typically a slow process in commercial properties. The management of small apartment projects can change hands rather quickly, but medium and large commercial projects seldom switch management without careful thought and planning. Therefore, the property manager should devote time to some form of business development each day. Once contact has been established with a potential client, the manager should keep the contact active. It is not unusual for six months or more to lapse from the initial discussion on a new commercial account to the actual start of the management contract. Property managers cannot wait until they lose one management contract before they start looking for a new one.

When a property owner selects a management company, he or she is hiring not a company, but an individual. Therefore, owners of property management firms must market themselves. The successful property manager has a reputation for honesty, integrity, knowledge of the market, proven results, and product knowledge. That reputation is generally the vehicle for new business. It is important that the property manager let owners know about the new company. There are several ways to do so.

1. Personal Contact. The most effective tool the property management company has is personal contact. The property manager can target a specific building or group of buildings, obtain the owners' names from tax records, mail them a brochure, and follow up with a phone call to set a meeting. Tracking a property's sale with a follow-up letter to the buyer can also be effective. Attending ICSC, IREM, or BOMA meetings where owners are likely to be present is another excellent way to make contacts. Very little in commercial real estate happens quickly, so after contacting an institution and discussing the company's services, the property manager should keep in touch in an effort to build a relationship.

2. Identifying Property Ownership. One of the most effective approaches to developing property management accounts is to use tax records to identify the owners of commercial properties. It usually takes a fair amount of time to see results with this approach. When calling potential clients the talents and abilities of the new firm should be presented in a positive way, but the existing property management company should not be criticized. After all, the owner may be managing in-house.

3. Publishing and Speaking. Writing articles for trade journals can be an effective strategy, especially if reprints are mailed to a select list of prospective clients, followed with a phone call. Being a panelist or guest speaker at professional association's meetings is excellent exposure and allows people to get to know the manager over a period of time.

4. Referrals. Referrals are one of the most effective entrees the property manager can have. Current clients can be a great help if they are aware that the manager is looking for business.

5. Press Releases. Any time the property manager accomplishes anything newsworthy, a press release should be distributed. News items can include taking on new business, negotiating a significant lease, obtaining a professional designation, or hiring a new staff member.

6. Civic Activities. Civic activities give a return to the community that supports the property manager. They also put the property manager in touch with other civic leaders, who are often good business contacts.

7. Advertising. Generally, advertising in local newspapers and mass media is not very effective. The owners of a multimillion dollar property are not likely to place their assets in the hands of an unknown manager based on an ad. A recurring ad may help establish a presence in the marketplace, but generally personal contact is necessary.

8. Brochure. A professionally designed brochure can be an excellent introduction to new clients. It can convey the image of success by indicating years of experience, specific credentials, and properties currently under management. A brochure should be followed up with personal contact.

Most fee management companies in the United States are relatively small in size and are able to concentrate on specific markets while providing a good living for the owner. On the other hand, commercial property management deals with very large investments, complex buildings, and sophisticated owners. This is not an area for the neophyte to jump into hoping to grow with the situation.

§ 2.5 COMPANY EXPANSION

What size should our company be? Can we become more profitable if we grow, or will we just have more problems? Both questions are frequently pondered by owners and directors of property management firms.

Expanding a company provides for potential increased profits, additional recognition, a more stable base of operations, increased company expertise, and personal gratification. However, if the expansion is not planned, it can easily become a disruptive force within the company and a financial burden.

The first step in expanding a company is to develop a three- to five-year growth strategy that focuses on expanding the company's market niche. Once the direction for expansion has been determined, a plan is developed to accommodate the changes to the operations of the company. Expanding a company's management portfolio will impact its space requirements; clerical, administrative and management staffing; computer capacity; equipment requirements; and operating expenses. The owner and the director of property management must be willing to commit time to the expansion effort.

The first consideration is to decide in which area the company should grow. Should the growth be within the present market niche, or should the market niche be expanded? Should the growth extend to providing services in addition to property management (e.g., leasing, consulting, brokerage, or appraisals)?

The most likely expansion is to broaden the property type managed in the present market niche. First consider the property types that have considerable crossover of responsibilities and expertise. A company specializing in suburban office buildings can consider expanding into industrial properties. There is less crossover of responsibilities and expertise between office buildings and shopping centers. The least amount of crossover is between residential and commercial properties.

Broadening the company's portfolio of property types may require modifying the management and accounting reports. For instance, shopping centers require a detailed analysis of each tenant's sales and a different approach to tenant's bill-back charges. The most drastic changes to the reporting program would be adding residential properties to a commercial management company, or vice versa. The manager can learn about various types of property by studying this book and the suggested reference materials, by attending property management and leasing seminars, and by joining professional organizations that represent different property types.

Another growth strategy is to expand the geographic area in which the company operates. In many areas it is possible to expand by increasing the sphere of operation. For instance, in southern California, a company could expand from Los Angeles County to Orange County to Riverside County to San Diego County. In other areas, expansion may require giant geographical leaps. For instance, a company in the Seattle area could expand east across the Cascade Mountains to eastern Washington, south to Portland and, in a major move, north to Anchorage, Alaska. A move of this magnitude would require either developing a program for managing properties from afar, discussed later in this chapter, or incurring the expense to open a branch office. In any event, expansion into another state may requires obtaining a real estate license in that state. An analysis of the market and competition would tell a company whether there were sufficient opportunities to enter the market without having any management accounts in the new area.

An immediate means of entry into another area is by purchasing a local property management company. The regional or national brokerage firms and developers who are operating in several areas can bring their property management division into an area to support an established brokerage or development operation.

A more long-term expansion strategy is to broaden the client base. A firm that specializes in managing for local owners and developers may expand its client base to institutional owners. Institutional owners tend to be more sophisticated and demanding. They might visit the property manager less frequently because they are usually absentee owners, but their reporting requirements are more extensive, especially accounting reports. In addition, they usually have a larger real estate staff with a range of experience.

A major consideration when expanding a company is staffing the three levels—executive or supervisory, property managers, and administrative support. The first consideration is whether additional properties can be managed without additional personnel. Since most property management companies operate near or at maximum capacity, it is unlikely that more than one or two additional properties can be added without additional staff. During a growth period, a company adapts from being understaffed when a few additional properties are added to the management portfolio to being slightly over staffed when employees are hired after a few more properties are added, to being adequately staffed when another one or two properties are added. If the company continues to expand, this cycle will start over again.

The existing executive or supervisory staff can usually handle the growth. If the growth is an expansion into a new property type—for instance, a shopping center—a new position can be created when the portfolio justifies it. One consideration: If the expansion is geographic, will a property management supervisor be needed for a branch office?

The most difficult decision is to determine how growth will effect the property management staff. The company must decide if it has the expertise to expand into another property type. If not, a property manager will probably need to be hired to market the new property division. A company cannot always afford to hire experienced managers, but if only entry-level managers are hired, the company becomes a school for property managers. If the company is amply staffed with experienced managers, it might consider hiring an entry-level person who would be assigned to one of the experienced managers. If the most recent hiring has been entry-level managers, an experienced manager may be needed to provide a depth of experience.

Care must be used when determining which level of experience is needed in the new property manager. The level of service a company has established can greatly deteriorate if the expertise and experience are not maintained at the same level for each property type.

Increasing the portfolio will require added clerical, administrative, and accounting staff. The management level staff will work harder and longer during a period of growth until a new manager is added. However, it is unrealistic to expect clerical, administrative, and accounting staff to work longer hours over an extended period of time. There is a maximum amount of work that the staff can produce in a normal work week. Fortunately, it is possible to hire part-time and temporary personnel.

§ 2.6   MANAGING NEW ACCOUNTS

The addition of a new account is an exciting event for the management company because it represents a transfer of trust from the owner to the manager. However, it can be a confusing time for tenants. The property manager must act immediately to show the owner his or her expertise and to assure the tenants that their property is being managed by a professional manager and a professional company. The manager must take time to evaluate the property and to establish management systems and procedures. Although the ideal situation is to receive a thirty-day advance notice, the company should be prepared to assume the management of a property on a day's notice. If a new account is assumed in a haphazard manner, the ongoing management will always be flawed. It can take from one week to three months of intense effort to get a commercial property fully on-line and reasonably understood by the property manager and the administrative staff. This is a critical period, for the firm will never get a second chance to make a first impression on the property owner and the tenants.

There are six areas that need to be addressed when assuming the management of an office building or industrial property, and a seventh to consider when assuming the management of a shopping center. The seven areas are: property ownership, property operations, tenants, administration, leasing, tenant improvements and, for shopping centers, the merchants' association/promotional fund/marketing fund.

The property manager and controller should meet with the owner or asset manager to discuss the owner's goals and objectives for the property. The property manager can then develop the management plan. A management agreement must be executed between the parties before the company assumes management responsibilities. The most immediate items of agreement are the management company's spending authority, the due dates of reports, and the names of the owner's representatives. The property manager should also establish the frequency of meeting with the owner.

Leasing responsibilities must be established during the meeting with the property owner. What are the parameters for leasing? What are the minimum rental rates, the minimum and maximum square footage, and the tenant allowance package that the property manager can offer a prospective tenant without the owner's prior approval? Who will prepare and pay for the marketing materials? If the management company's lease form is to be used, the property owner should review and give written approval. If the property management company will not handle leasing, what will its responsibilities be in interfacing with the broker? If the property manager is responsible for supervising the leasing agent, will a commission override be paid to the property management company?

The next area of concern is construction. Who will handle the tenant's improvements? Will the property manager act as a general contractor, supervise the general contractor, or have no direct construction responsibility? If the property manager will be responsible for bidding, contracting, and supervising construction, a list of at least three contractors should be approved by the owner. If unit pricing is used, the property manager must bid each item for unit pricing. A space planner needs to be selected for office buildings and industrial properties. Construction plans should be obtained.

Administrative responsibilities start with knowing the owner's required accounting format and due dates. Prior years' and the current year's budget and tenant billings, list of delinquencies, and invoices not paid should be transferred to the property manager. The leases must be summarized with a report of lease restrictions, first right of refusal, exclusives, right of cancellation, options, and expiration date.

The manager must arrange for a thorough property inspection. This is an opportunity to prepare an inventory of equipment and a map showing all shutoffs and electrical panels. A project data book (discussed in § 2.23) is prepared for the property. Having completed the inspection, the manager then obtains the property's construction plans and a list of the general contractors and subcontractors who built the project. All maintenance contracts are summarized. If there are on-site personnel, employment records are obtained. The property management staff is immediately familiarized with the property. A tenant kit and emergency procedures are developed.

The property manager visits with each tenant as soon as possible, but first the owner sends each tenant a letter introducing the new manager and informing the tenants where to send their rental payments. If tenants have any complaints, this is the time to find out. It is better to hear all complaints immediately and respond to them than to have disgruntled tenants.

If the new property is a shopping center, the manager must find out his or her responsibilities regarding the merchants' association or promotional fund. What is the budget? When does the group meet? What activities are planned? Who coordinates the activities? Who are the officers of the merchants' association?

A new account checklist shown in Exhibit 2.1 is an effective tool for ensuring that everything is done properly and in logical sequence.

§ 2.7 TERMINATING A PROPERTY MANAGEMENT ACCOUNT

An account can be terminated for any number of reasons. The property may have been sold, and the new owner will manage it in house, or the owner may have accepted a lower management bid from a competitor. A property management company might give up an account if it is not profitable or if there is a philosophical difference between the manager and the owner. Regardless of the reason, termination is no less important than taking over a new account.

The management transition should be orderly and complete. A sloppy termination can expose the property manager and the company to criticism, tarnish their reputation, sever a relationship, and even cause legal action. The areas that the owner is most concerned with are the accounting records, leases, and the transfer of funds. The accounting department will play a major role in the transfer of a management account. It is not unusual for extra compensation to be charged for a takeover or termination of a management account. This often occurs when an extraordinary account of time is needed to organize a property in disarray or to assist the new manager assuming the account.

The checklist in Exhibit 2.2 can help to ensure that all administrative, accounting, and personnel issues are handled properly when a management account is terminated.

§ 2.8 STAFFING AND ORGANIZATION

Like other service industries, property management covers a broad spectrum of services ranging from rent collection, simple accounting, and responding to maintenance problems to providing sophisticated reports, developing a maintenance management plan, implementing a tenant retention program, developing and implementing a comprehensive marketing and leasing program, and rehabbing a property. It is necessary to develop the company's policies and procedures and staff the company for its particular level of service.

EXHIBIT 2.1

New Account Checklist

Commercial Property

Date of Commencement

Project Name _____ of Management _____

Property Manager _____

Management's Office _____ Property Owner _____

In order to establish a new property management account, the cooperation of management, accounting, personnel, and payroll departments is necessary to insure a smooth transition into our system.

A checklist for the establishment of a property management account will be initiated by the property manager to whom the account is assigned.

After all the required departments have completed their functions, a copy of the checklist will be sent to the director of property management for filing in the property's permanent records, with a copy retained in the files of the property manager.

	Initials	Date Completed
I. Administrative		
A. Execute management agreement.	_____	_____
B. Send copies of signed contract to regional manager/branch office.	_____	_____
C. Inform accounting department of new account/management fee information.	_____	_____
D. Obtain current operating budgets for preceding and current year.	_____	_____
E. Send form letters to tenants including request for new insurance certificates.	_____	_____
F. Send form letters to suppliers/vendors.	_____	_____
II. Property Data		
A. Record lot sizes.	_____	_____
B. Show type of construction.	_____	_____
C. Obtain set of "as-built" plans.	_____	_____
D. Compile all manufacturer's information regarding facilities and amenities (e.g., heating, air-conditioning, fire sprinkler systems) and originals of all warranties that apply to all mechanical equipment.	_____	_____
E. Obtain inventory of personal property.	_____	_____
F. Complete project insurance changeover.	_____	_____
G. Obtain keys to vacant space.	_____	_____
H. Obtain master keys (office building).	_____	_____
I. Record location of shutoffs, timers, etc.	_____	_____

EXHIBIT 2.1 *(Continued)*

	Initials	Date Completed

III. *Income Data*
    A. Record information on all lessees, including name/phone number of tenant contract and billing address if different from premises. _____ _____
    B. Show unit sizes (square footage). _____ _____
    C. Compile monthly rental (rent roll). _____ _____
    D. Record rental due dates. _____ _____
    E. Compile current list of delinquencies. _____ _____
    F. Obtain copies of all leases and pertinent information. _____ _____
    G. Obtain insurance certificates. _____ _____
    H. List current vacancies. _____ _____
    I. Compile prospective tenant list. _____ _____
    J. Show other income (CAM, escalation, % rent, utilities, parking lot, etc.). _____ _____
    K. Total past year's gross sales for tenants. _____ _____

IV. *Operating Expense Data*
    A. Obtain copy of current and all past tax bills. _____ _____
    B. Obtain copy of most recent licenses and tax changes. _____ _____
    C. List all outstanding bills on hand with special instructions as to payment. _____ _____
    D. Obtain copies of most recent annual operating statements at least as far back as earliest base year for escalation. _____ _____
    E. Obtain copies of last tenant escalations bills. _____ _____
    F. Obtain copies of previous sales reports. _____ _____
    G. Establish supplier list. _____ _____

V. *Operations* (Expenses billed back to tenants)
    A. Record salaries, payroll taxes, etc. for on-site maintenance personnel. _____ _____
    B. List on-site office expenses. _____ _____
    C. Purchase on-site furniture and/or supplies. _____ _____
    D. Record vehicle/mileage allowance (on-site vehicle registration, license, insurance). _____ _____
    E. Obtain original copies of all agreements with each contractor, monthly charge, and address/phone number. _____ _____
        1. Elevator _____ _____
        2. Escalator _____ _____

EXHIBIT 2.1 (*Continued*)

	Initials	Date Completed
3. Janitorial	_____	_____
4. Landscaping	_____	_____
5. Music	_____	_____
6. HVAC	_____	_____
7. Parking lot sweeper	_____	_____
8. Snow removal	_____	_____
9. Sprinkler contractor	_____	_____
10. Pest control	_____	_____
11. Equipment maintenance contractor	_____	_____
12. Tenant improvement contractor	_____	_____
13. _____	_____	_____

F. Obtain copies of all certificates of insurance for current project contractors.   _____   _____

G. List service companies and suppliers, including names/addresses/phone numbers.

    1. Plumber   _____   _____
    2. Electrician   _____   _____
    3. Roofer   _____   _____
    4. Utility repairs   _____   _____
    5. Parking lot repairs   _____   _____
    6. Painter   _____   _____
    7. _____   _____   _____

VI. *Accounting*

A. Assign project number and notify property manager.   _____   _____
B. Set up bank account.   _____   _____
C. Prepare bank cards, signatures.   _____   _____
D. Order checks, deposit slips, endorsement stamps.   _____   _____
E. Enter management fee information on computer.   _____   _____
F. Establish type of operating statement that owner requests.   _____   _____
G. List security deposits being held (how held: cash, savings account, etc.).   _____   _____
H. Set up loan payment information.   _____   _____
I. Set up supplier list.   _____   _____
J. Verify ledger card.   _____   _____
K. Obtain copies of any audits performed on tenants in past years.   _____   _____
L. Obtain owner's federal tax ID number.   _____   _____
M. Summarize leases.   _____   _____

VII. *Payroll/Personnel Departments*

A. Set up employees on payroll.   _____   _____

EXHIBIT 2.1 (*Continued*)

	Initials	Date Completed
B. Set up employee permanent files.	_____	_____
C. Set up employees on group insurance.	_____	_____
D. Provide employees with benefit handbook.	_____	_____
E. Establish time card procedures for on site personnel.	_____	_____
VIII. *Emergency Procedures*		
A. Analyze property's security needs.	_____	_____
B. Review property's security program.	_____	_____
C. Develop emergency procedures plan.	_____	_____
D. Develop emergency procedures handbook for property management staff.	_____	_____
E. Develop emergency procedures handbook for tenants.	_____	_____
F. Notify police and fire departments of property manager's name and phone number.	_____	_____
G. Walk the project.	_____	_____
H. Conduct practice emergency response with management staff.	_____	_____
I. Conduct practice emergency response with tenants.	_____	_____
J. Review emergency procedures handbook with tenants.	_____	_____
K. Conduct building evacuations.	_____	_____
L. Notify answering service of whom to call after hours and in emergency.	_____	_____
IX. *Construction*		
A. Obtain as-built plans.	_____	_____
B. Hire a space planner (office and industrial properties).	_____	_____
C. Develop list of contractors to bid.	_____	_____
D. Obtain list of general contractor and subcontractors who built project.	_____	_____
X. *Miscellaneous*		
A. List any pending litigation regarding property.	_____	_____
B. List owner's insurance agent.	_____	_____
C. List owner's attorney.	_____	_____
D. List owner's accountant.	_____	_____
E. Obtain copy of property sign criteria.	_____	_____
F. Conduct energy audit.	_____	_____
G. Review tax assessment.	_____	_____

EXHIBIT 2.2

Termination of a Property Management Account Checklist

Date of Termination
Project Name _____ of Contract _____

Project Number _____ Project Type _____

Date Notice Is Given to Owner_____ Received from Owner _____

Property Manager/Branch _____

A complete and efficient transfer of a property management account requires the cooperation of the property manger, accounting, and personnel/payroll departments. The procedure to be followed and functions performed by each department are listed below:

A checklist for the termination of a property management account will be completed by the property manager for every account to be terminated.

The completed checklist that has been initialed and dated as each procedure is accomplished will be placed in the permanent account files.

After the accounting department has completed Section II, it will forward its completed copy to the office headquarters for review and filing in the property's permanent records, retaining one copy for the property file in the accounting department.

When notice for termination of a property management account is given to the property manager by an owner, it will be necessary for all departments to expedite these procedures. The property management agreement requires 30 days' notice, but is the exception rather than the rule to receive a full 30 day's notice. When notification is received, the property manager should immediately review the property management agreement for any special clauses regarding termination.

	Initial	Date Completed
I. *Administrative*		
A. Property manager receives notice of cancellation of account by owner.	_____	_____
B. Property manager notifies by telephone:		
Branch manager	_____	_____
Regional manager	_____	_____
Accounting/Controller	_____	_____
President	_____	_____
C. Property manager prepares backup memorandum with pertinent information and sends to:		
Controller	_____	_____
President	_____	_____
Regional manager	_____	_____
Payroll department	_____	_____
D. Property manager shall prepare a form letter and send to all suppliers and vendors. Copies of these form letters shall be sent to existing owner, branch office file, on-site		

EXHIBIT 2.2 *(Continued)*

	Initial	Date Completed

manager (if applicable). This letter shall accomplish the following:

1. Establish final date responsible for debts incurred as managing agent. _____ _____

2. Request final billing and/or disbursement, to close account. _____ _____

3. Provide new ownership contact if available. _____ _____

4. Follow up letters to utility companies with a phone call to identify meter reading date and respective billings. _____ _____

E. Conduct a personal review with project's employees to determine whether employees will be terminated or retained and transferred to another project. The following will then be accomplished:

1. Send a form letter as a follow-up to the personal interview to all project employees notifying them of their employment status. Send copies to owner of project and payroll department. _____ _____

2. Obtain final time cards from all employees and forward to payroll department. _____ _____

3. Prepare cover letter identifying status of each employee and forward to payroll department along with appropriate personnel status change forms, which are to include: _____ _____

   a) Total salary due through termination date

   b) Settlement of vacation time due

   c) Incentive commission due

F. Property manager or owner will prepare a form letter to the tenants regarding termination of management. This letter should contain information concerning future rent checks. Send copy of letter(s) to owner. _____ _____

G. Update personal property inventory list and provide to management office files and owner. _____ _____

H. Remove from the project site all supplies, etc. that have not been paid for by the project. _____ _____

I. Notify local police and fire departments that property manager will no longer be responsible for the property. Provide specific date of termination. _____ _____

J. Notify answering service (office/project) of change in management and specific date of termination. _____ _____

EXHIBIT 2.2 *(Continued)*

	Initial	Date Completed

K. For purposes of proration, property manager shall have information available to be able to coordinate final accounting of payables and receivables, which would include: _____ _____
  1. Receivables _____ _____
    a) Rent collected
      (1) Base rents
      (2) Percentage rents
    b) Prepaid rents collected
    c) Deposits collected (for security or keys)
    d) Other income collected
      (1) Utility reimbursements (as part of tenant rebilling process)
      (2) Vending machine income
      (3) Tax bill-back reimbursements (as part of tenant rebilling process)
      (4) CAM reimbursements (as part of tenant rebilling process)
      (5) Insurance reimbursements (as part of tenant rebilling process)
      (6) Increased operating cost reimbursements (as part of tenant rebilling process)
  2. Payables _____ _____
    a) Prepaid utility accounts
    b) Prepaid service accounts
    c) Unpaid bills
    d) Prepaid operating permits
L. Property manager shall meet with on-site manager to accomplish the following: _____ _____
  1. Reconcile petty cash fund.
  2. Determine mileage reimbursement due.
  3. Define outstanding physical problems.
  4. Review inventory.
  5. Determine tenant prospects in process.
  6. Determine any tenants that may be leaving in the near future.
M. Return policies and procedures manuals. _____ _____
N. Property manager shall meet with new operator on project to turn over information. Property manager must receive a written receipt for: _____ _____
  1. All personal property as shown on original physical inventory

EXHIBIT 2.2 *(Continued)*

	Initial	Date Completed

2. All pertinent on-site records
    a) Leases
    b) Tenant correspondence
    c) CAM records
    d) Tax bill-back records
    e) Insurance bill-back records
    f) Tenant sales records
    g) All operating permits
    h) Copies of current contracts
    i) Tenant roster
3. Project keys   _____ _____
4. Listing of paid deposits held and being transferred, prepaid rents, and delinquent rents   _____ _____

II. *Accounting*
  A. Property manager gives notification that the account is to be terminated.   _____ _____
  B. Determine the cash balance, if any, for the account versus bills on hand.   _____ _____
  C. Discuss with prospective property manager any unpaid bills in the system. If there is insufficient cash in the account, the property manager is to provide a written priority list indicating which bills are to be paid.   _____ _____
  D. Consider audit fees and payments due for: _____ _____
    1. Property management fee   _____ _____
    2. Payroll charges   _____ _____
    3. Leasing commissions   _____ _____
  E. Verify deposits to be transferred.   _____ _____
  F. Resolve petty cash on hand.   _____ _____
  G. Arrange project audit by member of accounting department.   _____ _____
  H. Notify new owner or owner's agent in writing of any loan payments or other normal recurring payments.   _____ _____
  I. Ascertain disposition of rental checks received after termination date.   _____ _____
  J. Ascertain disposition of any unpaid bills still in system or received after date of termination.   _____ _____
  K. If new owner will agree in writing to assume full liability for bills, bank charges, and any bad checks, close the account approximately ten (10) working days after the last day of the month. Maximum time to close would be fifty (50) days after termination of contract.   _____ _____
  L. Prepare the final statement of the account and submit to the new owner or agent.   _____ _____

EXHIBIT 2.2 (*Continued*)

	Initial	Date Completed
III. *Personnel/Payroll*		
A. Upon receipt of employee status change, process transfer or termination of employees.	————	————
B. If termination date is other than a normal payday, prepare special paychecks immediately.	————	————
C. Mail or deliver final checks to property manager.	————	————
IV. *Miscellaneous*		
A. Send copy of this checklist, when completed, to the director of property management.	————	————
B. Obtain signoff from owner or representative upon termination that the above has been done.	————	————

(a) STAFFING CRITERIA

A number of variables interact in making decisions about the size of the staff, its level of experience, and the property manager's workload.

The first consideration is the need of the property owner. Those who live or work near their properties and assume some of the management functions do not need a high level of service, but absentee owners such as institutions may want full property management service. Because these owners often report to investors, they may need an annual management plan, monthly management and inspection reports, close tenant relations, an aggressive marketing and leasing program, and construction coordination. They are relying on the manager to enhance the property's value.

Along these same lines, it is wise to consider the accounting requirements of the property owner and of the property management company when making staffing decisions. Most institutional owners and pension fund advisors require sophisticated reports, while a private investor is usually satisfied with the management firm's basic accounting reports.

The level of staffing in a property management company also depends on the company's philosophy regarding the level of service needed for its market niche. If a company has established itself as a firm specializing in medium-sized commercial properties with a high level of service, each manager will handle only a few properties and have assistance from the support staff. If the company's niche is a low to medium level of service for smaller commercial properties, the level of service will be correspondingly less. A related issue is the experience of the staff, especially the property managers. An experienced manager can handle more properties than a novice.

By their nature, some types of properties require more management time. For example, shopping centers require more time than office buildings; office buildings need more time than industrial properties; and older properties usually require more maintenance supervision than newer properties. Problem properties also require additional management time and expertise. The problems may be in leasing, rent collections, maintenance, or insufficient cash available to operate the property.

The location of the property is another variable in determining the manager's workload. Time spent in traveling to the property reduces the amount of time available to manage the property. Properties that are more than a two-hour drive away or that must be reached by air transportation require additional travel time for each visit.

The number and type of tenants in a property also affect the manager's workload. The more tenants, the more time required by the accounting department for tenant billing, adjustments, and percentage rent adjustments. More tenants also require more of the property manager's time. A shopping center with a merchants' association or promotional fund will require more management time than one without these organizations.

The property manager can manage more properties if he or she has backup support. Secretarial and administrative support frees the property manager from routine clerical and troubleshooting duties. The accounting department can provide the manager with reports and a full range of accounting services.

There are no hard and fast rules about the number of properties an experienced manager with backup support can handle, but a guideline for a medium level of service is eight to twelve properties in the 50,000 square feet to 150,000 square feet range and five to seven properties at a high level of service. Obviously, seven 150,000 square feet properties would require more time than seven 50,000 square feet properties. Most on-site managers for large office buildings or malls have limited, if any, time to manage additional smaller properties.

The size of the on-site staff depends primarily on the size of the building. The manager of an enclosed community mall frequently serves as the marketing director and is responsible for re-leasing with the support of a secretary or administrative assistant. The regional and superregional mall will be staffed with from three to five management and administrative people. In larger malls, a manager, possibly an assistant manager, a marketing director, possibly an assistant marketing director, and a secretary will provide the basic staffing. These malls will frequently have a security chief and a maintenance supervisor.

Mid-rise and large low-rise office buildings are staffed with a manager and secretary; the high-rise office building will often add an assistant manager. The maintenance staff will include building engineers and day porters. If the property management company's accounting is decentralized, a bookkeeper will be included with the on-site administrative staff.

(b) ON-SITE MAINTENANCE STAFF

Neighborhood Centers

Few neighborhood centers can justify a full-time on-site maintenance person. An alternative is to have a part-time maintenance person on site who is responsible for cleaning the common area, landscape maintenance such as mowing or fertilizing, cleaning vacancies, changing filters in the HVAC units, and other minor maintenance duties. Pruning and spraying of plants should be handled by experts. The advantage to having an on-site maintenance person is immediate response to calls. Also, the common area will be cleaner with regular attention.

Community Malls

Community malls are usually staffed with a working maintenance supervisor and a maintenance person. The janitorial service for the common areas can be in house or contracted. The supervisor oversees all contracts and performs some maintenance tasks. Major HVAC maintenance should be contracted, filter changes and limited preventive maintenance inspections can be handled by the maintenance staff. Routine maintenance is the responsibility of the on-site maintenance staff.

Regional and Superregional Malls

The larger malls can justify management-level supervisors in maintenance, operations, and security. These malls generally have an operations manager and a security chief. The operations manager hires the maintenance crew, and the security chief hires and directs the security force. If the security is contracted, the mall's manager or assistant manager will work with the security company, and the security chief's position will be eliminated.

Mid- and High-Rise Office Buildings

Many high-rise office buildings will hire an in-house engineering staff. In these cases, the lead maintenance person is usually the building's chief engineer. The number of engineers depends upon the size of the building. A building that contracts all mechanical maintenance will have a working maintenance supervisor in lieu of a building engineer. Day porters are scheduled to keep the lobby and common areas clean while the building is open whether or not the building is staffed with engineers or a maintenance supervisor.

Multitenant Industrial Properties

Large multitenant industrial properties operate somewhat like community mall. They are staffed with a manager and a secretary. The manager may be responsible for the tenant improvement work, or a tenant improvement coordinator may be on site. Since maintenance is usually limited to common areas, an on-site maintenance supervisor is seldom needed.

§ 2.9 HIRING PROPERTY MANAGERS

Property managers are the heart of the management company. The owner or supervisor can develop an effective marketing program, establish state-of-the-art policies and procedures, and develop a capable support and accounting staff, but if the property managers cannot implement the programs, the company will not succeed.

Several factors must be considered when hiring a property manager: the manager's duties; number of other property managers and their level of experience; size and type of portfolio under management; the type of property ownership; and the compensation program. When all of these factors are considered, the decision can be made whether to hire an experienced or an entry-level property manager. If a company has an experienced staff of property managers, an entry-level property manager may be hired to manage the smaller properties or serve as an on-site assistant manager. On the other hand, if a property management company has only a few experienced property managers and is taking on a portfolio of properties owned by a sophisticated owner, it may prefer to have a seasoned manager.

The company has several excellent sources to choose from in locating a property manager. Most local chapters of IREM and BOMA publish monthly member newsletters and will accept notices of positions available. IREM publishes a national newsletter, *CPM Aspects*, which has a jobs section. Finding an executive-level property manager may require the use of a search firm that specializes in the real estate industry. Active participation in the three major commercial property management organizations—BOMA, ICSC, and IREM—is a good way to become aware of the property managers in the area and their expertise.

Entry-level positions can be filled by looking in house for administrative assistants or bookkeepers with management potential or by hiring people in related fields or college graduates. Some military positions are similar to property management positions, so retired military personnel are good candidates. Qualifications for a competent property manager include:

- Ability to handle a crisis
- Ability to handle several tasks at once
- Ability to return to one task when interrupted by another
- Ability to work with numbers
- Excellent people skills
- Self-motivated
- Team player
- Good business sense
- Understands legal terms in contracts and leases
- Sales skills
- Creativity
- Willing to be on call after hours
- Trustworthy and of high integrity
- Quick study

§ 2.10   RESPONSIBILITIES OF THE COMMERCIAL PROPERTY MANAGER

The general responsibilities of a commercial property manager for shopping centers, office buildings, or industrial properties are similar, but those responsibilities must be tailored to the requirements of the building, the property owner, and the structure of the property management company.

A general list of duties and responsibilities for commercial property managers follows:

1. Collect rents
   (*a*) Deposit rent (on-site manager only)
   (*b*) Report deposit slips (on-site manager only)
   (*c*) Complete tenant ledger card (on-site manager only)
   (*d*) Delinquency follow-up
2. Obtain sales reports from retail tenants
   (*a*) Collect tenants' sales reports
   (*b*) Record tenants' sales (on-site manager only)
   (*c*) Follow up on missing reports
   (*d*) Analyze the sales reports
   (*e*) Prepare and distribute mall's monthly sales reports
3. Conduct retail tenant audits
   (*a*) Contact tenants regarding audit

(*b*)   Evaluate audit

(*c*)   Meet with tenant and auditor for audit review

4.   Analyze store's sales, inventory levels, and store's operations

5.   Prepare and distribute monthly management report

6.   Prepare and distribute annual management plan

7.   Report all insurance claims

8.   Conduct monthly inspections and follow up on maintenance problems

9.   Assist with litigation

(*a*)   Work with the property's attorney

(*b*)   Follow up on all litigation

(*c*)   Prepare and distribute litigation report

10.   Develop and supervise maintenance management program

11.   Coordinate security program

(*a*)   Assess the need for a security program

(*b*)   Develop and supervise security program

(*c*)   Review daily security reports (properties with on-site security)

(*d*)   Review store opening and closing reports (on-site mall manager)

12.   Promote positive community relations

13.   Approve expenditures

(*a*)   Approve invoices

(*b*)   Forward invoices to payables

(*c*)   Review tax assessments

14.   Monitor budget vs. actual reports

(*a*)   Report on vacancies

(*b*)   Meet with maintenance staff

15.   Hire, train, supervise, and terminate administrative staff

16.   Develop emergency procedures

(*a*)   Instruct the staff on emergency procedures

(*b*)   Conduct tenant training sessions

17.   Coordinate leasing activity

(*a*)   Conduct market survey

(*b*)   Develop rent schedule

(*c*)   Maintain a state-of-the-art lease form

(*d*)   Negotiate leases and renewals

(*e*)   Develop and implement leasing plan

(*f*)   Analyze tenant mix periodically

18. Monitor tenant's insurance requirement per the lease
19. Develop and implement a marketing program
    (a) Install on-site signage
    (b) Develop marketing material
    (c) Keep brokers aware of property
    (d) Build rapport with the brokerage community
20. Develop a risk management program
21. Evaluate real estate tax assessments and coordinate appeal of assessed valuation
22. Develop a tenant retention program
23. Analyze rehabs and modernization possibilities
24. Supervise tenant improvements
25. Develop a public relations programs

§ 2.11   RESPONSIBILITIES OF THE SHOPPING CENTER MANAGER

Shopping center management includes the aforementioned responsibilities as well as responsibilities unique to managing a retail property. These include:

1. Manage community room
    (a) Market the rooms to the community
    (b) Schedule use
    (c) Distribute rules and regulations
    (d) Have agreement signed
    (e) Collect deposits (include self-addressed, stamped return envelope)
    (f) Inspect room after use and coordinate cleanup
2. Communicate with merchants
    (a) Visit merchants monthly
    (b) Prepare monthly newsletter
    (c) Prepare and review the tenant kit with the merchants
3. Participate in merchants' association/promotional fund
    (a) Attend member meetings
    (b) Attend board of director's meetings
4. Coordinate tenant services
    (a) Co-sponsor seminars with police on how to prevent shoplifting and credit card fraud
    (b) Coordinate retailing consultant service

§ 2.12   RESPONSIBILITIES OF THE MALL MARKETING DIRECTOR

1. Conduct periodic market research
2. Prepare annual advertising, marketing, and promotions calendar
3. Develop annual budget
4. Implement advertising, marketing, public relations, and promotions program
5. Maintain rapport with the media
6. Review and approve invoices
7. Develop and operate accounting system
8. Visit periodically with merchants
9. Maintain close working relationship with manager of major stores
10. Participate in merchants' association/promotional fund meetings
    (*a*) Prepare agenda for general membership meetings and board meetings
    (*b*) Provide meeting notice for membership and board meetings
11. Adhere to the bylaws or rules and regulations of the promotional fund or merchants' association
12. Develop a public relations program
13. Hire, train, administrate, and supervise staff

§ 2.13   RESPONSIBILITIES OF THE ADMINISTRATIVE ASSISTANT

The administrative assistant assists the property manager in the day-to-day management of the properties. Duties include:

1. Provide administrative support for leasing and marketing projects
    (*a*) Prepare leases
    (*b*) Review leases submitted by brokers
    (*c*) Prepare commission statements
    (*d*) Prepare mailings to brokers and prospective tenants
2. Compile insurance records
    (*a*) Obtain tenant's insurance certificate
    (*b*) Obtain contractor's insurance certificate
3. Coordinate maintenance
    (*a*) Expedite all maintenance calls
    (*b*) Periodically inspect the property
    (*c*) Provide emergency backup for after-hours calls

4. Maintain control of keys to vacancies
5. Perform all secretarial duties for the property manager
6. Prepare monthly management report and annual management plan for distribution
7. Establish and maintain tenant files
8. Obtain estoppel from tenants
9. Maintain project data book

§ 2.14   RESPONSIBILITIES OF THE ACCOUNTING PERSONNEL

1. Input property manager's income and expenses projections
2. Calculate base rent income based on lease-up predictions from property manager
3. Calculate tenant pass-through charges subject to the terms of each tenant's lease
4. Code accounts payable for projects to appropriate account numbers in the chart of accounts, and communicate with property manager regarding questionable coding
5. Deposit daily cash receipts from tenants
6. Record tenant sales reports
7. Reconcile bank statements
8. Type accounts payable checks
9. Summarize leases
10. Calculate consumer price index (CPI) increases
11. Track tenant's base rent step-up increases and CPI increases
12. Prepare and mail tenant rent invoices monthly
13. Calculate and compare year-end adjustments to actual expenditures for estimated tenant charges
14. File copies of accounts payable vendor checks
15. Calculate payments made to vendors for preparation of 1099 filing with IRS
16. Maintain general ledgers
17. Prepare budget vs. actual expenditures, income statements, balance sheets, expenditure journals, sales reports
18. Respond to tenant inquiries regarding accounts receivable amount disputes
19. Compile schedules and documentation for owner's auditors, state payroll tax auditors, state revenue auditor, federal income tax auditors, and state real estate licensing auditors
20. Prepare payroll checks and file payroll tax reports

§ 2.15   OFFICE ADMINISTRATION

Whether a company is small or large, it is important to define roles. Property management activities involve considerable overlap among, for example, accounting, leasing, and management. If these areas are not clearly defined, some duties could be overlooked, or conflicts could occur. Clear job descriptions provide guidance, and an organizational chart clarifies the company's staff structure.

Regardless of the size of the administrative staff, the same high standards should apply. Office equipment should be in good working order, files should be maintained in impeccable condition for maximum access, all documents leaving the office should be letter perfect, and visitors to the office should be treated warmly and efficiently. In short, the same care that the staff gives to the management of its properties should be given to daily office functions.

The executive understands that a collaborative atmosphere among staff members generates greater productivity. Even tedious filing or typing becomes a means to achieving a more successful company to which everyone can contribute. This team spirit, exhibited by clear and honest communication, strong conflict-management skills, and problem-solving models, takes time to develop but is well worth the effort.

§ 2.16   REAL ESTATE LICENSING REQUIREMENTS

In most states, a real estate license is required to manage or lease properties in almost every situation. This includes collecting rents. A company must be licensed to manage or lease properties owned by others. The company must have an individual who serves as the company's designated real estate broker, and each property manager must have either a salesperson's or a broker's license. When a company or person manages or leases a property without a required real estate license, the state can issue a cease and desist order and immediately stop their activity. A real estate license is not required to manage one's own properties, however, or to manage properties as an employee of the property owner.

There are some gray areas that may cause misunderstanding. For instance, if the Smith Development Company develops an office building owned by Broadway Office Building Partnership, of which Smith is a general partner, an employee of Smith Development Company would need to be licensed to manage or lease the property owned by Broadway Office Building Partnership. The property manager is an employee of Smith Development Company, not of Broadway Office Building Partnership. In this situation, Smith Development Company would need a designated real estate broker, and the property manager would need a real estate license to manage or lease the office building.

Another gray area in some states is whether a syndicator must be licensed to manage the properties syndicated. Some states have held that the manager must be licensed or have the same percentage of ownership as the general partner. While it is not a requirement in every state, it bears looking into if a syndicator plans to manage the property it syndicates.

Real estate laws are fairly similar from state to state, but there are variances. Prudent managers will check the licensing requirements for every state in which they operate.

§ 2.17   INSURANCE

The executive in charge of the management company should annually review the company's insurance coverage with its insurance agent. The types and limits of coverage will depend upon the philosophy of the company, the state the company does business in, and clients' requirements.

A listing of insurance coverage for property management includes: errors and omissions, fidelity bond, broad form money and securities bond, valuable papers and records, office personal property, comprehensive general liability, automobile liability, employer non-ownership automobile liability, data processing equipment, workers' compensation, and employee benefits (e.g., health, dental, life, disability). An excellent reference source defining insurance coverage is *Coverages Applicable* by Roy C. McCormick, The Rough Notes, Co., Inc., 1981. The Institute of Real Estate Management offers its members a source to apply for errors and omissions insurance.

§ 2.18   ATTORNEYS

One of the frustrating aspects of property management today is the proliferation of lawsuits. The relationship between landlord, tenant, and manager is a complex one. The owner of the property and the fee manager may have differing legal positions in a particular situation and could well become adversaries as the facts of a case unfold. Additionally, the public is an important part of commercial projects, and this increases legal exposure.

It is incumbent upon the owner and the manager to be properly insured for liability in the event something goes wrong. They should have access to good legal advice in the preparation of leases, contracts, agreements, procedures, and even approach. No attorney can guarantee that a client will not be sued, but a good attorney can provide safeguards and planning that will minimize the exposure. Representative attorneys should be named early to be available on a consulting basis. Attorneys should be selected for their knowledge and activity in the area in question. Bankruptcy, for instance, is a complex field, so the property manager would be better off with an attorney who specializes in that area. Another specialized area is employee relations, which have become a key issue in many industries.

One positive side of our current litigious society is that owners and managers are generally aware of the potential problems of lawsuits and make extra effort to maintain good relationships and negotiate harder to resolve disputes out of court.

§ 2.19 MANAGING PROPERTIES FROM AFAR

Properties that are at least a few hours drive from the property management office and that have no on-site manager present many potential problems that must be carefully evaluated before a management proposal is submitted and a management plan developed. Who will supervise the maintenance program? How will emergencies be handled? Can a rapport with the tenants be maintained? How can the property manager be aware of what is happening in the community? Will the owner trust that the property is receiving sufficient attention? All of these concerns are eliminated with an on-site manager; however, most small and medium-sized commercial properties do not have on-site managers.

Generally, if a property is more than a two-hour drive from the manager's office, it is considered to be managed from afar. When a property is at this distance or greater, the manager probably will not be able to respond quickly to problems that arise, and a plan must be developed to address the above-mentioned concerns.

Routine maintenance and emergencies must be handled by a person in the area or on site. In some cases, a tenant can be hired to be the eyes and ears of the property manager. A real estate office in the building would be a likely candidate to assume this responsibility.

An alternative is to hire a part-time working maintenance supervisor. This person could be a maintenance contractor, a construction worker, or a retired person. Duties would include supervising the maintenance contractor, conducting periodic inspections, responding to maintenance calls and emergencies, cleaning the parking lot, and arranging for snow removal. This person could also let prospective tenants into a space when the leasing agent is not in the area. A maintenance contractor in the area can be hired to handle emergencies and to visit the property periodically.

The use of a full- or part-time working maintenance supervisor is an expense of the common area/escalation budget, landlord's budget, or both. The lease will determine if the supervisory time is a cost of the common area/escalation expense or the owner's nonreimbursable expenses. If the cost is not passed on to the tenant according to the lease, then the management agreement will determine if the cost of this person is a management company expense or an owner's expense. It could be the management company's expense if these duties are normally performed by the property manager.

The property manager can develop a rapport with tenants by scheduling periodic visits to the property and spending a brief time with each tenant. Tenants should be introduced to the local maintenance person and given his or her phone number. The maintenance person must be equipped with a beeper and be accessible to both tenants and manager.

It is difficult but necessary to be aware of community activities and how they affect the property. The property manager can do this by subscribing to the local newspaper or joining the local chamber of commerce or board of realtors. The latter will provide information on local business concerns and an opportunity to attend board meetings. Periodic luncheon meetings with community leaders and regular meetings with the maintenance supervisor will provide worthwhile information about the property and community.

To assure that the property owner receives satisfactory attention, the property manager should meet with the owner and explain in detail how the property will be managed—for example, who will respond to maintenance problems and emergencies—and address all issues that may be of concern to the owner.

An alternative to the program outlined above is joint management with either a commercial or residential property management company in the area. This company would perform on-site management. Its responsibilities might also include collecting rent and working with tenants, thus requiring the lead property manager to spend less time at the property. The manager in this case works with the owner and maintains responsibility for accounting, budgeting, monthly and annual management reports, tenant relationships, and business decisions. Of course, the management fee must be competitive and split in a fair formula between the two companies.

When establishing a management fee for properties that are at a distance from the management office, several expenses should be included. Travel costs will be higher if air travel and lodging are necessary. Even a two-hour drive to a property is time that could be used more productively. Entertaining community leaders and maintaining membership in business organizations are two other costs. The maintenance supervisor may be a cost of the management company, charged to the project, or a shared expense. One additional cost is sharing the fee with another management company.

There are numerous opportunities to manage properties from afar. These opportunities are usually found in the smaller community where professional commercial property management is limited or where a relationship is established with an owner who prefers the services of a particular company over a local firm. Managing properties from afar is an effective means for a management company to increase its portfolio size and profitability, but care must be taken in establishing the management procedures, analyzing additional costs, and establishing a fee that is fair to both the owner and the management company.

§ 2.20 INCENTIVE PROGRAMS

Incentive programs are designed to reward employees for achieving a goal, to acknowledge outstanding performance, to motivate people, to express appreciation, and to promote team spirit within the staff. Each incentive program should be analyzed to determine if it meets the intended goal, is perceived as fair, and is cost-effective. These programs can take many forms.

(a) COMMISSIONS

A commission is the major incentive for leasing. Leasing agents who are not paid a salary are usually paid 50% or more of the commission paid to their broker. Property managers who are paid a salary must devote most of their time to managing the properties, but they will still have time to handle leasing and renewals. Since commission income often is the majority of the profit margin earned by a commercial property management company, a property manager who is motivated to lease space has a positive impact on the company's profits. A 20% to 35% share of the commission for new leases and renewals in addition to a base salary is an effective incentive program for managers. The percentage can be increased as additional space is leased.

(b) BONUS FOR ACQUIRING MANAGEMENT ACCOUNTS

A management company's growth is dependent upon acquiring new accounts, so many companies offer their managers an incentive to add properties to the company's portfolio. A common incentive is a bonus consisting of all or a portion of the first month's management fee. This incentive can also be offered to leasing agents or sales brokers in the community if they refer a management account to the company.

(c) EQUITY INTEREST IN PROPERTIES

This is a common incentive program for upper management and executive positions in development firms. A small ownership position is given in a property being developed or syndicated.

(d)   AWARDS FOR ACHIEVING PROFESSIONAL DESIGNATIONS

A professional designation enhances both the individual's and the company's reputation in the industry. The company can acknowledge the manager's achievement by sending out press releases; featuring the individual in the company newsletter; distributing a memo to all employees; marking the occasion with an in-house celebration; or presenting a gift such as a restaurant pass, a weekend getaway, or cash.

(e)   AWARDS FOR PERFORMANCE AND MEETING GOALS

A small monetary award or gift certificate can be given in recognition of individual accomplishments or for goals that have been met by a group. For example, a Pacific Northwest property management firm gives employees a gift certificate from a restaurant for sending out monthly management reports on time for all the properties for three consecutive months. Since preparing a monthly management report is a team effort, everyone works together to be on time with his or her portion of the report.

(f)   ANNUAL BONUS

A year-end bonus, often referred to as the Christmas bonus, is an excellent way to reward the property manager along with the administrative and clerical staff for their work during the year. The bonus should be based on the company's profits and the individual's performance. One caution: If the same amount is given each year regardless of these two criteria, it will be perceived as an additional paycheck and not as an earned bonus.

(g)   GIFTS OF APPRECIATION

Recognizing birthdays or employment anniversary dates is another opportunity to reward staff members. An informal get-together for coffee and presentation of a gift certificate or a congratulatory card is appropriate on an employee's anniversary. A management firm in the Northwest has a cake each month for all birthdays in that month. Employees are taken to lunch and given a $50 gift certificate to a department store on their employment anniversary.

(h)   COMMUNICATION

Because property management is a people-oriented business, good communication between and within departments is essential in promoting teamwork. Staff members need to feel that they are valued and appreciated not only by receiving external rewards, but by the goodwill of their coworkers. One way to foster cooperation and allow people to express themselves is to sponsor regular staff or department luncheons. Here staff members can discuss business concerns informally, brainstorm, and share suggestions while enjoying each other's company at a meal. Another opportunity is to take each department out to a monthly lunch to review departmental operations. The lunch can be at or near one of the properties managed so the staff can visit the property. Another way to foster better communication and a positive team spirit is to schedule social events throughout the year so that staff members and their families can meet as friends and enjoy one another away from the office. A committee can organize events ranging from river rafting, to a Halloween costume party, to a summer picnic, to a family night, to a formal Christmas dinner.

Countless books have been written on team building, motivation, conflict management, and overall human relations. Since organizational goals are more likely to be met when people feel they are valued members of the company, property managers should learn to use the people management skills found in these resources.

§ 2.21 PROCEDURE MANUAL

Property managers need considerable autonomy to be effective. Their wide range of responsibilities and the amount of time spent away from the office preclude constant supervision. Many of them work in branch offices or as on-site managers for a large commercial property with limited supervision.

In this autonomous structure, specific guidelines are needed to ensure that the manager operates within the framework of the company's policies and procedures. Property owners, too, have specific guidelines, which might include the length of maintenance contracts, rent collection, evictions, and leasing terms. The management company can develop a manual covering the policies and procedures of each property owner and those of the management company.

The procedure manual also details how each department functions and how all departments interact with one another. The manual may be used as a marketing tool when the property management company submits a proposal. It gives the owner, especially an institutional owner, a model of efficiency that inspires confidence in the company.

No two procedure manuals are alike because each is tailored to the philosophy and operation of the management company and to the type of properties manages. Exhibit 2.3 is a sample outline that can serve as a basis for a property management company's procedure manual.

EXHIBIT 2.3

Procedure Manual Outline

SECTION I.   MANAGEMENT AGREEMENTS

Each management agreement is summarized into the following sections:

Property description: Address, square footage, and major tenants

Ownership: Name, address, and phone number of the ownership and its representative

Management agreement terms: Length, commencement and expiration date, cancellation rights, management fees, other fees including who pays for on-site personnel

Leasing: Leasing agent, commission schedule, and parameters within which a lease can be negotiated without the owner's approval

Expenditure limits: The amount of nonbudgeted maintenance and equipment expenditures allowed without owner's approval

Reports: List of the type and frequency of the narrative and accounting reports. Date reports are due. Name and Address of those who will receive the reports.

Operating account: Minimum balance required by the bank in owner's operating account

Insurance: Insurance requirements and policy limits for the property and for the management company

Legal counsel: The approved attorney

SECTION II.   GENERAL OFFICE POLICIES AND PROCEDURES

Explains office procedures and policies.

II-A1	Main office management personnel
II-A2	Branch office personnel
II-A3	New employees
II-A4	Terminating employees
II-A4a	Authority for personnel action
II-A5	Pay periods
II-A6	Time cards
II-A7	Office hours
II-A8	Vacations
II-A9	Illness
II-A10	Holidays
II-A11	Absence other than illness
II-A12	Medical, disability, and life insurance
II-B	Postage meter and mail
II-C	Office supplies
II-D	Automobile accidents
II-E	Expense reports
II-F	Petty cash vouchers
II-G	Filing system

EXHIBIT 2.3 *(Continued)*

II-7   Travel arrangements
II-8   Continuing education

SECTION III.   PURCHASING POLICIES AND PROCEDURES

Explains methods for purchasing and approving invoices.

III-A   Chart of accounts
III-B   Vendor/contractors lists
III-C   Monetary approval limits
III-D   Nonbudget/over-budget expenses over $1,000
III-E1   Definition of documents
III-E2   Purchase order numbering system
III-E3   Purchase order, blanket purchase order, confirmation of
            purchase order
III-E4   Instructions for preparing purchase order, blanket purchase
            order, confirmation of purchase order
III-F   Change order
III-G   Check request
III-H   Extra vendor work request
III-I   Capital expense
III-J1   Tenant extra order
III-J2   Instructions for preparing tenant extra order
III-J3   Tenant extra order log sheet

SECTION IV.   MANAGEMENT COMPANY'S ACCOUNTING POLICIES AND PROCEDURES

Provides instructions to the accounting department and information to others
in the company about how the accounting department operates.

IV-A   Tenant invoices
IV-B1   Processing an invoice
IV-B1a   Code of approval stamp
IV-B2   Not to exceed purchase order
IV-B3   Fixed-price contract
IV-B4   Utility and telephone bills
IV-B5   Unit price contract
IV-B6   Travel and entertainment vouchers
IV-C   Abstracting of contracts and equipment
IV-D1   Petty cash accounts
IV-D2   Instructions for preparing petty cash accounts
IV-E   Building managers checking account
IV-F   Merchants' association accounting
IV-G   Material & labor releases

SECTION V.   LEASING POLICIES AND PROCEDURES

Outlines procedures for working with brokers to complete a deal and for
moving the tenant into the building.

V-A1   Recognition of outside broker's status
V-A2   Nonrecognition of outside broker's status

EXHIBIT 2.3 *(Continued)*

V-B	Owner approval procedure
V-C	Lease exclusive and conflicts
V-D1	Lease summary preparation
V-D2	Lease preparation
V-E	Lease addendum
V-F1	Lease, amendment of lease, assignment, assumption, and consent
V-F2	Sublease agreement
V-F3	Holdover and termination agreements
V-F4	Lease termination agreement
V-G	Tenant work prior to lease execution
V-H1	Space studies (office building and industrial properties)
V-H2	Working drawings
V-I1	Tenant move-in
V-I2	Instructions for preparing tenant move-in
V-I3	Storefront allowances
V-J1	Lease commissions
V-J2	Lease commissions statement
V-K1	Tenant move-out
V-K2	Instructions for preparing tenant move-out

SECTION VI.   BUILDING OPERATING POLICIES AND PROCEDURES

Explains daily operating policies and procedures.

VI-A1	New tenant
VI-A2	Tenant list
VI-A3	Vacating tenants
VI-B1	Delivery of notice
VI-B2	Notices to pay rent
VI-C	Notice of delinquency
VI-D	Enforcing late charges
VI-E	Delinquency charge assessment letter
VI-F	Notice of default in payment of rent
VI-G	Rent relief
VI-H	Notice of abandoning tenant
VI-I	Application of security deposit to rent
VI-J	Holidays
VI-K	Tenant name change
VI-L	Tenant construction
VI-M	Security
VI-N	Maintenance
VI-O1	Public use of community hall
VI-O2	Public use of community booth
VI-P1	Merchants' association bylaws
VI-P2	Promotional fund bylaws
VI-Q	Building keys
VI-R1	Tenant HVAC calls
VI-R2	Tenant HVAC maintenance service

EXHIBIT 2.3 *(Continued)*

VI-S	Tenant janitorial complaints
VI-T	Building's organizational chart
VI-U1	Mall community booth guidelines
VI-U2	Public use of shopping center
VI-V	Litigation report
VI-W	Advertising agency
VI-X1	Budget input form
VI-X2	Budget explanation form
VI-X3	Tenant roster
VI-X4	Tenant charges
VI-X5	Tenant common area and escalation calculations

SECTION VII. CONSTRUCTION POLICIES AND PROCEDURES

Explains how construction of tenant's improvements is handled.

VII-A1	Tenant improvement estimates
VII-A2	Tenant improvement budget
VII-B	Tenant extra order
VII-C	Contractor's insurance
VII-D	Tenant's contractor
VII-E	Contractor's work order
VII-F	Construction contractor's request for payment
VII-G	Notice to security
VII-H	Construction completion
VII-I	Unit prices
VII-J	Notice of nonresponsibility
VII-K	Notice of completion
VII-L	Stock depletion reporting

SECTION VIII. INSURANCE POLICIES AND PROCEDURES

Provides instruction and forms for landlord's, tenant's, and contractor's insurance requirements.

VIII-A	Insurance agent
VIII-B	Outline of coverage
VIII-C	Notifying insurance agent—various phases of development and construction (new projects)
VII-D	Notifying insurance agent—Personal property purchased or leased
VII-E	Notifying insurance agent—Increased construction cost
VIII-F1	Preparation of accident/damage report
VIII-F2	General guidelines for reporting an accident
VIII-F3	Automobile liability, public liability, and property damage accident reports
VIII-F4	Employee accident reports
VIII-F5	Reporting requirements
VIII-G	New tenant
VIII-H	Existing tenants

EXHIBIT 2.3 *(Continued)*

VIII-I   New service contractor
VIII-J   Existing service contractor
VIII-K   Promotional events

SECTION IX.   REPORTS

Lists accounting and narrative reports.

IX-A   Delinquency report
IX-B   Lease expiration and deferred conditions
IX-C   Tenant sales report
IX-D   Expenditure report
IX-E   Rent roll
IX-F   Market surveys
IX-G   Breakeven analysis
IX-H   Monthly rental report
IX-I   Manager's monthly report
IX-J   Comparative occupancy report
IX-K   Leasing prospects report
IX-L   Space available report
IX-M   Monthly building status report
IX-N   Annual management plan

SECTION X.   SAMPLE LETTERS AND FORMS

Provides sample letters and forms for property mangers and their assistants.

X-1   Recognition of broker's status
X-2   Nonrecognition of broker's status
X-3   Broker's agreement
X-4a   Tenant lease information
X-4b   Addendum tenant lease information
X-5   Letter of transmittal to tenant—Signature of document
X-6   Standard transmittal letter
X-7   Consent to alteration letter
X-8   Transmittal letter to tenant with signed documents
X-9   Substantial completion letter
X-10   Sublease agreement
X-11   Landlord's consent to sublease
X-12   Holdover agreement
X-13   Termination agreement
X-14   Transmittal letter—Executed documents
X-15   Authorization to proceed with improvements
X-16   Lease commission statement
X-17   Leasing commission transmittal letter
X-18   Tenant information and emergency procedures manual—Letter
X-19   Mall/lobby directory listing authorization
X-20   Emergency notification
X-21   Office building security card

EXHIBIT 2.3 *(Continued)*

X-22	Security pass
X-23	Door and floor directory sign order authorization
X-24	Memo to clean space
X-25	Notice of delinquency
X-26	Late charge warning letter
X-27	Notice of abandoning tenant
X-28	Notice applying security deposit to rent
X-29	Letter to tenant—Holiday hours
X-30	Letter to tenant—Name change
X-31	Daily security report
X-32	Theft/burglary report
X-33	Accident/injury/property damage report
X-34	Inspection report—Shopping center interior
X-35	Inspection report—Shopping center exterior
X-36	Inspection report—Office building and industrial property
X-37	Monthly activity report
X-38	License, release, and indemnity agreement—Short form
X-39	License, release, and indemnity agreement—Long form
X-40	Transmittal—Tenant improvement plans
X-40a	Tenant extra order
X-40b	Tenant extra order log sheet
X-41	Letter to contractor—Insurance requirements
X-42a	Insurance requirement letters—Request for certificate
X-43b	Insurance requirement letters—Notice of nonconformity to limits
X-43c	Insurance requirement letters—Notice of expiration
X-44	TV antenna/satellite disk agreement
X-45	Contractor's work order
X-46	Transmittal letter—Work order
X-47	Notice of nonresponsibility
X-48	Notice of completion
X-49a	Insurance requirements—Shopping center lease
X-49b	Insurance requirements—Office building lease
X-49c	Insurance requirements—Industrial property lease
X-50	Monthly delinquency report
X-51	Tenant sales analysis
X-52	Moving notices
X-53	Lease amendment letter agreement—Rent relief
X-54	Tenant improvements—Budget
X-55	Maintenance request (call slip)
X-56	Memo to cleaning company (complaint)
X-57	Notice of default letter (shopping center)
X-58	HVAC maintenance notification letter
X-59	Rent deferment agreement
X-60	HVAC calls
X-61	Janitorial calls
X-62	Litigation report
X-63	Authorization to proceed with working drawings
X-64	Letter to tenant—Preparation of working drawings

§ 2.22   THE MANAGEMENT AGREEMENT

The management agreement is the basis for the relationship between the property management firm and the property owner or advisor. The agreement will establish the company's duties, authority, and compensation. This agreement must be carefully prepared and negotiated. A poorly drafted agreement can result in misunderstandings and eventually a termination of the relationship. The real estate law in many states requires the property management firm to have an executed management agreement. Violation of this law can subject the company to disciplinary action by the real estate commission.

Most institutional owners and pension fund advisors require that their management agreement be used. Because these agreements are usually one-sided, they should be reviewed carefully. Although these clients are not willing to negotiate their entire agreement, they will modify certain clauses. The following clauses should be given particular attention: indemnification; reports after the agreement is terminated; commission fees on co-brokered deals; the party responsible for paying for marketing brochures. The item that is usually nonnegotiable is the client's accounting reports. The property manager must carefully analyze the time to prepare these reports and factor this cost into the management fees.

Exhibit 2.4 is a sample commercial property management agreement that can be modified to meet the specific needs of the property owner and the property. A review of salient points in this agreement follows:

1.   Exhibit B.   This exhibit is an attachment listing the easements; covenants, conditions, and restrictions; common area agreements;

restrictions; exclusives; and any other documents that effect the management and operations of the property. These agreements should be reviewed, and in some cases summarized, to assure that the rights conveyed to other parties are not violated and the owner's responsibilities are fulfilled.

   2. Exhibit C. This exhibit lists the lease commission rate and commission payment schedule.

   3. Appointment of Manager (Section 1.1). The property management company is appointed the exclusive managing and leasing agent for the property. This item also states that the owner pays any taxes assessed on the management and leasing fees.

   4. Office Space. If the property has an on-site manager, office space is provided for the property manager and administrative staff at no charge.

   5. Management Services of Manager (Section 2). The property management company is provided the books and reports necessary to operate the property.

   6. Specific Duties of Manager (Section 2.4). This sections lists the responsibilities of the property management company. The duties must be tailored to the property and analyzed when establishing the management fee.

   7. Repairs and Maintenance (Section 2.4d). A minimum balance is required in the property's operating account. This is to assure that sufficient funds will be available for operating the property. A spending limit is provided for nonbudgeted expenses, including equipment and supplies. Procedures are outlined to obtain authorization to exceed these limits.

   8. Insurance (Section 2.4g). The management company agrees to administer the property's insurance program. However, the company is not responsible for determining the type and amount of insurance because few managers have expertise in this field and do not want to assume liability if the insurance coverage is not sufficient to cover a loss. This section provides that the property management company is named additional insured or named-insured on the property owner's insurance company.

   9. Personnel (Section 2.4h). This section provides that all on-site maintenance personnel are employees of the property management company, not of the owner. Most owners, especially institutions, cannot or will not place these personnel on their payroll.

   10. Other Services (Section 2.4i). The property management company is allowed to negotiate a separate charge for services that are not included in the list of manager's responsibilities.

11. Additional Services (Section 2.5). The property management company is allowed to charge the tenants for services beyond the scope of the management agreement. For example, a tenant may request that the property management company remodel the tenant's offices or find a subtenant or assignee for the tenant's premises.

12. Money Management (Section 2.5c). This section covers the administrative fee in connection with the management company's providing money management services and relieves the company of any liability related to these investments. The management company's accounting department will be required to spend additional time to implement a money management program, and an additional fee should be assessed to cover these expenses.

13. Waiver and Indemnification (Section 2.9). The property owner indemnifies, defends, and holds harmless the management company for liability for damage to person and property, except as a result of gross negligence of the property manager.

14. Authority of Manager (Section 3). All property managers do not have the same experience and ability. Property owners are aware of this and may request a particular property manager with specific expertise. This section names the manager assigned to the property. It also addresses whether or not the property management company will be an agent of the owner. A subsection states the terms of agreements that the property manager enters into on behalf of the property owner. These agreements are usually for maintenance. Two items of particular concern are length of contract and cancellation rights.

15. Compensation for Management Services (Section 4). This agreement provides for a minimum fee vs. a percentage of the base and percentage rents. When this agreement is used in managing a shopping center, the administrative fee in the common area budget is paid to the property management company. The management fee can be structured several ways. Other fee structures are: a percentage of all income collected, including tenant's reimbursement of taxes, insurance, and common area charges; or a flat fee. This section allows a fee for handling the payroll of on-site maintenance personnel.

16. Accounting Records and Reports (Section 6). Each property management company has a standard accounting and reporting system, but for some owners, particularly institutional owners, it must be modified. This section states that the property management company will provide its standard accounting and reporting system and the dates the owner will be provided these reports. If the accounting reports vary from the property management company's standard reports, they should be explained in an addendum in the management agreement. The property management company is committed to providing an annual budget by a certain date. The owner has thirty days to request changes after which the property manager has the authority to operate the property based on this budget.

17. Term and Termination (Section 8). The term of the management agreement, cancellation rights, and penalties for cancellation are explained in this clause. The manner and time frame of the final accounting report are also stated.

18. Designated Agent (Section 10). Many properties have multiple owners. The owner must appoint a representative who will provide direction for the property and have the authority to make decisions. This clause also provides for compensation if the property owner hires one of the manager's employees or terminates the agreement.

In 1988, the Institute of Real Estate Management developed a general management agreement with an accompanying booklet explaining each clause.

§ 2.23   THE PROJECT DATA BOOK

Every property generates a multitude of information. Some of the information is used in the daily operations of the property, and some is used only occasionally or in an emergency. Information for the operation of the property needs to be summarized, compiled, and available for quick reference. This information is divided into two general areas: lease summaries (discussed in Chapter 8 on lease administration), and property information.

The property information is compiled and placed in a project data book like the one in Exhibit 2.5. The book's first section contains general information such as the property's address, ownership, owner's representative, architect, general contractor, leasing agent, management company, attorney, insurance agent, and accountant. Also included are the phone numbers for police, fire department, and utility companies.

The next section of the project data book consists of statistical data: number of acres, square footage, number of parking stalls, dates of construction commencement and completion, and the major tenants and their opening dates. A plot plan is marked with shutoff valves, lock boxes, and employee parking area.

Another section lists the square footage of each space or suite, the tenant's name and address, and the after-hours phone number of the tenant's manager. Additional information includes a list of vendors and contractors with business and after-hours phone numbers. If available, a similar directory of the original construction subcontractors is helpful.

It is important to keep the data book current. If the data are entered into a computer, the book can be revised and updated easily. A master copy of the project data books for all the properties managed by the

EXHIBIT 2.4

Sample Commercial Property Management Agreement

Owner:

_____

Manager:

TRF Management Corporation

EXHIBIT **2.4** *(Continued)*

TABLE OF CONTENTS

EXHIBIT 2.4 *(Continued)*

EXHIBITS

EXHIBIT 2.4 *(Continued)*

MANAGEMENT AGREEMENT

THIS **MANAGEMENT AGREEMENT** (the "Agreement") is made and entered into as of this _____ day of _____, 19___, by and between _____
_____, a
_____ (the "Owner"), and TRF MANAGEMENT CORPORATION, a corporation (the "Manager"):

W I T N E S S E T H:

WHEREAS, the Owner is the owner or ground lessee of that certain real property commonly known as "_____" located in _____, _____ County, _____, as more fully set forth in the legal description thereof attached hereto and made a part hereof as "Exhibit A" (the "Property"), on which Property is located certain real property improvements, parking spaces and related facilities (the "Buildings") which Property, Buildings and any other improvements now or hereafter located thereon shall hereinafter be collectively referred to as the "Project"; and

WHEREAS, the Owner wishes to retain the services of the Manager as manager of the Project with responsibilities for managing, operating, maintaining and servicing the Project as stated in this Agreement; and

WHEREAS, any easements, covenants, conditions and restrictions with respect to the Project now in effect are as more fully set forth in the Schedule of Basic Documents attached hereto and made a part hereof as "Exhibit B"; (all of the aforesaid documents together with all amendments and modifications now or hereafter made thereto hereinafter collectively called the "Basic Documents"), and

WHEREAS, the Manager is willing to perform such services with regard to the management, operation, maintenance and servicing of the Project and the obligations of the Owner as stated herein;

NOW, THEREFORE, in consideration of the foregoing and of the full and faithful performance by the Manager of all the terms, conditions and obligations imposed upon the Manager hereunder, the parties hereto agree as follows:

1.   **APPOINTMENT OF MANAGER.**

    1.1   **Appointment.**

        (a)   **Manager.** The Owner hereby appoints the Manager as the exclusive manager and the exclusive leasing broker and agent of the Project with the responsibilities and upon the terms and conditions set forth herein, and the Manager, by its execution hereof, does hereby accept such appointment.

        (b)   **Commission Schedule.** The Manager shall be paid a leasing commission as set forth in the Commission Schedule attached hereto and made a part hereof as "Exhibit C." It is understood and agreed that any and all sales, use, business and occupations tax, or other such taxes, charged or assessed against or attributable to the fees, costs and expenses charged by, or paid to, Manager shall be the obligation of Owner and shall be paid in full by the Owner.

EXHIBIT 2.4 *(Continued)*

1.2   Tax Numbers.   The Manager's tax identification number is _____. The Owner's tax identification number is _____.

1.3   Office Space.   If the Owner requires an on-site manager or administrative person for the Project, then the Owner shall provide rent-free office space in the Project to the Manager, which space shall be sufficient to accommodate the Manager, on-site manager and/or administrative person and its employees in the performance of its obligations hereunder.   All of the costs and expenses of operating and maintaining such office space shall be paid for by Owner, which costs and expenses shall include but not be limited to providing adequate office furniture, equipment and supplies, heat, electricity and air conditioning, refuse removal, and other utilities and other costs and expenses related to such office space.

2.   MANAGEMENT SERVICES OF MANAGER.

2.1   Orientation.

(a)   **General.**   The Manager hereby acknowledges receipt of certain books and records with respect to the operation of the Project, personal property on the Project belonging to the Owner, and all service contracts relating to the maintenance and operation of the Project, all as more fully set forth in the schedule thereof attached hereto and made a part hereof as "Exhibit D."

(b)   **Itemized Receipt.**   After the effective date of this Agreement, upon request by the Owner, the Manager shall prepare and submit to the Owner a complete list of all books and records of the Owner held by the Manager, a list of all service contracts and a complete inventory of all personal property received by the Manager.

2.2   Management of the Project.   The Manager shall devote its reasonable best efforts consonant with first-class professional management to serving the Owner as manager of the Project, and shall perform its duties hereunder in a diligent, careful and vigilant manner so as to manage, operate, maintain and service the Project as a first-class commercial property.   The services of the Manager hereunder are to be of a scope and quality not less than those generally performed by professional managers of other similar first-class complexes and properties in the area.   The Manager shall make available to the Owner the full benefit of the judgment, experience and advice of the members of the Manager's organization and staff with respect to the policies to be pursued by the Owner in operating the Project, and will perform such services as may be reasonably requested by the Owner in operating, maintaining, servicing, improving and leasing the Project.

2.3   Use and Maintenance of the Project.   The Manager agrees not to knowingly permit the use of the Project for any purpose which might void any policy of insurance held by the Owner or which might render any loss insured thereunder uncollectible, or which would be in violation of any governmental restriction, statute, ordinance, rule or regulation.   It shall be the duty of the Manager at all times during the term of this Agreement to operate and maintain the Project according to the highest standards achievable consistent with the expressed plan of the Owner.   The Manager shall use its best efforts to secure full compliance of all lessees and sublessees, concessionaires and others in possession of all or any part of the Project with the terms and conditions of their respective leases, subleases and/or concessionaire agreements; provided, that Manager is authorized to refund security deposits to each tenant as

EXHIBIT 2.4 *(Continued)*

required under the respective leases. The Manager shall be expected to perform such other acts and deeds as are reasonable, necessary and proper in the discharge of its duties under this Agreement.

2.4   Specific Duties of Manager.   Without limiting the duties and obligations of the Manager under any other provisions of this Agreement, the Manager shall have the following duties and perform the following services to the extent that Manager is in possession of sufficient funds from the Project:

(a)   Monies Collected.   Collect all rent and other payments due from lessees, sublessees, concessionaires and others in the Project and any other sums otherwise due the Owner with respect to the Project in the ordinary course of business. The Owner authorizes the Manager to request, demand, collect, receive and receipt for all such rent and other charges and to institute legal proceedings in the name of, and as an expense reimbursable by, the Owner for the collection thereof and for the dispossession of lessees, sublessees, concessionaires and other persons from the Project. Such expenses may include the engaging of counsel of the Manager's choice for any such matter. All monies collected by the Manager shall be forthwith deposited by Manager, at Manager's option (i) in a separate bank account or accounts established by the Manager in the Owner's name for such purpose, having such signatories, and in a bank, approved by the Owner (the "Separate Account"); or (ii) in the Manager's agency account. Funds deposited in such Separate Account shall not be commingled with any funds of the Manager. Funds deposited in the Manager's agency account may be commingled with other funds in said agency account. The Owner shall maintain a minimum balance of $_____ in the Manager's Separate Account or Manager's Agency Account with respect to the Project to pay the expenses of the Project. If at any time, the balance of the Separate Account, or the Owner's portion of the Agency Account, falls below said sum then the Owner shall immediately upon notice by Manager, deposit an amount in such account sufficient to restore said account balance, or Owner's portion thereof, to not less than the amount set forth above. In no event shall Manager be obligated to extend its own funds on behalf of Owner where the Special Account balance, or the Owner's portion of the Manager's Agency Account, falls below the above sum. The Manager shall be responsible for the collection, disbursement, handling and holding of the monies collected to the extent that a normal, reasonable and prudent businessman would be responsible for such collection, disbursement, handling and holding of monies.

(b)   Obligations Under Basic Documents.   To the extent that monies are available from the Project, to duly and punctually perform and comply with all of the obligations, terms and conditions required to be performed or complied with by the Owner under the Basic Documents relating to management, operation, maintenance and servicing of the Project, including without limitation, the timely payment of all sums required to be paid thereunder, all to the end that the Owner's interest in the Project and its interests as Landlord under the leases shall be preserved and no default chargeable to the Owner shall occur under the Basic Documents. After disbursement of all funds specified herein or in any other provision of this Agreement, and after establishing a reasonable cash reserve in an amount mutually determined by Owner, and Manager, any balance remaining at the time each monthly report is forwarded to the Owner (as described in Section 6.2) during the term of this Agreement, shall be disbursed or transferred to the Owner or to such other person as directed from time to time by the Owner.

(c)   Taxes and Insurance.   Duly and punctually pay on behalf of the Owner all real estate taxes, assessments and insurance premiums payable in

EXHIBIT 2.4 *(Continued)*

respect of the Project or any part thereof, such to be done prior to the time that any insurance policy would lapse due to nonpayment of the premium and prior to the time any penalties or interest would accrue upon any real estate taxes or assessments (except such interest as may accrue on an assessment payable on an installment basis which the Owner has elected to pay on an installment basis).

        (d)   **Repairs and Maintenance.** To the extent that monies are available from operation of the Project, to make all repairs and perform all maintenance on the Buildings, appurtenances and grounds of the Project as required to be made by the Owner under the Basic Documents and in accordance with standards acceptable to the Owner. For any individual item of repair or replacement, the non-budgeted expenses incurred shall not exceed the sum of $_____ unless specifically authorized in advance by the Owner, excepting, however, that emergency repairs immediately necessary for the preservation and safety of the Project or danger to life or property may be made by the Manager without the prior approval of the Owner; provided, that immediately after such emergency repairs, the Manager shall send the Owner a report of any repairs so made.

        (e)   **Equipment and Supplies.** Make all arrangements for the furnishing to the Project of utility, maintenance and other services and for the acquisition of equipment and supplies as necessary for the management, operation, maintenance and servicing of the Project as required of the Owner under the Basic Documents; provided, however, the non-budgeted purchase of any single piece of equipment or order of supplies in excess of $_____ shall not be made without the written consent of the Owner.

        (f)   **Tax Assessments.** Keep the Owner informed of any change in the amount of real or personal property assessments or taxes relating to the Project, and to recommend, from time to time, the advisability of contesting either the validity or the amount thereof.

        (g)   **Insurance Coverage.** If requested by the Owner, to cause to be placed and kept in force all forms of insurance required by law or any mortgage secured by all or any part of the Project to protect the Owner or any mortgagee, including but not limited to public liability insurance, fire and extended coverage insurance, burglary and theft insurance, and boiler insurance. All insurance coverage shall be placed with such companies, in such amounts, and with such beneficial interest appearing therein as shall be acceptable to the Owner and otherwise be in conformity with the requirements of the Basic Documents or any mortgage covering the Project, and, anything herein to the contrary notwithstanding, it is understood and agreed that the Manager shall have no responsibility, obligation or liability for determining the amount or type of insurance which is required with respect to the Project. Should the Owner elect to place such insurance coverage directly, the Owner shall provide the Manager with a duplicate copy of the original policy, and the Manager shall thereafter keep such insurance in force. The Manager shall promptly investigate and make a full timely written report to the applicable insurance company, with a copy to the Owner, as to all accidents, claims or damage relating to the ownership, operation and maintenance of the Project, any damage or destruction to the Project and the estimated cost of repair thereof, and shall prepare any and all reports required by any insurance company in connection therewith. All such reports shall be filed timely with the insurance company as required under the terms of the insurance policy involved. The Manager shall have no right to settle, compromise or otherwise dispose of any claims, demands or liabilities, whether or not covered by insurance, without the prior written

EXHIBIT 2.4 *(Continued)*

consent of the Owner. The Owner shall name Manager as an additional insured on the Owner's insurance policy or policies carried by Owner with respect to the Property and/or Buildings.

(h) **Personnel.** Employ such on-site maintenance personnel on behalf of the Owner as necessary in order to maintain the Project in a first-class condition. All such on-site maintenance persons shall be employees of the Manager. The costs and expenses of such employees shall be borne by the Owner, which expenses shall include but not be limited to salary, payroll expenses, withholding taxes, automobile allowances, and Manager's standard employee benefits. Any employees, whether employed by the Owner or Manager, who handle or who are responsible for funds belonging to the Owner shall be bonded by a fidelity bond in an amount of not less than $500,000.00.

(i) **Other Services.** Perform all other services necessary to comply with the provisions of this Agreement or as may be agreed to be provided by Manager. If the Manager provides any services to the Owner or any lessees or sub-lessees of the Project which are not provided for in this Agreement and for which a separate charge is made, then such separate charge shall be retained for the account of the Manager, all as more fully set forth below; provided, that Manager shall notify Owner prior to providing such special services to any lessee or sublessee; and, provided, further, that any special fees payable by Owner for such special services shall be subject to the mutual agreement of Owner and Manager.

2.5   Additional Services.

(a) **Additional Lessee Services.** Should the Manager provide any services to lessees or sublessees which are not customary services or services not required hereunder ("Additional Lessee Services"), then a separate charge for such Additional Lessee Services shall be made to the lessees or sublessees receiving such Additional Lessee Services and the separate charge shall be paid to and retained by the Manager for its own account and the Owner shall have no interest therein. The Manager shall pay all costs incurred in providing such Additional Lessee Services. All amounts received by the Manager from Additional Lessee Services shall be excluded from Gross Rental Receipts for purposes of the calculation of the Management Fee in accordance with Section 4 below.

(b) **Additional Owner Services.** Should the Manager provide any services to the Owner which are not customary services or services not required hereunder such as, but not limited to, services related to a rehabilitation, remodeling, repair or reconstruction of the Project or major tenant construction ("Additional Owner Services"), then a separate charge for such Additional Owner Services shall be negotiated between Owner and Manager before such services are performed by Manager.

(c) **Money Management.** In the event Owner shall desire Manager to invest any sums which come into possession of Manager by reason of this Agreement and the Manager's actions hereunder, then Manager shall invest such sums solely in compliance with specific written instructions given Manager by the Owner. Any such investment shall be at Owner's sole risk and Manager assumes no obligation or responsibility with respect to such investment except to comply with Owner's written instructions with respect to such investment of funds. Manager shall receive an administrative fee of ten percent (10%) of all interest or other sums earned by reason of such investments.

EXHIBIT 2.4 *(Continued)*

2.6   Concessions Income. Any income received by the Manager from vending or other coin-operated machines or concessions ("Concessions Income") shall be delivered to and retained by the Owner for its own account, and the Owner shall pay all costs in connection with Concessions Income. The Manager shall receive a Management Fee on all concession income as more specifically set forth below.

2.7   Compliance With Laws. The Owner shall fully comply with all statutes, ordinances, rules and regulations governing the Project and the business conducted therein; provided, that at Manager's election, the Manager may take such action as may be necessary to comply with any and all statutes, rules, regulations, ordinances, orders or requirements affecting the Project promulgated by a federal, state, county or municipal authority having jurisdiction thereover, and all applicable orders of the Board of Fire Underwriters or other similar bodies. Notwithstanding any voluntary action taken by Manager on behalf of Owner, the Manager shall be released from any responsibility in connection with any statute, ordinance, rule or regulation pertaining to the Project or the business conducted thereof and Owner assumes full and complete responsibility for compliance therewith and for the payment of any and all penalties, taxes, impositions and fines resulting from a failure to comply with such statute, ordinances, rules and regulations.

2.8   Notices. All notices from any mortgagee, ground lessor or other party to any of the Basic Documents given pursuant thereto or pertaining thereto and all notices from any governmental or official entity shall be forthwith delivered to the Owner by the Manager.

2.9   Waiver and Indemnification.

(a)   Waiver. It is understood and agreed that Manager makes no representations or warranties with respect to the profitability of the Property.

(b)   Indemnification.

(1)   Subject to the provisions of Section 2.9(c) below, the Owner shall indemnify, defend and hold Manager harmless from and against all suits in connection with the Property and from liability for damage to personal property and injury to or death of any person, except suits, damage, injury or death arising through the gross negligence or willful acts of the Manager. Owner shall carry at its own expense public liability and elevator liability (if elevators are part of the equipment on the Property) naming Owner and Manager which insurance shall be adequate to protect their respective interests, and shall be in such form, substance, content and amounts reasonably acceptable to Manager, and to furnish Manager certificates evidencing such insurance. Unless Owner shall provide such insurance and furnish such certificate within sixty (60) days from the date of this Agreement, the Manager may, but shall not be obligated to, place said insurance and charge the cost thereof to the account of the Owner. All such insurance polices shall provide that the Manager shall receive not less than thirty (30) days' written notice prior to cancellation of the policy.

(2)   Subject to the provisions of Section 2.9(c) below, the Owner shall indemnify, defend and save the Manager harmless from all claims, investigations, and suits, or from actions or failures to act of the Owner, with respect to any alleged or actual violation of state or federal labor laws, it being expressly agreed and understood that as between the Owner and the Manager, however, it shall be the responsibility of the Manager to comply with all applicable state or federal labor laws. The Owner's obligation under this Section 2.9(b) shall include the payment of all

EXHIBIT 2.4 *(Continued)*

settlements, judgments, damages, liquidated damages, penalties, forfeitures, back pay awards, court costs, litigation expense, and attorneys' fees.

(3)   Subject to the provisions of Section 2.9(c) below, the Owner shall pay all expenses incurred by the Manager, including, but not limited to, reasonable attorneys' fees and Manager's costs and time in connection with any claim, proceeding, or suit involving an alleged violation by the Manager or the Owner, or both, of any law pertaining to fair employment, fair credit reporting, environmental protection, rent control, taxes, or fair housing, including, but not limited to, any law prohibiting, or making illegal, discrimination on the basis of race, sex, creed, color, religion, national origin, or mental or physical handicap; provided, however, that the Owner shall not be responsible to the Manager for any such expenses in the event the Manager is finally adjudicated to have personally, and not in a representative capacity, violated any such law.   Nothing contained herein shall obligate the Manager to employ counsel to represent the Owner in any such proceeding or suit, and the Owner may elect to employ counsel to represent the Owner in any such proceeding or suit.   The Owner also agrees to pay reasonable expenses (or an apportioned amount of such expenses where other employers of Manager also benefit from the expenditure) incurred by the Manager in obtaining legal advice regarding compliance with any law affecting the Property or activities related thereto.

(c)   **Concurrent Negligence; No Indemnification.**   Notwithstanding the provisions of Section 2.9(b) above, in the event of the concurrent negligence of Manager, its agents employees, invitees or contractors on the one hand, and that of the Owner, its lessees, sublessees, concessionaires, partners, directors, officers, agents, employees, invitees or contractors on the other hand, which concurrent negligence results in injury or damage to persons or property and relates to the construction, alteration, repair, addition to, subtraction from, improvement to or maintenance of the Project, or any part thereof, the Owner's obligation to indemnity

3.   **AUTHORITY OF MANAGER.**

3.1   **Manager's Representative.**   The Manager's initial representative shall be _____ (hereinafter referred to as the "Representative"). All employees of the Manager, including the Representative, shall be authorized to act as the Owner's agents.   The Manager reserves the right to appoint a substitute representative who shall be acceptable to the Owner; provided, that the Owner shall have fourteen (14) days from receipt of written notice of such substitute representative within which to approve or reject said substitute representative.   A failure or refusal to approve or reject said substitute representative within said time shall be deemed approval.

3.2   **Execution of Contracts.**   Subject to the provisions of Section 3.3 below, the Manager shall execute all contracts, agreements, and other documents and may undertake action necessary in the performance of its obligations for the maintenance of the Project as an agent of the Owner, as follows and as may be appropriate.

(PROJECT NAME)
By Its Agent:

TRF MANAGEMENT CORPORATION

By: _____
(Designation of
Corporate Office)

EXHIBIT 2.4 *(Continued)*

or

(PROJECT OWNER),

A _____

By Its Agent:

TRF MANAGEMENT CORPORATION

By: _____

(Designation of
Corporate Office)

3.3 **Contracts and Agreements.** The Manager shall not execute and enter into and bind the Owner with respect to any contract or agreement having a term in excess of one (1) year, unless said contract or agreement contains a thirty (30) day

3.3 **Contracts and Agreements.** The Manager shall not execute and enter into and bind the Owner with respect to any contract or agreement having a term in excess of one (1) year, unless said contract or agreement contains a thirty (30) day cancellation provision, without the prior written consent of the Owner, including but not limited to contracts and agreements on behalf of the Owner for the management, operation, maintenance and servicing of the Project and the acquisition of utility, maintenance or other services or the furnishing of services to lessees or sublessees in the Project and in the case of casualty, breakdown in machinery or other similar emergency, if in the reasonable opinion of the Manager emergency action prior to written approval is necessary to prevent additional damage or loss of life or personal injury or a greater total expenditure or to protect the Project from damage or prevent a default on the part of the Owner as landlord under leases or the Basic Documents, in which event such action shall be taken only in concert with prompt notification by the Manager to the Owner.

3.4 **Use of Name.** The Owner authorizes the Manager to use the name " _____ " and " _____ " in the performance of its obligations hereunder and for the purposes of identification and advertising.

4. **COMPENSATION FOR MANAGEMENT SERVICES.**

4.1 **Management Fee.** Owner shall pay Manager as compensation for the management services rendered hereunder an amount (the "Management Fee") equal to (a) _____ percent (___%) of the "Gross Rental Receipts" collected; or (b) a minimum fee of $_____ per month, whichever is greater. The Management Fee for a particular month shall be paid on or before the last day of the month.

4.2 **Definition of Gross Rental Receipts.** The term "Gross Rental Receipts" as used herein shall mean and include all gross receipts (but not any sums which, under normal accounting practice, are attributable to capital) derived from the operation of the Project, including, without limitation, all rent (including the amount of any rental forgiveness, free rent or other rental concessions given to any tenant), percentage rent, concessions income, late payment charges, interest on note collections, and other sums and charges received from lessees, including payments from lessees and sublessees made in consideration of the cancellation, surrender or modification of any lease or made by reason of any default thereunder, or the

EXHIBIT 2.4 *(Continued)*

application of security deposits upon defaults or towards the repair of any damage to the Project; provided, however, that Gross Rental Receipts shall not include sums paid to the Manager for Additional Services, or any security or other deposits.

4.3 Administrative Fees. The Manager shall receive and retain for its own account, in addition to and not in substitution for, its Management Fee, any and all administrative fees for administrating the common areas.

4.4 Fee for On-Site Employees. In addition to its Management Fee and any administrative fees, as described above, a fee equal to five percent (5%) of the gross salary or salaries paid to the said on-site maintenance personnel and janitors shall cover the administrative payroll costs and expenses for such on-site maintenance personnel.

4.5 Sales Tax. It is understood and agreed that any and all sales, use, business and occupations tax or other such taxes charged or assessed against, or attributable to, the fees, costs or expenses charged by, or paid to, Manager shall be the obligation of the Owner and shall be paid in full by the Owner.

5. LEASING SERVICES OF THE MANAGER.

5.1 Brokers. It is understood and agreed that the Manager is the exclusive leasing broker and agent for the Project; provided, that the Manager may engage other brokers to assist Manager in leasing space in the Project (which brokers may be employees of Manager or an affiliated or related company) and otherwise supervise leasing arrangements for the Project and shall share in any brokerage fees payable with respect to such leasing arrangements.

5.2 Right to Approve. Owner retains the right in its sole discretion to approve the terms, conditions, and form of any proposed lease and to approve any prospective tenant.

6. ACCOUNTING, RECORDS, REPORTS.

6.1 Records. The Manager shall maintain its standard comprehensive system of office records, books and accounts, which shall belong to the Owner. The Owner and others designated by the Owner shall have at all times access to such records, accounts and books and to all vouchers, files and all other material pertaining to the Project and this Agreement, all of which the Manager agrees to keep safe, available and separate from any records not having to do with the Project.

6.2 Monthly Reports. On or before the _____ day of each month during the term of this Agreement, the Manager shall deliver to the Owner (i) a Profit and Loss Statement representing the income collected and payment of operating expenses for the property; (ii) a capital expenditure journal; (iii) an operating expense journal; (iv) a delinquency report for the preceding calendar month; and (v) a tenant sales report where applicable. The Manager shall use the Manager's standard chart of accounts and budgeting format in preparing the foregoing. The Manager shall not be responsible for providing the following schedules: interest accruals, depreciation or amortization of real or intangible assets or any other duty not provided by standard property management accounting.

EXHIBIT 2.4 *(Continued)*

6.3   Annual Budgets.

(a)   **Delivery of Budget.** No later than November 30 of each year, the Manager shall deliver to the Owner a statement setting forth in detail the estimated receipts and the estimated amounts required to be expended, on a cash basis, during the next succeeding calendar year, by the Manager in the performance of its duties hereunder, including without limitation the amount of real estate taxes, assessments, insurance premiums and maintenance and other expenses relating to the Project operations. The Manager shall further provide such other financial information as is reasonably requested by the Owner. The Manager will cooperate with and give reasonable assistance to any independent public accountant retained by the Owner to examine such statements or other records pertaining to the Project.

(b)   **Approval.** Within thirty (30) days of receipt of the above statement, the Owner shall either approve the same or provide the Manager with written notice setting forth those items which are unacceptable to Owner or advising Manager as to what additional information is required. Failure to provide such notice to Manager within said thirty (30) day period shall be deemed approval of the statement by Owner. Upon such approval, or in the event Owner shall fail to provide notice to Manager as set forth above, the Manager shall be authorized to operate and manage the Project in accordance with the budget provided to Owner for approval.

6.4   **Employment Laws.** Manager shall comply with all laws relating to the employment by the Manager of its employees.

6.5   **Tax Reports.** The Manager shall have no responsibility for the preparation or submission of any federal, state or local tax report or return on behalf of the Owner.

6.6   **Disbursements.** The Manager shall have the Option, as more fully set forth in Section 2.4(a) above, to deposit funds in a Separate Account or to commingle the Owner's funds in the Manager's agency account.

7.   EXPENSES.

7.1   **Expense of Owner.** All obligations or expenses incurred hereunder including but not limited to on-site maintenance personnel and wages, payroll costs and employee benefits with respect thereto shall be for the account of, on behalf of, and at the expense of the Owner. The Owner shall not be obligated to reimburse the Manager for the Manager's home office expenses for general office equipment or office supplies or telephone service of the Manager, for any overhead expense of the Manager incurred in its home office, for any salaries of any executives or supervisory personnel of the Manager, for any salaries or wages allocable to time spent on matters other than the Project, or for any salaries, wages and expenses for any personnel other than personnel working at the Project site or with respect to the Project.

7.2   **Reimbursement For Expenses.** Any payments made by the Manager in the performance of its duties and obligations under this Agreement shall be made solely out of such funds as the Manager may from time to time hold for the account of the Owner or as may be provided by the Owner. The Owner shall give adequate advance written notice to the Manager if the Owner desires that the Manager make payment, out of the proceeds from the Property, of mortgage indebtedness, general taxes, special assessments, or fire, steam boiler, or any other insurance

EXHIBIT 2.4 *(Continued)*

premiums. In no event shall the Manager be required to advance its own funds in payment of any such indebtedness, taxes, assessments, or premiums.

8.   TERM AND TERMINATION.

8.1   **Term.** Subject to the provisions of Section 8.2 below, this Agreement is for a term of _____ (___) years commencing on _____, 19___ (the "Commencement Date") and terminating at midnight on _____, 19___ (the "Termination Date"). This Agreement shall continue on a month-to-month basis after said Termination Date unless terminated in accordance with Section 8.2 or 8.3 below.

8.2   **Termination For Cause By Owner.** The Owner may, at all times during the term of this Agreement, and any extension thereof, and upon not less than ninety (90) days' prior written notice to the Manager, terminate this Agreement; provided, that in the event such right of termination is exercised during the initial term of this Agreement, then the Owner shall pay to Manager, on or before the effective date of termination of this Agreement, an amount equal to thirty-three and one-third percent (33-1/3%) of the remaining unpaid management fees for the balance of the initial term of this Agreement.

8.3   **Termination By Manager.** The Manager may terminate this Agreement upon not less than ninety (90) days' prior written notice to Owner.

8.4   **Manager's Obligations After Termination.** Upon the termination of this Agreement as provided above, the Manager shall:

(a)   **Deliver Records.** Deliver to the Owner, or such other person or persons designated by the Owner, copies of all books and records of the Project and all funds in the possession of the Manager belonging to the Owner or received by the Manager pursuant to the terms of this Agreement or of any of the Basic Documents; and

(b)   **Assignment.** Assign, transfer or convey to such person or persons all service contracts and personal property relating to or used in the operation and maintenance of the Project, except any personal property which was paid for and is owned by the Manager. The Manager shall, at its cost and expense, remove all signs that it may have placed at the Project indicating that it is the manager of same and replace and restore any damage resulting therefrom.

(c)   **Termination of Obligations; Right to Compensation.** Upon any termination pursuant to this Section 8, the obligations of the parties hereto shall cease as of the date specified in the notice of termination; provided that the Manager shall comply with the applicable provisions hereof; and, provided further that Manager shall be entitled to receive any and all compensation which may be due the Manager hereunder at the time of such termination or expiration. Such compensation shall include the Management Fee set forth in Section 4.1 above prorated to the date of termination, together with brokerage fees due Manager for leasing activities through the date of termination. In order to compute the brokerage fee due Manager, Manager shall deliver to Owner within thirty (30) days after the date of termination, a list of all prospective tenants contacted by Manager or other brokers and for which Manager is owed, or may be owed, all or some part of a leasing commission. Such list shall include the name, address and telephone number of each such prospective tenant together with all lease proposals and other pertinent information in Manager's

EXHIBIT 2.4 *(Continued)*

possession relating to such prospective tenant. In the event Owner shall within one (1) year of the date of termination, enter into a lease for space in the Project with a prospective tenant set forth on the list of prospective tenants given by Manager to Owner, then and in such event Manager shall be paid a leasing fee equal to the fee which would have been paid Manager pursuant to the Commission Schedule had the lease with such tenant been entered into prior to the date of termination.

(d) **Final Accounting.** In the event the Owner has paid the Manager all sums due Manager hereunder, the Manager shall, within thirty (30) days of the date of expiration or termination of this Agreement, deliver to the Owner the following: (i) an accounting reflecting the balance of income and expenses of and from the Project to the date of termination or expiration of the Agreement; (ii) any balance of monies of the Owner then held by the Manager; and (iii) all leases, receipts for deposits, insurance policies, unpaid bills, correspondence and other documents which are the property of Owner in the possession of the Manager. The Owner shall have fifteen (15) days from the date the Manager delivers the foregoing to Owner within which to deliver to the Manager a written statement approving the foregoing as (i) a correct accounting of the income and expenses of and from the Project; (ii) the correct balance of monies of the Owner then held by the Manager; and (iii) all leases, receipts for deposits, insurance policies, unpaid bills, correspondence and other documents which are the property of the Owner with respect to the Project or setting forth in reasonable detail why such approval cannot be given, including any inaccuracy in said accounting. Upon receipt of said written approval, or upon the expiration of said fifteen (15) day period in the event such approval is not given, the Manager shall be deemed to have fully performed all of its obligations under this Agreement and shall be fully released by Owner from any and all liability and obligation to Owner under this Agreement and the performance thereof by the Manager. The Manager may retain copies or duplicates of all documents, accountings, leases, and other papers delivered to the Owner that are required or to be maintained or retained under, or in order to comply with, the law of the state in which the Property is situated and/or the state in which the Manager's offices are located.

9. NO AGENCY.

The Manager shall be responsible for all of its employees or employees of any affiliate, the supervision of all persons performing services in connection with the performance of all of the Owner's obligations relating to the maintenance and operation of the Project, and for determining the manner and time of performance of all acts hereunder. Nothing herein contained shall be construed to establish the Manager as an employee of the Owner.

10. DESIGNATED AGENT; NOTICES.

(a) **Owner's Designated Agent.** The Owner hereby designates _____ whose mailing address is _____ _____ (the "Designated Agent") as the agent of Owner to whom Manager may deliver or mail all notices required or desired to be given Owner hereunder and from whom Manager shall receive all consents, direction, decisions and notices required or desired to be given by Owner hereunder, as set forth below. The delivery of notice or requests, correspondence, communication, consents, waivers or other matters to such Designated Agent, whether in person or by mail as set forth herein, and/or the service of process upon such Designated Agent shall be conclusively deemed as delivery of the same and service of process

EXHIBIT 2.4 *(Continued)*

upon Owner. The Designated Agent and/or office may be changed from time to time by the Owner upon not less than ten (10) days' prior written notice to the Manager.

(b) **Authority of Designated Agent.** All correspondence, communication, requests, notices, waivers, consents, direction and other actions of the Owner shall be through the Designated Agent and the Manager shall have the right to rely with acquittance upon any correspondence, communications, requests, notices, consents, directions or other actions received from, or demanded by, the Designated Agent.

(c) **Notices.** Unless otherwise specifically provided, all notices, demands, statements and communications required or desired to be given hereunder shall be in writing and shall be sent by registered or certified mail, if intended for the Owner, addressed to the Designated Agent at the Designated Agent's address set forth above, with a copy to:

_____

_____

_____

_____

and if intended for the Manager, addressed to the Manager at:

> TRF MANAGEMENT CORPORATION
> 12400 S.E. 38th Street
> P.O. Box 5727
> Bellevue, Washington 98006-5727

or to such other address as shall from time to time have been designated by written notice by either party to the other party as herein provided.

11. CAPTIONS; PLURAL INCLUDES SINGULAR.

The captions of this Agreement are inserted only for the purpose of convenient reference and do not define, limit, or prescribe the scope or intent of this Agreement or any part hereof. Words used herein shall include both the plural and singular, and the male shall include the feminine and neuter genders.

12. APPLICABLE LAW.

This Agreement shall be construed in accordance with the laws of the State in which the Property is situated.

13. ENTIRE AGREEMENT.

This Agreement embodies the entire understanding of the parties and there are no further agreements or understanding, written or oral, in effect between the parties relating to the subject matter hereof.

14. HAZARDOUS SUBSTANCES.

14.1 Manager's Obligations.

(a) **Presence and Use of Hazardous Substances.** Manager shall not knowingly and intentionally, without Owner's prior written consent, keep on or

EXHIBIT 2.4 *(Continued)*

around the Property, for use, disposal, treatment, generation, storage or sale any substances, wastes, or materials designated as, or containing components designated as hazardous, dangerous, toxic or harmful and/or which are subject to regulation by any federal, state or local law, regulation, statute or ordinance. With respect to any such Hazardous Substance, Manager shall:

(i)   Comply promptly, timely and completely with all governmental requirements for reporting, keeping and submitting manifests, and obtaining and keeping current identification numbers;

(ii)   Submit to Owner true and correct copies of all reports, manifests and identification numbers at the same time as they are required to be and/or are submitted to the appropriate governmental authorities;

(iii)   Within five (5) days of Owner's request, submit written reports to Owner regarding Manager's use, storage, treatment, transportation, generation, disposal or sale of Hazardous Substances and provide evidence satisfactory to Owner of Manager's compliance with the applicable government regulations;

(iv)   Allow Owner or Owner's representative to come on the area in which Manager is working or which is covered by this Agreement at all times to check Manager's compliance with all applicable governmental regulations regarding Hazardous Substances;

(v)   Comply with minimum levels, standards, or other performance standards or requirements which may be set forth or established for certain Hazardous Substances (if minimum standards or levels are applicable to Hazardous Substances present on the Property or any part thereof, such levels or standards shall be established by an on-site inspection by the appropriate governmental authorities and shall be set forth in an addendum to this Agreement); and

(vi)   Comply with all applicable governmental rules, regulations and requirements regarding the proper and lawful use, sale, transportation, generation, treatment, and disposal of Hazardous Substances.

Any and all costs incurred by Owner and associated with Owner or Owner's inspection of the Property and Owner's monitoring of Manager's compliance with this Section, including Owner's attorneys' fees and costs, shall be due and payable by Manager upon demand by Owner.

(b)   Cleanup Costs, Default and Indemnification.

(i)   Manager shall be fully and completely liable to Owner for any and all cleanup costs, and any and all other charges, fees, penalties (civil and criminal) imposed by any governmental authority with respect to Manager's knowing and intentional use, disposal, transportation, generation and/or sale of Hazardous Substances, in or about the Property.

(ii)   Manager shall indemnify, defend and save Owner, and Owner's respective officers, directors, shareholders and employees, harmless from any and all of the costs, fees, penalties and

EXHIBIT 2.4 *(Continued)*

charges assessed against or imposed upon Owner (as well as Owner's attorneys' fees and costs) as a result of Manager's knowing and intentional use, disposal, transportation, generation and/or sale of Hazardous Substances.

               (iii)   Upon Manager's default under this Section, in addition to the rights and remedies set forth elsewhere in this Agreement, Owner shall be entitled to the following rights and remedies:

               (A)   At Owner's option, to terminate this Agreement immediately; and/or

               (B)   To recover any and all damages associated with the default, including, but not limited to, cleanup costs and charges, civil and criminal penalties and fees, loss of business by Owner and by tenants in the Property, any and all damages and claims asserted by third parties, and Owner's attorneys' fees and costs.

15.   EQUAL OPPORTUNITY.

It is understood and agreed that Manager is an equal opportunity and non-discriminatory employer. The Owner and Manager agree that there shall be no discrimination against, or segregation of, any person, or group of persons, on account of race, color, creed, religion, sex, age or national origin in the lease, transfer, use, occupancy or enjoyment of the Property nor shall the Owner or Manager permit any discrimination or segregation with respect to the selection, location, number, use or occupancy of tenants of space within the Property.

16.   MANAGER'S EMPLOYEES.

Owner understands and agrees that the Manager has expended great amounts of time and effort in the selection, hiring and training of its employees and that the Manager's business, and the conduct thereof, is dependent to a large extent upon maintaining and retaining employees who have been trained by the Manager and that the Manager faces extreme hardship and monetary loss whenever such employees leave its service. For the above reasons, the Owner agrees that it shall not, directly or indirectly, during the term of this Agreement or for two (2) years after the expiration of the term of this Agreement, employ or solicit for employment, or otherwise engage, Manager's employees. Owner further agrees that the Manager shall be entitled to injunctive relief, monetary damages or both, upon the Owner's violation or breach of the foregoing.

IN WITNESS WHEREOF, the parties hereto have executed this Agreement as of the day and year first above written.

OWNER:

MANAGER:

TRF MANAGEMENT CORPORATION

By: _____

          _____, President

EXHIBIT 2.4 *(Continued)*

EXHIBIT A

Legal Description
Westgate Partners Limited Partnership

Tract One:

Parcels 1, 2, 3, A, B, C, D, E, F and G. As shown on that certain survey of a portion of Section 35, Township 21 North, Range 2 East of the W.M., Filed for record on May 20, 1987 under auditor's no. 8705200360, Records of Pierce County Auditor, in Mission County, Oregon.

Tract Two:

Lot 2, as shown on short plat no. 8510040312, filed with the Mission County Auditor, in Mission County, Oregon.

EXHIBIT B

Schedule of Basic Documents

TRF Management Corporation has been provided a copy of the Declaration of Restrictions and Grant of Easements dated February 22, 1985 and Common Area Maintenance Agreement dated March 15, 1985. TRF Management Corporation has also been provided with originals and copies of all existing leases, project correspondence files, maps, drawings, and specifications with respect to the project.

EXHIBIT C

Commission Schedule

For leases three (3) years in length or longer:

New Leases	$3.00 per square foot
Lease Renewals	$1.50 per square foot

For leases less than three (3) years in length:

New Leases	$1.00 per square foot per year
Renewal Lease	$.50 per square foot per year

Commission Payment:

New Leases	50% upon base execution and 50% when the tenant opens for business
Lease Renewals	100% upon execution of the lease for renewals

EXHIBIT 2.4 *(Continued)*

EXHIBIT D

Schedule of Service Contracts

I. Records: TRF Management Corporation
    - General Ledger
    - Cash Receipts Journal
    - Cash Disbursements Journal
    - Paid Invoices
    - Cancelled Checks
II. Contracts:
    - Parking Lot Sweeping Agreement with Sound Sweeper Service
    - Landscape Maintenance Agreement with TLC Landscaping
    - HVAC Maintenance Contract with Donald Miller for small tenant shops
    - General Maintenance Agreement (month-to-month) with Kirkwood Maintenance, Inc.

EXHIBIT 2.5

Project Data Book

Project No: 1234

LINCOLN PLAZA
Lincoln Way and Main Street
Redwood City, WA 90513

Owner:	Lincoln Plaza, a limited partnership 12400 SE Dolores Street Redwood City, WA 90513 Ronald Smith Manager Real Estate Investment Dept.	(123) 456-7811
Architect:	Smith and Jones 11 N. Elm Redwood City, WA 90513	(123) 567-8901
General Contractor:	Acme Construction PO Box 9889 Emporia, WA 90514	(123) 885-7824
Leasing:	Commercial Leasing Corporation Eric Muhlebach 1234 Broadway NE Redwood City, WA 90514	(123) 555-2241
Management:	Able Management Corporation Maria Rivera 4 N. Plaza Square Redwood City, WA 90514	(123) 456-0000

EXHIBIT 2.5 *(Continued)*

Attorney:	Kathy Muhlebach Thompson Building, Suite 450 Redwood City, WA 90514	(123) 555-8960
Insurance Agent:	North, Fuller, and Fry Thompson Building, Suite 222 Redwood City, WA 90514	(123) 555-0082
Accounting:	Lee Lloyd Associates 1464 S. Pine Street Redwood City, WA 90514	(123) 456-1040
Police Department:	Redwood City Police Station 411	Emergency: 911 Business: 555-1255
Fire Department:	Redwood City Fire District	Emergency: 911

Utilities

Water/Sewer:	Redwood City Water District No. 45 PO Box 78 Redwood City, WA 90514	555-8901
Gas:	Houston Natural Gas 11 Industrial Way Redwood City, WA 90514	555-0041
Electricity:	Redwood City Power and Light PO Box 667 Redwood City, WA 90514	555-3781

Statistical Data

Acres: 13.5
Square Feet: 148,702
Parking: 824
Construction Began: April 1980
Construction Completed: November 15, 1980
Opened: November 15, 1980
Major Tenants Open:
    Ace Supermarket   November 15, 1980
    SaveRite Drug Store   November 18, 1980
    Redwood Hardware   April 1, 1981

EXHIBIT 2.5 *(Continued)*

Property Management Subsystem
Current Date 4/22/87   Project No.: 3033
Page No. 1   Project Data Report   Shoppers Plaza

Tenant	Sq. Ft.	Trade Name (1) Tenant Addr/(2) Pref Mail Address	Telephone Contact #s
A	35,875	Dave's Home Center #250 Mgr: Dave Davis (1) 1717 Lincoln Way Suite #A Redwood City, WA 99456	(301) 255-4678 (301) 255-2063 Emergency ( ) -
A-04	2,400	Vacant Mgr:	( ) - ( ) -
A-08	1,600	Beauty Supply Shop Mgr: Sara Burdell (1) 1731 Lincoln Way Redwood City, WA 99456	(301) 255-6508 (301) 458-2013 Emergency ( ) -
A-10	1,620	Quality Homes Realty Mgr: Fred Goodsen (1) 1782 Lincoln Way Redwood City, WA 99456	(301) 256-4062 (857) 236-5437 Emergency ( ) -
A-02	2,420	The Paint Bucket Mgr: Mark Langdon (1) 1783 Lincoln Way Redwood City, WA 99456	(301) 256-2910 (857) 236-1039 Emergency ( ) -
A-06	1,600	The Happy Hobby Shop Mgr: Nancy Young (1) 1784 Lincoln Way Redwood City, WA 99456	(301) 256-3042 (301) 236-2075 Emergency ( ) -
B	21,875	Redwood Drug Store Mgr: David Smith (1) 1790 Lincoln Way Redwood City, WA 99456	(301) 256-3924 (206) 876-5689 Emergency ( ) -
B-02	2,420	Humpty Dumpty Computer Store Mgr: Bob Mills (1) 1782 Lincoln Way Redwood City, WA 99456	(301) 256-9856 (301) 236-6809 Emergency ( ) -
B-10	1,400	The Shoe Box Mgr: Robyn Kildere (1) 1783 Lincoln Way Redwood City, WA 99456	(301) 256-1037 (301) 627-4052 Emergency ( ) -
B-12	1,400	Showtime Video House Mgr: Steve Stodsen (1) 1784 Lincoln Way Redwood City, WA 99456	(301) 327-8019 (857) 236-2145 Emergency ( ) -
B-14	3,600	Susie's Cards and Gifts Mgr: Susan Hopson	(301) 256-3291 (301) 256-4687

EXHIBIT 2.5 *(Continued)*

Tenant	Sq. Ft.	Trade Name (1) Tenant Addr/(2) Pref Mail Address	Telephone Contact #s
		(1) 1786 Lincoln Way Redwood City, WA 99456 (2) Bob Smith 1025 6th Avenue Everett, WA 98203	Emergency (206) 362-7891
B-16	2,080	The Sound System Mgr: Howard Hanson (1) 1786 Lincoln Way Redwood City, WA 99456 (2) 20922 NE 81st Street Bothell, WA 98011	(301) 256-9876 (857) 236-0154 Emergency (349) 746-5183
B-18	2,740	Quality Health Foods Mgr: James Ingalls (1) 1787 Lincoln Way Redwood City, WA 99456 (2) 14400 Elm Street Centralia, WA 99934	(301) 256-3768 (301) 236-6929 Emergency (406) 294-6024
B-19	2,400	Half Price Shoes Store Mgr: Fred Foster (1) 1788 Lincoln Way Redwood City, WA 99456	(301) 256-6942 (857) 468-5437 Emergency ( ) -
B-20	1,600	Jessica's Hair Designs Mgr: Jessica Giovanni (1) 1790 Lincoln Way Redwood City, WA 99456 (2) 4442 Naples Way Woodinville, WA 98056	(301) 256-2059 (301) 248-3012 Emergency (206) 641-9690
B-21	1,600	Carol's Children's Clothing Mgr: Carol Young (1) 1791 Lincoln Way Redwood City, WA 99456 (2) 1212 Elm Street Centralia, WA 94657	(301) 287-7066 (857) 236-5437 Emergency (602) 348-8023
C-01	43,851	Super Giant Market Mgr: Bruce Harrison (1) 1782 Lincoln Way Redwood City, WA 99456 (2) 4316 120th SE Firndale, WA 96709	(301) 246-4052 (301) 246-5437 Emergency (301-245-6290
C-02	1,132	Posies Flower House Mgr: Jan Johnson (1) 1783 Lincoln Way Redwood City, WA 99456	(301) 256-3448 (301) 236-5300 Emergency ( ) -
C-04	1,132	The Pasta Plaza Mgr: Fred Goodsen	(301) 256-4062 (857) 236-8023

EXHIBIT 2.5 (Continued)

Tenant	Sq. Ft.	Trade Name (1) Tenant Addr/(2) Pref Mail Address	Telephone Contact #s
		(1) 1784 Lincoln Way Redwood City, WA 99456	Emergency ( ) -
C-06	894	Sew & Sew Shoe Repair Mgr: Sam Smith (1) 1785 Lincoln Way Redwood City, WA 99456	(301) 256-4062 (857) 236-5437 Emergency ( ) -

C-08	894	Triple A Insurance
		Mgr: Charles Simonson
		(1) 1786 Lincoln Way
		      Redwood City, WA 99456
		(2) 6489 124th SE
		      Oakdale, WA 98745
			(301) 286-9734
			(301) 246-1465
			Emergency
			(301) 245-6290

C-10	894	Vacant	( ) - ( ) - Emergency ( ) -
C-11	43,851	Flower Fresh Dry Cleaners Mgr: Robert Wilson (1) 1788 Lincoln Way Redwood City, WA 99456	(301) 346-2354 (301) 246-1587 Emergency (301) 245-6290

C-12	1,175	Redwood Chiropractic Clinic
		Mgr: Dr. Charles Hurt
		(1) 1787 Lincoln Way
		      Redwood City, WA 99456
		(2) 8096 Elm Avenue
		      Rosewood, WA 98054
			(301) 278-3267
			(301) 246-6598
			Emergency
			(301) 245-6290

Pad 1	2,875	Home Town Bank
		Mgr: James Richards
		(1) 1710 Lincoln Way
		      Redwood City, WA 99456
		(2) 12276 Green Street
		      Redwood City, WA 99456
			(301) 246-7008
			(301) 246-3432
			Emergency
			(301) 245-0554

Pad 2	3,550	The Pizza & Pasta Parlour
		Mgr: Catello Pagano
		(1) 1714 Lincoln Way
		      Redwood City, WA 99456
		(2) 12256 Maple Street
		      Redwood City, WA 99456
			(301) 246-5454
			(301) 246-8765
			Emergency
			(301) 245-6290

Pad 3	3,750	Down Home Dining Restaurant
		Mgr: Daniel Denning
		(1) 1716 Lincoln Way
		      Redwood City, WA 99456
		(2) 12067 5th Avenue
		      Firndale, WA 96709
			(301) 246-8956
			(301) 246-3446
			Emergency
			(301) 245-7860

	148,702	Total Project Sq. Ft. End of Project	

EXHIBIT 2.5 *(Continued)*

LIST OF VENDORS

JANUARY 1987

Electrical:	Burke Electric 3511 W. Greenview Way Kennewick, WA 99336	John Brown (509) 746-5489 (509) 582-7113**
Fire Sprinklers:	Safety Fire Protection PO Box 1567 Pasco, WA 99301	Richard Young (509) 547-3478 (509) 735-5698**
Glass:	Associated Glass 18956 Highway 95 Lynnwood, WA 09456	Bill Kirk (206) 546-3456 (206) 778-2387**
HVAC:	Brown Controls 3006 Northup Way Bellevue, WA 98004	Fred Jones (304) 567-9823 (206) 454-1278**
Janitorial:	Young's Janitorial Service 1010 Elm Street Kirkland, WA 98033	Robert Young (206) 821-5496 (206) 823-6897**
Maintenance:	Columbia Maintenance, Inc. 120 S. Main, PO Box 345 Woodinville, WA 98076	Russ Goldstone (509) 734-6253 (509) 783-1674**
Pest Control:	Allsafe Pest Control 26th E. 2nd Avenue Redmond, WA 98056	Richard Buford (509) 582-4198**
Plumbing:	Paula's Plumbing 1346 SE 132nd Street Kirkland, WA 98034	Paula Stone (206) 823-2698 (206) 823-4587**
Roof:	Master Coatings Route 1, Box 34 Woodinville, WA 98056	Darrell Fox (509) 546-1219
Towing:	R & J Towing 1416 Gillespie Redmond, WA 98045	Greg A. Showalter (203) 454-6872

**Home Phone Number

LIST OF SUBCONTRACTORS

Acoustic Treatment:	Acoustical Design, Inc. 1194 Andover Park W Seattle, WA 98189	Walt Cramer (206) 575-1923
Caulking:	Stark's Caulking 3225 S. 276th Auburn, WA 98002	Debbie Stone (206) 854-8334

EXHIBIT 2.5 *(Continued)*

LIST OF SUBCONTRACTORS

Ceramic Tile:	Expert Tile Company 9632 Midvale Avenue S Seattle, WA 98104	Gary Grice (206) 525-4885
Concrete Pouring & Finishing:	Beeks Concrete Co. Route 2, Box 2945 Bellevue, WA 98004	Thom Thum (206) 454-6790
Dock Equipment:	Westcoast Handling Systems PO Box 8834 Redmond, WA 98056	Dan Thomas (203) 454-3465
Hollow Metal Doors & Frames:	Brennan Supply 14032 S.E. 132nd Street Redwood City, WA 98045	Mike Estes (509) 546-8723
Rolling Steel Door:	Steel Door Company 1300 Columbia Center Blvd. Firdale, WA 98456	Steve Stark (509) 745-2098
Sliding Hollow Metal Doors:	Steel Door Company 1300 Columbia Center Blvd. Firdale, WA 98456	Steve Stark (509) 745-2098
Electrical:	Westside Electric Co. 2121 North 38th Street Seattle, WA 98014	Bill Rauch (206) 632-3467
Flashing & Sheet Metal:	Foster Sheet Metal, Inc. PO Box 6148 Bellevue, WA 98045	Lee Foster (206) 568-1156
Resilient Flooring:	William Willey Co., Inc. PO Box 80356 Woodinville, WA 98075	William Willey (206) 673-4567
Fire Sprinkler:	Fire Sprinkler Co., Inc. 10005 E. Montgomery Bellevue, WA 98034	Larry Garbe (509) 928-3498 Harold Harris (206) 454-2068
Glazing & Storefront:	Sparkling Glass Company 1120 W. Lewis Seattle, WA 98006	Simon Shoe (206) 456-9807
Finish Hardware:	Plaza Hardware Co. 1315 Plaza Street Seattle, WA 98010	Richard Simms (203) 823-6078
HVAC & Plumbing:	Smith & Sons Co., Inc. 11078 Pacific Highway Bellevue, WA 98044	Ron Smith (206) 763-8900

EXHIBIT 2.5 *(Continued)*

LIST OF SUBCONTRACTORS

Thermal Insulation:	Insulation Service Co. 9944 - 152nd Avenue NE Redmond, WA 98045	Bob Burton (206) 885-5145
Millwork:	Coastcraft Mill Work PO Box 1888 Tacoma, WA 98401	Larry Jacobs (206) 839-9578
Painting & Vinyl:	Smith & Son Painting Contractors 465 Park Avenue NW Renton, WA 98056	John Smith (206) 229-3597
Reinforcing Steel:	Strong Steel Corporation PO Box 668 Kirkland, WA 98045	Terry Strong (206) 827-5887
Roof Hatch:	Foster-Bray Co., Inc. PO Box 5432 Seattle, WA 98005	Ed Bray (206) 323-8787
Roof Structure:	Kirkland Structures, Inc. 10909 - 154th Avenue SE Kirkland, WA 98034	Kay Jones (206) 823-5698
Roof Trusses:	Roof Trusses, Inc. 3163 "C" Street SW Auburn, WA 98002	Randy Jones (206) 823-1050
Built-Up Roofing & Rigid Insulation:	Rogers Roofing & Insulation PO Box 1554 Kirkland, WA 98033	Roger Gates (506) 525-3045 (506) 821-6934**
Site Utilities:	Jones & Smith Construction 11156 E. Imperial Avenue Seattle, WA 98168	Betty Jones (206) 823-2387
Sitework:	L. W. Kidd Co., Inc. PO Box 345 Seattle, WA 98045	Alan Mason (509) 265-8954
Structural & Misc. Steel:	Big Time Welders 6820 - 178th SW Redmond, WA 98052	Pat Meek (206) 885-9622
Stucco & Drywall:	ABC Drywall 10607 E. Wesson Drive Seattle, WA 99035	Gary Black (509) 934-1732
Toilet Accessories:	Shiny Brite Accessories, Inc. PO Box 1234 Seattle, WA 98114	Cliff Bray (206) 546-8756
Prefinished Wallboard	William Willey Co., Inc. PO Box 80365 Bellevue, WA 98004	Karin Stromberg (206) 454-9008

company are kept in the manager's office for the staff's reference. Each on-site management office has a copy of the information for that property, and managers keep copies of the project data book at their desk, in their car, and at home. Because many maintenance calls and emergencies occur after business hours, it is essential that managers have the project data available wherever they are.

§ 2.24 TENANT IMPROVEMENTS

Tenant improvements can be as simple as laying new carpet in an office building or as complex as building a new restaurant on a shopping center pad or outlet. But whatever the scope, the completion of tenant improvements is an integral part of the manager's relationship with both landlord and tenant. Even if the manager does not have direct responsibility for them, tenant improvements that are not completed on time or according to plan will ultimately become a management problem. On the positive side, overseeing tenant improvements can become a profit center for the manager and enhance client relationships.

Some managers have the capability of providing full contracting services and charges for these services just as an independent contractor would. This involves a contractor's license and bonding requirements in most states. On the other hand, something as simple as arranging for painting a suite or cleaning drapes requires no special licenses and is often part of the management services.

Regardless of the degree of involvement, the manager should be aware of building limitations, local building codes, costs for construction items, and time involved. Enthusiasm and optimism can lead the parties to believe that construction can be performed faster and less expensively than is realistic, and the reality can cause hard feelings, expensive delays, and even lawsuits. Any time the building owner is completing work for the tenant there should be a written agreement as to what is being furnished and when it will be completed. Commercial leases generally have an Exhibit C that spells out the owner's responsibilities and clearly states that all other work is the responsibility of the tenant (see Exhibit 2.6).

§ 2.25 CONSULTING SERVICES

The property manager should not overlook the unique opportunity to provide consulting service. This is an opportunity to add profit to the company for little additional expense. One benefit of a consulting service is that it may lead to management accounts.

Consulting services can be marketed directly and indirectly. Direct marketing includes potential client contact and advertising. The firm

EXHIBIT 2.6

Description of Landlord's Tenant's Work

Landlord agrees that it will, at its sole cost and expense, commence the construction of the demised premises and pursue the completion (with the exception of delays or conditions beyond the Landlord's control) in accordance with Landlord's or Landlord architect's designs and plans, which construction shall include the items generally described in Landlord's work below:

Tenant agrees to prepare, or cause to be prepared, and to submit the Landlord's architect two sets of fully dimensioned one-quarter (¼") scale drawings showing the layout of the demised premises including store front, trade fixture plans and any other matters which would affect the construction design of the demised premises, within thirty (30) days after the date that this lease is fully executed. Said plans shall be in conformity with the hereinafter set forth description of "Tenant's Work."

LANDLORD'S WORK for which Landlord is obligated to initially construct and pay:

1. Exterior building walls, roof, all structural items, including store front, per Landlord's design and specifications.

2. A flat concrete floor slab to receive Tenant's finish floor. **Tenant to pay the cost for utility lines and undergrounding for Tenant's needs within the demised premises.**

3. One toilet room including plumbing with Landlord's standard toilet room fixtures to include standard toilet, lavatory, water heater above toilet room for lavatory only, and mirror, all in a location selected by Landlord and per Landlord's design and specifications. Wall and floor covering to meet Health Department codes.

4. Landlord's standard type finished 2' x 4' x ⅝" grid ceiling at a height of 8 feet or higher to cover the demised premises.

5. Demising partitions or walls, including common walls to major tenants, will consist of wood or metal studs (at Landlord's selection), sheet rock, taped and sanded, or unfinished concrete and/or block on rear walls to receive Tenant's finish, where shown on Landlord's drawings.

6. Installation of air conditioning and heating system per Landlord's plans and specifications, adequate to condition, in accordance with the **A.S.R.A.E.** guideline for the geographical location, a standard retail store having electrical fixtures and equipment consuming no more than two and one-half (2.5) watts per square foot of leased area. If Tenant's requirements are in excess thereof, Tenant shall pay the increased cost.

7. Electrical. All electrical work not expressly provided for below shall be a part of Tenant's work.

    (a) An electrical panel at the rear of the space as applicable:

0 - 1200 s.f.	100 amp	Single phase	
1200 - 2250 s.f.	100 amp	3 phase	4 wire
2250 - 2800 s.f.	125 amp	3 phase	4 wire
2800 - 3375 s.f.	150 amp	3 phase	4 wire
3375 - 4500 s.f.	200 amp	3 phase	4 wire

    (b) Convenience outlets (fed from the Tenant's panel) located approximately 15 feet on center on the side demising partitions.

    (c) Four tube recessed 2' x 4' fluorescent light fixtures per Landlord's plans and specifications. Light fixtures shall be provided at a ratio of not greater than one (1) per eighty (80) square feet of floor area of the demised premises.

    (d) Conduit and "J" box for the Tenant's sign.

    (e) "J" box, conduit, wiring and fixture for incandescent light and exhaust fan in the toilet room.

8. Landlord will provide a means of supplying telephone service to the Tenant's space.

9. Landlord will install sprinklers in the demised premises at the rate of one (1) head per 125 square feet without any interior partitions. Any additional sprinklers and/or changes required as a result of Tenant improvements, by local fire codes other than the Landlord's standard layout will be at the cost of the Tenant, and must be made by Landlord's contractor.

10. Standard aluminum and glass store front, 8 feet or higher (at Landlord's option), with a single-acting entrance door to include mail slot, not to exceed a maximum of 3'0" in width.

TENANT WORK:

1. Tenant shall provide, administer and pay for any and all work done to the demised premises other than that provided under LANDLORD'S WORK hereinabove. Tenant shall procure and pay for any and all plans, drawings, permits, etc., necessary to do said work in a legal and workmanlike manner. Upon completion of Tenant's work, Tenant shall provide Landlord a copy of the certificate of occupancy issued by the appropriate governmental agency.

2. Should the Tenant request, in writing, and the Landlord agree, in writing, to have Landlord's contractor perform any of the Tenant's work, it is agreed that the Tenant shall pay for all costs of said work in accordance with Landlord contractor's requirements. In addition, Tenant shall make arrangements for said work on or before _____. If said arrangements are not made by said date, then Landlord or Landlord's contractor shall have no obligation to provide for said work.

Landlord's Initials   _____

Tenant's Initials   _____

must first determine the primary and secondary geographic areas it plans to service. For instance, a Seattle firm's primary market may be the Northwest and Alaska, and its secondary market the rest of the western United States or even the rest of the country. Next, the property manager identifies potential clients in the market (e.g., pension fund advisors, small developers, institutions, government agencies, and lenders). The person responsible for property management or leasing in each organization is identified. A letter is sent to the prospective client detailing specific consulting services that would meet the needs of the client. A letter to a developer might address the firm's ability to assist in organizing a property management department. A letter to a lender with properties in a depressed area might focus on the firm's expertise in managing and leasing problem properties. The information packet should include a brochure and a brief description of the firm. This is followed by a phone call and a request for a meeting.

Indirect marketing is one of the most effective ways to promote one's consulting services. Serving on committees and holding office in local chapters of IREM or BOMA, teaching, and writing are the best indirect ways to market consulting services.

There are countless opportunities to teach. The major real estate organizations are usually looking for speakers for their local miniseminars. A property manager can develop a topic from his or her experience or participate in a panel. Community colleges, too, often look for guest speakers and instructors to teach a property management course. IREM has developed two community college courses—Introduction to Property Management (201) and Apartment Management (202). IREM provides the instructors with a course outline, lecture outline, exams, and textbook. If the local community college doesn't offer either of these courses, someone in the management firm might want to contact the school to discuss the possibility of doing so. Serving on the national faculty of one of the real estate organizations provides the most worthwhile teaching experience.

Writing is another good way to indirectly market consulting services. Local business magazines and daily newspapers are often interested in receiving general interest articles on real estate. After conducting a market survey of, for example, suburban office buildings, a property management firm can develop a feature article from the data. Another possibility is to turn a unique experience into an article for a national magazine. The authors of this book, after providing consulting services for five years, wrote the first article on property management consulting, "The Property Manager as Consultant," in the *Journal of Property Management*, July/August 1986.

Consulting fees are based on an hourly rate, a monthly retainer, or an agreed-upon amount. For example, a property manager in California was hired at a fixed fee to analyze the management and leasing operations of a failing community mall in the Northwest. Another manager was paid an hourly rate by a shopping center developer to review plans for a proposed office building. A property management firm was paid a monthly retainer for six months to develop the management and leasing plan and to supervise the on-site staff of an office building until the developer established its property management department.

When negotiating a consulting assignment, the property manager and client must agree on the type and frequency of reports. Reports will vary from a short, written and oral presentation when the assignment is completed, to monthly written reports, to an extensive management plan. Preparing and presenting the reports can be time consuming, and the manager must factor in that time when establishing a fee. The consulting agreement must explicitly address the service that will be provided, including the type and frequency of reports (see Exhibit 2.7).

§ 2.26 DEVELOPING A COMPANY EDUCATION PROGRAM

Commercial property management is a dynamic profession. Each element in the effective management of a property is constantly changing. These changes in accounting, leasing, merchandising, insurance, maintenance, administration, and legal matters are precipitated by a number of factors, including industry innovation, government and tax regulations, economic conditions, technological advances, legal rulings, and shifts in society's values.

Obviously, no individual can be an expert in every field. Property managers can master some of these elements and have a working knowledge of the others. The administrative and clerical staff must be proficient at their particular responsibilities and have a general familiarity with the other areas.

A company education program is an effective way to maintain a high level of professionalism for the entire staff. It can inform the staff about other aspects of property management and create a flow of shared information throughout the company. The education program can include membership in professional organizations, subscriptions to relevant publications, classes at local educational institutions and real estate organizations, and participation in in-house seminars.

The core of an effective education program is the in-house seminar. Staff members may meet annually for a one- or two-day presentation on chosen topics of interest. Depending upon the size of the company, the group will be divided into sections to cover a variety of subjects according to job responsibility, or presentations may be given to the entire group followed by small group discussions.

An effective in-house seminar must be carefully prepared. A committee with a representative from each department is formed and solicits

EXHIBIT 2.7

Sample Consulting Agreement

THIS CONSULTING AGREEMENT (hereinafter referred to as the "Agreement") is made and entered into this _____ day of _____, 19____, by and between TRF MANAGEMENT CORPORATION, a Washington corporation (hereinafter referred to as "Consultant") and _____ (hereinafter referred to as "Owner"):

WHEREAS, Owner is the ground lessee or fee owner of certain real property situated in _____ (city, state), which real property is more fully described in the legal description hereof attached hereto and made a part hereof as Exhibit "A"; and

WHEREAS, Owner has purchased or developed certain improvements on and to said real property for the purpose of conducting thereon and therein a Shopping Center known as _____; and

WHEREAS, said real property and improvements are referred to herein as the "Property"; and

WHEREAS, Owner has or will employ an individual to act as its on-site manager of the Property (hereinafter referred to as "Manager") for the leasing of space in the Property, the collection of rents, day-to-day management of the Property, and the management and control of the association formed or to be formed among Owner and tenants of space in the Property (hereinafter referred to as the "Merchants' Association"; and

WHEREAS, the Owner desires to employ Consultant as an independent contractor and consultant to provide Owner with advisory, consultative, and supervisory services concerning management of the Property as hereinafter set forth;

NOW, THEREFORE, in consideration of the mutual terms and conditions set forth herein and for $_____ and other good and valuable consideration, the receipt and sufficiency of which is hereby acknowledged, the parties hereto hereby agree as follows:

1. *ENGAGEMENT OF CONSULTANT; TERM*

(a) The Owner hereby employs and engages Consultant, and Consultant hereby accepts such employment and engagement, as an independent contractor to provide the consulting services described below. It is understood and agreed that Consultant is not an employee of Owner and is not, except to the extent set forth herein, Owner's agent for any purpose.

(b) *Term.* The term of the Agreement shall be for _____ and shall commence on _____, and terminate at 12:00 midnight on _____.

(c) *Cancellation.* Either party may cancel this Agreement upon not less than sixty (60) days prior written notice to the other.

2. *CONSULTING SERVICES*

(a) *Services.* Consultant shall provide Owner with advisory, consultative and supervisory services, including without limitation, supervision of the on-site Manager employed by Owner (hereinafter "the Services") and assistance in the development and implementation of the procedures and operational standards which are reasonably required for the management of the Property as a

EXHIBIT 2.7 *(Continued)*

shopping center and the establishment and operation of a Merchants' Association (hereinafter "Management Procedures").

The Services to be performed by Consultant in accomplishing the foregoing shall consist of the services set out in the Schedule of Services attached hereto and made a part hereof as Exhibit "B". The Management Procedures shall be established and the Services shall be performed as deemed reasonably necessary and appropriate for the efficient and successful management and operation of a shopping center of a size and type similar to that constructed on the Property.

(b) *Scope*. For the purposes hereof, the Services to be performed by Consultant shall include meetings by authorized employees of Consultant with Owner and/or Manager to be conducted at reasonable times upon reasonable notice taking place during the initial term on an average of _____ times each calendar month and consisting of up to _____ per month of actual meeting time; provided that Consultant shall participate in additional meetings and devote additional hours in the case of emergencies. Consultant shall have no obligation to undertake any unreasonable action or activity in order to accomplish its obligations hereunder. Consultant shall be under no obligation to maintain any employee or agent on the Property.

3. *FEE.*

For its services hereunder, Owner shall pay to Consultant a consulting fee in the amount and manner set forth on Exhibit "C", attached hereto, on or before the last day of each month during the term hereof. In addition to the consulting fee to be paid Consultant, the Owner agrees to pay in advance, or upon demand, as Consultant may determine, all of Consultant's actual expenses in performing its obligations hereunder.

For the purposes hereof, the term "actual expenses" shall include transportation expenses and airline tickets to and from _____ for all the meetings with the on-site Manager, and from Seattle to _____ for emergencies or other special trips, meals, lodging, and similar expenses and costs incurred in performing services on behalf of Owner.

4. *LAW.*

This Agreement shall be interpreted and enforced pursuant to the laws of the State of _____.

5. *WAIVER.*

It is understood and agreed that Consultant makes no representations or warranties with respect to the effectiveness of any of the Management Procedures or the profitability of the Property. Owner specifically assumes all risk of the use of any or all of the Management Procedures. Further, Owner hereby waives and releases and indemnifies Consultant, its agents, and employees from any and all claims, costs, losses, expenses, injuries, or damages suffered, incurred, or claimed by any person, entity, partnership, or joint venture and arising by reasons of the Agreement or the Management Procedures except if caused as a result of the negligence, breach, or misconduct of Consultant or any agent, employee, or associate of Consultant in performance or non-performance of Consultant's duties under this Agreement.

EXHIBIT 2.7 *(Continued)*

6. *COMPETITION.*

Nothing herein contained shall in any way prohibit Consultant from engaging in the management of, or entering into any other consulting agreements with respect to, other properties or ventures of any type or kind whatsoever even though the same may be in direct or indirect competition with the business conducted by Owner on the Property.

7. *ATTORNEYS' FEES.*

In the event either party shall commence any action to enforce its rights hereunder, then the prevailing party in such action shall recover against the other, reasonable attorneys' fees in addition to any costs incurred in the defense or prosecution of such action.

8. *NO ASSIGNMENT.*

This Agreement and the rights, benefits, and obligations hereunder shall not be assignable by any party hereto.

EXHIBIT B

Schedule of Services

Advisory, consultative, and supervisory services to be provided by Consultant:

1. Assist on-site Manager with training and direction for day-to-day shopping center management.
2. Assist in preparing annual operating budget and periodic review of budget.
3. Assist in setting up a maintenance management program, which includes bidding services and recommending vendors for selection.
4. Periodically supervise vendors and janitorial/maintenance operation.
5. Prepare monthly gross sales reports and analysis. Tenants' sales reports shall be obtained by the mall Manager and provided to Consultant.
6. Conduct tenant-mix analysis and make leasing recommendations.
7. Make recommendations to Owner for project improvements, both in physical modifications and in management/operation procedures.
8. Review Merchants' Association budget with income/expenditure plans.
9. Assist on-sit Manager in operation of Merchants' Association and development of an advertising and promotion plan.
10. Attend a monthly Merchants' Association meeting.
11. Prepare monthly deferred conditions. Lease summaries will be prepared by the mall Manager and provided to Consultant.
12. Provide Consultant's standard shopping center (mall) lease and management agreement. Said contracts will be reviewed by _____ (attorney) before they are used.
13. Provide and instruct the mall Manager in the use of Consultant's management forms.
14. Provide training to mall personnel at the Bellevue and Anchorage offices of Consultant.

Source: R. F. Muhlebach & A. A. Alexander, "The Property Manager as Consultant" 51 *J. Prop. Mgmt.* (July/August 1986). Copyright © 1986 by the Institute of Real Estate Management. Reprinted by permission.

topic suggestions from staff members. In collaboration with the director of property management, speakers are contacted and a program formulated.

Suggested topics for staff seminars include:

1. **Insurance.** Reporting claims, review of property coverage, review of employee benefits. Guest speaker: company's insurance agent.

2. **Legal Issues.** Eviction procedures, effects of bankruptcy laws on the landlord/tenant relationship, explanation of lease clauses. Guest speaker: company's legal counsel.

3. **Maintenance.** Roofing and parking lot inspections, landscaping, heating, ventilation and air-conditioning. Guest speaker: contractors or consultants. Film and slides are available from the Asphalt Institute, Asphalt Institute Building, College Park, MD 20740.

4. **Accounting.** New tax laws. Guest speaker: company's accounting firm.

5. **Asset management.** Review needs of the asset manager. Guest speaker: a local asset manager.

6. **Advertising and Public Relations.** Guest speaker: ad agency representative.

7. **Leasing.** Review state of the art in commercial leases, marketing techniques. Guest speaker: attorney discussing lease clauses.

Another portion of an in-house seminar is a presentation given by one or several staff members. For example, the company's controller can review the procedures for approving and paying bills and explain what causes bills to be held. Other talks could include: a property manager reviewing procedures for handling emergencies; a leasing agent reviewing market conditions; or the director of property management reviewing monthly management reports and annual management plans.

Depending on the seminar's structure, department sessions may run concurrently during the day, with a summary meeting for the entire group to conclude the session.

Another useful in-house educational program is the year-end review. This may be either an all-company or a single department meeting at which employees are given an opportunity to assess the year just passed, to give feedback on current operating practices, and to offer suggestions for improvement in the future. Staff members can also recognize company and personal accomplishments. An excellent format combining an informal and formal agenda is a two-hour session beginning at noon with lunch provided.

The property management company that does not have an ongoing education program will slowly lose its competitive edge. Providing a varied program of educational opportunities in a property management company benefits both the individual staff member and the company as a whole.

§ 2.27 CONCLUSION

Most property management companies are small, and it is easy to become so engrossed in managing properties that managing the company is overlooked. However, a small company requires the same attention to its administration and development that larger firms enjoy.

Three

Budgeting: Income and Expense Components

§ 3.1 THE PURPOSE OF A BUDGET

The effective budget is a financial road map of the property. The purpose of a budget is to provide financial guidance to the property manager and the property owner. A good budget will not prevent problems from happening, but it will allow the manager to anticipate and properly respond to financial changes.

For example, if the property will not have sufficient funds to pay the first tax installment, this will be obvious when the budget is developed. The property owner then has sufficient time to plan for the cash shortfall. Conversely, if the property will generate a positive cash flow by midyear, the property owner can plan how these funds will be used.

Without a budget these two situations would go unnoticed until either the property ran out of funds or the owner realized more cash was available than anticipated. In either case, the owner is likely to be surprised. The property manager is responsible for minimizing or eliminating surprises for the property owner.

§ 3.2 TYPES OF BUDGETS

All but the most simple commercial properties have subbudgets that make up the entire budget. In a complex situation, a property can have several of the following subbudgets:

Expense

1. Capital expenditure budget
2. Owner's expenses
3. Common area—parking lot
4. Common area—mall
5. Escalation expenses—office building
6. Merchants' association/promotional fund/marketing fund
7. Property taxes
8. Insurance
9. Utility reimbursement
10. Reimbursement for repairs

Income

1. Base rent
2. Percentage rent
3. Reimbursement of tenant charges
4. Merchants' association/promotional fund/marketing fund
5. Miscellaneous income

1. Capital Expenditure Budget. The capital portion of the budget includes those items not generally expensed in one year and that are amortized over more than one year. These will include major repairs, tenant improvements, and leasing commissions.

2. Owner's Expenses. These expenses are paid by the owner and not reimbursed by tenants. They generally include merchants' association or promotional fund dues, legal expenses, business licenses, office expenses, and property management fees.

3. Common Area—Parking Lot. In an enclosed mall, all tenants commonly share the parking lot expenses, and only those tenants on the mall share the mall expenses. Parking lot expenses are exterior items of maintenance, including parking lot sweeping, landscaping, security, and utilities for the parking lot.

4. Common Area—Mall. These expenses are generally shared by tenants whose stores open onto the mall. Major tenants are not always required to share these expenses, which include janitorial services, air-conditioning, maintenance, utilities, security, and interior landscaping.

5. Escalation Expenses—Office Building. Office tenants will share in the expenses of operating the building. These escalation charges include janitorial service, building repairs, insurance, property taxes, pest control, utilities, and, in some situations, management fees.

6. Merchants' Association/Promotional Fund/Marketing Fund. The owner's contribution to either the merchants' association or promotional fund is generally budgeted in this category. If the landlord collects the merchants' dues and pays the bills, it is generally not a part of the overall property budget but is handled separately.

7. Property Taxes and Insurance. Most owners want a careful evaluation of the amount of taxes and insurance being paid and the percentage being recaptured from the tenants. In the typical commercial lease, tenants will reimburse the landlord for their pro rata share of these expenses.

8. Utility Reimbursement. The owner may pay for the utilities in bulk—known as a master meter—or have a central plan and recover the costs from the tenants on a pro rata basis.

9. Reimbursements for Repairs. Large properties often have an on-site maintenance staff to provide repairs for a fee for tenants, who are responsible for the cost of the work.

§ 3.3   BUDGET DEVELOPMENT AND EVALUATION

One important factor in evaluating a property manager's performance is his or her ability to develop accurate income and expense projections. Although the budgeting process is not difficult, it can be time-consuming, and it requires a thorough knowledge of budget development and evaluation.

The budget must be consistent with the property owner's goals and objectives. This means that the manager must meet with the owner to discuss both short- and long-term goals. Was the property purchased for long-term appreciation? If so, the owner will want to invest in preventive maintenance and capital improvements. Does the owner have cash flow problems? Does the owner live off the property's income and need all the cash for personal use? In both these situations, the owner would be reluctant to spend any more money than was necessary to maintain the current status of the property.

The property manager should bring to the owner's attention all of the major maintenance and capital improvements and justify the need for this work. The property manager reviews the necessity of the work and recommends which items should be completed in the budget period and which can be deferred. It is an exercise in futility to develop an operating budget and then discover that the budget is not consistent with the owner's goals and objectives for the property.

(a) BUDGET TEAM

Developing an accurate budget requires the input of several members of the property management company along with outside consultants. The property manager is primarily responsible for developing the budget and should use the knowledge and experience of maintenance personnel, contractors, the accounting department, the leasing agent, the property's insurance agent, consultants, and the manager's supervisor.

The maintenance supervisor is often most familiar with the maintenance and mechanical operations of the property, yet this person's input is sometimes overlooked when the budget is developed. The maintenance supervisor should meet with the maintenance personnel to review the property's condition and then submit a brief status report to the manager.

Smaller commercial properties seldom have on-site maintenance personnel. They generally contract all maintenance, whereas most large properties contract only specific maintenance. The property manager should meet with all contractors to review their area of maintenance and solicit their opinion on future maintenance needs. For example, the HVAC service contractor may make recommendations for repairs beyond the preventive maintenance contract or recommend upgrading the filters. (See Chapter 9 for more information on maintenance agreements.)

Consultants may be added to the budget team for specific expertise, such as parking lot maintenance or roofing. Consultants are hired to analyze, make recommendations, develop specifications, and estimate costs for specific work.

The leasing agent should provide the leasing projections. The property manager needs to know the occupancy level in order to estimate janitorial and utilities costs in an office building. The manager also needs to know which spaces will be leased, the required amount of tenant improvements, and the amount of space that will be leased and renewed to project commission expense.

The property manager and the insurance agent should meet with the owner to discuss the existing insurance program and the cost of alternative insurance coverage.

The accounting department is an integral part of the budget team. The bookkeeper will provide historical expenses and actual expenses for the current period combined with the property manager's estimate of the expenses for the balance of the current budget period to arrive at the estimated expenses for the current year or budget period. Besides calculating the tenant's charges and reimbursements, the bookkeeper may be asked to determine specific expenses such as real estate taxes.

(b) BUDGET SCHEDULE

A budget is developed over a two- to four-month period. Each commercial property has multiple income components and up to four operating budgets. Every source of income in each income component and every line item expense in each operating budget must be analyzed to prepare an accurate net operating income (NOI) projection.

Multiply the time required to develop one property's income and expense projections by the number of properties managed and it is obvious that cooperation among the staff and close internal budgeting control are critical. Losing control of the budgeting process will result in inaccurate projections, missed deadlines, loss of confidence in the property manager, frustration in the office, and the possibility of losing management accounts.

The budgeting process must be planned, communicated to everyone involved in the budgets, and monitored. As a first step in developing the plan, the controller reviews the management agreements to determine when each budget is due to the owner and then prepares a proposed timeline for each budget. The timeline is developed in reverse chronological order, starting with the date the budget is due to the property owner, and includes the following steps: mail budget to owner, complete final review and corrections, submit for review by property manager's supervisor, type and edit written narrative, obtain income and expense data from the property manager, obtain historical and current data from the accounting department.

The timeline should be distributed to all staff members, and progress should be monitored. One staff person, such as an administrative assistant, can act as coordinator to keep the process flowing smoothly. Delays should be identified and corrected immediately. Staff members also should be recognized for meeting each deadline. Teamwork is essential.

Exhibit 3.1 is a sample budget timeline. This form is just one of many ways to organize the budgeting process. Each company must develop a timeline that suits its operations. Following is an explanation of the terms on the timeline:

Numbers to the project administrator—The property manager provides the income and expense projections to the project administrator (bookkeeper) who enters the numbers in the computer.

Numbers to the property manager—The project administrator provides the property manager with a spread sheet showing the income and expense projections on a monthly basis.

Typist—The budget, along with the annual management plan narrative, is given to the typist for first-draft typing.

Property manager and supervisor review—The property manager's supervisor reviews the first draft of the management plan and budget. The management plan is proofread for errors.

EXHIBIT 3.1

1989 Budget Timeline

No.	Project Name	PA/PM	Expense Numbers to PA	Income Numbers to PA	Numbers to PM	To Typist	PM/Super Review	Corrections	Mail to Owner
8186	Anch Bus Pk	Debbie/Charlene	7-15	8-17	8-31	9-10	9-10	9-11	9-12
8187	Anch Dist I	Thom/Charlene	7-15	8-7	8-31	9-10	9-10	9-11	9-12
8213	Anch Dist II	Jane/Charlene	7-15	8-17	8-31	9-10	9-10	9-11	9-12
3083	A5A	Thom/Jo	8-3	9-2	9-8	9-14	9-15	9-16	9-17
3065	Belgate	Billie/Jessica	9-18	10-20	10-24	10-30	10-31	11-3	11-4
3016	College Pl	Jane/Jessica	8-21	9-22	9-25	10-1	10-2	10-3	10-6
3026	Copper City	Marla/Rick	10-2	11-3	11-6	11-12	11-13	11-14	11-17
3075	Cottonwood	Billie/Marsha	8-14	9-15	9-18	10-6	10-7	10-8	10-9
3091	Crossroads	Rick	2-2	3-2	3-8	3-14	3-15	3-18	3-22
3007	Ellensburg	Marla/Jessica	10-2	11-3	11-7	11-11	11-12	11-13	11-14
1101	Fifth & I	Billie/J.D.	9-30	10-30	11-6	11-11	11-16	11-19	11-20
3056	Forest Park	Thom/Rick	7-1	7-31	8-7	8-14	8-18	8-21	8-28
3044	Frontier	Debbie/J.D.	9-15	10-15	10-22	11-3	11-4	11-5	11-6
3001	JAFCO	Melody/Bob	9-4	10-6	10-10	10-15	10-16	10-17	10-20
2089	Kennewick	Billie/Bob	8-4	9-4	9-17	9-24	9-25	9-28	9-30
3067	Mill Creek	Melody/Rick	9-18	10-20	10-23	10-29	10-3	10-31	11-3
4015	Mountain Sq.	Rick	9-3	3-2	3-8	3-14	3-15	3-18	3-22
3012	Northway	Jane/Terry	8-7	9-8	10-5	10-19	10-20	10-22	10-23
3079	Oak Tree	Marla/Bob	9-11	10-13	10-17	10-23	10-24	10-27	10-28
1290	Overlake E.	Billie/Rick	8-3	9-3	9-10	9-14	9-16	9-23	9-25
3064	Regional	Melody/Terry	9-1	10-1	10-8	10-19	10-21	10-22	10-26
3011	Silverada	Billie/Bob	8-21	9-22	9-25	10-1	10-2	10-3	10-6
PR607	Spanaway	Marla/Rick	8-7	9-7	9-14	9-21	9-25	9-28	9-29
2020	Sunset Vil	Marla/Bob	10-9	11-9	11-14	11-17	11-18	11-19	11-22
3077	TRF Annex	Marla/Jessica	9-25	10-27	10-31	11-4	11-5	11-6	11-7
2095	TRF Office	Marla/Jessica	8-28	9-29	10-5	10-9	10-12	10-13	10-14
3063	Twin Lakes	Jane/Jessica	10-9	11-10	11-13	11-20	11-21	11-24	11-25
3033	Wash Plaza	Melody/Bob	8-14	9-15	9-28	10-6	10-8	10-29	10-30
3040N	Westgate N	Thom/Diana	9-21	10-21	10-24	10-30	10-31	11-3	11-4
3040S	Westgate S	Melody/Diana	9-4	10-7	10-10	10-16	10-17	10-20	10-21
3000	Westwood	Marla/Rick	10-16	11-17	11-19	11-21	11-24	11-25	11-26
3028	Woodinville	Debbie/Rick	9-4	10-6	10-9	10-15	10-16	10-17	10-20

PA - Project Administrator   PM - Property Manager   PM/Super - Property Manager Supervisor

Corrections—The typist makes corrections.

Mail to owner—Before mailing to the owner, the property manager makes a final review of the management plan.

§ 3.4   DEVELOPING THE OPERATING EXPENSE BUDGET

Each item in the operating expense budget needs to be analyzed on a month-by-month basis to arrive at the total expenses for each month. A budget input form is used for each operating budget. Exhibit 3.2 is an example of a shopping center common area maintenance budget. By listing each expense for each maintenance item on a monthly basis, the manager develops a month-by-month operating expense. Combining all the operating budgets, landlord's and common area maintenance (CAM), along with the expenses for taxes, insurance, and any other expenses provides a month-by-month operating and capital expenses budget. When the monthly operating expenses are subtracted from the monthly income components, the result is a month-by-month net operating income (NOI) projection.

With this budget format, any month with a negative NOI or negative cash flow after debt service can be identified in advance and the timing of some expenses, especially major nonrecurring expenses, can be shifted to a period with positive cash flow. Identifying months with negative cash flow allows the property owner to plan for cash shortages. Conversely, positive cash flow projections are monitored for cash management planning.

The property manager must consider seven elements before arriving at expense numbers.

(a)   INSPECTIONS

It is impossible to develop an accurate and meaningful budget without an inspection. The property manager reviews prior inspection forms, and notes future maintenance items and capital improvement items on these forms. The manager then inspects the property. If major maintenance or capital improvement is needed, such as roof repair or replacement, a consultant is hired to analyze the problem.

(b)   HISTORICAL DATA

One method of developing an operating budget is to add an inflation factor to the current year's budget. However, this method doesn't take into consideration nonrecurring expenses, capital improvement, the market's impact on the property, and major cost adjustments for specific expenses

EXHIBIT 3.2

Budget Input Form

Operating Expenses

PROJECT NO.: 3032 PROJECT NAME: Washington Plaza PERIOD: 1989 PREPARED BY: RFM DATE: 11/15/88

GEN. LEDGER ACCT. NO.		DESCRIPTION	JAN.	FEB.	MARCH	APRIL	MAY	JUNE	JULY	AUG.	SEPT.	OCT.	NOV.	DEC.	TOTAL YEAR	% Gross Sched @ 100%	$/SQ. FT.
2-748	20	Admin. Fee	305	298	358	298	290	3C9	317	309	317	302	305	298	3,706		
2-811	00	Electricity	800	800	750	750	650	650	650	650	650	750	800	800	8,700		
2-814	00	Water	75	75	75	125	125	200	200	200	200	150	75	75	1,575		
2-815	00	Sewer	50	-	50	-	50	-	50	-	50	-	50	-	300		
2-832	50	Security	225	225	225	225	225	225	225	225	225	225	225	225	2,700		
2-835	00	Trash Removal	200	200	200	200	200	200	200	200	200	200	200	300	2,500		
2-835	50	Bldg. Supplies	35	35	35	35	35	35	35	35	35	35	35	35	420		
2-854	00	Landscaping	400	400	700	400	400	500	500	500	500	400	400	400	5,500		
2-860	000	Janitorial	250	250	250	250	250	250	250	250	250	250	250	250	3,000		
		PAGE TOTAL	2,340	2,283	2,643	2,283	2,225	2,369	2,427	2,369	2,427	2,312	2,340	2,283	28,401		
		CARRY FORWARD	-	-	-	-	-	-	-	-	-	-	-	-	-		
		TOTAL	2,340	2,283	2,643	2,283	2,225	2,369	2,427	2,369	2,427	2,312	2,340	2,283	28,401		

INPUT DATE: _____ REVISION DATE: _____ APPROVED BY: AAA DATE: 11-20-88 such as substantial increases in electrical rates. This budget approach is not usually accurate.

Former President Carter popularized the zero-based budget that required analyzing each expense without consideration for past and current expenditures. The budget method that will be outlined in this chapter is similar to a zero-based budget. However, historical expenses and current expenditures will provide a frame of reference when developing the operating budget.

Historical and current expense data can assist in developing the operating budget in the following ways:

- Comparing the proposed budget to prior budgets on a per-item basis will ensure that an expense category is not missing from the proposed budget.

- Through use of historical data trends may be identified. For example, an older medical building was undergoing continued plumbing repairs. This trend suggested that a major plumbing problem was about to occur.

- Expenditures over several years can be used for reference to validate bids. If the janitorial costs have been around 80 cents per square foot per year, and the janitor's new bid is in the high 90-cent range, the present janitorial contractor may be overly confident about winning the contract award. In this case additional bids are necessary.

- Historical data can indicate that either the maintenance specifications are wrong or a contractor misinterpreted the bids. For instance, if full-service landscaping service has been costing $1,000 a month and some bids are coming in at $600 to $800 a month, the property manager should check the bid specifications against the contractor's specifications for missing items such as pruning or weed control.

(c) PUBLICATIONS

Publications researched and distributed by real estate associations are another source for comparing operating expenses. The Institute of Real Estate Management (IREM) publishes *Office Buildings Income and Expense Analysis* (Exhibit 3.3), and Building Owners and Managers Association (BOMA) publishes the *Experience Exchange Report* (Exhibit 3.4). These two annual publications analyze office building operating expenses for every major metropolitan area and several secondary cities in the United States. Analyses are classified by size and age of buildings. The International Council of Shopping Centers (ICSC) routinely publishes the *Shopping Center Operating Cost Analysis Report* (Exhibit 3.5).

This report provides operating expenses for strip centers and enclosed malls within different regions. Samples of reports found in these three association publications are shown in Exhibits 3.3 to 3.5.

All of these publications are used to compare expenses. A major variance in an expense category in one of the publications indicates the expense should be further analyzed. For instance, if real estate taxes in these publications average 75 cents per square foot per year for the city in which the property is located and the current projected tax expense is $1.10, this variance should be further analyzed and possibly a tax consultant called in to compare the assessed valuation with comparable building valuation. If there is no apparent justification for the variance, the taxes may be appealed.

(d) COMPARING EXPENSES WITH BUILDINGS IN THE AREA

Information is shared freely in the property management profession. Active membership in IREM, ICSC, and BOMA provides an opportunity to meet other property managers and to share experiences. It is common for managers to seek information from each other. This professional network is invaluable when developing a budget for a building when historical expenses are not available or for a building under construction or proposal.

(e) CURRENT YEAR'S EXPENSES

A budget is usually developed some time between the middle to the end of the current budget period and is finalized a month or two before the current budget period ends. Some of the most helpful information for developing a budget can be obtained from the current budget period's actual and estimated expenses. The actual expenditures and estimates of the expenses for the remaining budget period are the best guidelines for preparing a budget.

The property manager takes the current year's expenses to date and estimates the expenses for the remaining budget period. Actual and projected expenses are combined to obtain accurate estimates for the current year's budget. The property manager then reviews the budget explanation information (Exhibit 3.6) and determines if the reasoning for the remaining expenses is still valid or if the situation has changed and new assumptions will require revised estimates.

(f) COMPETITION'S IMPACT ON THE BUDGET

Outside influences may impact a building's operating and capital budgets. This in turn affects the marketing and leasing of the building. New developments and upgrading of existing competition always require

EXHIBIT 3.3

Operating Expenses for Suburban Office Buildings

Selected Metropolitan Areas

METROPOLITAN ANALYSIS BY RENTAL RANGE   SUBURBAN

| SUBURBAN OFFICE BUILDINGS | | | | RENTAL RANGE DALLAS, TX | | | $0.01 - $9.99 | | |

CHART OF ACCOUNTS	\$/GROSS AREA OF ENTIRE BLG.			\$/GROSS RENTABLE OFFC. AREA			\$/NET RENTABLE OFFC. AREA		
	BLGS SQ. FT. (10000)	MED.	RANGE LOW HIGH	BLGS SQ. FT. (10000)	MED.	RANGE LOW HIGH	BLGS SQ. FT. (10000)	MED.	RANGE LOW HIGH
INCOME									
OFFICES	35 589	7.62	6.55 8.81	14 181	7.53	6.90 9.08	32 513	8.45	6.96 9.02
GROSS POSSBLE INCOME	35 589	7.51	6.47 8.82	14 181	7.33	6.67 8.31	32 513	8.50	7.22 9.09
VACANCY/DELIN.RENTS	35 589	2.23	.16 2.83	14 181	1.97	.02 2.83	32 513	2.40	.45 3.07
TOTAL COLLECTIONS	35 589	5.44	4.43 6.56	14 181	6.43	5.07 7.10	32 513	6.20	5.18 7.16
EXPENSES									
SUBTOTAL UTILITIES	35 589	1.22	1.00 1.43	14 181	1.42	1.11 1.54	32 513	1.37	1.10 1.56
JAN.PAYROLL/CONTRACT	34 583	.35	.25 .46	13 175	.37	.33 .57	31 507	.38	.28 .45
SUBTOT JAN/MAINT/RPR	35 589	.93	.75 1.15	14 181	1.05	.72 1.20	32 513	.99	.84 1.26
MANAGEMENT FEE	35 589	.29	.21 .36	14 181	.30	.26 .34	32 513	.30	.21 .38
SUBTOTAL ADMIN/PAYRL	35 589	.86	.60 1.07	14 181	.87	.44 1.11	32 513	.98	.66 1.13
INSURANCE	33 501	.11	.09 .13	14 181	.12	.10 .14	30 435	.11	.08 .13
SUBTOTAL INSUR/SRVCS	35 589	.47	.36 .54	14 181	.52	.36 .66	32 513	.52	.41 .59
NET OPERATING COSTS	35 589	3.64	2.97 3.99	14 181	3.80	3.39 4.26	32 513	3.86	3.47 4.26
REAL ESTATE TAXES	35 589	.90	.72 1.03	14 181	.87	.73 .92	32 513	.95	.84 1.04
TOTAL OPERATNG COSTS	35 589	4.53	4.09 4.98	14 181	5.00	4.26 5.29	32 513	4.91	4.47 5.29

| SUBURBAN OFFICE BUILDINGS | | | | RENTAL RANGE DALLAS, TX | | | $10.00 - $12.99 | | |

CHART OF ACCOUNTS	\$/GROSS AREA OF ENTIRE BLG.			\$/GROSS RENTABLE OFFC. AREA			\$/NET RENTABLE OFFC. AREA		
	BLGS SQ. FT. (10000)	MED.	RANGE LOW HIGH	BLGS SQ. FT. (10000)	MED.	RANGE LOW HIGH	BLGS SQ. FT. (10000)	MED.	RANGE LOW HIGH
INCOME									
OFFICES	31 548	11.13	10.21 11.70	12 231	12.00	11.57 12.50	25 471	11.51	10.70 12.00
GROSS POSSBLE INCOME	31 548	11.58	10.55 12.19	12 231	12.46	11.71 12.82	25 471	11.95	11.48 12.27
VACANCY/DELIN.RENTS	31 548	2.95	.46 3.60	12 231	1.84	.46 2.38	25 471	3.29	1.13 4.13
TOTAL COLLECTIONS	31 548	8.53	7.19 10.18	12 231	10.76	9.15 11.57	25 471	9.02	7.43 10.52
EXPENSES									
SUBTOTAL UTILITIES	31 548	1.34	1.11 1.62	12 231	1.51	1.34 1.63	25 471	1.48	1.19 1.64
JAN.PAYROLL/CONTRACT	31 548	.47	.36 .54	12 231	.47	.44 .52	25 471	.49	.37 .57
SUBTOT JAN/MAINT/RPR	31 548	1.19	.94 1.33	12 231	1.31	1.12 1.38	25 471	1.19	1.02 1.38
MANAGEMENT FEE	31 548	.30	.26 .40	12 231	.36	.27 .42	25 471	.34	.27 .43
SUBTOTAL ADMIN/PAYRL	31 548	.88	.73 1.07	12 231	.81	.76 1.02	25 471	.95	.80 1.22
INSURANCE	31 548	.09	.07 .13	12 231	.10	.06 .12	25 471	.11	.08 .16
SUBTOTAL INSUR/SRVCS	31 548	.43	.42 .48	12 231	.46	.42 .48	25 471	.47	.44 .56
NET OPERATING COSTS	31 548	3.86	3.49 4.21	12 231	3.80	3.71 4.36	25 471	4.01	3.71 4.94
REAL ESTATE TAXES	31 548	.98	.89 1.14	12 231	1.06	.95 1.18	25 471	1.12	.98 1.25
TOTAL OPERATNG COSTS	31 548	5.03	4.40 5.36	12 231	5.03	4.69 5.41	25 471	5.25	4.50 6.00

| SUBURBAN OFFICE BUILDINGS | | | | RENTAL RANGE DALLAS, TX | | | $13.00 - $15.99 | | |

CHART OF ACCOUNTS	\$/GROSS AREA OF ENTIRE BLG.			\$/GROSS RENTABLE OFFC. AREA			\$/NET RENTABLE OFFC. AREA		
	BLGS SQ. FT. (10000)	MED.	RANGE LOW HIGH	BLGS SQ. FT. (10000)	MED.	RANGE LOW HIGH	BLGS SQ. FT. (10000)	MED.	RANGE LOW HIGH
INCOME									
OFFICES	22 641	12.98	12.70 13.52	11 346	13.85	13.44 13.93	18 385	14.34	13.67 15.05
GROSS POSSBLE INCOME	22 641	13.55	12.92 15.40	11 346	14.33	13.56 15.09	18 385	15.06	14.31 16.22
VACANCY/DELIN.RENTS	22 641	3.19	1.42 5.57	11 346	5.07	1.14 6.00	18 385	3.40	1.53 5.91
TOTAL COLLECTIONS	22 641	10.01	8.20 12.23	11 346	9.67	7.04 12.47	18 385	12.26	9.42 14.55
EXPENSES									
SUBTOTAL UTILITIES	22 641	1.31	1.16 1.40	11 346	1.45	1.22 1.46	18 385	1.42	1.22 1.57
JAN.PAYROLL/CONTRACT	22 641	.48	.39 .53	11 346	.46	.32 .56	18 385	.52	.42 .60
SUBTOT JAN/MAINT/RPR	22 641	1.14	.93 1.37	11 346	1.15	.94 1.41	18 385	1.18	1.08 1.48
MANAGEMENT FEE	19 563	.32	.23 .55	9 320	.34	.24 .49	15 316	.39	.27 .56
SUBTOTAL ADMIN/PAYRL	21 640	.91	.68 1.05	10 345	1.08	.71 1.11	17 384	.97	.67 1.22
INSURANCE	22 641	.11	.08 .14	11 346	.13	.10 .15	18 385	.13	.09 .16
SUBTOTAL INSUR/SRVCS	22 641	.54	.36 .67	11 346	.57	.36 .61	18 385	.60	.41 .70
NET OPERATING COSTS	22 641	3.97	3.49 4.18	11 346	4.19	3.29 4.34	18 385	4.29	3.77 4.41
REAL ESTATE TAXES	22 641	1.31	1.11 1.43	11 346	1.40	1.06 1.45	18 385	1.42	1.22 1.70
TOTAL OPERATNG COSTS	22 641	5.33	4.80 5.61	11 346	5.33	4.74 5.95	18 385	5.63	5.19 6.15

FOOTNOTE: SQUARE FOOTAGE FIGURES (SQ.FT.) ARE REPORTED IN MULTIPLES OF TEN THOUSAND. SEE GUIDELINES SECTION FOR EXPLANATION OF REPORTS AND INTERPRETATION OF DATA. COPYRIGHT 1989, IREM.

Income/Expense Analysis: Office Buildings, Downtown & Suburban (1989)

Source: Reprinted with permission from the Institute of Real Estate Management.

EXHIBIT 3.4

1989 BOMA Experience Exchange Report

CITY ANALYSES 1988   **U.S. PRIVATE SECTOR**

Washington, DC
DOWNTOWN 50,000-100,000 SQ. FT.

	TOTAL BUILDING RENTABLE AREA					TOTAL OFFICE RENTABLE AREA					OCCUPANCY INFO.		BLDS
	7 BLDS	561,014 SQ. FT.					550,357 SQ. FT.						
	#	DOLLARS/SQ. FT.		MID RANGE		DOLLARS/SQ. FT.		MID RANGE			AVG SQFT/OFFICE TENANT	4479	7
INCOME	BLDS	AVG	MEDIAN	LOW	HIGH	AVG	MEDIAN	LOW	HIGH				
OFFICE AREA	6					21.01	22.04	15.27	26.88				
RETAIL AREA	3	33.47	25.79								AVG SQFT/RETAIL TENANT	1526	3
OTHER AREA	2	8.56	9.79										
TOTAL RENT	6	21.21	23.01	15.27	26.27						AVG SQFT/OFFICE WORKER	272	6
MISCELLANEOUS	4	.28	.34	.15	.41								
TOTAL INCOME	6	21.39	23.21	15.27	26.56								
EXPENSE											AVG % OFFICE OCCUPANCY	92.0	7
CLEANING	7	1.12	1.14	1.02	1.19	1.14	1.17	1.04	1.23				
REPAIR-MAINT	7	1.59	1.61	1.37	1.97	1.62	1.70	1.39	2.01		AVG % RETAIL OCCUPANCY	84.3	3
UTILITIES	7	2.30	2.02	1.91	2.52	2.34	2.12	1.96	2.56				
RDS/GRNDS/SEC	7	.41	.51	.18	.55	.42	.54	.19	.55				
ADMINISTRATIVE	7	.81	.80	.51	1.02	.82	.80	.52	1.07				
TOTAL OPER EXP	7	6.25	6.46	5.68	6.74	6.37	6.80	5.79	6.91				
FIXED EXPENSES	7	3.23	3.45	3.12	3.52	3.29	3.55	3.14	3.62		AVG $ RATE YR-END RENT	25.74	7
TOTAL OPER + FIX	7	9.48	9.87	8.58	10.35	9.67	10.40	8.78	10.61				
LEASING EXP	6	2.34	.54	.37	5.54								
TOTAL PAYROLL	7	.96	.76	.70	1.23						RENTABLE/GROSS SQFT	.90	5
TOTAL CONTRACT	7	2.26	2.13	1.41	3.08								

DETAIL*	AVERAGE	BLDS	DETAIL*	AVERAGE	BLDS	DETAIL*	AVERAGE	BLDS	DETAIL*	AVERAGE	BLDS	DETAIL*	AVERAGE	BLDS
CLEANING TOTAL	1.12	7	**UTILITIES TOTAL**	2.30	7	SECURITY TOTAL	.43	5	**FIXED EXP TOTAL**	3.40	6	**TOTAL PAYROLL**	.96	7
PAYROLL	.53	2	ELECTRICAL	1.79	7	SEC PAYROLL			REAL ESTATE TAX	3.08	6	CLEANING	.53	2
CONTRACT	1.04	6	GAS	.08	6	SEC CONTRACTS	.37	5	BUILDING INS	.17	6	REPAIR/MAINT	.75	7
SUP/MAT/MISC	.02	6	FUEL OIL	.43	3	SEC OTHER			PERS PROP TAX	.00	2	RDS/GROUNDS		
TRASH REMOVAL	.07	6	PURCH STEAM						OTHER TAX	.14	6	SECURITY		
REPR/MAINT TOTAL	1.59	7	PURCH CH WTR			**ADMIN TOTAL**	.81	6				ADMINISTRATIVE		
PAYROLL	.75	7	COAL			PAYROLL			**LEASING EXPENSES**	2.71	5			
ELEVATOR	.17	7	WATER/SEWER	.30	6	MGMT FEES	.80	5	ADV/PROMOTION	.24	3	**TOTAL CONTRACTS**	2.26	7
HVAC	.18	7	**RDS/GNDS/SEC**	.39	6	PROF FEES	.13	3	COMMISSIONS	.56	3	CLEANING	1.04	6
ELECTRICAL	.05	6	TOTAL			GEN OFC EXP	.05	5	PROF FEES			REPAIR/MAINT	.49	7
STRUCT/ROOF	.09	4	RDS/GNDS TOTAL	.06	4	OTHER ADM EXP	.04	5	TENANT ALTS	1.78	4	RDS/GROUNDS		
PLUMBING	.07	5	RDS/GNDS PAYRL						BUY-OUTS			SECURITY	.37	5
FIRE/LIFE SFTY	.01	2	RDS/GNDS CONTR	.05	4				OTHER LEASING	1.39	3	ADMINISTRATIVE	.88	5
OTHER MAINT/SUP	.35	7	RDS/GNDS OTHER	.02	3									

*TOTAL BUILDING RENTABLE AREA-AVERAGE DOLLARS/SQ. FT.   ©1989 BOMA Experience Exchange Report

DOWNTOWN 100,000-300,000 SQ. FT.

	TOTAL BUILDING RENTABLE AREA					TOTAL OFFICE RENTABLE AREA					OCCUPANCY INFO.		BLDS
	46 BLDS	8,694,819 SQ. FT.					8,033,078 SQ. FT.						
	#	DOLLARS/SQ. FT.		MID RANGE		DOLLARS/SQ. FT.		MID RANGE			AVG SQFT/OFFICE TENANT	6798	46
INCOME	BLDS	AVG	MEDIAN	LOW	HIGH	AVG	MEDIAN	LOW	HIGH				
OFFICE AREA	42					22.72	21.81	18.20	26.89				
RETAIL AREA	36	20.69	22.29	15.36	30.94						AVG SQFT/RETAIL TENANT	3045	39
OTHER AREA	15	6.56	9.40	5.22	10.82								
TOTAL RENT	45	22.62	22.11	18.60	26.04						AVG SQFT/OFFICE WORKER	328	22
MISCELLANEOUS	44	.45	.17	.03	.40								
TOTAL INCOME	45	23.06	22.35	18.88	26.44								
EXPENSE											AVG % OFFICE OCCUPANCY	94.1	46
CLEANING	46	.99	1.02	.92	1.08	1.06	1.08	.97	1.16				
REPAIR-MAINT	46	1.25	1.23	1.00	1.45	1.34	1.31	1.06	1.55		AVG % RETAIL OCCUPANCY	91.4	39
UTILITIES	43	1.67	1.69	1.50	1.88	1.75	1.75	1.60	1.96				
RDS/GRNDS/SEC	46	.27	.25	.11	.35	.29	.26	.11	.38				
ADMINISTRATIVE	46	1.04	1.09	.90	1.24	1.12	1.22	.91	1.35				
TOTAL OPER EXP	42	5.18	5.33	4.60	5.81	5.61	5.82	5.04	6.19				
FIXED EXPENSES	46	3.49	3.62	3.07	4.07	3.78	3.91	3.47	4.35		AVG $ RATE YR-END RENT	25.52	36
TOTAL OPER + FIX	42	8.65	8.91	7.89	9.75	9.37	9.56	8.72	10.43				
LEASING EXP	44	.81	.27	.11	.64								
TOTAL PAYROLL	42	.75	.71	.59	.90						RENTABLE/GROSS SQFT	.95	40
TOTAL CONTRACT	42	2.47	2.62	2.15	2.91								

DETAIL*	AVERAGE	BLDS	DETAIL*	AVERAGE	BLDS	DETAIL*	AVERAGE	BLDS	DETAIL*	AVERAGE	BLDS	DETAIL*	AVERAGE	BLDS
CLEANING TOTAL	1.00	42	**UTILITIES TOTAL**	1.69	39	SECURITY TOTAL	.19	40	**FIXED EXP TOTAL**	3.58	42	**TOTAL PAYROLL**	.75	42
PAYROLL	.13	10	ELECTRICAL	1.53	39	SEC PAYROLL	.14	7	REAL ESTATE TAX	3.19	42	CLEANING	.13	10
CONTRACT	.92	41	GAS	.04	15	SEC CONTRACTS	.16	40	BUILDING INS	.15	41	REPAIR/MAINT	.63	41
SUP/MAT/MISC	.02	32	FUEL OIL	.05	24	SEC OTHER	.18	11	PERS PROP TAX	.00	22	RDS/GROUNDS		
TRASH REMOVAL	.06	42	PURCH STEAM						OTHER TAX	.26	37	SECURITY	.14	7
REPR/MAINT TOTAL	1.24	42	PURCH CH WTR			**ADMIN TOTAL**	1.06	42				ADMINISTRATIVE	.12	26
PAYROLL	.63	41	COAL			PAYROLL	.12	26	**LEASING EXPENSES**	.85	40			
ELEVATOR	.14	42	WATER/SEWER	.11	39	MGMT FEES	.80	41	ADV/PROMOTION	.04	35	**TOTAL CONTRACTS**	2.47	42
HVAC	.15	42	**RDS/GNDS/SEC**	.26	42	PROF FEES	.15	38	COMMISSIONS	.38	36	CLEANING	.92	41
ELECTRICAL	.03	38	TOTAL			GEN OFC EXP	.02	42	PROF FEES	.03	8	REPAIR/MAINT	.46	42
STRUCT/ROOF	.15	31	RDS/GNDS TOTAL	.05	35	OTHER ADM EXP	.04	36	TENANT ALTS	.17	32	RDS/GROUNDS	.05	35
PLUMBING	.02	37	RDS/GNDS PAYRL						BUY-OUTS			SECURITY	.16	40
FIRE/LIFE SFTY	.01	19	RDS/GNDS CONTR	.05	35				OTHER LEASING	.37	13	ADMINISTRATIVE	.92	42
OTHER MAINT/SUP	.16	42	RDS/GNDS OTHER	.01	19									

*TOTAL BUILDING RENTABLE AREA-AVERAGE DOLLARS/SQ. FT.   ©1989 BOMA Experience Exchange Report

Source: Reprinted with permission of Building Owners and Managers Association (BOMA) International, Washington, DC.

EXHIBIT 3.5

Shopping Center Operating Analysis Report, 1989

Item	N	Mean	Median	Q1	Q3
Maintenance & Repair	46	0.621	0.441	0.270	0.713
Exterior	26	0.690	0.286	0.102	0.489
Parking Lot	26	0.253	0.150	0.094	0.211
Janitorial	19	0.168	0.108	0.063	0.196
Repairs	13	0.113	0.065	0.036	0.188
Landscaping	17	0.146	0.097	0.047	0.207
Miscellaneous	12	0.165	0.094	0.057	0.191
Building/Structural/Systems	22	0.070	0.059	0.021	0.091
Exterior Electricity	15	0.035	0.027	0.011	0.046
Insurance	24	0.073	0.054	0.036	0.096
Fire	12	0.048	0.037	0.024	0.081
Liability	13	0.042	0.025	0.015	0.067
General & Administrative & Marketing	43	0.414	0.293	0.198	0.465
Leasing & Management Fee	30	0.260	0.230	0.166	0.302
Leasing Fee	20	0.120	0.108	0.070	0.146
Management Fee	28	0.219	0.204	0.149	0.257
Professional Fees	19	0.069	0.047	0.020	0.096
Legal Fees	15	0.031	0.020	0.014	0.048
Marketing	11	0.036	0.024	0.016	0.038
Miscellaneous Aggregations:					
Interior & Exterior (M&R)	28	0.339	0.286	0.138	0.428
Interior & BSS (M&R)	23	0.094	0.082	0.024	0.140
Exterior & BSS (M&R)	30	0.374	0.327	0.146	0.533
Water & Sewer (Utilities)	11	1.205	0.084	0.018	0.167
Payroll & G&A&M	31	0.259	0.223	0.167	0.293
M&R & Security	47	0.640	0.465	0.276	0.722
G&A&M & Security	43	0.417	0.293	0.196	0.500

Source: International Council of Shopping Centers

EXHIBIT 3.6

Budget Explanation Form

PAGE 1 OF 1

PROJECT NO: 3032 PROJECT NAME: Washington Plaza PERIOD 1989 PREPARED BY: RFM DATE: 11-15-88

Common Area Maintenance

GENERAL LEDGER ACCT. NO.	DESCRIPTION	
2-74820	Admin. Fee	15% of the actual CAM expenses
2-81100	Electricity	Parking lot and canopy light usage same as prior year. Utility company projects 5% increase effective Jan.
2-81400	Water	Usage same as prior year. Water company projects 10% increase effective January.
2-81500	Sewer	Fixed rate of $50 every other month.
2-83250	Security	Drive-by patrols after center is closed.
2-83500	Trash removal	No increase over last year. Extra pick-ups in December.
2-85400	Landscaping	$400/monthly maintenance contract; $300 weed control and spraying-March; Flowers in planters - $100 in June, July, August, and September
2-8600	Janitorial	Contract 2 hr/day policing parking lot and sidewalks

INPUT DATE: REVISION DATE: APPROVED BY: AAA DATE: 11-18-88 careful analysis of a building's marketing features. The property manager drives through the area in which the competition is located looking for new and upgraded buildings. These buildings should be toured, compared, and assessed for their impact on the subject building. A site that is vacant when the budget is developed can become a competing building ready for occupancy during the budget period. Low-rise office buildings, industrial properties, and shopping centers can be constructed in less than a year.

It is important to consider such additional competition from new developments and upgraded buildings in formulating a building's leasing and occupancy projections. The city or county building department will usually provide information on plans for new developments. The property manager analyzes the impact of these plans on his or her building and considers whether additional improvements to the building must be included in either the operating or the capital budget.

(g) MARKET CONDITIONS

Market conditions will affect the operating and capital budgets and the income projections. In a soft leasing market, capital improvements and/ or upgrading maintenance is often necessary to maintain or improve the building's market position. A market survey, which is part of the management plan, needs to be conducted in the early stages of the budget process. (See Chapter 7 for more information on market surveys.) The market survey will provide the data necessary to project leasing activity and occupancy, which in turn are needed to project all of the income components. This information is helpful when determining whether to upgrade the common areas and the exterior of the building.

(h) CHART OF ACCOUNTS

The chart of accounts can be limited to a few expense items or extended to an unlimited breakdown of operating expenses. The property management company needs to develop a chart of accounts that adequately identifies the expenses. Regardless of the management company's procedures, most institutional owners will require that the property manager uses its own chart of accounts.

A prefix may be added to the chart of accounts number to identify the particular budget. For instance, the landlord's nonreimbursable budget prefix is number 1; common area parking lot maintenance, number 2; common area mall maintenance, number 3; escalation expenses, number 4; merchants' association/promotional fund/marketing fund, number 5. A painting expense charge to the landlord's nonreimbursable budget for painting a vacancy would be 1-86100, while painting the lobby in an office building would be charged to escalation budget 4-86100.

Exhibits 3.7 and 3.8 show how a chart of accounts can be organized by numerical codes or alphabetically by expense items.

§ 3.5 ANALYZING OPERATING EXPENSES

Each expense item is analyzed separately. When analyzing each expense, do not determine the annual cost and divide this number by twelve to arrive at a monthly expense. Since an expense is seldom a constant amount for every month, each expense has to be analyzed on a month-by-month basis. Even when a maintenance contract has a fixed monthly price for full service such as landscape maintenance, there is usually periodic maintenance that is not part of the contract, or a need may arise for emergency repairs that cannot be included in the base contract.

An analysis of several expense components follows. Once the manager understands the process and rationale behind each item, any expense item can be analyzed and budgeted.

(a) AUDIT FEES

The landlord's expenses may include a partnership audit fee. Consult with the property owner for the cost of this service. Retail tenants' sales should be audited periodically to ensure that they are submitting accurate sales figures and paying the correct amount of percentage rent. After determining the number of tenants to audit, the property manager can obtain cost estimates from firms specializing in tenant audits.

(b) COMMISSIONS

Commissions are estimated by first determining the amount of new space that will be leased and the amount of space that will be renewed. Next, the property manager reviews the leasing agreement to determine the commission schedule for new space, renewals, and pad tenants. These two variables are used to compute the commission expense.

(c) ELEVATORS

Most property managers know less about elevator maintenance than they do about HVAC maintenance, so they usually rely on a maintenance contractor. Bid specifications must be carefully prepared or, if they originate with the bidders, they must be carefully compared. Will the contract be a full maintenance contract? If a local small contractor with a lower bid than a national contractor is hired, the property manager must determine if the contractor has an adequate supply of parts and sufficient service people available for emergency and after-hours service.

EXHIBIT 3.7

Chart of Accounts

NUMERICAL LIST

Administrative — 71000

71100	Advertising
71101	Merchants Assoc. Contributions
71105	Entertainment & Promotion
71110	Contributions
74105	Automobile Lease Expense
74108	Parking/Ferry Tolls
74110	Automobile Repairs & Maintenance
74810	Management Fees
74875	Management Fees - Cash
75510	Insurance Expense
76100	Air Freight
76105	Bank Charges
76110	Dues and Subscriptions
76115	Office Equipment Rental
76120	Office Supplies
76125	Postage
76130	Repairs and Maintenance
76135	Telephone Expenses
76140	Miscellaneous Expense
77100	Accounting Fees
77105	Consulting Fees
77110	Legal Fees
77115	Architect Fees
77120	Leasing Commissions
78100	Business Tax
78105	Licenses
78110	Permits
78115	Personal Property Tax
78120	Real Estate Tax
78125	Sales Tax on Capital Additions
79100	Air Fare
79105	Car Rental
79110	Lodging
79115	Meals
80100	Salaries
80105	Payroll Taxes
80110	Profit Sharing Expenses
80115	Insurance - Life
80120	Insurance - Medical/Dental
80130	Gasoline
80135	Management Training

Utilities — 81000

81100	Electricity
81200	Gas
81300	Oil
81400	Water
81500	Sewer
81900	Other Utilities

Building Supplies — 83000

83100	Licenses & Permits
83150	Alarm
83200	Music
83250	Security
83300	Signs
83350	Supplies
83400	Tools/Equipment/Uniforms
83450	Rentals
83500	Trash Removal

Repairs & Maintenance — 84000

84110	Salaries
84120	Payroll Taxes
84130	Employee Benefits
85100	Building Repairs/Maintenance
85200	Flooring
85300	Ceilings
85400	Landscaping
85410	Window Maintenance
85500	Roof
85600	Elevator/Escalator
85700	Plumbing/Sprinklers
85800	Parking Lot
86000	Janitorial
86100	Painting
86200	Sweeping/Snow Removal
86300	Electrical
86400	HVAC
86500	Insurance Damage
86600	Reserve Account

Tenant Costs — 89000

89100	Tenant Repairs
89200	Tenant Improvements
89220	Landlord Improvements
90000	Rent Expenses
96000	Federal Income Tax Expense

EXHIBIT 3.8

Chart of Accounts

ALPHABETICAL LIST

Administrative —71000

Accounting Fees	77100
Advertising	71100
Air Fare	79100
Air Freight	76100
Architect Fees	77115
Automobile Lease Expense	74105
Automobile Repairs & Maintenance	74110
Bank Charges	76105
Business Tax	67100
Car Rental	79105
Consulting Fees	77105
Contributions	71110
Dues & Subscriptions	76110
Entertainment & Promotion	71105
Gasoline	80130
Insurance - Life	80115
Insurance - Medical/Dental	80120
Insurance Expense	75510
Leasing Commissions	77120
Legal Fees	77110
Licenses	78105
Lodging	79110
Management Fees	74810
Management Fees - Cash	74875
Management Training	80135
Meals	79115
Merchants Assoc. Contributions	71101
Miscellaneous Expense	76140
Office Equipment Rental	76115
Office Supplies	76120
Parking/Ferry Tolls	74108
Payroll Taxes	80105
Permits	78110
Personal Property Tax	78115
Postage	76125
Profit Sharing Expenses	80110
Real Estate Tax	78120
Repairs & Maintenance	76130
Salaries	80100
Sales Tax on Capital Additions	78125
Telephone Expenses	76135

Building Supplies —83000

Alarm	83150
Licenses & Permits	83100
Music	83200
Rentals	83450
Security	83250
Signs	83300
Supplies	83350
Tools/Equipment/Uniforms	83400
Trash Removal	83500

Repairs & Maintenance —84000

Building Repairs/Maintenance	85100
Ceilings	85300
Electrical	86300
Elevator/Escalator	85600
Employee Benefits	84130
Flooring	85200
HVAC	86400
Insurance Damage	86500
Janitorial	86000
Landscaping	85400
Painting	86100
Parking Lot	85800
Payroll Taxes	84120
Plumbing/Sprinklers	85700
Reserve Account	86600
Roof	85500
Salaries	84110
Sweeping/Snow Removal	86200
Window Maintenance	55410

Tenant Costs —89000

Federal Income Tax Expense	96000
Landlord Improvements	89220
Rent Expenses	90000
Tenant Improvements	89200
Tenant Repairs	89100

Utilities —81000

Electricity	81100
Gas	81200
Oil	81300
Other Utilities	81900
Sewer	81500
Water	81400

Should the property manager enter into a long-term maintenance agreement, usually five years, to receive a discount?

All of these issues must be considered when developing elevator maintenance costs. A light-load credit should be negotiated in the contract. This provides a discount for occupancy below a certain level and is usually a series of discounts based on different occupancy levels.

(d) HVAC MAINTENANCE

This is another area in which property managers generally rely on an HVAC contractor. When bidding the preventive maintenance, the contractor usually will provide the maintenance specifications, which can vary significantly from contractor to contractor. Each bid must be compared for frequency of maintenance, the items to be inspected and how often, and the type of filters provided by the contractor.

The property manager may hire a consultant to develop the preventive maintenance specifications. The manufacturer of the equipment may also provide such specifications. Some buildings hire building engineers to perform all HVAC maintenance. In Los Angeles, the building engineers' union has an education program for its members, and many buildings hire these engineers for an in-house maintenance program. If this is the case, the budget will reflect the number of engineers or chief engineers and their payroll costs.

The HVAC contractor can usually estimate accurately the cost of nonpreventive maintenance work and work not covered in the maintenance contract.

(e) INSURANCE

Insurance expense is based on the type of coverage and its cost, which depends on the type of building, the building's features, and its location. The property owner will determine the type and limits of coverage for the building, and the insurance agent will provide the estimated cost of the coverage.

(f) JANITORIAL

Janitorial costs for office space may be determined by dividing the cost into two areas—common areas and occupied spaces. The cost to clean the common areas is not affected by occupancy unless a floor is totally vacant. Obtain a cost, either a dollar amount or a cost per square foot, for the common area. Then obtain a cost per square foot for occupied space. The common area cost for occupied floors is added to the cost to clean the tenants' spaces. To determine the cost to clean the tenants' spaces, multiply the cost per square foot per month to clean the occupied spaces times each month's projected occupancy.

Another approach is to obtain a price to clean the entire building based on 100% occupancy and allow a credit for each square foot of vacant space.

Shopping centers have only common areas to clean. The property manager determines the number of janitors needed each day and their schedule. The number of janitors will vary based on weekdays, nights, weekends, and peak selling seasons. The janitorial company will bid on these hours and the specifications for cleaning. If the janitorial service is in house, the property manager can calculate janitorial expense by determining the payroll cost of each janitor, the number of hours worked each week, and the cost of the supervisor.

(g) LANDSCAPING

There are three components to the landscape expense: the monthly maintenance contract fee or monthly in-house maintenance cost, periodic maintenance expenses, and the cost of replacing and upgrading planting materials. When developing the monthly maintenance cost, the property manager must carefully review the contractor's specifications. Some specifications will provide for full maintenance, including pruning, weed control, and spraying, while others will provide for the minimum monthly maintenance.

After calculating the monthly charge, the cost of the periodic maintenance, pruning, and weed control is determined if it is not included in the monthly maintenance service.

The third variable is plant replacement and upgrading. The property manager should inspect the property with a landscaper, checking for plants and trees that have been damaged or stolen. The manager reviews the landscaping needs and decides if upgrading is necessary to maintain the property's image or to be more competitive in the market. An estimate from a landscaper is submitted with the list of new planting materials.

(h) LEGAL FEES

Legal fees are usually the result of evictions or landlord-tenant disputes. Current cases are reviewed with an attorney to estimate what it would cost to resolve the disputes. The delinquencies are reviewed to determine which tenants will require legal action and, based on present legal costs, an estimate can be determined.

(i) MAINTENANCE PAYROLL

Maintenance employees' costs include salaries, payroll costs, and employee benefits. These are estimated by determining the specifications or job requirements, the number of maintenance personnel needed, the salaries for each person, the number of hours each staff person will work, cost of overtime, and the hours for replacement help for vacations and sick leave. The cost is usually constant each month except for additional personnel added for specific maintenance jobs, seasonal needs such as the Christmas period for shopping centers, possible bonuses or incentive pay, and periodic salary reviews.

(j) MANAGEMENT FEE

The management fee is relatively easy to estimate for properties with a high occupancy. Management fees are generally a percentage of income collected or a flat fee. In some cases, the management fee is a percentage versus a minimum fee, whichever is greater.

First review the management agreement, which will define how the management fee is calculated. If the fee is a percentage of income, it is either a percentage of the base rents and percentage rents collected or a percentage of all income collected. All income will include the base and percentage rent plus the income from tenant charges such as escalation or common area maintenance charges and reimbursement for taxes and increased expenses.

After estimating the income components, multiply these components by the management fee percentage. Apply this formula to each monthly income component to arrive at a monthly management fee. If the building is in a lease-up stage, the process is the same but the accuracy of the estimated management fee is based on the accuracy of the lease-up projections. When the management fee is a minimum fee rather than a percentage, the minimum fee is budgeted for the months the percentage fee is less than the minimum fee.

(k) MERCHANTS' ASSOCIATION/PROMOTIONAL FUND/MARKETING FUND

If the shopping center has a merchants' association or promotional fund, the landlord is usually a major contributor. The tenant's lease generally stipulates both the landlord's and the tenant's obligation. Landlords usually pay between 25% and 33% of what the tenants contribute.

The property manager must first total the contributions from all the tenants and then multiply this amount by the percentage of the landlord's contribution. If the center opens with a low occupancy, the landlord may be willing to pay dues based on a 100% occupancy to provide the association or fund with operating capital.

If the center is new, the tenants and landlord may have a grand opening contribution. In this case, the method for calculating the landlord's obligation is the same. If the center is opening with a low occupancy, some landlords will contribute the tenant's grand opening dues and collect this amount from tenants that open within one year of the center's grand opening. However, it is difficult to collect grand opening dues from tenants who open a year later.

(l) PAINTING

Painting expense consists of contract painting and painting supplies. Before developing the numbers for the budget, the property manager inspects the property and identifies areas that will need painting and bids these jobs. On-site maintenance personnel will need painting supplies for small jobs and touch-ups.

(m) PARKING LOT MAINTENANCE

The parking lot must be thoroughly inspected for signs of cracking, raveling, or alligatoring. If major repairs are needed, a parking lot consultant should develop specifications for repair and their estimated cost. If only minor repairs are needed, a reliable asphalt or concrete contractor can provide a cost estimate for the budget. A month or two before the work begins, the job is bid by three or more contractors, including the contractor who provided the estimate for the budget.

The Institute of Real Estate Management publishes two excellent bulletins on parking lot maintenance: Bulletin 365, *Pavement Rehabilitation*, by Edward Cook; and Bulletin 381, *Effective Maintenance of Asphalt Paving*, by David J. Garber, CPM. The Asphalt Institute in College Park, Missouri, has produced an audiotape series on asphalt maintenance. This series is excellent for an in-house seminar. Such instructional materials help the property manager identify problems and take corrective action. Accurate projections of parking lot maintenance costs are essential in developing this line item expense.

(n) REPAIRS AND MAINTENANCE

This category is often divided into several accounts, such as plumbing, electrical, and painting. If no major problem exists or is anticipated in these areas, historical expense data are usually a good reference in estimating the expenses for the next budget period. If inspection or service requests indicate major problems in any of these areas, a consultant or contractor should inspect the building to determine the problem, possible solutions, and the estimated cost for each solution.

(o) ROOFS

The process for budgeting roof maintenance is the same one used for budgeting parking lot maintenance. The International Council of Shopping

Centers publishes an excellent bulletin on roof maintenance titled *The Worry-Free Roof*. The Institute of Real Estate Management publishes three bulletins on roof maintenance: Bulletin 354, *Roof Repair and Maintenance*, by Kai W. Adler; Bulletin 367, *Why Comprehensive Roof Inspection?* by H.Z. Lewis, P.E.; and Bulletin 374, *The Maintenance Roof*, by Heydon Lewis, P.E. These bulletins explain how to conduct a roof inspection, what to look for, and how to develop a roof maintenance program.

(p) SECURITY

The security needs of the building must be regularly assessed. Security can be a drive-by patrol, part-time to full-time on-site guards, and monitoring devices. Once the property manager has analyzed the building's security needs, the security program is bid. If on-site guards are part of the security program, the property manager must develop the hours per day the guards will be on site and provide the schedule to security companies bidding the assignment. Most security contracts are bid on an hourly rate. The rate for drive-by security patrols is usually based on the number of times the property is visited each night. (See Chapter 4).

(q) SNOW REMOVAL

Snow removal is one of the most difficult expenses to estimate because it is dependent primarily upon the weather. However, even with this uncontrollable factor the property manager can develop a prudent and economical strategy.

The first step is to develop a snow removal strategy as outlined in § 9.15. Next, the cost to remove the snow, push the snow to a different area of the parking lot, and clear the sidewalks can be calculated. Then the property manager must determine how often per month each of the above will be required during a normal year's snowfall.

(r) SUPPLIES

Paper supplies are either provided by the janitorial company and included in the janitorial costs or purchased by the property manager. The amount of paper products used by the tenants depends upon the occupancy of the building. The company that supplies the paper products can usually provide a fairly accurate estimate of the amount of paper products used if the property manager tells the supplier how many people work in the building. Another approach to estimating paper cost is to compare the estimated occupancy for the budget period with occupancy for the current year and adjust the cost of paper products accordingly.

The amount of paper products used in a mall's common area doesn't change significantly from one year to the next unless the mall expands or the occupancy level drops. If the amount of products consumed is approximately the same, the other variable is a change in the cost of the product caused by a price increase or by changing suppliers.

Other types of supplies such as hardware, tools, or uniforms are usually insignificant expenses that do not vary from year to year but need to be estimated and included in the budget.

(s) PARKING LOT SWEEPING

Parking lot sweeping is usually contracted. The property manager determines the frequency of sweeping, develops sweeping specifications, and accepts bids. In many areas, sweeping is dependent upon the weather. Sweeping is not needed when snow is on the ground, but a major spring cleanup is necessary to remove dirt and gravel that build up during the snow season. In other areas, sweeping is needed more frequently during the windy winter months than in the summer months.

(t) TAXES

Estimating real estate taxes is similar to estimating utility costs in that all of the information often is not available when the budget is prepared. The two factors required for estimating this expense are the assessed valuation and the millage rate. The safe method of estimating the assessed value for a new building is to combine the cost of construction and the land value and multiply this amount by the projected millage rate. It is highly unlikely that the first year's assessed value will exceed this estimate.

When a building is assessed while it is under construction, the assessed value represents the value of the land and the cost of the construction as of the date the building is assessed. In this situation, the property manager confirms with the assessor's office the date the building will be assessed and estimates the cost or value of the construction as of that date. Some municipalities assess all buildings on the same date— December 31, for example. Existing buildings have the benefit of the current year's valuation for reference.

The other factor is the millage rate. This rate is set by the city or county government. If the new millage rate hasn't been established, the property manager can review the changes in the millage rate over the past five years to establish trends along with proposed increases as reported in the local newspaper. Multiply the millage rate by the assessed valuation to determine the tax amount.

If the property was recently sold, the assessor may use the sale price as the market value and hence the assessed value. The property manager must constantly monitor the property's assessment to assure that it is fair and consistent with the assessment of comparable properties. Budgeting the real estate tax estimate provides an additional opportunity to review the current year's assessment. The fairness of the assessed value can also be reviewed when the assessment is received.

(u) TELEPHONE AND ANSWERING SERVICE

There are a few telephone charges that can be classified as either an escalation/common area expense or a landlord's expense. All elevators should have a telephone connected directly to a 24-hour answering service or a 24-hour guard station. The telephone and answering service expense is a building's escalation expense. If the building has an on-site management office, the answering service, which is needed for after-hours emergencies, is a building expense.

(v) TRASH REMOVAL

This expense is somewhat like a utility expense. Seldom does the property manager select the trash removal company. Either the municipality removes trash or a private contractor has an exclusive contract with the municipality to serve an area. Rates are determined by frequency of service and/or volume of trash removal and are established or approved by the municipality.

The volume of trash removed from the building is determined by the building's occupancy level and use. The property manager must determine the frequency of trash pickup and/or the size and number of trash receptacles. After determining this, the trash removal company can quote a monthly fee. Community and regional shopping centers may need to budget for additional trash removal during the Christmas season and other peak selling periods.

(w) UTILITIES

The two factors to consider when estimating utility expense are the billing rate and consumption. Keep in mind, however, that billing rates can change during a budget period and that consumption during lease-up time is difficult to predict.

When estimating the rate, the property manager should contact the utility company's representative for the property's area. The representative can provide the current billing rate and information concerning any rate increase during the budget period. This information cannot usually be obtained by just calling the utility company, so the property manager needs to develop a working relationship with the utility company's local representative. One way to build rapport is to request an energy audit of the building. Another opportunity is to work with the utility company when developing the building's emergency procedures.

If the projected rate increases cannot be obtained from the utility company, the property manager will project a rate increase by analyzing the rate increases during the past three to five years. Special note should also be given to recent rate adjustments and news stories about the local and national cost of energy as well as the financial condition of the utility company.

The other factor in estimating utility cost is the building's monthly consumption, which is based on the number and types of fixtures, the mechanical equipment, the occupancy rate, and the type of occupant.

Estimating utility costs for a shopping center differs from estimating an office building's costs. A shopping center's utility costs include common areas, vacancies, and utilities that are master-metered to all the tenants. The parking lot common area utilities include electricity for lighting and water for irrigation. To estimate parking lot lighting, calculate the hourly kilowatt usage and the number of hours the lights will be on each month. The type and number of fixtures will provide the amount of kilowatts consumed each hour. The property manager can estimate the hours the lights will be on each day. In the southern part of the United States, these hours will be fairly constant year round; in the northern states, parking lot lighting hours vary as much as four to five hours per night from summer to winter.

The formula for determining water consumption is not as simple as that for electricity consumption. The total expense for water can usually be obtained from the landscaper or the water company's representative. If the property is more than a year old, both the electricity and the water usage amounts are available for the prior twelve-month period. In this case, the property manager need only apply the projected billing rate to the prior year's usage.

The utilities for an enclosed mall are the lighting, water for irrigation, and the gas/electricity for the HVAC units. The manufacturer or installer of the HVAC equipment can estimate the kilowatts of electricity or BTUs of gas that will be consumed in an hour and the number of hours the equipment will operate during each month. This information, along with the billing rate, will provide the utility cost for the HVAC equipment. Again, if the shopping center has been in operation for more than a year, the historical utility consumption is available.

If a utility—water, for example—is master-metered, the property manager can provide the utility company with a list of the types of businesses in the center, and the utility company will estimate the average consumption for each business.

In an office building, the utility consumption includes interior common area lighting, parking lot or garage lighting, lighting for occupied spaces, gas or electricity to operate the mechanical systems, and water consumption. The common area lighting and mechanical systems usage is estimated the same way as the shopping center common area utilities and HVAC units are estimated. The occupied space consumption is based on the average usage per 1,000 or 10,000 square feet with adjustment for tenants with overstandard usage.

Another way to estimate usage for new buildings is to request the utility consumption from other property managers who manage similar buildings. Estimating utility consumption on existing buildings with a history of usage is fairly simple; estimating consumption for a new building or a building in lease-up is difficult. The utility's cost will vary each month based on consumption, and the monthly variance can be significant.

(x) VACANCY EXPENSE

Vacant spaces incur expenses. Vacancies in shopping centers and industrial properties have more direct expenses than vacancies in office buildings. Because of the separate utility metering and the street frontage of shopping center and industrial space, these spaces have a utility cost. Most municipalities assess a minimum meter charge whether or not the utility is used. In cold-weather regions, the space must be heated during the winter to prevent water freezing in the pipes. Since these are street front spaces, the exterior of the windows must be washed monthly or quarterly, and the inside windows washed semiannually.

It is important to the leasing effort that all vacancies be placed in condition to "show" as soon as possible because a dirty and unattractive space is difficult to lease. The interior of all vacant spaces must be cleaned periodically. Some spaces may need walls or ceiling repaired and painted and windows and floor coverings cleaned.

(y) WINDOW WASHING

In an office building, the property manager must determine how often interior and exterior windows should be washed and whether the ground floor windows need to be cleaned more frequently. Once the specifications have been developed, bids are requested from contractors. Industrial and shopping center tenants are responsible for cleaning their windows. For a mall, the property manager budgets the window washing in the common areas.

(z) EXPENSE EXPLANATION

Budgets are developed a few months before they go into effect. Each property has at least two operating budgets: the common area maintenance or escalation budget and the landlord's non-reimbursable budget.

Each budget has multiple expense categories. Multiply the amount of data for each budget by the number of properties managed by a property manager and it becomes obvious why it is almost impossible to remember all the budgeted items, why they were included, how each expense was determined, and when each expense is to be incurred.

The budget explanation form (Exhibit 3.6) can be used to list each expense, how it was determined, and how the budget amount will be used. For example, under the landscaping category for a mall, a monthly $500 maintenance expense is budgeted, but lilies are added at Easter at a cost of $300, poinsettias are added in December at a cost of $400, and new plants are added in January for $750. The budget explanation form provides a quick and accurate explanation for each expense item and is a reminder of why an amount was budgeted.

§ 3.6 CAPITAL BUDGET

A capital expenditure is one that is expected to yield benefits in future accounting periods. Capital expenditures are recorded as assets and amortized over the periods believed to be benefited.

Capital improvements are usually nonrecurring expenses. Most capital improvements to a property are major expenses. Examples include carpeting over a concrete mall floor, replacing a roof, remodeling a lobby, installing extensive energy conservation or life safety equipment, and making tenant improvements.

The same principles used in developing an operating budget are applied to developing a capital budget. All budgets start with a property inspection. Many capital improvements, such as the ones listed above, require an expert's opinion and recommendation since few property managers have an in-depth knowledge of construction and engineering. When a consultant is needed, monies should be budgeted for the consultant's time.

Capital improvements to marketing features of the building, such as lobbies, restrooms, elevators, and lighting in a building's exterior and center court areas, have a direct impact on the leasing. Maintaining a building's competitive position is essential to maintaining its occupancy level and rental rates. The property manager, whether serving as the leasing agent or not, must continually analyze market conditions and be aware of the building's position in the market. One way to keep apprised of the building's position in the market is to compare its features with the competition's. The office building market survey form in Chapter 7 (Exhibit 7.2) provides a checklist of features for comparison.

After inspecting the building and determining its position in the market, the manager compiles a list of suggested capital improvements and develops estimates to present to the owner. The property manager must prepare thoroughly for this meeting to be able to explain why the expenditures are needed. The owner will often take the manager's recommendation under advisement and consider the expenditure in relation to the goals of the property and the owner's ability to fund the cost of the improvements. When the owner approves any of the recommended capital improvements, the property manager will have specifications for the work prepared and bid the job.

Property owners and their accountants do not always agree on whether an expense is a capital expense or an operating expense. One owner may take an aggressive position on how an expense should be treated, while another may take an opposite view. The property manager needs to understand how the owner treats these expenses.

§ 3.7   DEVELOPING INCOME PROJECTIONS

Each income component must be analyzed and projected on a monthly basis along with the operating expenses to develop a month-by-month net operating income and cash flow. The first step in developing the income projection is to review the tenants' lease summaries, which state the obligation to pay rent, percentage rent, and tenant charges. Exhibit 3.9 is a sample tenant roster that summarizes the terms of each lease in the Washington Plaza shopping center. The CAC column is for common area charges. "Yes" indicates that the tenant pays those charges.

(a)   BASE RENT

The base rent is the easiest income component to project. The lease summaries are reviewed to determine the monthly rent during the budget period. Careful attention is given to any fixed step-ups in the rent. If a lease expires during the budget period, the property manager ascertains whether the tenant will renew and estimates the renewal rate. If the tenant is not renewing, or the landlord refuses to renew, the property manager must estimate how long the space will remain vacant and during which months. Since it is wise to initiate renewals at least six months before the lease expires, only tenants whose leases expire later in the budget period will need to be contacted.

Another determination in projecting base rents is the tenant's rent payment history. Financially weak tenants may move out before their lease expires, may make only partial payment, or may stop paying rent altogether. If any tenants fall in this category, the property manager needs to decide what course of action to take. Usually the tenant is evicted, and legal action is taken to recover the lost income. If the market conditions and the area's economy warrant, a retail tenant may be offered rent

EXHIBIT 3.9

Tenant Roster

Bldg. Washington Plaza

Date 5-1-89

TENANT	SUITE #	TYPE OF STORE	SQ. FT.	RENT			SECURITY DEPOSIT	TERM YEARS	LEASE DATE	COMMENCE-MENT	TERMINA-TION DATE	% RENT	SPECIAL NOTES	C.A.C.
				YEAR	$/S.F.	MONTH								
J & B Supermarket	A-1	Supermarket	40,000	201,000	5.03	Step-up	-	30	1984	4-1-85	3-31-15	2	Option	Yes
Ice Cream Store	A-2	Ice cream	1,200	15,600	13.00	1,300	1,300	7	1985	4-15-85	4-14-92	6	-	Yes
Karen's Beauty Supply	A-3	Beauty products	1,000	12,480	12.48	1,040	1,000	5	1985	6-1-85	5-30-90	6	-	Yes
Tony's Pizza	A-4	Restaurant	2,400	26,400	11.00	2,200	2,200	10	1985	7-15-85	7-14-95	5	Option	Yes
Cats and Dogs	A-5	Pet store	1,800	23,400	13.00	1,950	1,950	5	1985	6-1-85	5-30-90	6	-	Yes
Discount Shoes	A-6	Shoe store	2,400	22,800	9.50	1,900	1,000	7	1985	4-1-85	3-31-92	4	-	Yes
Hair Cuts	A-7	Barber shop	500	7,500	15.00	625	625	5	1985	4-1-85	3-31-90	8	-	Yes
Saver's Drugs	B-1	Drug store	20,000	120,000	5.00	10,000	10,000	20	1985	4-1-85	3-31-05	2	Option	Yes
Vacant	B-2	-	1,200	-	-	-	-	-						-
Family Video	B-3	Video rental	2,400	31,200	13.00	2,600	2,600	5	1985	10-1-85	9-31-95	5	-	Yes
White's Cleaners	B-4	Cleaner	1,200	17,400	14.50	1,450	1,450	7	1986	2-1-86	1-31-93	7	-	Yes
Elegant Fabric	B-5	Fabric store	3,000	33,000	11.00	2,750	2,750	6	1985	11-1-85	10-31-91	6	-	Yes
Western Bank	B-6	Bank	1,800	27,000	15.00	2,250	2,750	10	1988	4-15-89	4-14-99	-	-	Yes
Vacant	B-7	-	1,100	-	-	-	-	-					-	Yes
Burgers and Burgers	P-1	Fast food	3,540	30,000	Pro/rent	2,500	5,000	20	1987	2-1-88	1-31-08	3	Option	Yes

relief. In either case, the property manager must consider the financial impact of such adverse situations on the base rent income projections.

Each tenant's monthly rent for the budget period is recorded on a budget input form (Exhibit 3.10). After calculating the income that will be received each month from each space, the property manager totals each monthly income column. If the management company is computerized, it can print a monthly rent projection.

Note in Exhibit 3.10 that the supermarket rent stepped up in July. The form lists vacancies and the month in which a new tenant commences paying rent. Note that one space was projected to remain vacant until June and another until September. Adding each tenant's rent by month provides the monthly base rent income projection.

A similar analysis is prepared for percentage rent, escalation or CAM income, reimbursement of taxes and insurance, and any other income components. Adding all the income component budgets together provides a month-by-month income projection.

(b) LEASE-UP AND VACANCY PROJECTIONS

Vacant space will not remain vacant forever. The property manager must estimate when the space will be leased, at what rate, and when the rent will commence. The leasing agent is consulted for this projection. If the property manager is the leasing agent, a market survey must be conducted to determine the property's market rental rate and to project the amount of space that will be leased in the building and when.

Each vacant space is analyzed for its desirability, the rental rate it can command, and its probable lease date. For example, a shopping center has four vacancies: two 1,400-square-foot spaces, an 1,800-square-foot space, and a 5,500-square-foot space. The property manager projects that one 1,400-square-foot space will be leased in March with the tenant opening April 15 with one and one-half months' free rent. Rent payments begin June 1. The 1,800-square-foot space is projected to be leased in July with tenant occupancy in September and rent to commence October 1. There is little demand for the odd-shaped space of 5,500 square feet, which is projected to be leased in November with three months' free rent, which extends beyond the budget period. No base rent is projected for this space during this budget period. The second 1,400-square-foot space is expected to remain vacant during the entire budget period.

The lease-up of a new office building is projected in a similar way, except that the manager looks at square footage instead of spaces leased. For instance, a 95,000-square-foot office building opens with 30,000 square feet occupied. With 7,500 square feet per month projected to be leased during the first six months and 5,000 square feet per month projected leased over the next three months, the building's occupancy is expected to stabilize at 90,000 square feet. Just as in the shopping center

EXHIBIT 3.10

Budget Input Form

Income

Project No.: __3032__   Project Name: __Washington Plaza__   Period: __1989__   Prepared by: __RFM__   Date: __11-5-89__

Base Rent Income Projection

GEN LEDGER ACCT. NO.	DESCRIPTION	JAN.	FEB.	MARCH	APRIL	MAY	JUNE	JULY	AUG.	SEPT.	OCT.	NOV.	DEC.	TOTAL YEAR	% Gross Sched @100%	$/SQ. FT.
	J & B Supermarket	16,500	16,500	16,500	16,500	16,500	16,500	17,000	17,000	17,000	17,000	17,000	17,800	201,000		
	Ice Cream Store	1,300	1,300	1,300	1,300	1,300	1,300	1,300	1,300	1,300	1,300	1,300	1,300	15,600		
	Karen's Beauty Sup	1,040	1,040	1,040	1,040	1,040	1,040	1,040	1,040	1,040	1,040	1,040	1,040	12,480		
	Tony's Pizza	2,200	2,200	2,200	2,200	2,200	2,200	2,200	2,200	2,200	2,200	2,200	2,200	26,400		
	Cats and Dogs	1,950	1,950	1,950	1,950	1,950	1,950	1,950	1,950	1,950	1,950	1,950	1,950	23,400		
	Discount Shoes	1,900	1,900	1,900	1,900	1,900	1,900	1,900	1,900	1,900	1,900	1,900	1,900	22,800		
	Hair Cuts	625	625	625	625	625	625	625	625	625	625	625	625	7,500		
	Saver's Drugs	10,000	10,000	10,000	10,000	10,000	10,000	10,000	10,000	10,000	10,000	10,000	10,000	120,000		
	Vacant	-	-	-	-	-	1,400	1,400	1,400	1,400	1,400	1,400	1,400	9,800		
	Family Video	2,600	2,600	2,600	2,600	2,600	2,600	2,600	2,600	2,600	2,600	2,600	2,600	31,200		
	White's Cleaners	1,450	1,450	1,450	1,450	1,450	1,450	1,450	1,450	1,450	1,450	1,450	1,450	17,400		
	Elegant Fabric	2,750	2,750	2,750	2,750	2,750	2,750	2,750	2,750	2,750	2,750	2,750	2,750	33,000		
	Western Bank	2,250	2,250	2,250	2,250	2,250	2,250	2,250	2,250	2,250	2,250	2,250	2,250	27,000		
	Vacant	-	-	-	-	-	-	-	-	1,375	1,375	1,375	1,375	5,500		
	Burgers & Burgers	2,500	2,500	2,500	2,500	2,500	2,500	2,500	2,500	2,500	2,500	2,500	2,500	30,000		
	PAGE TOTAL	47,065	47,065	47,065	47,065	47,065	48,465	48,965	48,965	50,340	50,340	50,340	50,340	583,080		
	CARRY FORWARD															
	TOTAL	47,065	47,065	47,065	47,065	47,065	48,465	48,965	48,965	50,340	50,340	50,340	50,340	583,080		

INPUT DATE: _____   REVISION DATE: _____   APPROVED BY: AAA   DATE: 11/18/89 example, after projecting the amount of space that will be leased each month, the property manager tries to anticipate how long it will take to build out the tenant's space, when the tenants will move in, how much free rent will be offered, and when they will commence paying base rent.

Vacancy and lease-up projections are the most complex income projections. They are more likely to be accurate if the manager takes time to study the market, know the building and its competition, evaluate the leasing effort, and understand the owner's ability to make a deal.

(c) PERCENTAGE RENTS

Percentage rent is a significant income component in many shopping centers. Office buildings and multitenant industrial buildings can have percentage rental income from retail or service tenants such as restaurants and health clubs.

Percentage rent is also a difficult income component to project because the property manager has limited influence over the tenant's sales volume. A quick but imprecise way to project percentage rent is to increase every tenant's sales by a given percent over the prior year and compare that estimate with the tenant's breakpoint (the breakpoint is determined by dividing the tenant's annual rent by the percentage rate). The amount of sales in excess of the breakpoint is multiplied by the percentage rate to arrive at the percentage rent owed.

A more accurate method is to analyze each tenant separately to estimate its sales for the budget period. The first step in this process is to compare each tenant's breakpoint with its sales for the most recent twelve-month period. Tenants whose sales either exceed or are within 20% of their breakpoint are then analyzed. The remainder of the tenants have little if any chance of their sales exceeding their breakpoint and paying percentage rent.

Several criteria are used to estimate the sales of those tenants who are likely to pay percentage rent, including:

- Sales projections. This is the best source, but some managers and store owners will not share this information.
- Sales trends. If the tenant's sales have increased between 6% and 8% during each of the past five years, a similar increase is probable.
- New competition. A local hamburger restaurant is experiencing 10% increases every year; but if a new McDonald's comes into the area, the local restaurant's sales will undoubtedly drop.
- Tenant mix. If a shopping center is adding another major tenant, the center will have additional traffic, and the other tenants' sales can be expected to increase. Conversely, if a major tenant vacates the center, the other tenants' sales probably will decline.

- Product demand. The property manager must be aware of fads in the marketplace. Hula hoops and drive-in carhops on roller skates were popular in the 1950s, and in the early 1980s tanning salons and take-and-bake pizza operations were popular. However, novelties wane over the years, and many businesses that were once the rage lose their popularity and close.
- Managerial change. An exceptionally good store manager may be promoted to regional manager and replaced with an inexperienced and less capable person. Or, the reverse can happen: a store with poor sales growth may replace its management with an aggressive person, and sales will increase dramatically.
- Merchandise or design changes within the store. Has the store remodeled or added new lines of merchandise? Has merchandise of lesser quality replaced quality items? These moves will affect sales.

The above information can be used to estimate the tenant's sales for the budget period. If sales exceed the breakpoint, this amount is multiplied by the tenant's percentage rate.

Before the estimated amount of percentage rent can be included in the income projection, the property manager must check the tenant's lease for rights to recapture percentage rent. In the 1950s and 1960s many national tenants, especially major tenants, negotiated the right to recapture some or all of their tenant charges—common area maintenance, taxes, and insurance, for example—from their percentage rent. This right has seldom been granted a tenant since the 1970s.

An example of a tenant's percentage rent estimate follows:

Last year's sales	$650,000
Projected sales increase	+ 52,000
Projected per annum sales	$702,000
Tenant's breakpoint	− 600,000
Sales in excess of breakeven point	102,000
Percentage rate 6%	× .06
Percentage rent	$ 6,102
Recapture from percentage rent	-0-
Percent rent projected	$ 6,102

This analysis is applied to each tenant whose sales are likely to exceed its breakpoint or breakeven point.

After estimating the percentage rent, the manager must project which months the tenant will pay it. Remember, percentage rent is paid when sales are reported, usually a month after they take place.

Some national tenants pay on a quarterly basis, and major tenants usually pay annually. Most tenants will pay their percentage rent in

December and January for November and December sales. Some tenants, such as a candy store where sales peak in February, April, June, November, and December, may pay percentage rent several months of the year, whereas a restaurant's sales and percentage rent can be constant each month. The tenants' monthly sales will indicate the months they are likely to pay percentage rent.

The last factor to consider in this income component is percentage rent refunds. Even though most tenants report sales figures monthly and pay percentage rent on a monthly basis, their sales are annualized. If a tenant's sales exceed the breakpoint one month, with payment of percentage rent the following month, but sales are below the breakpoint on an annualized basis, the percentage rent paid is then refunded.

A tenant's breakeven point is determined by dividing the percentage rate into the annual rental rate for the annual breakeven point and dividing this number by twelve to determine the monthly breakeven point.

The rent paid in excess of the base or minimum rent is known as percentage rent or overage rent.

(d) CONSUMER PRICE INDEX (CPI)

The consumer price index (CPI) is a monthly measure of changes in the prices of goods and services consumed by urban families and individuals. Compiled by the Bureau of Labor Statistics, the index is based on about 125,000 monthly quotations of prices, rents, and property tax rates collected from about 65,000 sources. The items range from food to automobiles and from rents to haircuts. The relative importance given to individual items in the index is based on periodic surveys of consumer expenditures. Current prices are expressed as a percentage of average prices during 1967. The monthly index is prepared for the nation as a whole, for each of 17 large metropolitan areas, for individual items, and for commodity and service groupings. All data are published in the U.S. Department of Labor's *Monthly Labor Review*.

Many leases have rent adjustments based on the increases in the CPI. The tenant's rent can be adjusted over any period of time, such as annually or every three years. The increase can be based on the percentage increase in the CPI or a fraction of that increase.

Most commercial leases use the CPI for metropolitan areas. All items are indexed for the nearest geographical area published for the population area of the property. The CPI adjustment is determined by comparing the current month's index for the selected city with the same index in the preceding year. Below is an example of an adjustment in the San Francisco area CPI:

June 1987 CPI	347.3
June 1986 CPI	− 338.1
Index adjustment	+ 9.2

To calculate the percentage adjustment in the CPI, divide 9.2 (the index adjustment) by 338.1 (the preceding year's index) for an increase of 2.7%.

If a tenant's rent was $1,000 per month, with an annual increase based on the June CPI increase, the increase in base rent would be $27 ($1,000 × 2.7%). The tenant's adjusted monthly rent would become $1,027.

If the increase was based on two thirds of the increase in the CPI, the increase would be 1.8% (2.7% × 0.66%). The increase in monthly rent would be $18.

(e) COMMON AREA MAINTENANCE (CAM) INCOME

The property manager determines what percent of the CAM budget will be collected. Each tenant's lease summary states the tenant's share of the CAM budget. The percentages for all tenants are totaled for each month. The CAM budget is divided by twelve, and each month the percent of space that will pay reimbursements is multiplied into one month's CAM budget. If a tenant is not required to pay a pro rata share of a particular expense, such as security, the landlord will not be reimbursed for that portion of the expense. These figures can be calculated in minutes if the accounting system is computerized. Chapter 4 on shopping centers explains in detail the exceptions to a tenant paying the full pro rata share of CAM charges. The common area calculations form in Exhibit 3.11 is designed for easy calculation of each tenant's pro rata share of all tenant charges. The form indicates how each calculation was derived. Note that the denominator for the CAM is larger than the denominator for taxes and insurance by 3,540 square feet. Burgers and Burgers (P-1) is a pad tenant that pays its pro rata share of CAM but has a separate tax parcel and maintains its own insurance coverage. HVAC (heating, ventilating, and air-conditioning) is a charge from the landlord for the cost to contract the HVAC maintenance. The two major tenants—the supermarket and the drugstore—and the pad tenant maintain their own HVAC units.

After the percentages are established, tenant charges can be calculated in dollar amounts as shown in Exhibit 3.12. This type of form is used when quoting estimated charges to prospective tenants.

(f) ESCALATION INCOME

Escalation income is billed to the office building tenants in one of three methods: base year, stop clause, or triple net charge. First, develop the building's operating expenses. Then review each tenant's lease summary to determine the method of billing and which expense items are treated as escalatable operating expenses. Calculate each tenant's pro rata share of the operating expenses. If the tenant pays a base year escalation, establish the expenses for the base year and subtract them

EXHIBIT 3.11

Tenant Common Area Calculations

Bldg: Washington Plaza

Tenant	Suite #	CAM			CAM Mall			Taxes			Insurance			Merchant Assoc.			Misc.
		T.T. Sq.Ft.	Denom.	%	T.T. Sq.Ft.	Denom.	%	T.T. Sq.Ft.	Denom.	%	T.T. Sq.Ft.	Denom.	%	T.T. Sq.Ft.	$/S.F.	$	H.V.A.C.
J & B Supermarket	A-1	40,000	83,540	47.9	-	-	-	40,000	80,000	50.	40,000	80,000	50.	40,000	.15	5000	-
Ice Cream Store	A-2	1,200	"	1.4	-	-	-	1,200	"	1.5	1,200	"	1.5	1,200	.50	600	180
Karen's Beauty Supply	A-3	1,000	"	1.2	-	-	-	1,000	"	1.3	1,000	"	1.3	1,000	.50	500	180
Tony's Pizza	A-4	2,400	"	2.8	-	-	-	2,400	"	3.0	2,400	"	3.0	2,400	.50	1200	360
Cats and Dogs	A-5	1,800	"	2.2	-	-	-	1,800	"	2.3	1,800	"	2.3	1,800	.50	900	240
Discount Shoes	A-6	2,400	"	2.9	-	-	-	2,400	"	3.0	2,400	"	3.0	2,400	.50	1200	360
Hair Cuts	A-7	500	"	0.6	-	-	-	500	"	0.6	500	"	0.6	500	.50	250	100
Saver's Drugs	B-1	20,000	"	24.0	-	-	-	20,000	"	25.	20,000	"	25.	20,000	.25	5000	-
Vacant	B-2	1,200	"	1.4	-	-	-	1,200	"	1.5	1,200	"	1.5	1,200	.50	600	180
Family Video	B-3	2,400	"	2.8	-	-	-	2,400	"	3.0	2,400	"	3.0	2,400	.50	1200	360
White's Cleaners	B-4	1,200	"	1.4	-	-	-	1,200	"	1.5	1,200	"	1.5	1,200	.50	600	180
Elegant Fabric	B-5	3,000	"	3.6	-	-	-	3,000	"	3.8	3,000	"	3.8	3,000	.50	1500	400
Western Bank	B-6	1,800	"	2.2	-	-	-	1,800	"	2.3	1,800	"	2.3	1,800	.50	900	240
Vacant	B-7	1,100	"	1.3	-	-	-	1,100	"	1.4	1,100	"	1.4	1,100	.50	550	180
Burgers and Burgers	P-1	3,540	"	4.2	-	-	-	-	-	-	-	-	-	3,540	.50	1770	-
TOTAL		83,540						80,000			80,000			83,540			

EXHIBIT 3.12
Tenant Charges

Bldg: Washington Plaza

| TENANT | Suite # | RENT | | | | .34/s.f. C.A.M. | | .60/s.f. Taxes | .50/s.f. MISC. | | HVAC |
		Security Deposit	Annual	Monthly	%	Parking Lot	Mall		Ins.	M.A.	Other
J & B Supermarket	A-1	-	201,000	16,500 / 17,000	2	13,600	-	24,000	20,000	6,000	-
Ice Cream Store	A-2	1,300	15,600	1,300	6	408	-	720	600	600	180
Karen's Beauty Supply	A-3	1,000	12,480	1,040	6	340	-	600	500	500	180
Tony's Pizza	A-4	2,200	26,400	2,200	5	816	-	1,440	1,200	1,200	360
Cats and Dogs	A-5	1,950	23,400	1,950	6	612	-	1,080	900	900	240
Discount Shoes	A-6	1,000	1,900	22,800	4	816	-	1,440	1,200	1,200	360
Hair Cuts	A-7	625	7,500	625	8	170	-	300	250	250	100
Saver's Drugs	B-1	10,000	120,000	10,000	2	6,800	-	12,000	10,000	5,000	-
Vacant	B-2	-	-	-	-	408	-	720	600	600	180
Family Video	B-3	2,600	31,200	2,600	7	816	-	1,440	1,200	1,200	360
White's Cleaners	B-4	1,450	17,400	1,450	7	408	-	720	600	600	180
Elegant Fabric	B-5	2,750	33,000	2,750	6	1,020	-	1,800	1,500	1,500	400
Western Bank	B-6	-	27,000	2,250	-	612	-	1,080	900	900	240
Vacant	B-7	-	-	-	-	374	-	660	550	550	180
Burgers and Burgers	P-1	5,000	30,000	2,500	3	1,204	-	-	-	1,770	-

133

from the projected operating expenses for the budget period. Multiply the increase in operating expenses above the base year by the percentage of space occupied by the tenant to determine the tenants' share of the escalation budget.

When the operating expense stop clause is used, the dollar per square foot of the stop is subtracted from the dollar per square foot of operating expenses for the budget period. The tenant's square footage is multiplied by the increase in operating expenses per square foot above the stop expense. The resulting number is the amount of escalation income the tenant will pay.

Triple net leases are common in single-tenant industrial properties, but some office buildings also use this method of escalation charge. The tenant's percentage of occupancy of the building is multiplied times the building's operating expenses.

When reviewing the lease summary, the property manager checks for caps on the escalation charges. For instance, a tenant may pay its full pro rata share of the escalation charge but not exceeding $1 per square foot during each of the first three years of the lease.

A source of escalation income that is easy to overlook is space that will be leased during the budget period. The lease-up projection is reviewed, and tenants who will occupy space that was recently vacant and commence paying escalation charges in the budget period are included in the escalation income projections. Escalation income, like all other income components, is estimated on a month-by-month basis.

(g) TAXES AND INSURANCE

Real estate taxes and building insurance are not included in the shopping center common area maintenance budget and usually are billed separately in industrial properties. Although most office buildings include these expenses in their escalation budget, some office buildings separate one or both of these expenses from the escalation budget. In each of the above situations, except where these expenses are included in the escalation budget, the tenants must be billed separately for real estate taxes and insurance expenses.

Most commercial leases require the tenants to pay their full pro rata share of these costs. In the 1950s and 1960s, tenants often paid these expenses above a base year. Both of these methods of charging tenants are explained in the escalation billing section.

Most leases allow a special tax assessment, known as a Local Improvement District (LID) or bonded indebtedness, which is a charge for street improvements such as traffic lights and sidewalks, to be included in the real estate tax billings.

The tenant's insurance clause must be reviewed carefully to determine if the tenant pays a pro rata share of all of the landlord's insurance coverage. Some leases, especially with major tenants, will exclude certain coverage or place a limit on the amount of liability insurance they will reimburse the landlord.

(h)   TENANT EXTRA SERVICES

Office building leases allow for a charge if the tenants request extra services. These services can consist of overstandard janitorial services, maintenance that is the responsibility of the tenant, and other miscellaneous jobs. This income component is projected by reviewing the tenant's extra service charges in the current year and determining if any new tenants will have a similar need.

(i)   UTILITY INCOME

In the 1960s and early 1970s, several types of developments, particularly enclosed malls, billed electricity to tenants for a profit. The developer would contract with the utility company to purchase electricity that was metered on one master meter. The developer then paid the cost to run lines to submeters for each tenant. Tenants were billed the same rate they would be charged if they purchased the power directly from the utility company. The developer earned a profit by purchasing the electricity at a bulk rate (similar to a wholesale rate) and charging the tenants a retail price. Developers justified their profit by stating that it was a return on their investment of installing at their cost the utility lines and submeters. When managing a property with this situation, the manager must monitor the billing rate to ensure the tenants are being billed based on the correct rate.

(j)   OVERSTANDARD UTILITIES

Some office building tenants consume more utilities than is normal for their space size, and most leases allow the landlord to bill the tenants for their overstandard usage. This extra usage is usually the result of special equipment, an excess of equipment consuming an inordinate amount of electricity, or after-hours use of lighting and HVAC service. The property manager must monitor the tenant's use of utility. When a tenant has additional utility requirements, a consultant may be called in to determine the amount in excess of standard usage. The income received is credited to the building's escalation expenses because the expense will be charged to the escalation expenses. A simpler method is to separately meter the tenant's premises.

(k) OVERSTANDARD HVAC

Overstandard HVAC is a need of tenants who must keep their offices open beyond the building's hours of operation and tenants who need supplementary cooling. The property manager determines an hourly cost for HVAC, which includes the cost of electricity, the wear on the equipment, and the cost of the building engineer's time if he or she is required to be on site while the equipment is operating. The income generated is credited to the building's escalation expenses because this is where the expense is charged.

(l) TENANT IMPROVEMENT PROFIT

When tenant improvement work is performed by the building owner or property management company, a profit is added to the cost of the work. The profit is the typical profit a general contractor would earn and is either credited to the building owner or the property management company or is shared.

The property manager estimates the amount of tenant improvement work based on the amount of space that is projected to be leased and renewed, the type of tenant build-outs that new tenants are likely to need, and the improvements, if any, that will be required to renew leases. Tenant improvement fee is usually a percentage of the construction cost. Office tenants and most industrial tenants in multitenant buildings will require that tenant improvement be performed by the landlord. Shopping center tenants almost always perform their own tenant work.

(m) INTEREST INCOME

Interest income is a component that can easily be overlooked. Income received from each property should be deposited in an interest-bearing account. The property manager determines the average balance each month and multiplies this number by the interest rate paid on that account.

§ 3.8   RESERVES FOR REPLACEMENT

In any large income-producing property, major components will have to be replaced or major repairs will be needed at some point. It is prudent to estimate these needs, quantify them, and set aside sufficient cash to cover them.

Many owners choose not to set aside cash reserves. They prefer to use available monies as they are earned and worry about major repairs or replacements when they are needed. This is not an irresponsible approach, since the owner is counting on either increased cash flow, the likelihood of refinancing, or the probability of secondary financing or a line of credit.

Even if the final decision is not to reserve for replacement, the prudent manager will still estimate the reserves that may be needed and share this information with the property owner. It is not uncommon for a manager to evaluate the cash flow and arbitrarily set aside a percentage for reserves. Such a figure is more likely to be what the manager believes the property could afford rather than what the property may really need.

Taking a slightly different approach, the manager may set a reserve based on cents per square foot per year. A common reserve figure in shopping centers is five cents per square foot per year. Obviously, a large reserve is not built up in this short time frame.

(a) NEEDS ESTIMATE

The most effective method of determining reserves that will be needed is to consider each major building component.

First, review which major components must be analyzed. In a strip shopping center, these components include the roof, the parking lot, and the exterior painting. Tenants are generally responsible for the air-conditioning unit.

The holding period of the property must be taken into consideration. No owner is going to worry about what work will have to be done after the property is sold. For easy calculations, our example will be a 100,000-square-foot strip shopping center. The owners will hold the center for ten years. The evaluation of each component is as follows:

- *Roof.* An evaluation of the roof indicates that it is generally in good condition, but one large section of 25,000 square feet will have to be replaced within five years. The estimated cost for this repair in five years is $30,000. To reserve for this cost, the $30,000 is divided by the five years available to accumulate the monies, for an annual reserve in the amount of $6,000. Dividing the cost by the square footage of the center—100,000 square feet—provides a reserve of six cents per foot per year.
- *Exterior Painting.* A physical inspection indicates that the center will need a complete paint job at the end of the eighth year. The estimated cost will be $80,000. Again, $80,000 divided by the years to accumulate the reserve indicates $10,000 per year will be needed. On a square footage basis the reserve is ten cents per square foot per year.
- *Major Parking Lot Repairs.* The parking lot is sound, but after three years it will need patching, resealing, and restriping. The

cost is estimated to be $30,000. The annual reserve is $10,000, and the per square foot reserve per year is ten cents.

(b) COLLECTION OF RESERVES

To establish a reserve fund, the center manager would set aside twenty cents per square foot for the next three years and ten cents per square foot for the following three years. These funds would likely be held in an interest-bearing account during this time. The manager would calculate the interest to be earned and reduce the amount set aside by the interest earned so that the interest and the actual reserves would provide the needed cash. Another approach would be to allow the interest to accumulate as a cushion if the original cost estimate were too low.

If the reserves for common area items are to be paid by the tenants, the method of calculation would be the same. However, the leases must permit charging a reserve for replacement to the tenants. Most major or anchor tenants will not pay into a reserve. They will pay their pro rata share when it is due rather than have the landlord hold their funds.

If the leases do allow for the collection of reserves, those monies should be placed in a trust or escrow account earning interest and held in the tenants' behalf until major work is done. If the center is sold, the trust account should be transferred to the new owners to be held on behalf of the tenants. If a tenant has paid into reserves but vacates before the monies are spent, the tenant does not receive a refund of the reserves paid.

§ 3.9 REVIEWING AND REVISING THE BUDGET

About sixty days before the budget period begins, the budget is completed and approved by the property owner based on the best information available at the time. Ideally, the budget will be accurate for the entire year with no revisions necessary.

It is possible, however, that changes will occur that will require revision. A major tenant may move out. An unusually heavy snowfall may result in being significantly over budget. A long-term, difficult vacancy may be filled unexpectedly. A major replacement of a building component may substantially reduce operating expenses. In all cases, the budget should be revised, for the change is likely to be significant. When such a change occurs, the new assumptions are incorporated into the budget, the budget is dated, and the owner is given a new cash flow projection.

Even if no major changes have taken place, the budget should be carefully evaluated periodically. Some owners of income property zero out all budgets at midyear. The actual income and expenses become the budget for that period, and all accounts are in balance, or "zeroed" out.

This is intended to prevent the manager from borrowing from one account to support another. Any excess funds are automatically withdrawn.

It is more common, however, for the manager to prepare an analysis of income and expenses at midyear, evaluate what the current position means for the balance of the year, and report that position along with recommended changes to the owner. Such a midyear adjustment allows the manager and owner to plan the balance of the year so that the desired goals will be reached, given the existing circumstances.

Should income be running ahead of budget, and it appears that such will be the case at year-end, the decision may be made to proceed with some capital expenditures that were shelved due to lack of funds. Conversely, if funds appear to be running behind schedule, some discretionary expenditures may be eliminated from the budget for the balance of the year.

A "deep pocket" owner may not be too concerned that the budget is under expectations for the year, whereas a "cash flow" owner may be keenly aware of every dollar. It is important for the property manager to understand the owner's position and be sure that the owner is informed of anything that might have an impact on that position.

Because of the very real possibilities of large swings in the cash flow of commercial properties, it is critical that the actual figures be compared with the budget on a monthly basis and that those comparisons be analyzed for significant differences. Most owners will accept a variance between 5% and 10% in any one line item without too much concern. Quite often the manager is not even asked to comment on variances less than 10%. However, the current monthly variance may be indicative of a larger problem coming up. The manager must be sensitive to this possibility and inform the owner even if the current variance is within the agreed-upon range.

When the monthly operating statements are forwarded to the owners, the statements should contain a narrative report that evaluates the numbers for the owner. Numbers by themselves do not always give a complete picture.

§ 3.10 CONCLUSION

Budgeting is not a difficult process, but it can be time-consuming. Once the property manager understands how to determine each income and expense component, an accurate NOI or cash flow projection can be developed. This is needed to maintain financial control over the property. All property owners require accurate budgets.

Four

Shopping Center Management

§ 4.1 INTRODUCTION

While shopping centers as we know them are only about fifty years old, the concept is as old as society itself. In the past, farmers came to town on the weekend and traded, bought and sold at a common market. The market was located in the center of town to be accessible to the greatest number of people. The farmers grouped together because collectively they could offer more and attract more people—the basic concept of the shopping center.

While many aspects of the management and leasing of shopping centers are quite similar to office buildings, industrial parks, and even apartment buildings, there are significant differences. The major difference is the interdependence between the tenants and the shopping center for their success. The involvement of management in selecting the right tenant for the center and then maximizing that tenant's sales potential and, therefore, the center's potential through high sales and percentage rents provides a unique approach to real estate leasing and management.

In a poll conducted by the Institute of Real Estate Management (IREM), members were asked to rank the management difficulty of various properties. Shopping centers were ranked as the most difficult to manage. Reasons cited were complexity of the tenant mix, the element of percentage rents, and involvement with tenants in promoting and advertising the shopping center. Despite its complexity and difficulty in operation, however, the shopping center also provides tremendous satisfaction when the results are positive.

Management has little involvement with office or industrial tenants beyond collecting the rent, establishing an emergency procedures program, making sure the tenant is not doing anything detrimental to the facilities or other tenants and developing a tenant retention program. In the shopping center, the landlord's challenge is to select tenants whose merchandise and marketing program complement the demographics of the trade area and the other tenants in the center.

Once the tenant mix has been established, steps must be taken to assure that the tenant generates high sales. High sales usually bring increased customer traffic, helping all of the tenants in the center. Furthermore, the tenant's success produces increasingly higher rents, both minimum and percentage, over a longer period of time.

The astute shopping center manager will be knowledgeable in many areas, including leasing, operations, security, business law, contract law, real estate law, human relations, accounting, finance, promotions, community relations, demographics, and maintenance.

While there are many sources for this information, one stands out—the International Council of Shopping Centers (ICSC), the trade association for the shopping center industry. The ICSC has been in existence for more than thirty years and was founded on the premise that sharing ideas makes all members more knowledgeable in the field.

ICSC conducts excellent training in all aspects of shopping centers. Its University of Shopping Centers offers intensive classes in almost every facet of the business, from marketing to management to development. The ICSC also offers management, marketing and maintenance institutes, seminars on construction, legal issues, accounting, leasing, and other topics. ICSC is responsible for testing and certifying shopping center managers and marketing directors. Managers are recognized with the Certified Shopping Center Manager (CSM) designation. Marketing directors receive the Certified Marketing Director (CMD) designation, formerly Accredited Shopping Center Promotions Director (ASPD).

For several hundred years, downtown was the center of social and retail activity until the end of World War II, when the exodus to the suburbs began. Sears, with its freestanding buildings, was the first major retailer to move to the suburbs to be closer to the customer. As more and more shoppers showed preference for the suburbs, small centers were built there to accommodate their needs. Developers and the retail industry followed the market, and shopping centers proliferated throughout the United States.

§ 4.2 SHOPPING CENTER CLASSIFICATIONS

Shopping center classifications have traditionally been based on the size of the shopping center and the type of major tenant that anchors it. The size of the shopping center is determined by the amount of gross leasable area (GLA)—the area occupied by the tenants. All other areas in the shopping center are referred to as common areas.

(a) BY SIZE AND MAJOR TENANT

The following are the major classifications of shopping centers as defined by GLA and major tenant.

Neighborhood Center

The neighborhood center ranges in size from 50,000 to 150,000 square feet of gross leasable area and is usually anchored by a supermarket. Some neighborhood centers may have a drugstore or home improvement store as additional major tenants. The small shops are generally service tenants such as laundromats, cleaners, videotape rentals, and food services such as restaurants and specialty food stores. The neighborhood center usually has one to three pads for use by restaurants or banks. A pad is a parcel of land within the shopping center that is either leased or sold to a tenant. The merchants of the neighborhood center offer primarily convenience goods and services.

Community Center

The community center ranges in size from 150,000 to 400,000 square feet of GLA. The community center is anchored by a junior department store and one or a combination of the following: supermarket, drugstore, home improvement center, and variety store. The small shops are a combination of convenience and service stores, restaurants, and general merchandise and fashion stores.

Regional Center

The regional center ranges in size from 400,000 to 1,000,000 square feet of GLA. It is anchored by at least one full-line department store and is tenanted predominantly by fashion, gift, and general merchandise stores, and restaurants. The regional shopping center was originally developed as an open-air mall, but most regional malls developed since the early 1970s are enclosed malls. Most open-air malls have been converted to enclosed malls.

Superregional Center

The superregional center is in excess of one million square feet of GLA. The superregional center is anchored by four or more full-line department stores with more than 100 small shops like those in a regional mall.

Specialty, Theme Center, or Festival Center

The specialty or theme center is either a conversion of an existing nonretail facility or a center developed around an architectural theme such as an Old World or nautical theme. The festival or specialty center is generally tourist oriented. Ghiradelli Square in San Francisco is a specialty center that was converted from an old chocolate factory. Trolley Square in Salt Lake City is an old trolley barn converted to a specialty center. The specialty center usually doesn't have a major tenant; however, a restaurant or various food services frequently serve as the center's main draw. The center is tenanted by specialty and boutique stores such as a music box store or a leather goods shop. Such stores require a tremendous amount of traffic to survive, as their merchandise appeals to a limited number of people and most of the items are not necessities. Specialty or theme centers typically range in size from 50,000 to 300,000 square feet of GLA.

Outlet, Off-Price, and Discount Center

Outlet, off-price, and discount centers are generally classified as one type of center, but each category is slightly different. The outlet merchant is the manufacturer who is also selling merchandise in retail stores, but at a bargain price. The off-price merchant is selling branded merchandise such as Dior and Jordache at less than traditional retail prices. The discount merchant sells merchandise at less than traditional retail prices, but it is not necessarily branded merchandise.

The size of these centers ranges from neighborhood centers to community centers. They are anchored by a junior department store with merchandise falling in one of the above categories. The anchored store ranges in size from 30,000 to 100,000 square feet. The rest of the center is tenanted by merchants who also sell discounted or off-price merchandise, and food service tenants.

These centers are usually located well away from traditional shopping centers to avoid conflicts with the suppliers of traditional retailers and to keep the rental factor lower as demanded by these tenants with low margins. A lower rental rate is also achieved by the developer by limiting the amenities in the center.

Promotional or Power Center

The promotional or power center is a relatively new type of shopping center. The anchors or major tenants are heavy promotional and price promotional merchants. These major tenants, ranging in size from 15,000 to 50,000 square feet of GLA, have a following of small shop tenants who market to the same customer and prefer to locate in the same centers. They include high volume stereo stores, home improvement centers, discount woman and mens apparel, and import stores. These centers range in size from 50,000 to 500,000 square feet of GLA.

Unanchored Centers

The unanchored center is the newest concept in the industry. Centers of up to 150,000 square feet of GLA are being built without traditional anchors such as a supermarket or drugstore. The size of the center, its location, and the mix of merchandise is intended to provide the attraction and the traffic.

(b) BY MARKET SERVED

Another consideration in classifying shopping centers is how the center operates in the marketplace. A center that has the square footage and anchor tenants of a community mall may function as a regional mall. For instance, until the late 1980s, Anchorage had no regional center. Three centers in that city were anchored by, respectively, a junior department store, a supermarket, and a super drugstore, with 50 to 100 small shops. Although the centers met the size and major tenant criteria of community malls, they functioned as regional malls. The small-shop tenant mix in these community centers is similar to the regional center's. These centers also are managed, leased, and marketed like regional malls.

A center that meets the size criteria of a neighborhood center but is located in a rural area may have a tenant mix similar to a community center and serve the area as a community center.

It is more important that the property manager understand how the shopping center functions in the community than it is to classify a shopping center by its size. The tenant mix must meet the needs of the shopping center's trade area. Once this has been determined, the manager can develop and implement an effective leasing program.

§ 4.3 DOWNTOWN REDEVELOPMENT

The late 1970s and early 1980s saw a move to revitalize downtown areas to create a shopping district similar to shopping centers. Municipal governments and redevelopment agencies assist in assembling land, provide low-cost loans, help in abating or deferring real estate taxes, provide infrastructure at no cost to the project, and even help with ongoing maintenance costs. Downtown revitalization has had mixed results throughout the country. Like shopping centers, downtown areas, even when revitalized, must have market support and the conveniences that shoppers demand.

§ 4.4 PARKING REQUIREMENTS

A shopping center's size is determined primarily by the amount of gross leasable area the developer can build on a parcel of land. The developer will usually build the maximum amount of GLA allowable. The amount of buildable GLA is restricted by the parking ratio (the number of parking stalls per GLA) and the amount of landscaping that is required by the municipality. The more GLA that can be built on a site, the more income that property will produce.

Parking restrictions for shopping centers are determined by the municipality. The city, county, or borough will have a parking code stating the minimum number of parking stalls per 1,000 square feet of GLA for a shopping center. A parking ratio of six per thousand (6/ 1,000) means that six parking stalls are required for each 1,000 square feet of GLA.

Other parking restrictions may be found in the tenant's lease. Seldom would a small tenant's lease address parking requirements; however, the major tenant's lease may require either a minimum number of parking stalls for the entire shopping center or a specific parking ratio of stalls per GLA. A major tenant wants to be sure that adequate and convenient parking exists for its customers.

Parking requirements also may be found in the reciprocal easement agreement (REA), the covenants, conditions and restrictions (CC&R), or common area agreements. These agreements place various restrictions on the use of the property. (See § 4.7.)

Most of the parking ratios for shopping centers were created several years ago and are outdated. This is evident by the fact that very few neighborhood centers have days when the entire parking lot is full; even most regional and superregional malls have very few days during the year when all stalls are occupied.

The International Council of Shopping Centers, under the auspices of the Urban Land Institute (ULI), funded a study on parking requirements for shopping centers. In 1982 the ULI published its findings in *Parking Requirements for Shopping Centers: Summary Recommendations and Research Study Report*. This 136-page report concluded that adequate parking for a typical shopping center would require:

- Four spaces per 1,000 square feet of GLA for centers having a GLA of 25,000 to 400,000 square feet

- Four to five spaces in a lineal progression with an average of 4.5 spaces per 1,000 square feet of GLA for centers having 400,000 to 600,000 square feet
- Five spaces per 1,000 square feet of GLA for centers having GLA of over 600,000 square feet

Additional parking was recommended for shopping centers with office space, cinemas, or food services exceeding a predetermined percentage of the shopping center's GLA. The significance of this report is that the parking requirements of many municipalities exceed the recommendations in the ULI report.

§ 4.5   CREATING ADDITIONAL INCOME AND GLA ON EXISTING CENTERS

An opportunity may exist to create additional income by building additional GLA if a shopping center's parking ratio exceeds ULI recommendations. Additional GLA can be created by adding onto an existing building, constructing another building, or creating a pad for a restaurant or bank in the parking lot. Creating and leasing additional GLA will generate additional income, thus increasing the income of the shopping center and its value. For instance, if a pad were created by changing the parking requirements, and the pad were ground leased to a national fast-food restaurant for $30,000 per year, the additional income generated from this pad would be just under $30,000 per year after subtracting expenses associated with the increased income such as increased management fees. The net operating income would be increased by approximately $30,000; if the center was valued at a cap rate of 10%, the value of the center would increase approximately $300,000.

If the municipal code's parking requirements are higher than those in ULI's report, property managers should consider obtaining a variance or working with the building department for possible changes to the municipal code. It may be easier to obtain a variance for one shopping center than to request the municipality to change its code for all present and future shopping centers.

Before action is taken to add GLA to the shopping center, the property manager must review the tenant's leases, the REA, CC&Rs, and common area agreements for parking restrictions. If any of these documents have a parking restriction, the property manager must obtain an agreement with the signators of these documents amending the parking requirements before changing the center's parking ratio.

Another possible restriction would be a tenant's lease or any of the above mentioned documents that may provide a tenant, usually the major tenant, with the right to approve the redesign of a shopping center. The addition of a pad or additional buildings would probably be considered as redesigning the shopping center.

The property manager should be well prepared when pursuing a change in the parking code or a variance with the municipality amending the tenant's lease or the REA, CC&Rs, and common area agreements. In addition to using the ULI report, the property manager may need to hire a consultant to conduct a parking survey of the shopping center. A survey of the percentage of vacant parking stalls at different times on different days could provide invaluable information. The property manager may also want to obtain aerial photos of the parking lot taken at different times of the day.

In addition to obtaining a variance in the parking ratio for the shopping center, the property manager may ask the municipality for a change in the number of compact parking stalls that can be provided in the shopping center. The ULI *Parking Requirements for Shopping Centers* has estimated that by the 1990s, most automobiles in use will be compact cars. Creating compact parking stalls out of regular-sized ones will yield more total parking stalls and provide more efficient use of the parking area, thus allowing for more buildable GLA.

The property manager should evaluate the shopping center's parking requirements, and if the number of parking stalls exceeds the recommendations in the ULI report, the manager should consider reducing the ratio of parking stalls per GLA. This reduction will provide additional building opportunities and generate further income for the shopping center, thus enhancing the value of the center.

§ 4.6 OPERATING AGREEMENTS

There are agreements that place restrictions on the landlord's and tenants' use of shopping centers and assign rights and obligations to the landlord and the major tenants. These restrictions, rights, and obligations are usually found in the shopping center's reciprocal easement agreement, common area agreement, or covenants, conditions, and restrictions.

(a) RECIPROCAL EASEMENT AGREEMENT

The REA is an agreement between the landlord and the major tenants that describes the property, defines the common area, and establishes the rights and obligations of the major tenants and the landlord. This agreement will appoint the landlord as the manager of the common area, establish the maintenance standards for the common area, and provide the major tenants with the right to remove the landlord as the manager of all or a portion of the common area if the maintenance does not meet the agreement's standards. The major tenants are given rights to approve changes or additions to the common area.

These rights may even include the major tenant's approval of the landlord's plans for remodeling the property. When major tenants own their building and the adjacent parking areas, this agreement provides crossover rights to use each other's common area. Occasionally the lender is a party to these agreements. REAs are most often found in regional and community shopping centers.

(b) COMMON AREA AGREEMENT

The common area agreement is a document between the landlord and the major tenant(s) describing the common areas and buildable area and establishing the rights and obligations of each party within these areas. A common area manager is appointed, usually the landlord. Each party's pro rata share of the expenses of the common area is established. The agreement provides the major tenants with approval rights to changes to the common area. These agreements, which are most often found in neighborhood or community centers, include the following provisions:

- Recitals
- Maintenance standards
- Lighting
- Taxes
- Maintenance director
- Reimbursement of maintenance director
- Billing for expenses
- Effect of sale by owner
- Default in payment of expenses
- Lien for expenses or taxes
- Right to maintain parcel separately
- Responsibility if no maintenance director
- Sale and leaseback of the major tenant's parcel
- General provisions
- Sale and sale-leaseback purchaser

(c) COVENANTS, CONDITIONS, AND RESTRICTIONS

CC&Rs are restrictions on the use of the property. They convey the rights and obligations to the owners of the property.

These various operating agreements can easily be violated. For example, the REA may restrict kiosks, the use of common areas for selling, or the leasing of the common area to a temporary tenant. Adding a pad tenant to the common area may violate the common area agreement. The courts have found that ignorance is no excuse for violating a tenant's rights.

Violations of these agreements, whether intentional or not, can be costly to the landlord and possibly the property management company. The property manager should meet with the owner of the shopping center to determine if the property has any of these agreements. If it does, the property manager should request a copy of the agreement and determine the landlord's rights and obligations as they effect the operation, development, and leasing of the property. If the owner is not familiar with the agreements, the owner's attorney should review them and summarize the rights and obligations of the parties that are signator to the agreement.

§ 4.7 THE CUSTOMER SURVEY

One of the critical elements of any shopping center's success is serving its trade area properly. The market survey, in contrast to the customer survey, provides most of the necessary information on demographics, competition, traffic, ingress, and egress, but it does not evaluate customer response to a particular shopping center. If the center does well in sales and occupancy, it can be assumed that the center is serving the area well. Even in this situation, however, it is possible that the center might do even better if it were more responsive to consumers' needs. The customer survey provides a way to determine shoppers' perceptions of the center and to invite suggestions for improvement.

Before a customer survey is conducted, specific goals must be developed. Is the purpose to evaluate maintenance and cleanliness of the center? Is it to define tenant mix and determine just what the public thinks is missing? Is it to measure the impact of outside events, such as teenage cruising, major street work, or the opening of a competing center, on the success of the center? Once goals are defined, the survey must be carefully drafted to assure that the responses will provide the necessary information.

Surveys can take various forms. The most expensive and extensive survey is an interview in the customer's home. Less expensive is a customer interview conducted on site or focus groups. Visiting civic clubs and neighborhood groups for discussions can be very productive and provide opportunity for a dialogue rather than just filling in blanks on a form.

Professional marketing organizations have the background and experience to design the survey, formulate the correct questions, recommend the methods of polling, and determine the proper number of customers to contact to validate the survey. A comprehensive customer survey for a regional shopping center with known problems can easily cost in excess of $40,000 and take months to develop and evaluate.

At the other end of the spectrum, an owner or manager of a small center can use a simple customer survey to determine what the customer wants and to evaluate maintenance and management. A simple questionnaire like the one in Exhibit 4.1 can be prepared and, when filled out and deposited in one of the center's stores, becomes an entry blank for a prize drawing. A small ad in the local paper or placards in each store promote the program and keep the cost low.

A neighborhood shopping center may conduct a survey in conjunction with one or more major tenants. For example, if the tenant is a supermarket, the survey asks questions about the center and the supermarket. The survey forms are placed in the customer's shopping bag at the supermarket and a free loaf of bread is presented if the form is returned within ten days. The cost of the bread and copying the forms is minimal, and is shared by the supermarket and the center.

Questionnaires provide focus and can be handed out by all merchants or mailed to the trade area or zip code residents. The decision about which form to use will be influenced by the degree of the problem to be resolved, the owner's resources, outside or out-of-pocket costs, and the time frame in which the information is desired.

Another method of evaluation is to attend civic group meetings to obtain impressions of the center. A contribution to the group's favorite charity or local civic program may help gain entrance, the expenditure justified by gaining worthwhile information. The group can be approached with a questionnaire to be filled out and then discussed, or those in attendance can be questioned. In any case, questionnaires should be brief or customers may become annoyed and not complete them.

A license plate survey can be very effective in determining where customers are coming from. One method is to note license numbers for every fourth car in the lot using random times and days. Be careful to avoid employee automobiles. After collecting 500 to 800 license numbers, submit them to the state motor vehicle department which will, for a fee, provide addresses. The addresses are then plotted on a map of the area, giving a good approximation of the center's trade area. Independent companies also survey license plates for a center and compile useful data.

Most owners/managers spend upwards of 70 hours in their stores and talk with hundreds of customers. Hence a survey of merchants can yield valuable information about center maintenance, customer preferences, effective advertising media, lighting, security problems, and even problems with other tenants (see Exhibit 4.2). Care must be exercised in evaluating merchant responses, for they can be self-serving.

Generally, the center's owners pay for these surveys because merchants' association funds are usually limited and because the owner will

EXHIBIT 4.1

Customer Survey

1. What is the primary purpose of your visit to this shopping center today?
   - (1) Specific purchase
   - (2) Work in store
   - (3) Specific store/restaurant
   - (4) General shopping
   - (5) Special shopping center or store event
   - (6) Other purpose (specify) ⎯⎯⎯⎯⎯⎯⎯⎯⎯⎯⎯
2. What is your next destination?
   - (1) Other shopping area
   - (2) Work
   - (3) Home
   - (4) Other
3. Which of the following categories best describes the length of your shopping visit?
   - (1) Less than 1 hour
   - (2) 1 to less than 2 hours
   - (3) 2 to less than 3 hours
   - (4) 3 hours or more
4. How did you get to this shopping center today?
   - (1) Taxi
   - (2) Walk
   - (3) Tour bus
   - (4) City bus
   - (5) Car
   - (6) Bicycle
   - (7) Other
5. Did you come to this shopping center today from home, work, another shopping area, or some other place?
   - (1) Work
   - (2) Other shopping area
   - (3) Home
   - (4) Other
6. Which of these categories best describes the total amount you spent at the center today, including expenditures for food?
   - (1) Nothing
   - (2) Less than $10
   - (3) $10–$24.99
   - (4) $25–$49.99
   - (5) $50–$99.99
   - (6) $100–$199.99
   - (7) $200–$399.99
   - (8) $400–$599.99
   - (9) $600 or more
7. Which of the following stores did you visit today?
   - (1) Restaurant
   - (11) Bicycle shop

EXHIBIT 4.1 *(Continued)*

(2)	General merchandise	(12)	Telephone equipment
(3)	Shoe store	(13)	Fish & seafood market
(4)	Yogurt shop	(14)	Video store
(5)	Print shop	(15)	Optometrist
(6)	Fabric store	(16)	Beauty supply
(7)	Dentist office	(17)	Apparel shop
(8)	Electronic equipment	(18)	Post office
(9)	Cleaners	(19)	Gift & card shop
(10)	Pizza parlor	(20)	Computer store

8. What is the primary reason for your being in downtown Happytown today?
   (1) Employed in office or store in the center
   (2) Work in downtown
   (3) Conducting business downtown
   (4) Shopping
   (5) Live downtown
   (6) Other (specify): _____
   (7) Visiting (tourist)
   (8) Visiting (conventioneer/conference attendee/out of town business traveler)

9. How often would you say you visit the following shopping centers or areas for shopping/dining?

	Frequently Once/week or More	Occasionally Once/Month or More	Seldom Less Than Once Month	First Time/ Once	Never
(1) Happytown Plaza	5	4	3	2	1
(2) Happytown Mall	5	4	3	2	1
(3) City Center	5	4	3	2	1
(4) Riverfront Commons	5	4	3	2	1
(5) Downtown stores	5	4	3	2	1

10. Where do you work?
    Cross streets _____ and _____ .

11. Which stores did you make purchases in:

(1)	Restaurant	(11)	Bicycle shop
(2)	General merchandise	(12)	Telephone equipment
(3)	Shoe store	(13)	Fish & seafood market
(4)	Yogurt shop	(14)	Video store
(5)	Print shop	(15)	Optometrist
(6)	Fabric store	(16)	Beauty supply
(7)	Dentist office	(17)	Apparel shop
(8)	Electronic equipment	(18)	Post office
(9)	Cleaners	(19)	Gift & card shop
(10)	Pizza parlor	(20)	Computer store

12. Which of these publications do you read regularly?

(1)	*Happytown Weekly*	(3)	*Morning News*
(2)	*Great Area Gazette*	(4)	*Happytown Shopper*

EXHIBIT 4.1 (Continued)

13. When you go to the shopping center, why do you choose it over some other shopping centers?
    (1) No reason
    (2) Close to home or work/convenience
    (3) Like stores/restaurants generally
    (4) Like specific center store or restaurant. Specify: _____
    (5) Other reason. Specify: _____
14. Which of these radio stations do you listen to regularly?
    (1) WZRR-AM (800)
    (2) WPON-FM (91)
    (3) WKKY-FM (99.9)
    (4) WERT-AM (610)
    (5) WYZZ-FM (103.1)
15. Why don't you visit this shopping center more often for shopping/dining?
    (1) Don't have enough time
    (2) Prefer other centers
    (3) Too confusing to find my way around the center
    (4) No reason
    (5) Too far to drive/walk
    (6) Not open weekday evenings
    (7) Cannot find merchandise I'm looking for
    (8) Too tourist oriented
    (9) Don't shop anywhere often
    (10) Other centers closer
    (11) Too expensive
    (12) Not open Sundays
    (13) Don't like stores
    (14) Parking too difficult
16. If the center had a multiscreen movie theatre, would you patronize it?
    (0) Don't know/No response   (2) Probably no   (4) Definitely yes
    (1) Definitely no   (3) Probably yes
17. Which of these television programs do you watch on a regular basis?
    (1) 5:30 P.M. News,   WAJY Channel 12   (ABC)
    (2) 6:00 P.M. News,   WERT Channel 30   (NBC)
    (3) 6:00 P.M. News,   WKYT Channel 21   (CBS)
    (4) 11:00 P.M. News,   WQZV Channel 17   (ABC)
    (5) 11:00 P.M. News,   WERE Channel 35   (NBC)
    (6) 11:00 P.M. News,   WSTS Channel 10   (CBS)
    (7) CBS Morning News,   WUYU Channel 19   (CBS)
    (8) Good Morning America, WNCR Channel 37   (ABC)
    (9) Today Show,   WPPT Channel 6   (NBC)
18. What additional stores, services, or eating places would you like to see added to the center? _____
    _____

19. What other improvements or changes would you like to see at the center or in the stores? _____
    _____

EXHIBIT 4.1 (Continued)

20. How many children under age 18 live in your household?
    1   2   3   4   5   6 or more   7 no children
21. Which of the following categories best describes the number of years of education you have completed?
    (1) Up to 11 years   (4) 4 years college
    (2) Completed high school   (5) Graduate school
    (3) 1–3 years of college   (6) Refused/No answer
22. What is the zip code of your home?

    _____ _____ _____ _____ _____

23. Which of these categories best describes your age?
    (1) 12–16   (2) 17–21   (3) 22–29   (4) 30–44   (5) 45–54
    (6) 55–64   (7) 65–Plus   (8) Refused/No answer
24. Which of these categories best describes the total annual income of everyone in your household?
    (1) Less than $10,000   (5) $35,000–$49,999
    (2) $10,000–$14,999   (6) $50,000–$74,999
    (3) $15,000–$24,999   (7) $75,000 or more
    (4) $25,000–$34,999   (8) Refused/No answer
25. Describe your occupation

    _____

    _____

26. Gender
    1 Male   2 Female
27. Race
    1 White   2 Black   3 Hispanic   4 Oriental   5 Other

EXHIBIT 4.2

Shopping Center Merchant Survey

(To be completed by on-site store manager or store owner, if applicable)

Note: Some aspects of this questionnaire may not apply to your specific store.

Store/Management Profile

1. What store within the Happytown trade area do you consider to be your primary competition?

   _____

2. What are your store's peak hours at Happytown? _____
   Which of these categories best reflects your store's total advertising budget during 1986?
   ____ Don't know   ____ $1,000 to $5,000   ____ $10,000 or more
   ____ Less than $1,000   ____ $5,000 to $10,000

3. Does your firm conduct regularly scheduled selling training programs for managers?
   ____ No ____ Yes—How often? _____

4. How many people are employed in your store?
   Full time _____
   Part time _____

5. Please list which credit cards your store accepts. _____

   _____

6. How long have you (manager/owner) been employed with your company?
   ____ Less than one year   ____ Five years to less than ten yrs
   ____ One year to less than two yrs   ____ Ten years or more
   ____ Two years to less than five yrs

7. Does your firm conduct regularly scheduled selling training programs for employees?
   ____ No ____ Yes—How often? _____

8. Check those which best describe your store's advertising program.
   ____ National advertising   ____ Local advertising
   ____ Regularly scheduled   ____ Regularly scheduled
   ____ Sporadic   ____ Sporadic

9. Please list all of your stores' locations in the Happytown market and rank them in order of sales volume.

                                                          Rank

   _____   _____

   ____ _____   _____
   ____ _____   _____
   ____ _____   _____
   ____ _____   _____

10. Does your store maintain a mailing list of active customers?
    ____ Yes ____ No

11. Are you provided with a store plan for merchandising/display?
    ____ No ____ Yes

12. If yes, how often? _____
    Do you have flexibility to make changes?   ____ No ____ Yes

EXHIBIT 4.2 *(Continued)*

13. What is your (manager/owner) highest level of completed education?
    ____ Some high school   ____ Master's degree
    ____ Graduated high school   ____ Doctor's degree
    ____ Some college   ____ Associate or business degree
    ____ Bachelor's degree

14. Please describe your merchandise return policy? _____
    _____
    _____

15. Does your store use professional visual merchandising display services?
    ____ No ____ Yes—In House ____ Outside Resources ____

16. Do you offer merchandise layaways? ____ Yes ____ No

17. What are the best aspects of the Happytown Center?
    _____
    _____
    _____

18. What are the worst aspects of the Happytown Center?
    _____
    _____
    _____

19. What additional services should be offered to customers/merchants by the Happytown Center?
    _____
    _____
    _____

20. What suggestions for center improvements do you have?
    _____
    _____
    _____

21. What additional stores, services and eating places are needed at this center?
    _____
    _____
    _____

22. Please rate the following aspects of the Happytown Center.

	No Opinion N/A	Excellent	Above Average	Average	Below Average	Poor
Center Management						
Common area maintenance	6 ____	5 ____	4 ____	3 ____	2 ____	1 ____
Security	6 ____	5 ____	4 ____	3 ____	2 ____	1 ____
Heating, ventilating, air-conditioning	6 ____	5 ____	4 ____	3 ____	2 ____	1 ____
Communications with center management	6 ____	5 ____	4 ____	3 ____	2 ____	1 ____
Management responsiveness to store problems	6 ____	5 ____	4 ____	3 ____	2 ____	1 ____

EXHIBIT 4.2 (Continued)

Management responsiveness to mall problems	6 ___	5 ___	4 ___	3 ___	2 ___	1 ___

Center Marketing

Quality of execution and effectiveness of: Events	6 ___	5 ___	4 ___	3 ___	2 ___	1 ___
Decor	6 ___	5 ___	4 ___	3 ___	2 ___	1 ___
PR/community relations	6 ___	5 ___	4 ___	3 ___	2 ___	1 ___
Advertising campaign	6 ___	5 ___	4 ___	3 ___	2 ___	1 ___
Advertising media placement	6 ___	5 ___	4 ___	3 ___	2 ___	1 ___
Other merchant participation in: Center events	6 ___	5 ___	4 ___	3 ___	2 ___	1 ___
Center group Advertising	6 ___	5 ___	4 ___	3 ___	2 ___	1 ___
Competiveness with other centers	6 ___	5 ___	4 ___	3 ___	2 ___	1 ___
Communications with marketing staff	6 ___	5 ___	4 ___	3 ___	2 ___	1 ___
Marketing staff responsiveness	6 ___	5 ___	4 ___	3 ___	2 ___	1 ___

Center Qualities

Length of center hours	6 ___	5 ___	4 ___	3 ___	2 ___	1 ___
Uniformity of store hours	6 ___	5 ___	4 ___	3 ___	2 ___	1 ___
Traffic in center	6 ___	5 ___	4 ___	3 ___	2 ___	1 ___
Traffic in your area of the center	6 ___	5 ___	4 ___	3 ___	2 ___	1 ___
Tenant mix	6 ___	5 ___	4 ___	3 ___	2 ___	1 ___

23. If you advertise, in which media?

Publications	Radio	Television
___ Courier Journal	___ WHAM-FM	___ WTZZ (12)
___ Happytown Times	___ WAFC-AM	___ WTTY (1)
___ Business Journal	___ WCCR-FM	___ WQQM (42)
___ Happytown Magazine	___ WPOI-AM	___ WSAS (54)
___ Happytown Sun	___ WTRE-FM	___ Billboards
___ Other _____	___ WTUI-AM	___ Other _____
		___ Other _____
		___ Other _____

24. Please estimate the percentage of sales volume this demographic group contributes to your store sales:

    By age group
    Persons under 22 years   _____%
    Persons 22 to 44 years   _____%
    Persons 45 plus years   _____%
    Total   100%

EXHIBIT 4.2 *(Continued)*

25. Please estimate the percentage of sales volume this demographic group
    contributes to your store's sales:
       By racial group
    White   _____%
    Blacks   _____%
    Hispanics   _____%
    Orientals   _____%
    Other races   _____%
    Total   100%

26. Please estimate the percentage of sales volume this demographic group
    contributes to your store's sales:
       By gender
    Male   _____%
    Female   _____%
    Total   100%

27. Please estimate the percentage of sales volume this demographic group
    contributes to your store's sales:
       By household income group:
    Income earners under $15,000   _____%
    Income earners $15,000 to $34,999   _____%
    Income earners $35,000 plus   _____%

28. In which of the following merchandising/advertising programs can your
    store participate?

	Can/Could		Already Do/Could	
Group Ads in				
Newspaper tabloids	___ Yes	___ No	___ Yes	___ No
Newspaper sections	___ Yes	___ No	___ Yes	___ No
Magazine sections	___ Yes	___ No	___ Yes	___ No
Coupons	___ Yes	___ No	___ Yes	___ No
Direct mail catalogs	___ Yes	___ No	___ Yes	___ No
Direct mail flyers	___ Yes	___ No	___ Yes	___ No
Radio advertisements	___ Yes	___ No	___ Yes	___ No
Television advertisements	___ Yes	___ No	___ Yes	___ No
Group Merchandising Events				
Sales events	___ Yes	___ No	___ Yes	___ No
Fashion shows	___ Yes	___ No	___ Yes	___ No
Contests	___ Yes	___ No	___ Yes	___ No

use the information for management and leasing considerations in addition to the merchandising interests of the tenants. If the survey is to be used for leasing, it should include a disclaimer on the accuracy of the information and how it was obtained.

A potential customer survey for a center yet to be built may be conducted, but such a survey is more likely to be used if there is a problem in an existing center, a rehab is contemplated, or a major tenant is leaving and additional input is needed about what the customers want or need.

The customer survey (Exhibit 4.1) is meant to evaluate many aspects of the center. Questions 1, 2, 4, 5, 7, and 8 explore what brings customers to the center. Questions 12, 14, and 18 evaluate advertising media for the center's customers. Questions 7, 11, 13, 17, and 19 will help management evaluate the current tenant mix and determine the nature and thrust of future leasing efforts. Questions 22, 24, 25, 26, 27, and 28 seek to identify the customer of the center so that amenities and tenant mix can be matched to customer preferences.

§ 4.8 TENANT MIX

The concept of tenant mix is not limited to shopping centers but is more critical to the success of a shopping center than it is to office buildings, medical buildings or industrial parks. Tenant mix must be consistent with the trade area as well as within the center itself.

No one formula exists for correct tenant mix, but there are helpful guidelines to determine the most likely mix for a given shopping center. The best tenant mix for a specific shopping center will provide the broadest range of goods and services consistent with the shopping patterns of the people in the trade area. If customers in the trade area are affluent, the shops are more likely to cater to higher income tastes. If, on the other hand, the trade area is made up of families at the lower end of the income spectrum, the successful shops are more likely to carry lower cost merchandise. It does not make sense to put K-Mart in Beverly Hills or Saks Fifth Avenue in a blue-collar neighborhood.

Sources such as *Sales and Marketing Management's Annual Survey of Buying Power* detail how people spend their money in every major metropolitan area of the country. By evaluating that information, a tenant mix can be developed. If, for example, a study of supermarket sales shows higher than average figures, an opportunity may exist for another supermarket. Studying the average sales per square foot of existing supermarkets can indicate whether a new store in this category will be successful. Exhibit 4.3 compares sales in several women's wear shops, men's wear shops, and restaurants.

Multiplying the number of people in the trade area by the average purchases per person to arrive at the potential sales in the area. We can

EXHIBIT 4.3

Sales Comparisons by Stores

	SEPTEMBER '72		OCTOBER '72		NOVEMBER '72		DECEMBER '72		JANUARY '73		FEBRUARY '73	
	Sq. Ft.	%	Sq. Ft.	%	Sq. Ft.	%	Sq. Ft.	%	Sq. Ft.	%	Sq. Ft.	%
WOMEN'S WEAR												
A	4.33	- 12.3	4.37	.04	4.96	+ 9.2	13.37	+ 2.7	4.20	+ 21.8	3.27	- 10.2
B	6.18	+ 61.6	4.25	+ 28.9	5.80	+ 26.2	13.61	+ 71.2	3.33	+ 68.9	3.77	+ 78.9
C	5.83	- 0 -	6.51	+ 31.6	7.77	+ 47.7	23.70	+ 35.4	4.61	+ 57.8	5.51	+ 78.9
D	11.28	+108.2	7.56	+ 47.7	8.22	+ 36.2	15.51	+ 41.2	4.69	+ 61.9	4.67	+ 67.9
E	6.56	- 29.5	4.40	- 13.2	6.07	+ 26.3	14.35	+ 42.2	4.39	+ 42.6	4.56	+ 51.0
F	5.00	- 6.6	4.80	- 12.8	5.50	- 19.2	11.76	- 19.1	3.22	- 14.4	4.76	+ 3.3
G	4.56	+ 155.8	4.62	+ 32.0	5.44	+ 27.5	11.41	+ 26.8	3.91	+ 58.0	3.68	+ 45.6
H	11.63	+ 76.6	11.26	+ 85.6	12.48	+ 69.8	22.17	+ 66.0	6.37	+ 23.5	7.20	- 4.3
I	4.78	- 7.1	3.66	+ 44.1	3.50	+ 9.9	6.86	+ .5	1.65	- 40.2	2.67	+ 16.0
J	6.92	+ 18.5	6.68	+ 31.6	8.47	+ 32.1	11.68	+ 38.5	5.77	+ 65.2	7.74	+ 38.4
K	5.60	- 6.7	4.59	- 3.2	5.48	+ 23.6	15.28	+ 41.3	4.37	+ 16.9	5.41	+ 57.1
L	6.20	- 0 -	4.77	- 0 -	7.64	- 0 -	11.98	- 0 -	5.83	- 0 -	5.06	- 0 -
M	5.06	+129.3	5.53	+ 65.2	5.90	+ 57.8	13.10	+ 44.7	6.46	+ 83.7	5.00	+ 28.9
N	5.61	- 9.0	5.29	+ 25.3	5.65	+ 52.7	9.97	+ 22.8	2.63	+ 66.9	3.98	+111.2
O	4.57	- 0 -	3.82	- 0 -	5.08	+213.0	11.09	+ 54.9	3.46	+ 62.3	3.52	+133.8
P	3.50	+ 18.9	3.28	+ 90.8	3.79	- 34.3	8.77	+ 6.9	3.19	+ 21.0	2.65	+ 11.7
Q	6.49	+ 8.8	5.53	+ 35.9	6.27	+ 25.8	15.00	+ 20.4	3.87	+ 23.1	4.46	- 2.3
R	4.00	- 0 -	4.28	+ 15.5	5.39	- 0 -	9.16	- 0 -	2.97	- 0 -	3.62	+ 31.7
Category Average	5.62	+ 25.9	4.95	+ 26.0	5.64	+ 37.0	13.19	+ 31.2	4.07	+ 37.8	4.24	+33.6
MEN'S WEAR												
A	4.79	- 12.6	4.39	+ 15.4	5.36	+ 10.7	11.68	- 8.1	3.39	+ .7	3.55	- 11.0
B	4.40	- 0 -	4.59	- 0 -	7.17	- 0 -	12.45	- 0 -	4.48	- 0 -	7.17	- 0 -
C	7.43	+ 38.0	5.47	+ 2.6	9.16	+ 26.2	17.81	+ 27.2	3.55	- 9.9	9.27	+ 85.5
D	4.13	- 0 -	4.16	- 0 -	4.59	- 0 -	12.78	- 0 -	4.43	- 0 -	3.11	- 0 -
E	- 0 -	- 0 -	- 0 -	- 0 -	2.72	- 0 -	10.03	- 0 -	3.67	- 0 -	3.57	- 0 -
F	4.34	+ 2.3	3.25	+ 4.9	7.17	- 17.0	14.14	+ 17.0	1.80	+ 19.8	3.70	+ 46.8
G	16.20	- 0 -	8.48	- 0 -	11.21	- 0 -	31.85	- 0 -	8.92	- 0 -	8.90	- 0 -
H	4.32	- 0 -	4.23	- 5.1	6.11	- 46.2	10.62	- 13.8	3.02	- 21.5	2.79	- 19.3
I	3.86	+. 45.7	4.62	- 1.7	5.81	+ 1.9	14.60	- 7.3	3.93	+ 28.6	3.99	+ 21.5
Category Average	5.42	+ 14.8	4.58	+ 2.6	5.88	- 2.3	14.00	+ 6.0	4.08	- 6.7	4.49	+ 32.0
RESTAURANTS												
A	10.01	- 12.3	8.53	- 13.2	10.12	- 7.2	17.22	- 5.0	7.56	- 7.5	7.17	- 19.1
B	8.84	+ 62.5	8.75	+ 19.0	9.38	+ 25.7	11.16	+ 20.5	8.73	+ 16.5	8.79	+ 28.2
C	8.90	- 1.8	9.01	. 01	9.18	+ 3.6	11.01	+ 9.9	8.77	+ 5.7	8.32	+ 5.9
Category Average	8.99	+ 17.0	8.84	+ 5.9	9.36	+ 10.8	11.72	+ 11.4	8.63	+ 8.8	8.41	+ 11.9

160

then estimate the sales of the existing market. Sales tax figures can also be used to determine if the area has excess potential that would suggest support for a new supermarket.

Studying how people in the trade area spend their money reveals percentages of sales in various uses such as women's wear, men's wear, shoes, and restaurants (see Exhibit 4.4). These percentages are then modified based on the competition and type of center involved. Every category of merchandise can be evaluated in the same way. The sales potentials indicated by this type of study are meant to be a guideline and not an absolute figure. Analyzing the area's growth rates, traffic patterns, and quality of existing competition provides additional indicators for probable success.

A supermarket and drugstore serve as anchor tenants in a neighborhood center. They provide the traffic to support the smaller merchants. Both should be either high end or low end rather than appealing to different market segments.

The actual placement of specific tenants within a given center is not a science. The property manager's experience and general know-how play an important part in determining tenant mix. The goal, however, is to mix goods and services to encourage impulse shopping while the customer is looking for something specific. Beauty and barber shops do not usually need a high traffic location as they are a destination-type tenant. A jewelry store will usually want to be in a high traffic location so customers can see something they like and buy on impulse.

A pet store or hair salon is not a good neighbor for a restaurant because unpleasant odors may flow into the restaurant. A record store is not a good idea next to a bookstore since bookstore patrons could be disturbed by loud music from the adjoining premises. Placing an auto parts store between two dress shops will not benefit any of the retailers involved.

The center's management must also take great care not to put in tenants that would cause customers discomfort or would take away from the overall shopping experience (see § **4.14** for a discussion of potential problem tenants).

§ 4.9 PERCENTAGE RENT ADMINISTRATION

Rent paid above the minimum rent is referred to as percentage rent or overage rent—rent over the minimum rent. The theory is that merchants in a shopping center should be able to generate more sales than they would if they were freestanding without the drawing power of the additional merchants. The payment of percentage rent by a tenant is meant to recognize the increased sales realized by combining the merchants in the shopping center environment. The landlord should benefit if the retail environment results in the tenant's achieving higher sales.

EXHIBIT 4.4

Sales Comparisons by Store Categories

	September 1971	September 1972	October 1971	October 1972	November 1971	November 1972	December 1971	December 1972	January 1972	January 1973	February 1972	February 1973
WOMEN'S WEAR	203,894.00	256,745.71	192,290.00	242,277.78	222,297.00	304,550.02	524,967.00	688,742.20	145,922.02	205,207.33	170,508.55	227,765.89
% Change		+25.9		+26.0		+37.0		+31.2		+37.8		+33.6
MEN'S WEAR	46,584.00	53,480.82	56,555.00	58,050.92	94,664.00	92,541.64	170,952.00	181,264.14	42,569.33	39,716.83	49,556.01	65,420.31
% Change		+14.8		+2.6		-2.3		+6.0		-6.7		+32.0
RESTAURANTS	103,366.00	121,016.26	112,390.00	119,039.05	113,713.00	126,064.79	141,540.00	157,775.85	106,662.07	116,131.08	101,103.09	113,220.05
% Change		+17.0		+5.09		+10.8		+11.4		+8.8		+11.9
FOOD TO GO	39,420.00	27,540.25	44,560.00	40,843.96	103,375.00	108,910.51	200,198.00	240,619.68	76,333.45	120,095.33	97,819.91	128,971.76
% Change		-30.2		-8.4		+4.9		+20.1		+57.3		+31.8
SHOES	166,626.00	193,412.74	125,485.00	157,946.07	142,027.00	176,526.69	273,147.00	301,311.24	121,870.89	152,004.97	110,862.46	157,297.81
% Change		+16.0		+25.8		+24.2		+10.3		+24.7		+41.8
JEWELRY	59,850.00	53,087.97	43,646.00	72,485.22	69,843.00	120,159.56	224,722.00	366,000.87	39,506.05	57,328.55	44,830.14	64,967.88
% Change		+33.2		+66.0		+72.0		+62.8		+45.1		+44.9
GIFTS	30,009.00	28,376.60	26,027.00	27,398.85	38,727.00	50,242.40	140,382.00	176,623.82	24,687.36	29,456.89	29,955.73	37,715.00
% Change		-5.5		+5.2		+29.7		+25.8		+19.3		+30.3
GENERAL MERCHANDISE	161,921.00	174,965.05	155,079.00	183,237.23	214,204.00	286,380.37	511,229.00	691,877.09	176,165.61	232,228.38	179,500.67	238,267.03
% Change		+8.0		+18.1		+33.7		+35.3		+31.8		+32.7
CENTER TOTAL	791,670.00	908,625.40	756,032.00	901,279.08	999,210.00	1,265,375.98	2,187,137.00	2,804,214.89	733,717.38	952,169.38	783,136.51	1,033,625.73
% Change		+14.7		+19.2		+26.6		+28.2		+29.7		+31.9

6 MONTHS TOTAL   Sep – February – 6,250,902.51
                 Sep – February – 7,865,290.46

% Change   25.8%

Percentage rent is administrated on three levels: (1) accounting for any percentage rent due, (2) measuring the success of each tenant and of the center as a whole, and (3) collecting the monies due.

The percentage rental rate for any given tenant is based on the profit margin of that type of business. A supermarket has a very low profit margin and the lowest percentage rental rate in the industry at 1% to 1 1/2% of sales. Most retail soft goods, shoe stores, restaurants, and specialty stores are in the midrange of profit margins and pay from 5% to 7% of gross sales. Service tenants such as beauty and barber shops have a higher profit margin and will pay 7% to 10% of sales (see Exhibit 4.5). These figures are all negotiable but should be kept within reasonable ranges to be fair to both landlord and tenant. Percentage rental rates are applied to gross sales, less sales tax and any negotiated exclusions (see below).

Typically, the tenant will pay minimum rent on the first of each month and any percentage rent due above the minimum as called for in the lease. The point at which a tenant is obligated to pay percentage rent is known as the *breakpoint,* which can either be a natural breakpoint or a negotiated breakpoint.

EXHIBIT 4.5

Percentage Rent Record

Tenant	Footage	Percent	Notes
Friendly Market	42,000	1.5	Reports & pays 45 days end calendar year
Kathy's Kards	2,000	7.0	Reports 20 days, pays end calendar quarter
Today's Styles	1,500	5.0	Reports 10 days, pays end month
White Cleaners	1,600	6.0	Reports 20 days, pays end lease year 6/30
Advance TV	2,000	0	No requirement
Vacant	700		
Kings Hardware	5,000	3.0	Reports 10 days, pays end of month
Pizza Plus	3,200	6.0	Reports 10 days, pays end of month
Fast Sell Realty	1,500	0	No requirement
Goodies Ice Cream	1,700	5.0	
Fancy Fabrics	3,400	4.5	
Slim & Trim Salon	3,200	7.0	
Family Shoes	2,600	3.0	
Speedy's Bikes	1,600	5.5	
Discount Drugs	22,000	3.0	
Dine 'n Dash	3,600	6.0	
Home Town Bank	2,400	0	
Totals:	100,000		

The natural breakpoint is determined by dividing the minimum rent by the percentage rental rate. Example: $12,000 minimum annual rent ÷ 6% percentage rental rate = $200,000 annual breakpoint. If the tenant's sales are less than $200,000—$175,000, for example—percentage rent is not owed ($175,000 annual sales × 6% = $10,500 total percentage rent vs. $12,000 minimum annual rent = no balance due). If, however, the tenant's sales were $240,000 for the year, the annual percentage rent would be $2,400 ($240,000 annual sales × 6% = $14,400 total percentage rent – $12,000 minimum rent paid = $2,400 percentage rent due).

Tenants in a shopping center pay either a minimum rent or a percentage of their sales, whichever is greater. The percentage rent for a tenant whose rent is $12,000 a year with a 5% rate and sales of $300,000 is $3,000 ($300,000 × 5% = $15,000 – $12,000 = $3,000 percentage rent). If the same tenant's sales were $200,000, there would be no percentage rent ($200,000 × 5% = $10,000 – $12,000 = no percentage rent).

Major tenants will report sales and pay the percentage rent owed annually. Smaller shop tenants should report their sales and pay the percentage rent owed monthly. After the year ends, the tenant's sales are adjusted based on the tenant's annual sales, which even out the seasonal highs and lows of the year. Even though a tenant may pay percentage rent in April and December, the annual basis sales may be below the breakpoint. In this case, the percentage rent paid would be refunded.

(a) NEGOTIATING PERCENTAGE RENT RATES

Percentage rent calculations can vary. The breakpoint can be negotiated up or down; one percentage rate can be used to determine the breakpoint and another for sales above the breakpoint; there can be a declining rate; or the tenant may have the right to deduct taxes, insurance, and common area costs from percentage rents.

Negotiating the Breakpoint Downward

The tenant may demand a higher level of interior improvements to the store than the landlord is willing to provide and is unwilling to pay a higher rent to offset the cost of these improvements. The landlord may propose that the breakpoint be lowered to offset the landlord's additional investment. In the above example, the natural breakpoint of $200,000 could be negotiated to a $150,000 breakpoint. If the tenant generated $50,000 in sales above the breakpoint at a 6% rate, $3,000 in additional percentage rent would be paid to the landlord.

Negotiating the Breakpoint Upward

A tenant may be forced to pay market rent for a space that is in poor condition. As an inducement, the landlord might agree to move the natural breakpoint up to allow the tenant to recapture the additional cost to improve the premises. For example, a natural breakpoint of $200,000 negotiated to a $230,000 breakpoint is $30,000 above the natural breakpoint times 6% percentage rate provides the tenant with $1,800 a year to offset the additional improvements.

Higher Percentage Rate to Breakpoint and Lower Percentage Rate Thereafter

Sometimes the landlord and the tenant cannot agree on the percentage rental rate. The tenant might want 5% and the landlord 6%. A compromise, aside from the obvious rate of 5.5%, is 6% to the breakpoint and 5% thereafter ($12,000 minimum rent ÷ 6% percentage rate = $200,000 natural breakpoint; $12,000 minimum rent ÷ 5% percentage rate = $240,000 natural breakpoint).

Calculate the breakpoint by dividing 6% into the annual rent and multiplying the sales in excess of the breakpoint by 5%. The result is the amount of percentage rent. To determine the total rent, add the minimum rent to the percentage rent. (For example, sales are $500,000. $12,000 minimum rent ÷ 6% = $200,000 breakpoint. $300,000 is subject to percentage rent at 5%: $300,000 × 5% rate = $15,000 percentage or overage rent + $12,000 minimum rent = $27,000 total rent.)

Declining Rate

A high volume tenant might be willing to pay percentage rent, but not at the same rate for all sales. A declining rate may be the answer. For example, a 30,000-square-foot supermarket generates $18 million in annual sales—very high volume by industry standards. The tenant may feel the percentage rent paid based on a constant rate is too high under the circumstances. A compromise might be 1% for the first $12 million ($12,000,000 × 1% = $120,000); .75% for the next $3 million ($3,000,000 × .75% = $22,500); and .50% thereafter ($3,000,000 × .50% = $15,000.) Total rent is $157,500.

Deductions from Percentage Rent

While it is rare today to allow a tenant to deduct expense items from percentage rent due—known as recapture—some major tenants demand, and get, the right to do so. In the example following, the tenant is allowed to deduct (recapture) its share of the taxes and insurance from any percentage rent owing.

Total sales		$5,000,000
1.5% gross		75,000
Less minimum rent		50,000
Percentage rent due		$ 25,000
Less taxes paid	$18,000	
Less insurance paid	9,000	
	$27,000	
Actual percentage rent owed		-0-

(b)   ACCOUNTING

Generally, the accounting department needs a lease or a billing to trigger a receivable. In the case of percentage rent, the accountant first has to collect sales reports from the tenants. A master list of all tenants should be prepared indicating whether sales reports are required and, if so, when they are due and at what point will percentage rent be due (see Exhibit 4.6).

It is helpful to provide sales report forms to less sophisticated tenants. The due dates of sales reports for all tenants should be recorded in a tickler file and, if not received as agreed, the tenant should be notified. A close follow-up on sales reports can improve cash flow substantially.

Once the reports are received they should be checked by the accounting personnel for mathematical accuracy and any percentage rents due. If monies are due, the tenant should immediately be billed and the amount entered on the tenant ledger card or on the computer so that the billing is not lost in the system. The bookkeeper would then pass the report on to the property manager for sales evaluation and possible tenant audit (see § 4.9(f)).

(c)   SALES ANALYSIS

The astute manager will use tenant sales reports to measure an individual tenant's success, the success of a category of tenants, the success of a portion of the center, and the success of the center itself. The larger the center, the more sophisticated the analysis of the tenants' sales, a valuable resource in making management and leasing decisions.

The best comparative measure of tenant sales in the shopping center industry is *Dollars and Cents of Shopping Centers*, published every three years by the Urban Land Institute (see Exhibit 4.7). This book has excellent comparative figures on various aspects of retail leases of interest to the shopping center manager. The book is organized by center

EXHIBIT 4.6

Tenant Roster

Date _____

Bldg. Neighborhood Center

TENANT	SUITE #	TYPE OF STORE	SQ. FT.	RENT YEAR	RENT $/S.F.	RENT MONTH	SECURITY DEPOSIT	TERM YEARS	LEASE DATE	COMMENCEMENT	TERMINATION DATE	% RENT	SPECIAL NOTES	C.A.C.
Friendly Market	A-1	Super Market	42,000	147,000	3.50	12,250	None	30	4-15-77	2-1-78	1-31-08	14	Options	Cap.
Kathy's Kards	A-2	Cards & Gifts	2,000	19,000	9.50	1,583.33	1583.33	5	2-1-78	3-1-78	3-31-83	6		Yes
Today's Styles	A-3	Hair Styling	1,500	14,625	9.75	1,218.75	2437.50	5	1-15-78	4-15-78	4-14-83	7½		Yes
White Cleaners	A-4	Dry Cleaners	1,600	15,600	9.75	1,300	1300.00	5	1-8-78	4-1-78	3-31-83	7		Yes
Advance T.V. & Radio	A-5	TV, Radio, Stereo	2,000	19,000	9.50	1,583.33	1583.33	5	1-20-78	4-1-78	3-31-83	4		Yes
Vacant	A-6		700	7,700	11.00	641.66								
King's Hardware	A-7	Hardware	5,000	43,750	8.75	3,645.83	3645.83	10	10-10-77	2-1-78	1-31-88	4		Yes
Pizza Plus	A-8	Pizza Rest.	3,200	29,600	9.25	2,466.66	2466.66	15	9-12-77	4-1-78	3-31-94	5	CPI 5&10 yr	Yes
Fast Sell Realty	A-9	Real Est. Office	1,500	17,250	11.50	1,437.50	2875.00	5	4-3-80	5-1-80	4-30-85	-	+ 10% 3rd yr.	Yes
Goodies Ice Cream	A-10	Ice Cream Parlor	1,700	16,150	9.50	1,345.83	1345.83	10	2-1-78	4-15-78	4-14-88	5	CPI 6th yr	Yes
Fancy's Fabric	A-11	Fabric	3,400	31,450	9.25	2,620.83	2620.83	5	4-10-78	6-15-78	6-14-83	5		Yes
Slim & Trim Figure Salon	A-12	Figure Salon	3,200	30,080	9.40	2,506.66	2506.66	5	4-5-78	6-1-78	5-31-83	7		Yes
Family Discount Shoes	A-13	Family Shoes	2,600	26,000	10.00	2,166.66	2166.66	5	9-20-78	11-1-78	10-31-83	6		Yes
Speedy's Bikes	A-14	Bike Sales/Service	1,600	16,400	10.25	1,366.66	1366.66	5	10-6-78	11-15-78	11-14-83	5		Yes
Discount Drugs	A-15	Drugs & Sundries	22,000	79,200	3.60	6,600	None	30	5-3-77	2-15-78	2-14-08	3-2-1	Options	Yes
Dine 'n' Dash	P-1	Family Restaurant	3,600	57,600	16.00	4,800	9600.00	20	6-12-77	5-10-78	5-9-98	5	Options	Yes
Home Town Bank	P-2	Bank	2,400	48,000	20.00	4,000	8000.00	20	10-3-77	6-20-78	6-19-98	-	Option	Yes

EXHIBIT 4.7

Comparative Measure of Tenant Sales

U.S. NEIGHBORHOOD SHOPPING CENTERS
Hobby/Special Interest, Gifts/Specialty

Tenant Classification	No. in Sample	GLA in Sq. Ft. Median	GLA Lower Decile	GLA Upper Decile	Sales per Sq. Ft. Median	Sales Top 10 Percent	Sales Top 2 Percent	Rate of Percentage Rent Median	Rate Lower Decile	Rate Upper Decile
Cameras M04	18	1.630	920	2.900	217.67	268.96	281.22	5.00	2.00	6.00
National Chain	5	1.600								
Local Chain	2									
Independent	11	1.766	920	2.900						
Toys M05	13	1.900	150	5.250	82.10	107.07	151.59	6.00		
National Chain	0									
Local Chain	5	3.260								
Independent	8	1.750			82.10			6.00		
Bike Shop M06	16	1.350	970	3.312	103.93	139.98	159.54	5.00	4.00	6.00
National Chain	0									
Local Chain	3									
Independent	13	1.350	900	3.312	103.93			5.00		
Arts and Crafts M07	28	1.200	900	10.400	69.11	104.76	138.83	6.00	5.00	8.00
National Chain	3									
Local Chain	4									
Independent	21	1.200			60.29			6.00		
Coin Shop M08	5	1.032								
National Chain	0									
Local Chain	2									
Independent	3									
Outfitters M09	9	1.378			127.06					
National Chain	0									
Local Chain	4									
Independent	5	1.400								
Imports N01	7	2.800								
National Chain	0									
Local Chain	1									
Independent	6	2.800								
Cards and Gifts N03	84	2.310	1.200	3.600	73.87	133.44	170.00	6.00	5.00	8.00
National Chain	9	3.000			80.46			6.00		
Local Chain	17	2.310	1.352	3.000	63.67	109.38	120.77	6.00	5.00	7.00
Independent	58	2.200	1.200	3.515	75.26	132.03	170.00	6.00	5.00	8.00

Source: Urban Land Institute, *Dollars and Cents of Shopping Centers,* 192–193 (1987.)

Total Rent per Sq. Ft.			Common Area Charges per Sq. Ft.			Property Taxes and Insurance per Sq. Ft.			Total Charges per Sq. Ft.			Total Charges as Percent of Sales		
Median	Top 10 Percent	Top 2 Percent	Median	Top 10 Percent	Top 2 Percent	Median	Top 10 Percent	Top 2 Percent	Median	Top 10 Percent	Top 2 Percent	Median	Lower Decile	Upper Decile
9.24			.41			.54			10.03			5.57		
	14.49	16.26		.88	1.88		1.01	1.25		15.74	17.08		3.18	13.80
9.75			.41			.77			11.31					
9.03			.37			.32			9.33					
	9.84	10.50		.63	.74					10.56	13.53			
8.83			.63			.63			10.53			15.79		
	14.00	20.07		2.08	2.73		1.06	1.15		16.96	22.54		6.29	31.31
5.93									6.86					
9.60			.73			.63			10.92			18.67		
8.06			.80			. 63			10.79			8.64		
	11.96	12.70		1.74	1.61		1.06	1.06		13.99	14.64		4.65	19.98
8.06			.72			.63			10.79			8.55		
	11.28	11.96		1.46				1.74		1.309	13.99			
9.00			.60			.61			10.00			12.29		
	12.21	14.40		1.32	1.81		1.18	1.32		14.16	16.01		6.80	41.06
8.76			.57			.61			9.68			12.29		
	11.00	12.00		1.08	1.18		.96	1.16		12.23	12.59		5.16	41.06
8.25									8.55					
12.00			.62			.24			12.24			7.75		
12.00						.24			13.84					
9.16			1.04			.51			10.41					
9.16			1.04			.51			10.41					
8.75			.62			.65			9.88			13.29		
	12.49	18.67		1.46	1.73		1.28	2.17		14.55	20.51		6.73	27.61
7.25			.80			.95			10.08			12.97		
9.18			.81			.80			11.04			13.29		
	11.00	12.49		1.73	1.73		1.16	1.93		14.52	14.55		5.91	31.10
8.70			.53			.61			9.63			14.68		
	12.00	15.00		1.03	1.73		1.22	1.92		13.73	16.36		6.99	27.61

types, geographic areas, and tenant types. It provides store size ranges, sales ranges and medians, percentage rental rate ranges and medians, and occupancy cost ranges and medians. By comparing a center's or tenant's sales with those in *Dollars and Cents*, the property manager can get a good idea of how well the tenants are performing. It is often necessary to extrapolate and interpret the information in light of individual situations, but the guide is helpful in analyzing existing tenants as well as prospective tenants.

(d) EVALUATING EXISTING TENANTS

Each tenant's sales should be compared with national averages and with similar uses within the center. For example, a neighborhood center has a national chain 45,000-square-foot supermarket. It produces $9,360,000 in sales, which is $280 per square foot. *Dollars and Cents of Shopping Centers* (1987) indicates that a supermarket will average $281.25 per square foot. A comparison shows that the store is average for a national chain and above average for supermarkets in general.

In larger centers, a form like the one in Exhibit 4.3 would be used to evaluate a specific tenant. Comparing the tenant with the category reveals whether the tenant is doing well, poorly, or average. The manager must also consider store size, specific type of merchandise, time of year, and any store changes that have taken place.

Once the sales figures are gathered, the property manager should schedule a meeting with each tenant to open up a dialogue. The tenant in the supermarket example above should not be a future rent collection problem: It is generating very good sales, is number two in its category, and is well above average in its percentage of increases. Congratulations are in order during the meeting.

(e) EVALUATING PROSPECTIVE TENANTS

Sales comparison figures can also be used to evaluate prospective tenants. For example, in a negotiation with two prospective men's wear stores, assume that Prospect 1 is negotiating for lower rent and that Prospect 2 seems willing to accept your terms. Prospect 1 has another shop averaging $350 per square foot in sales and feels she will do at least that volume in your center. Prospect 2 believes he will average sales of $120 per square foot but will pay your asking rent of $12 per square foot per year. Men's wear stores generally pay about 5% of sales. Prospect 1 would pay a total rent of $17.50 per square foot based on her sales, if the rent would be 5% of gross sales, a very comfortable rent-to-sales ratio. Prospect 2 would produce only rent of $6 per square foot based on projected sales, but the minimum rent is $12 and the ratio of rent to sales is 10%. All things being equal, Prospect 1 would make the better long-term tenant. Note: Rent-to-sales ratio is determined by dividing the tenant's sales into its rent. When a tenant's rent-to-sales ratio exceeds 10% to 12%, the tenant is probably not generating a profit and is a candidate for failure.

(f) EVALUATING THE CENTER'S SALES

Sales figures can be used not only to evaluate each tenant but to evaluate the center as a whole and to measure the success of various merchandise categories within the center (see Exhibit 4.3). Each category is totaled, averages set, and each tenant in the category compared with the whole. Comparisons can be made on sales per square foot as well as sales increases or decreases.

Great care must be taken not to reveal individual tenant's sales figures to others in this process. If there are three or fewer merchants in a category, revealing the total sales would automatically provide each tenant with the sales of the others. For that reason, it is very difficult to calculate category breakdowns in neighborhood centers. Sales analyses in such centers are limited to confidential individual tenant analysis and an overall center analysis. If the center is in a state where sales taxes are collected, those figures can be used to measure the market share of an individual center on an ongoing basis (see Exhibit 4.8).

(g) AUDITING TENANT SALES

In any shopping center that has percentage rent provisions in the leases, the property manager must consider the accuracy of the sales being reported. The potential exists for a tenant to deliberately understate sales, to underreport sales through a misinterpretation of the lease, or to miscalculate the amount due. This results in a financial loss to the owners, reducing net operating income and actual cash flow and ultimately reducing the value of the shopping center. The property manager will want to minimize or eliminate inaccurate percentage rent payments.

The first step in auditing a tenant's sales is a good lease clause. The typical shopping center lease will state that the audit is an expense of the landlord unless the sales reported are off by 2% or greater, in which case it is the cost of the tenant.

Once the property manager has the appropriate lease language and the tenant's sales reports, evaluation and follow-up can take place. Regular store visits and discussions with the operator will provide clues to the tenant's sales volume. A comparison of the tenant's volume with the industry average will provide additional insights into the tenant's performance.

Dollars and Cents of Shopping Centers is the best reference source for percentage rent evaluation. Certain situations will suggest an audit:

EXHIBIT 4.8
Sales Analysis

CENTER Neighborhood Center

MONTH: _____

MERCHANT	AREA	MONTHLY SALES COMPARISON					YEAR-TO-DATE COMPARISON					BREAK-POINT	OVERAGE POTENTIAL EVALUATION					
		MONTH 1981	MONTH 1980	% CHANGE	SQ. FT.	SQ. FT.	CURRENT YEAR	PREVIOUS YEAR	% CHANGE	SQ. FT.	SQ. FT.		CURRENT MONTH			YEAR-TO-DATE		
													1981	1980	%CHANGE	1981	1980	%CHANGE
Supermkt	A-1	885,000	835,500	5.9	21.07	19.89	5,640,111	5,258,211	8.4	84.29	77.58	816,667	1,025	282	363	4,102	0	-
Balls Cards	A-2	34,380	29,101	18.14	17.19	14.55	120,380	101,353	18.85	60.17	50.68	27,783	396	79	500	351	0	-
Styles	A-3	7,315	6,812	7.38	4.88	4.54	28,500	27,150	4.90	19.00	18.10	17,000	0	0	0	0	0	0
Cleaners	A-4	10,150	9,230	9.97	6.34	5.77	40,510	38,003	6.59	25.32	23.75	19,529	0	0	0	0	0	0
TV & Stereo	A-5	44,144	38,887	13.51	22.07	19.44	175,312	161,200	8.75	87.66	80.60	41,675	99	0	-	344	0	-
Hardware	A-7	37,500	34,111	9.93	7.50	6.82	149,012	137,800	7.41	29.80	27.56	96,350						
Pizza	A-8	61,500	57,111	7.68	19.22	17.84	245,500	228,211	8.53	76.72	70.49	52,000	475	256	185	1,875	1,016	184
99 Flavors	A-10	18,312	1.66	10.77	10.60	70.151	69,135	1.47	41.28	40.67	26.917	29,040						
Fabric	A-11	38,900	33,612	15.73	11.44	9.89	135,000	114,120	13.33	39.71	35.04	55,260						
Salon	A-12	19,151	17,999	6.40	5.98	5.82	76,011	72,003	5.57	23.75	21.18	40,000						
Shoes	A-13	41,512	33,667	23.38	14.97	12.95	158,333	135,898	16.51	69.90	52.27	37,917	216	0	-	4,000	0	-
Bikes	A-14	18,858	19,312	(2.35)	11.79	12.07	74,312	75,889	(2.08)	46.45	47.43	28,000						
Drug	A-15	285,011	245,811	15.95	12.96	11.17	1,100,101	895,994	22.89	59.00	30.73	244,433	1,217	46	252	6,603	46	1,376
Dine	P-1	101,560	97,013	4.69	26.95	26.95	400,850	385,666	3.43	111.34	907.11	108,000	122	0	-	-	-	-

Remaining merchants report yearly.

- Tenant's sales have steadily increased in a specific pattern but have leveled off just below the breakpoint for percentage rent.
- The tenant paid percentage rent last year but is now reporting sales just below the breakpoint.
- The store is always busy, but the sales volume does not seem to match the activity.

The property manager should pay close attention to sales when the center has been remodeled, expanded, or has added a major tenant and the given tenant's sales do not increase. Even if nothing seems to be amiss, auditing a tenant who is close to the breakpoint may reveal enough additional sales to require paying percentage rents. Auditing the most vocal tenant in the center can produce excellent results because as other tenants find out about the audit they often take more care in reporting their sales.

Physical observation of a store can turn up questionable activities. One drugstore operator was observed diverting cash sales to a cigar box in a drawer below the cash register. It was also noted that some of the store's employees were stealing from the cigar box.

A useful technique in auditing tenants' sales is to send a letter to all tenants in the center announcing a routine audit of a percentage of all tenants' sales on a regular basis. This starts tenants thinking about the accuracy of their sales reports. In states with sales taxes, the property manager may ask for a copy of the tenant's state sales tax reports and compare them with the sales reports made to the center. If the tenant cannot explain any discrepancies, it is prudent to conduct an audit.

In deciding who should audit tenants, several factors should be considered. The property manager's accounting staff provides the greatest flexibility and is the least expensive. However, unless they are knowledgeable in retail accounting important items might be overlooked such as missing cash register tapes, missing invoices, imbalance between inventory and sales. In addition, the tenants might not take the staff accountant as seriously as they would an outside auditor.

The use of a large national CPA firm specializing in tenant audits has advantages if the tenant has many locations and the books are centrally located. Using a nationally recognized company also indicates the serious nature of the audit because these companies have the expertise to find clever manipulations or obscure errors. If a national company is used, however, it will often schedule the audit for its convenience rather than the shopping center's.

A local CPA firm generally knows more about the area's business climate, is more flexible in schedule, and can return for another look if the situation warrants.

Unless there is reason to believe there may be many auditing problems in a center, it is suggested that not more than 10% of the tenants should be audited in any given year because of the expense of conducting audits. Even though a tenant may be suspected of not accurately reporting sales, there are times when an audit is not indicated. If the tenant's actual sales are not likely to produce percentage rent, and the lease is expiring shortly, there is no point in spending money on an audit. The same holds true if the tenant is underreporting but sales are not likely to exceed the breakpoint. Also, as a practical matter, if the tenant and landlord are having ongoing problems concerning other matters, an audit can easily aggravate an already difficult situation.

The auditor should send a completed written report outlining any problems, the scope of the problem, and recommendations for prevention. As quickly as possible, the property manager should meet with the tenant, review the report, and make appropriate requests for any monies due and procedural changes to prevent future discrepancies.

If the discrepancies are large enough, or deliberate in nature, the manager may need to consider a possible lease default, checking with legal counsel before proceeding. Whatever the outcome of an audit, it is personal business between tenant and management and not a topic to discuss with other tenants or outsiders.

§ 4.10   THE MERCHANTS' ASSOCIATION

No matter how small the shopping center, it can always benefit from a good merchants' association. Although they do have problems, and many owners would just as soon not have the merchants organized for any reason, an effective association is worth any small problems it may cause.

The purpose of a merchants' association is to advertise and promote the center and to foster good business practices, thereby encouraging the public to shop at the center. It is not the purpose of the association to operate the common areas, oversee leasing efforts, supervise on-site employees, or set rents and center hours. It is critical for the long-range success of the association that these purposes be kept clearly in mind and that the property manager maintain sufficient control to see that the association does not deviate from its intended purpose.

When properly run, the merchants' association benefits all parties. The merchants gain the benefits of joint advertising and reach a larger audience for less individual investment, particularly when the landlord contributes toward their advertising efforts. The merchants' association also provides a forum to discuss good business practices and share common concerns.

The owner gains by having this forum to help guide the center in an effective merchandising program. The owner will see direct benefits in terms of high center sales, which produce additional percentage rents.

Even the community gains when a center has an organized promotional effort. The public becomes aware of merchandising events, sales, and community interest programs. Large centers put on shows and events with broad public appeal, often at little or no cost to the customer.

There are three traditional approaches to advertising and promoting shopping centers: merchants' association, promotional or marketing fund, and owner-sponsored program.

(a) TRADITIONAL MERCHANTS' ASSOCIATION

For many years, the traditional merchants' association was the choice of almost all shopping center owners. This association is set up by the center's owners or developers as a nonprofit corporation. Nonprofit status gives the association effective buying power because they do not pay taxes and, as a corporation, the association's liability is limited.

There are three approaches to membership. The most effective is mandatory membership in the association as a lease requirement. The second approach, and a weaker one, is a lease provision that requires a tenant to join the association if 80% of the merchants belong. The last and least effective is voluntary membership. In all cases, tenants who are members of the merchants' association are required to pay minimum dues set by the landlord and often are required to participate in a minimum number of advertising campaigns each year.

The association is governed by bylaws prepared by the owners and administered by a board of directors elected by the merchants. The owner or property manager always has a permanent seat on the board of directors and has veto rights over programs in the common areas that are deemed undesirable for the center.

Major tenants often refuse to join a merchants' association, causing a split between large and small tenants. This is one reason for setting the participation level at 80% rather than 100%. The major tenant is generally one of the largest advertisers in the center and does not want to be controlled by the smaller tenants.

The most effective merchants' associations allow one vote for each merchant rather than weighted votes for store size. Some centers allow for one vote per 1,000 square feet of leased space, which may seem equitable but can cause serious problems if five smaller tenants in favor of a program are voted down by a 14,000-square-foot tenant acting alone. Although the property manager can veto any activity in the common area because the landlord controls that space, the veto should be used only when absolutely necessary. Tenants will feel that they have no real say if they are continually overruled.

The association generally meets monthly to plan programs for the future and discuss items of mutual interest. In smaller centers, merchants may be reluctant to participate. Many are small business owners who already spend long hours at their stores. The property manager needs to encourage participation and show consistent support for the association without appearing to control it. For this reason, the manager would be ill advised to act as an officer of the association or to take on many of the administrative tasks.

In very large shopping centers, the merchants' association is administered by a full-time professional marketing director. The International Council of Shopping Centers (ICSC) has a program for training and certifying marketing directors. The professional designation is Certified Marketing Director (CMD), which recognizes a high level of experience and training in that field.

The bylaws of the association should give the landlord the right and obligation to hire, fire, and oversee the marketing director. The cost is generally part of the owner's contribution to the association, if the owner makes a contribution. The marketing director is not a member of the board but carries out most of the business of the association and serves as its executive director.

Because of limited funds available, promotions and advertising in smaller centers are handled in various ways. The center can hire a part-time marketing director who is paid an hourly or monthly fee, or it can retain the services of a public relations or marketing company.

The least effective approach, often used in neighborhood centers, is for the merchants to run the association. Although better than no effort at all, this arrangement does not work very well. Merchants lack experience in shopping center advertising and promotion and are already too busy to devote much time to further activities. However, when merchants are in charge, the property manager generally types and mails minutes, meeting notices, annual calendars, and other administrative materials so that the merchants can concentrate on advertising and promotion.

(b) PROMOTIONAL OR MARKETING FUND

A more recent innovation in handling shopping center advertising and promotions is the promotional or marketing fund. In the late 1970s, a number of regional and superregional malls set up an advertising or promotional fund in lieu of a merchants' association. This method has been fairly effective in large centers; in smaller centers it is not as workable since merchants may resent paying into a fund with little or no say in its disposition.

If the center has a promotional or marketing fund, the lease will require each merchant to contribute. The landlord then administers the fund in the best interests of the center. Although there is no association and no monthly merchant meetings, an advisory committee of merchants will provide guidance and ideas for the fund's administrator.

Merchants can also meet quarterly to review past promotions and suggest future events.

(c) OWNER-SPONSORED PROGRAM

The center's owner has the largest single investment in the center and must be concerned with its long-term success even if the merchants are not enthusiastic about advertising and promotions. The third approach is for the landlord to advertise and promote independently with no support or involvement from the merchants. In a problem property, where the merchants seem unwilling to cooperate in advertising and promotion, this may be the only alternative. In this case the landlord independently sets up a program, implements it, and pays the costs.

One effective advertising program is a weekly ad that uses a standard format but features different merchants or events each week. This keeps the center's name in front of the public and attracts prospective tenants. The landlord in this case arranges for centerwide sales, civic programs, or paid promotions throughout the year.

(d) DUES STRUCTURES

Dues vary widely but will generally range from 35¢ per square foot per year to as high as $2 per square foot per year in specialty centers. Neighborhood center dues usually range from 35¢ to 50¢ per square foot per year. Regional mall dues will vary from 50¢ to $1.50 per square foot per year.

The amount of dues is generally spelled out in the lease. Dues for major tenants are usually negotiated at a lower rate per square foot than for smaller tenants. It is not unusual for major tenants to have a permanent seat on the board of directors.

There should be an automatic mechanism for increasing dues over the term of the lease to keep up with inflation. This can be an agreed-upon annual increase—3% or 5%—or an increase tied to the consumer price index (CPI). The main idea is to protect the purchasing power of the association. The dues are paid either quarterly or monthly. In neighborhood centers they are administered by the association and in larger centers by the marketing director or owner. It a problem arises, it is the landlord's responsibility to collect the dues because they are a provision in the lease agreement.

(e) GRAND OPENING DUES

New or revitalized centers usually plan a grand opening or reopening. It is not unusual to require each merchant to contribute to the grand opening. Dues vary widely, but 25¢ to $1 per square foot is most common. This is generally paid at the time the lease is signed.

The grand opening is usually arranged by the owners because the merchants are not organized at that point to handle it themselves. Tenants who open up to one year after the grand opening are also assessed grand opening dues. Quite often the landlord will contribute the share allocated to vacancies. This amount is reimbursed when the space is leased.

(f) OWNER'S CONTRIBUTION

It is difficult to have an effective merchants' association or promotional/ marketing fund without a contribution by the owner, usually between 25% and 33% of what the association collects from the merchants. The contribution can be cash or "in kind," such as providing the services of a marketing director. Cash contributions should be timed to coincide with dues collection from tenants so that the association has a steady and predictable cash flow.

(g) USE OF FUNDS

Regional and superregional shopping centers have annual budgets that allow for television advertising, shuttle buses, ads in tourist publications, national celebrity visits, full-scale theme productions, extensive community involvement activities, direct mail brochures and Christmas decorations. Smaller centers cannot generate the income for such a broad approach and must use their funds carefully.

In both cases, the funds are generally allocated over the year on the basis of the center's sales distribution (see Exhibit 4.9). The largest expenditures are saved for November and December, when most centers will do 20% to 25% of the year's business. Most centers will allocate the least amount of funds for February because it is the lowest month in terms of sales. Those tenants who do well on Valentine's Day will be the exception. It becomes very important to prepare an annual budget and program to be sure the association is not out of funds in December when it needs them most (see Exhibit 4.10).

Small centers generally have direct-mail programs, coupon advertising, shared newspaper ads, Boy Scout or 4H activities, art shows, car shows, sidewalk sales, community promotions such as a used book collection for a library, and local celebrities. The National Research Bureau publishes a monthly report of effective shopping center advertising and promotion.

(h) STARTING A MERCHANTS' ASSOCIATION

The property manager should take the lead in starting the merchants' association. The first step is to review tenant leases and determine which

EXHIBIT 4.9

Month	Department Stores	Jewelry Stores	Men's and Boys' Wear	Women's Apparel and Accessory Stores	Gift Shops
Jan.	7.4	6.2	6.7	6.5	4.2
Feb.	7.4	6.6	6.0	6.2	4.9
Mar.	7.9	6.7	6.8	7.5	5.5
Apr.	7.9	6.2	7.1	7.9	5.8
May	8.3	7.3	7.7	8.0	6.8
June	8.1	6.6	7.9	7.2	6.6
July	8.3	6.1	7.0	7.5	5.7
Aug.	8.5	6.5	8.5	8.7	6.5
Sept.	8.1	6.5	7.6	8.3	6.1
Oct.	8.8	7.5	8.7	9.1	8.0
Nov.	8.8	9.4	10.0	9.3	13.2
Dec.	10.5	24.4	16.0	13.8	26.7
Total	100	100	100	100	100

Source: Shopping Center World

EXHIBIT 4.10

Simplified Small Center Annual Budget Merchants' Association

			Percent of Budget
Dues Income 58,000 feet × .35		$20,300.00	
Owners Contribution 30%		6,100.00	
Total Income		$26,400.00	100
January	January Sidewalk Sale & Clearance Ad & Banners	2,100.00	8
February	Valentines Day—Coloring Contest	2,300.00	9
March	No activity	-0-	-0-
April	Spring Mailer	500.00	3
May	Mother Day—Coloring Contest & Newspaper Ad	2,400.00	9
June	Summer Boat Show & Vacation Contest	2,200.00	8
July	Anniversary Promotion	3,000.00	11
August	Back to School Ad—Posters & Banners	3,200.00	12
September	Art Show—No cost to Association	-0-	-0-
October	October Clearance Direct Mailer and Window Signs	2,200.00	8
November & December	Christmas Decorations Christmas Kick Off Ad	8,500.00	32
Totals		$26,400.00	100

tenants are required to join. Next, select a date and a place to hold the first meeting. This can be a landlord-sponsored breakfast, lunch, or dinner meeting. Prior to the meeting, the property manager should call or visit each merchant to explain the purpose of the association and to invite the merchant personally to the first meeting. If the tenant's lease requires membership and dues, the property manager simply reminds the tenant of this obligation. If the lease is silent on the issue, the property manager must persuade the tenant to join on a voluntary basis.

The property manager prepares an agenda for the meeting that includes the following:

- The purpose of the merchants' association
- An income projection
- Statement on the landlord's role as major dues payer with the right to veto activities in the common area
- Suggested activities
- Suggested committees
- Nomination of officers.

The manager then chairs the first meeting, making sure to limit discussion to the subjects on the agenda. If issues not included on the agenda are raised, the property manager must be able to deal with them; unresolved items can destroy a merchants' association before it even gets off the ground.

(i) POTENTIAL PROBLEMS

The following are some typical problems that can beset a merchants' association meeting. *The meeting becomes a gripe session.* The main fear landlords have of merchants' associations is that meetings will turn into gripe sessions. Tenants will complain that the common area maintenance charges are too high, or the parking lot sweeper is doing a poor job, or the landlord should be spending time leasing the vacancies and not in a merchants' meeting. The property manager should not allow these unrelated issues to be discussed at a merchants' association meeting.

The manager can prevent this by clarifying the purpose of the merchants' association and stating at the outset that questions or discussions that are not related to advertising or promotion will not be allowed. The property manager should indicate willingness to meet with merchants at any other time either at the property manager's office or at the merchants' store to discuss issues related to the merchant or the shopping center. If a tenant insists on discussing an unrelated item, the property manager should firmly but politely inform the tenant that the matter will be discussed at a later date and continue with the meeting. The manager can state that he or she will not bring up landlord's concerns, such as, delinquent rent or other lease violations and the tenant's shouldn't bring up their problems with the landlord during these meetings.

"Why should I pay dues when the major tenants don't?" Some major tenants refuse to belong to the merchants' association, and seldom is the landlord in a strong enough position during lease negotiations to include mandatory membership in the major's lease. The property manager should inform the small shop merchant that the landlord was unable to persuade the major to join the association and remind the tenant that the major tenant spends millions of dollars on advertising and is the main traffic draw to the center. The manager also should let the tenant know that he or she will continue to encourage the major tenant to join on a voluntary basis. As a compromise, the manager may be able to solicit the major tenant's participation by contributing to specific events such as Christmas decorations or turkeys for a giveaway the week before Thanksgiving.

"Why should I be involved when my neighbor never attends a meeting?" A simple and direct reply from the property manager is, "Why should a few tenants who either do not care or do not have the time to participate cause the rest of us to lose the benefits of working together and the benefits of the merchants' association?"

"We're tired of doing all the work." As with all organizations, a few members do most of the work. The property manager needs to encourage participation from a sufficient number of merchants so that there is a regular change of officers and committee chairpersons. Two or three active committees will relieve the board of much work and provide a training place for future board members. If the workload is too heavy for a few merchants, the small center's association could hire either an advertising agency or a person to work part time as the marketing director.

"The dues are too high." Inform tenants that they will receive a return in advertising and promotional benefits far greater than their individual dues. By combining the tenants' dues and the contribution of the landlord, the association can purchase more advertising and promotional activities than the tenants could afford individually. In addition, advertising rates for the association are usually lower than the tenant could purchase individually.

"A few merchants run the association." This statement is usually overcome by inviting the tenant to join or chair a committee or by having the tenant nominated to the board of directors.

(j) COMMUNICATING WITH MERCHANTS

It is important that the property manager and the shopping center marketing director communicate regularly with the merchants to keep them informed on upcoming events. A monthly newsletter, usually only a few pages in length, informs the merchants about new retailers in the center, new managers, the shopping center sales comparisons by category, the leading store in each category, upcoming events, copy deadlines, and miscellaneous information about the shopping center and merchants. These newsletters usually have catchy names such as "Mall Talk" or "S'mall Talk," and merchants are encouraged to submit information about their stores and their employees.

Larger shopping centers develop marketing calendars listing the advertising and promotional events through the year. The calendar gives the dates of each event, a brief description of each, deadlines for ad copy, and a projected budget for each event.

The merchants' association handbook includes a directory with phone numbers of all the stores and the name of their managers; shopping center hours; employee parking information; meeting dates of the merchants' association; and information on the community booth, community room, information booth, and the center's gift certificate program. The handbook also includes a marketing plan that outlines the association's objectives, strategy, and tactics. The marketing plan exemplifies the shopping center's primary, secondary, and tertiary trade areas and describes the demographics of each. It explains the marketing budget and analyzes income and expenses in a monthly breakdown. The handbook is an excellent addition to the leasing package because it shows the prospective tenant the aggressive advertising and promotional program of the center. Smaller shopping centers can scale down the handbook to suit their particular needs.

An advertising session informs the merchants of media publishing dates and media contacts at the newspaper and radio station. It may list all upcoming events and the association's plans for supporting the events with print or electronic media advertising.

§ 4.11   LANDLORD-TENANT RELATIONS

Landlord-tenant relations are more critical in the shopping center than most other types of properties. In a shopping center the property manager must be concerned with the best tenant mix and within that mix must find the best operator for each category of merchant. The property manager then must make every effort to create an environment where the tenant can maximize their sales.

The landlord's approach to leasing, management, and maintenance will have a direct impact on the tenant. Tenants often overstate that impact and use it as an excuse for nonperformance of the lease. Hence, a relationship with tenants should be established very early. It is of the utmost importance that tenants clearly understand their obligations and charges, the landlord's obligations, the purpose of each tenant's expense, and which items are the landlord's expenses. The lease documents, especially the construction exhibits, should spell out who is responsible for what.

One area that can cause tenant relations problems is the condition of the space when it is turned over to the tenant. Several arrangements are possible in the construction of the premises: the tenant provides all improvements in a pad location; the tenant takes the existing premises "as is"; the landlord completes the space except for floor covering and interior partitions; the landlord provides a turn-key store that has all improvements except trade fixtures and interior decor. The more precise the lease and construction exhibits, the less likely there will be disputes in the future.

Tenants are almost always responsible for maintaining the premises, which generally includes exterior doors, glass, and utility lines serving the premises even if they are outside the tenant's premises. Pad tenants will most likely handle their own roof repairs. In-line tenants will pay for their share of roof repairs, but the landlord is responsible for the work. In some leases the landlord repairs the roof at his or her own expense.

Once the lease is signed, the leasing agent should introduce the tenant to the property or center manager. This person should be prepared to explain the tenant's next steps and provide guidance where necessary, advising the tenant of critical construction and grand opening information. To protect tenants from unpleasant surprises, as part of the introductory program they should receive a statement showing their rents and tenant charges (i.e., common area maintenance, taxes, insurance, and merchants' association or marketing fund dues), and information on payment procedures. This information can be included in a welcoming booklet or tenant information kit. This information can be mailed, but delivering it in person gives the manager and the tenant an opportunity to get acquainted and begin their relationship. Tenants also appreciate a gift and congratulations from the landlord when their store is opened. Just before the tenant opens for business, the manager should conduct a walk-through of the premises. This shows the tenant that the owner or manager cares, and it allows them to agree on any work to be completed. Obviously, at that point it is in everybody's best interest to have any necessary work done as quickly as possible.

Each retail tenant should be visited at least once a month. The purpose of the visit is to establish communication, so the manager must refrain from using this time to complain about late rents, poor sales, or parking violations. The visit should be short; if the tenant is busy with a customer, a nod and a wave will suffice.

A common complaint from tenants is that they only see the property manager when something is wrong. When it is necessary for the manager to bring an infraction or default to the tenant's attention, the tenant should be given the benefit of the doubt, at least for the first time. Tenants may not have understood the situation, or perhaps circumstances were beyond their control.

A clause in the lease prohibiting certain actions should not be stated as the reason for a rule. Rather, tenants should be informed of the business reasons underlying the lease clauses. For example, if the lease does not allow tenants to park in front of their store, referring to the employee parking clause is generally not productive. It is more beneficial to tell tenants that the reason for employee parking requirements is to allow two to four customers per hour the convenience of close-in parking.

Tenants often ask property managers for favors above and beyond the landlord lease requirements. There is no reason not to be understanding and sympathetic. Rather than responding with a flat no or chastising the tenant for asking more than the lease agreement calls for, the manager should reply sympathetically: "I'm sorry but I cannot do what you ask." If the manager decides to grant the request because it is an important tenant or a fair request, the tone should be sincere and gracious. Legitimate tenant requests should be acted on promptly. When complaints are ignored, tenants build up resentment that the landlord does not care or that they are not important. The property manager should either deny the request in a timely fashion or perform the work promptly.

All tenant billings should have sufficient detail to assure tenants that their billing is in accordance with the lease. Tenants should be given courteous, complete, and accurate answers to specific questions. Many local small shop tenants, in particular, sign leases with little real understanding of what they are signing. A complex common area billing is routine to the sophisticated manager, and it is easy to become impatient with tenants who appear to be questioning not only the billing itself, but the property manager's honesty and integrity. Patience and an understanding of the tenant's position will serve the property manager in this situation than impatience.

When disputes arise between tenants, especially if they are related to lease requirements, the property manager should step in to mediate the dispute. Feuding tenants have a way of polarizing the other tenants, and part of that feud often winds up being antimanagement.

Finally, the manager should avoid communicating by sending "Dear Tenant" letters. Tenants like to think they are respected as successful business people as well they should be. If group letters must be sent, address them to "All Merchants" or, even better, to individual operators.

The tenant is the landlord's customer and should be treated as such. Every effort should be made to maintain an open businesslike communication with all tenants all of the time. Even when a tenant is being difficult, it is in the manager's best long-term interest to stay cool and rational and move any disagreements in a positive direction.

§ 4.12 TENANT REPAIRS

Most modern shopping center leases require tenants to maintain their premises at their own expense. It is not advisable to perform repairs that the tenants are responsible for and bill them back to the tenant. When this is done, the property manager often winds up defending costs or procedures. There are exceptions, however. Quite often it is desirable to have one contractor or owner's employee maintain the roof air conditioners to be sure that they are properly maintained and to prevent excess traffic on the roof. If possible, the landlord should control the maintenance work but have the contractor bill the tenants directly.

If the landlord provides the services through his or her staff, a profit is allowable, but the total cost of the service should be competitive in the marketplace, and the tenant is entitled to know the basis of the billings. Quite often the problems mentioned above far exceed the potential profits.

If general repairs are provided to the tenants for a fee, it is suggested that all work be performed on the basis of a written request by the tenant. The billing should be detailed and reflect the original request. If work is required over and above the original request, it should be discussed with the tenant before proceeding and the tenant should authorize in writing the additional work.

§ 4.13 FINANCIALLY TROUBLED RETAIL TENANTS

When merchants experience problems, the shopping center experiences problems. Merchant failures can give a shopping center a negative image among both existing and potential tenants, as well as customers. When tenant failures occur in conjunction with a soft leasing market, shopping centers are in serious trouble. Faced with the potential deterioration of a shopping center, a property manager needs to search for practical short-term solutions that will enable the shopping center to endure this difficult economic period. Solutions to this problem can be both monetary and nonmonetary assistance to the financially troubled tenant.

The most obvious symptom of potential failure is late rent payment, but earlier indications may be obtained by monitoring a tenant's sales. The property manager should compare the tenant's sales with national averages found in *Dollars and Cents of Shopping Centers*. If the tenant's sales are appreciably below the national averages, the tenant is probably operating the business at a loss. The tenant's sales should also be compared with prior periods to determine sales trends. If the sales are consistently declining, the tenant either now or in the near future will experience financial difficulties.

Other symptoms of potential tenant failure are reductions in inventory, store hours, staffing, advertising, and a lower merchandise turnover. When tenants have financial problems, they may be unable to purchase new inventory. Low inventory or old inventory that is not selling will continue the downward sales spiral. Tenants may respond to financial difficulties by attempting to reduce operating expenses. A reduction in store hours, staffing, and advertising generate immediate cost savings but result in the continuing sales decline.

A more effective means of monitoring a tenants' operations is to develop a good rapport with tenants so that they will inform the manager of potential problems.

The property manager must analyze the impact of various factors on the shopping center before deciding whether to offer monetary relief to a tenant. The most important consideration is the condition of the leasing market. Are there existing vacancies and, if so, how long will it take to lease them? If any tenants fail, how long will it take to re-lease their space? In estimating the time it will take to re-lease a space, the space in question should be analyzed in terms of its desirability; the adjacent tenants; visibility from common areas and fronting streets; and its size, configuration, and location. The property manager must also know the local retail leasing market.

Once the vacancy period for the space has been estimated, the property manager must consider what effect a vacancy might have on the tenant mix of the shopping center. Will the shopping center's ability to draw customers be significantly weakened if a tenant moves out? What effect would one tenant failure, or several tenant failures, have on the leasing program? In a soft leasing market it is difficult to find replacement tenants, and that difficulty is compounded when potential tenants notice vacancies and tenant failures in a center. A further consideration: Is the center developing a reputation among the merchants in the community as a place where a retailer is doomed?

Another consideration is the cost of replacing a tenant, which includes: loss of rent, rental concessions in the form of free rent or tenant allowances, remodeling costs, leasing commissions, possible legal fees, and possible lower percentage rents from other tenants resulting from reduced sales of merchants affected by the vacancy. Still another consideration is the financial position of the shopping center. At least partial rent payment may be essential for the normal operations of the shopping center.

If the property manager determines that the cost to replace the troubled tenant is too high, or if the tenant deserves assistance because of prior contributions to the shopping center, a temporary rent relief program should be considered.

(a) RENT RELIEF

Rent relief is designed to help a tenant overcome financial difficulty. Commonly used rent relief programs are: deferred rent, percentage rent only, waived rent, and use of security deposit.

Deferred Rent

The merchant's current rent and an agreed-upon amount of future rent are reduced, and repayment is deferred to a later date. For example, a tenant's rent might be reduced from $1,000 per month to $400 per month for six months, then increased by $600 per month for six months later in the lease term. Delinquent rent can also be deferred to a later date. Many property managers prefer not to charge interest on the deferred rent because it hinders the tenant's recovery.

Percentage Rent Only

The tenant's minimum base rent is eliminated for a specific period, and monthly rental payments are based on a percentage of the tenant's sales. The percentage used can be either a rate already established in the lease or a renegotiated rate, which generally is higher.

Waived Rent

Past, present, or future rent is waived entirely. All or a portion of each month's rent for a period of time may be waived.

Use of Security Deposit

All or a portion of the security deposit may be applied either to rent owed or future rent. Little is sacrificed with this method because the security deposit would be applied to delinquent rent or future rents if the tenant vacated before the lease expired. A condition of a rent relief program may be that the tenant spends a percentage of the waived or deferred rent on additional advertising or inventory.

When rent relief is granted to a tenant, the property manager is always concerned that the tenant will inform all the other tenants of the landlord's assistance and the other tenants will seek a similar program.

Generally, most tenants are not going to tell their neighboring merchants that their sales are so poor that the landlord is granting them rent relief for their survival. Nevertheless, if the tenant does talk, and the property manager receives other requests for assistance, the other tenants should be informed that each tenant's situation is analyzed individually. The property manager and the landlord are the sole arbiters in granting a tenant's request.

When offering a rental concession to an existing tenant, a property manager can reopen lease negotiations. The lease may have one or more clauses detrimental to the shopping center, and the offer of rent relief can be contingent upon the tenant's agreeing to modify or eliminate these clauses.

(b) LEASE CLAUSES IN RENTAL CONCESSIONS

Lease clauses that might be revised or eliminated include:

- *Options.* Either eliminate the option or tie the rental rate in the option period to the adjustment in the consumer price index or other predetermined increase.
- *Restrictions.* Eliminate the provision allowing tenants to approve remodeling or expansion plans of the center.
- *Exclusive.* The tenant's lease may prohibit similar uses within the shopping center. Such restrictions should be eliminated.
- *Use.* It may be desirable to place more restrictions on the tenant's use.
- *Assignment/subletting.* Assignment or subletting should be subject to the landlord's prior written approval.
- *Merchants' association.* Membership in the merchants' association or contribution to the marketing fund should be mandatory.
- *Signage.* Conformance to the shopping center's sign criteria should be required.
- *Store hours.* The tenant should be required to maintain the same business hours as the rest of the shopping center.
- *Cancellation clause.* The landlord may obtain the right to cancel the lease if the tenant's sales do not meet or exceed an agreed-upon minimum amount.

An amendment to the lease is required to formalize any modifications. If a portion of the deferred rental payment is due after the lease expires, the tenant should sign a promissory note for this amount.

Offering a tenant rent relief may be a distasteful solution to some owners or property managers, but sometimes it is the only way to save a shopping center's most valuable asset—its tenants.

(c) NONMONETARY ASSISTANCE

Nonmonetary programs can be an alternative to monetary relief or used in conjunction with the rent relief program. The first consideration is, how can the property manager help the tenant reduce operating expenses without affecting sales? Reducing the tenant's square footage will reduce base rent, pro rata tenant charges, utility costs, and possibly the size of the tenant's staff. If the tenant's sales do not depend on walk-by traffic, the tenant could be relocated to a less desirable area of the center where the rent is lower. This solution is practical only if the tenant's fixturization costs are nominal. A hair salon could not afford to relocate because of the expense of the plumbing for its fixtures, but a shoe repair store could easily relocate.

It may be beneficial to expand the tenant's use clause. If the tenant is the only restaurant in the center, the tenant's use clause could be broadened to include other food-related items. The property manager must be certain, however, that this will not have a negative effect on the tenant mix of the shopping center or on the sales of other tenants.

If the tenant's problem stems primarily from mismanagement, a new operator may be able to turn the business around. Thus, permitting a lease assignment may be a simple solution.

Many small merchants do not have strong backgrounds in retailing and do not have the opportunity to seek professional retailing instruction. Consequently, the merchant's employees do not usually receive the necessary sales training. The property manager should consider asking the shopping center owner to hire a retail consultant to provide seminars and individual consultations for tenants and their employees. These programs should not only be motivational training sessions, but also provide insight into the development of a merchandising plan, markdown policies, in-store signage, displays, budgeting, selling techniques, and other important retailing concepts and principles. The tenants benefit by acquiring valuable retailing techniques, and their employees receive professional sales training.

Most owners and managers who have provided this service to their tenants consider the expense an investment in the financial strength of the center. Through strong sales they can expect higher percentage rent and fewer tenant failures.

(d) LEASE TERMINATION

When the probability of a tenant's recovering from financial problems is slim, even though the landlord has assisted with either rent relief or nonmonetary assistance or a combination of the two, it may be best to seek a termination of the lease. Terminating the lease enables the property manager to regain possession of the premises and place the space back on the market. The lease can be terminated by eviction or mutual consent.

A mutual lease termination may be offered to the tenant for financial consideration. The property manager should request a current financial statement from the tenant before agreeing to the lease cancellation. If the tenant is a corporation, and the lease has personal guarantees, a financial statement should be requested of the corporation and the guarantors. If both party's financial statements are weak, a mutual cancellation with either no cancellation payment or a nominal payment to the landlord would be most practical.

One school of thought says that it is fruitless to incur the cost of taking a tenant to court for back or future rent if the tenant has no assets. Another approach is to file a judgment and wait for the day when the tenant gains financial stability. If the tenant's financial statement is healthy, the property manager can either negotiate a lease buy-out on the part of the tenant or enforce the lease, including the payment of rent and other tenant charges, until the space is re-leased. This is an area in which it is impossible to establish a standard operating procedure. Each case must be analyzed individually and with flexibility.

Although rent relief is not advocated by all property managers, it offers a temporary solution to an immediate problem. In fact, in some cases rent relief may be the only solution. But if problems are spotted early enough, less drastic solutions may be employed effectively.

§ 4.14   POTENTIAL PROBLEM TENANTS

Customers will avoid a shopping center that they find distasteful. Shoppers can be offended by the type of merchandise or service provided, and the actions of one merchant in the shopping center can disrupt another merchant's business. Customers can also be frightened by the patrons of a particular store or loiterers in the mall or parking lot. The property manager should avoid leasing to tenants who might cause problems, or structure the tenant's lease to prevent the problems from occurring, or provide the landlord with the right to cancel the lease if the problem persists.

Several uses can create problems. The property manager should carefully evaluate whether or not these uses should be included in the center's tenant mix. If they are included, the manager should have the above-mentioned lease restrictions to alleviate potential problems. Following is a list of tenants that can cause problems for a shopping center along with suggested lease modifications to alleviate these problems.

(a) VIDEO ARCADES

Few property managers take a middle ground regarding this use; they either hate video arcades or they find them to be an acceptable use in a shopping center. Astute managers recognize that this tenant will pay top dollar for a space, with the potential for percentage rent.

Video arcades present few problems when they are located in an enclosed mall and must close when the shopping center closes. The video arcade in an enclosed mall does not face onto the parking lot, and young people do not have the opportunity to hang out in front of the arcade or in the parking lot in front of the arcade. Also, most malls have security guards who handle loiterers. Video arcade problems usually arise in open centers, particularly neighborhood and community centers.

The biggest potential problems with video arcades are excessive noise and unruly teenagers. The lease should call for additional insulation, especially above the ceiling and extending to the roof, to minimize the transfer of noise from the video machines to adjacent tenants. One center in the Northwest was sued by a craft merchant adjacent to a video arcade who claimed that the video arcade noise prevented the store from holding craft classes and thus reduced its sales and profits. The noise problem can be alleviated by stating that the tenant is required to take the necessary action to prevent noise from carrying over to the neighboring tenant spaces. If the tenant refuses to correct this problem, the lease should allow the landlord the right to make the corrections and bill the tenant for the cost of the work.

The potential problem with unruly teenagers and preteens also can be addressed in the lease by stipulating that an adult attendant must be on site during store hours and that the store must close at a specific time. The lease can state that at the request of the landlord the tenant will hire a uniformed security guard at the tenant's expense. The ultimate control the landlord can have is the right to cancel the lease if the tenant is unable to correct the problem within a specific period of time.

(b) VIDEO STORES

The popularity of the VCR in the early 1980s has created a proliferation of video stores throughout the United States. Most of these video stores opened in neighborhood shopping centers and are not a source of problems, but some customers might be offended by the explicit promotional posters and photos on X-rated videotape boxes. To prevent this potential problem, the property manager can state in the lease that the X-rated tapes will be placed in the rear of the store and not be visible from the storefront.

(c) TAVERNS

Opinions are mixed on whether taverns should be in a shopping center. Some of the major tenants' leases in neighborhood and community centers either restrict taverns from the shopping center or restrict their location within a specific distance from the major tenant's premises. The concern with the tavern in a shopping center is the possibility of rowdy behavior in the parking lot and the negative image that this will create for the shopping center. Another concern is the littering of beer bottles and other trash in the shopping center late at night and into the early morning. This can be a serious problem if the shopping center is not swept daily and the litter accumulates in the parking lot. If the property manager decides to enter into a lease with a tavern, the lease restrictions may require the tavern to have a uniformed security officer on site during specific hours at the request of the landlord.

A further concern with taverns is the possibility of the tavern converting to a topless bar. Although this is unlikely, if it did occur it would have a tremendous negative impact on the center and its image. To prevent this from happening, the lease should restrict the type of live entertainment allowed on the premises. The property manager may find it prudent to seek an alternative use for a large space rather than leasing to a tavern.

(d) RECORD SHOPS AND HEAD SHOPS

Record shops are an acceptable use in a shopping center and a positive addition to a shopping center's tenant mix. The concern with a record shop is that the merchant might sell drug paraphernalia usually found in a head shop. To prevent a record shop from selling such items, the use clause should be very specific on which items can be sold. It should not state that the tenant may sell records, tapes, and "other related items or accessories," thus leaving the related items or accessories up for debate.

(e) ADULT GIFT STORES

In the early 1980s a number of adult gift stores opened throughout the United States. These stores sell a combination of lingerie, adult cards, and adult gifts and may generate unpleasant controversy in the community. If adult stores are allowed in a shopping center, the property manager may want to specify in the lease that the X-rated materials and adult gifts be displayed in the back of the store.

(f) AUTOMOBILE SERVICE

Another use that became very popular in the early 1980s is instant oil and lube service for automobiles. These uses are usually freestanding buildings where an automobile is lubed and the oil changed while the owner waits. The operators of most of these establishments are generally very professional, and their buildings are attractive and well maintained. A concern might be the number of cars that are parked in the shopping center to be serviced for pickup later in the day. The lease may restrict the number of cars that the operator can place in the shopping center.

(g) SERVICE STATIONS

Service stations have always been an acceptable pad use for shopping centers. The concern with service stations is the number of cars that are parked in the lot and the cleanliness of the service station. These items should be addressed in the tenant's lease.

(h) OFFICES

More and more office users are finding shopping centers an attractive alternative to an office building. The shopping center provides the office user with good exposure, comparable or lower rental rates than office buildings, more amenities, and free and abundant parking. The concern of the property manager is the long-term parking requirement of office users. Some major tenant leases will restrict office uses within a specific distance of their premises. The lease for the office user should designate the areas where employees may park.

(i) HAIR SALONS

Hair salons are found in most shopping centers. The problem that can arise with this use is the odor from the permanent wave solution that can filter into the adjacent tenant's space. The lease should require the tenant to have proper ventilation and address the maintenance of the HVAC unit.

(j) PET STORES

Pet stores are another acceptable use in all shopping centers. The concern with this use is unpleasant odors. The tenant must keep the store's cages and grooming area clean and have proper ventilation.

Most tenants do not create a problem for the customers or adjacent tenants. When a problem does arise, it can ruin a shopping center's image and create havoc with the other tenants and take a long time to correct. The property manager can alleviate potential problems by anticipating these concerns and addressing them in the tenant's lease. The placement of a pet store, along with a hair salon, can create problems. These stores should not be located next to a food operator.

§ 4.15   MERCHANDISING VACANT SPACES

A shopping center's vacancies should be merchandised to alleviate their negative impact on the customers, the merchants, and potential tenants. Vacancies in a shopping center are unlighted and give the appearance of a blank wall instead of a prospering business with interesting displays and activities. Vacancies also create pocket areas of little or no traffic and cause tenants in nearby spaces to lose some of the benefits of the shopping center environment. This loss is multiplied with each additional vacant space.

These vacancies can be viewed as an opportunity to help existing tenants merchandise their stores and to create goodwill in the community. These goals can be accomplished at very little expense.

The property manager should consider offering the vacant space or spaces to merchants in the center to display their merchandise. The merchants can decorate the show windows and have their merchandise displayed in another area of the shopping center. This offer is contingent upon the tenant's moving out of the vacancy on short notice, keeping the premises clean, abiding by the landlord's sign criteria, and relieving the landlord of all responsibility for missing or stolen items. The merchant should enter into a license agreement covering these and other obligations. The merchant should be encouraged not to display expensive items that are likely targets for theft. The selection of tenants to display their merchandise in the vacancies is based on which tenants can best utilize the space, which tenants need the most assistance, and the location of the tenant's space in relationship to the vacancy. Tenants may be offered the space on a rotating basis or on a longer term use.

(a)   COMMUNITY'S USE OF VACANT SPACE

An alternative to merchandising vacant spaces is to allow community groups the opportunity to use the vacancies. If the spaces are anticipated to be vacant for a short period, they can be offered to groups for a specific short-term purpose such as a haunted house the week before

Halloween, a white elephant sale, a collection area for toys at Christmas, or a dropoff point for a food drive. Organizations may use the space for their membership drive or to register children for sporting activities, such as Little League sign-ups. Other organizations such as the Girl Scouts, Boy Scouts, and the 4-H clubs can use the vacancies to display their activities and promote their organizations.

If the center is in an economically depressed area or is a distressed center with vacancies anticipated for an extended period, these spaces may be offered to community organizations on a long-term basis. Space may be offered to the community college or the high school adult education program for a classroom or to the chamber of commerce for a temporary office. The property manager should have the right to relocate these organizations to another vacancy or to terminate the use with sufficient notice to enable the organization to either complete its function or find another location.

Another use is to convert a vacancy into a community room. Even if the shopping center already has a community room, a second community room may be considered if demand justifies its use. If the community room is a temporary use, the property manager should not allow organizations to reserve the room more than two months in advance. Community groups should also enter into a license agreement for the use of the vacancy.

(b) CHARGING FOR VACANT SPACE

The property manager must decide whether to charge for the use of the vacancy. When the space is offered to community groups it should be provided at no charge. If the community group will use the space on a long-term basis, the group should be responsible for the utility costs and the costs to maintain the heating, ventilating, and air-conditioning unit. When tenants use the space to display their merchandise, the space should be provided free of all charges.

How will prospective tenants know that the vacancies are available to lease when they are temporarily occupied? This concern can be alleviated by maintaining a For Lease sign in front of the shopping center and a small For Lease sign located on the premises where it doesn't detract from the window display. Most prospective tenants are able to distinguish a permanent user from a temporary user.

If the vacancies are spaces that have never been occupied, the property manager must weigh the cost to finish these spaces against the benefits mentioned above. The cost to finish vacancies in a regional mall can be considerable. Many regional malls lease their spaces in an almost completely unfinished condition. The space is turned over to the tenant with a dirt floor, no ceilings, demising walls, store fronts, sprinkler system, or heating, ventilating, and air-conditioning duct work. If the regional mall has a high percentage of vacancies, the manager should consider selecting spaces in key areas of the mall that will have a severe negative impact on the mall if they remain vacant. Allowing long-term temporary tenants the right to occupy vacant space may be necessary to create a flow of traffic to areas of the mall that have few merchants. The landlord must reserve the right to relocate the temporary tenant.

There are no industry standards for finishing out spaces in neighborhood centers. One extreme is to turn space over to the tenants in the condition described above. The other extreme is for the landlord to build out, or finish, the space except for the floor covering and wall treatment. In between these extremes are countless ways to finish the tenant premises. If the spaces are built out in a near complete state, the property manager has little to do to turn the space over to a temporary tenant. If the use is for a short term or the space is being used by an existing tenant, the property manager should paint the walls. The user can be required to build the display platform. If the use is for a longer term, the user may be required to paint the walls and provide flooring. When the property manager incurs the expense to finish the space, the improvements may enhance the marketability of the space, and the improvement costs may be recaptured by leasing the space sooner than projected.

§ 4.16   SEMINARS FOR TENANTS

The success of a shopping center is dependent upon the success of its tenants. A center's base rent is in part determined by the potential or actual sales volume of the tenants. A shopping center in which most tenants' sales volume greatly exceeds the national average can justify charging a higher base rent than a shopping center in which the tenants' sales are at or below the national average.

The higher the tenants' sales volume, the higher the rental rates that can be achieved on vacancies and during lease renewals. When a tenant exceeds the breakpoint for paying percentage rent, additional rent in the form of percentage rent or overage rent will be paid. And when tenants' sales are stronger, there is less likelihood of tenant failure. Costs associated with tenant failure are lost rent, commission expense, and marketing costs.

Tenant failures are a major concern of the property manager because they give the shopping center a reputation that businesses cannot be successful in that location. Statistics prove that the most likely tenant to fail is the small, independent business, with the first year being the most critical period. According to Dunn & Bradstreet, more than half of the approximately 57,000 businesses that failed in 1985 had been operating for less than six years. Twenty-nine percent of the failures occurred in the business's first two years. During the next three years, 28% of these businesses failed. Only 20% of the failures occurred after the business's tenth year.

The property manager can help tenants maximize their sales by sponsoring retailing seminars designed to improve their business and merchandising skills and improve their sales volume. Such programs are of particular importance in distressed centers and in areas with a weak economy.

The seminar program should be designed around the needs of the shopping center tenants. Those who need the most assistance are the local "mom and pop" retailers who, unlike managers of regional and national chain stores, do not have the opportunity to attend professional retailing seminars. They also do not have the retailing expertise of a large, sophisticated chain.

The property manager can offer many seminars to tenants free of charge. Through business contacts the property manager often can tap into valuable community resources. For example, the local police department can present information on shoplifting. The Small Business Administration (SBA) can provide speakers on specific topics ranging from budgeting to market research, and lenders are generally willing to present seminars on cash management and financing. The display manager of a department store may be willing to teach a seminar on window displays. A professor from the local university might speak on motivational sales training. The cost of these one- to two-hour seminars is nominal.

Retail consultants can present classes on specific retailing subjects and meet with the merchants on an individual basis. These consultant's fees are usually paid by the landlord. Occasionally the merchants' association will share the expense, but usually the association's budget cannot afford this expense. The merchants are never charged for the general seminar or the individual sessions with the consultant. If the tenant requests additional individual consulting, it is at the tenant's expense.

Topics for group sessions might include: in-store promotions, visual merchandise, personnel management, retail salesmanship, customer policies, return policies, sales forecasting, inventory planning, open-to-buy, and stock pricing.

Even though the retail program is free to the merchant, many merchants need to be convinced to attend. Often small retailers have limited time available, do not believe the program will be worthwhile or, even worse, believe that they know all there is to know about their business. The seminar should be publicized to all merchants; a bulletin with pertinent information will be a first step toward gaining their interest. The property manager should then meet with each merchant to discuss the program and the benefits of participating in it. The manager should outline the program, provide the credentials of the instructors, and explain how the program worked at other shopping centers. If the property manager is assisting a tenant with a rent deferment program, financial assistance should be contingent upon the tenant's participation in the program.

The seminars should be held either in the morning, before the stores open, or in the evening. Two hours per session is the maximum length. The seminars should be held on site in a vacancy, the community room, or the conference room of a major tenant. Light refreshments should be provided at each class.

Advisors to Business Management (ABM) in Long Beach, California, has developed a program of successful seminars for merchants. ABM will conduct three two-hour seminars and will meet individually with merchants for a two-hour session. Most chain stores do not participate in individual consulting sessions, but many send representatives to the seminars.

The property manager should attend the seminars and the individual consulting sessions to gain an understanding of retailing and its problems, to learn to distinguish a poor tenant from a good one, and to gain insight into an individual tenant's strengths and weaknesses.

A resource library on retailing can be developed at the property management company's office or at the shopping center's on-site management office. The Small Business Administration and many leading banks have publications, pamphlets, and books for the small business. Examples are Bank of America's series called *The Small Business Reporter* and the National Retail Merchant Association's outstanding publications on retailing. ICSC publishes *The Retail Challenge Tips For Shopping Center Retailers*. A quarterly newsletter that many shopping center owners provide to their tenants.

Subscribing to the leading retail trade journals is not only an excellent way to collect information for the library, but also a way for the property manager to stay abreast of current trends in retailing. Included among these publications are *Nation's Restaurant News*, and *Chain Store Age Executive*, published by Lebhar-Friedman, Inc.; *Shopping Centers Today*, published by International Council of Shopping Centers; *Shopping Center World*, published by Communication Channels, Inc.; *Fairchild's Book and Visuals*, Fairchild Publications; Newspaper Advertising Bureau, Inc., for newspaper advertising plan book; Merrill Lynch's *How to Read a Financial Report;* NCR Corporation, Customer and Support Education, for its education publications catalog. Retailing consulting firms such as Robert Morris Company in Cleveland provide operating statement analysis, and Retail Merchandising Services Automation in Riverside, California, provides merchandising information systems for retailers.

Retail seminars can be used as a marketing tool in the shopping center leasing program. These educational opportunities tell prospective tenants that the manager and the landlord are concerned about the success of the tenants and are willing to take the lead in offering unique programs for them. The landlord should view the retail seminar program as an investment that will pay great dividends by helping tenants become better retailers who have higher sales and pay greater percentage rent.

§ 4.17 COMMUNITY SERVICES

(a) COMMUNITY ROOM

A community room gives the shopping center a chance to provide a service to the community, to promote positive public relations, to generate additional traffic to the center, and in some situations to merchandise a vacancy. It is a large room, sometimes a converted vacant space, that is offered as a meeting place at no charge to community groups and for a small fee to businesses. Community rooms are usually found in community or regional centers. If they are designed within the mall, they are located in an area that would be difficult or impossible to lease, and away from the storefronts and traffic areas. They are furnished with folding chairs, long folding tables, and a wall writing board. The facility is promoted through news releases to the media, direct mail invitations to community groups, information provided to merchants, and brief statements regarding the facility in the shopping center's advertisements.

The property manager must develop guidelines for the use of the community room. The guidelines have two purposes: to allow maximum use by the greatest number of organizations, and to maintain control over all aspects of the room's use. The guidelines will limit the times a group can schedule the room to prevent some groups from monopolizing it. A group might be allowed to reserve the room at least seven days but no more than ninety days in advance; or the room may be used by a group for a maximum of four days within any given thirty-day period.

If the community room is located in a mall, the use may be limited to mall hours. If the room has direct access from the parking lot or if security guards or maintenance personnel are available, they can provide access to the mall beyond business hours. Groups should be required to clean the room after using it and should not be allowed to affix any materials such as handbills to the walls. Public address systems or disturbing activities are not allowed, and the property manager always retains the right to reclaim the room for other uses.

When community rooms are located in a mall, the maintenance or security personnel are given the room's daily schedule and are responsible for unlocking and locking the room for each group. If the community room is located in a shopping center without on-site personnel, a key to the room may be left with one of the tenants. The groups can be instructed where to pick up and return the key and how to secure the room. The room should be cleaned daily by the shopping center janitorial staff or a maintenance contractor.

The property manager can promote the mall to the captive audience in the community room by posting in the room a list of the merchants, a separate listing of the restaurants, including those that deliver, photos and ads of past and current promotions, and a calendar of upcoming promotional and merchandising events.

Organizations using the community room may be required to sign a license agreement or a hold harmless agreement.

(b) COMMUNITY BOOTH

Since the early 1970s, there have been conflicting rulings by the courts on all levels as to the public's right to use the shopping center as a public forum. The property manager must check with legal counsel on the rights of the public and the obligations of the property owners in each state regarding the public's access and right to use public property for noncommercial uses.

Many shopping center owners addressed this issue by building a community booth in the shopping center's common area as a public forum facility for individuals or groups. These booths are usually located against a blank wall in an area with ample pedestrian traffic. Managers of small centers that do not have a permanent booth can designate locations on the sidewalk where individuals or organizations may set up a table to distribute information.

The property manager must develop guidelines and enforce them equally with all individuals and organizations. The guidelines will include how an individual or organization applies for consent to use the shopping center's community booth. The application process may require that the booth be reserved a minimum number of days prior to the use. The application may ask for the name, address, and telephone number of the organization or individual sponsoring the activity and the names of the individuals participating in the activity. The guidelines may prohibit the sale of merchandise or service and limit the activities to the community booth. Signs may be restricted to a specific size. Individuals and organizations are responsible for cleaning the area inside and outside the booth. Public address systems or voice amplifying devices should be prohibited.

The property manager must stay current with the changing laws regarding the public's right to use private property, particularly shopping centers, as a forum to disseminate information to the public. The International Council of Shopping Centers is the best source of information on this issue.

If the property manager has followed the appropriate guidelines, the community booth can provide a public service to the community without creating problems for the shopping center.

(c) INFORMATION BOOTH

The information booth is an area in a mall that can provide customers with general information regarding the mall and its merchants. The staff of the information booth also can provide operational support for the mall's management and marketing staff. Information booths are usually found in larger shopping centers that have a budget to support this service.

The information booth can provide a variety of services to the customer, including information on mall hours, store locations, and upcoming events. The information booth can also handle lost and found items, deal with lost children or parents, issue wheelchairs, and rent strollers. A listing of positions available in the stores can either be kept or posted at the booth. The community booth staff can receive emergency calls to the management office and answer questions regarding the mall. The staff of the information booth may also serve as radio dispatchers for the mall's security and maintenance personnel.

The information booth can be a convenient place to sell mall gift certificates, which are valid in any mall store. Certificates can be sold in dollar increments, such as ten-dollar increments, or for a specific amount. In either case, they should state that they are valid only at the mall.

There are several approaches to the gift certificate. One approach is to sell it like a money order or check. The certificate is signed by a mall representative, a purchase is made at a mall store, and the store fills in its name as the payee. Depending on the program, the payee either deposits the check in its account or is reimbursed by the management office. The money received from selling the gift certificates is deposited in a special account.

The information booth's staff should be trained to handle emergencies, ranging from helping a customer find his/her car to coping with a bomb threat. The booth should have a procedure manual that lists emergency phone numbers, details the dress code, discusses the above-mentioned duties, includes procedures for personal calls and visits, and explains how to deal with the public and with irate customers.

The information booth is an opportunity to provide service to customers that is not found in most shopping centers.

§ 4.18 SECURITY

A shopping center's success depends on its acceptance by the community, but the community will not accept a center in which it does not feel safe. The property manager needs to constantly monitor the security needs of the shopping center. Most people feel safer at a shopping center than on the city streets, and the property manager must maintain this feeling by monitoring the center's security needs.

(a) NEIGHBORHOOD CENTER SECURITY

Strip centers and neighborhood centers seldom have a security problem other than minor vandalism in the parking lot and graffiti on the back walls of the center. Security problems that do occur are usually a result of one or a combination of four factors: (1) The shopping center is located in a high-crime area, and the problems at the shopping center are a reflection of the problems in the neighborhood. (2) Youth are using the shopping center as a place to hang out. (3) A rash of burglaries occurs in a short period as the burglars move from one area of the community to another. (4) A tenant is attracting a clientele that is causing the problems.

When there are no security problems other than minor vandalism, the property manager's security program will consist of asking the tenants and maintenance personnel to report suspicious people and loiterers. The property manager should develop a rapport with the police precinct captain and ask that officers drive through the shopping center periodically.

Graffiti should be removed or painted over immediately or it will encourage more vandalism. If graffiti is an ongoing problem, the manager should try to determine when it is occurring—for instance, after school or late in the evening. The property manager should then ask the police to drive through the shopping center during those hours. If that does not solve the problem, a private security patrol may be needed during the period of the day or evening when the problem occurs until it stops.

Another problem may be teens cruising the parking lot. One approach to this problem is to request that the police enforce the motor vehicle code with regard to noise, speed, and drinking while driving.

A deterrent to vandalism and other security problems is good lighting in the common areas. Problems occurring in the evenings or early morning hours indicate that the property manager must give extra attention to the shopping center lighting. Visiting the center in the evening, walking throughout the parking lot, behind the shopping center, and on all sidewalks will help the manager find areas that need better illumination.

(b) COMMUNITY MALL SECURITY

Smaller malls and enclosed community malls usually do not need security guards on duty twenty-four hours a day. Their security needs are similar to those of the nonenclosed neighborhood center with the exception that the mall will attract more shoppers and is a convenient place for teens to gather. If either of these situations warrants on-site security guards, the property manager can schedule them based on the traffic and activities in the mall. A security program may be needed for the hours the mall has most of its traffic and the hours school is out. For instance, a security guard may be scheduled from 2:00 P.M. to 10:30 P.M., Monday through Friday, and during the hours the mall is open on the weekends, plus one-half hour after the mall closes. When school is out for the summer and during holidays, the starting time may be adjusted to an earlier hour. After mall hours, the night janitorial staff can clean the common areas, and the maintenance personnel can start their shift when the night janitorial crew leaves. Combining the maintenance and janitorial personnel and the security guards in such a manner provides on-site personnel twenty-four hours a day.

The property manager develops a security program by first analyzing the hours the guards will be needed for each day of the week. Then additional guards are scheduled for peak selling seasons and special events. The cost of the guard service can be easily determined by multiplying the number of hours by the hourly rate.

The security schedule in Exhibit 4.11 is for an enclosed community mall. Note that the schedule provides security during the peak traffic periods of the week and takes into account the additional security needs for special events, the peak selling season, and evenings, when the probability of vandalism is greater.

The community mall security guard schedule provides guards during the peak mall traffic times each day of the week. Additional guards are on duty on New Year's Eve and Halloween, the two days when there is most likely to be vandalism. Three promotions—sidewalk sales, moonlight sales, and community bazaars—will generate extra traffic in the mall, and additional security is scheduled to handle this traffic.

The extra security for the Christmas season starts the Friday after Thanksgiving. Traditionally, this is the busiest shopping day of the year, which means additional security is needed on the three-day Thanksgiving weekend. Many malls extend their hours the two weekends before Christmas Day, and the security schedule reflects the longer Saturday and Sunday mall hours. A security guard is placed in the parking lot to direct

EXHIBIT 4.11

Security Guard Schedule and Budget

Monthly Security Guard Schedule

Monday–Friday	1 guard	4:30 P.M. to 10:30 P.M.	= 6 hr × 5 days	= 30 hr
Saturday	1 guard	10 A.M. to 10 P.M.	= 12 hr.	= 12 hr
Sunday	1 guard	noon to 7 P.M.	= 7 hr	= 7 hr
				49 hr/wk

49 hr/wk × 4.33 wk/mo = 212 hr/mo

Additional Security Guards

Halloween night	1 parking lot guard	3 P.M. to 6 A.M.	= 15 hr
	1 guard in mall	3 P.M. to 9 P.M.	= 6 hr
			21 hr
New Year's Eve	1 guard	10 P.M. to 6 A.M.	= 8 hr
January Sidewalk Sale	1 guard	noon to 6 P.M.	= 6 hr
July Moonlight Sale	1 guard	6 P.M. to midnight	= 6 hr
September			
Community Bazaar	1 guard	10 A.M. to 5 P.M.	= 7 hr
			27 hr

Christmas Season

Thanksgiving weekend

Friday	1 mall guard	10 A.M. to 9 P.M.	= 11 hr
	1 parking lot guard	10 A.M. to 9 P.M.	= 11 hr
Saturday	1 mall guard	10 A.M. to 6 P.M.	= 8 hr
	1 parking lot guard	10 A.M. to 6 P.M.	= 8 hr
Sunday	1 mall guard	11 A.M. to 6 P.M.	= 7 hr
	1 parking lot guard	11 A.M. to 6 P.M.	= 7 hr
			52 hr

Second week before Christmas

Monday–Friday	1 mall guard	noon to 10 P.M. = 10 hr × 5 days =	50 hr
	1 parking lot guard	noon to 10 P.M. = 10 hr × 5 days =	50 hr
Saturday	1 mall guard	10 A.M. to 6 P.M. =	8 hr
	1 mall guard	noon to 7 P.M. =	7 hr
	1 parking lot guard	10 A.M. to 7 P.M. =	9 hr
Sunday	1 mall guard	noon to 6 P.M. =	6 hr
	1 mall guard	1 P.M. to 6 P.M. =	5 hr
	1 parking lot guard	noon to 7 P.M. =	7 hr
			142 hr

Week before Christmas

Monday–Friday	1 mall guard	10 A.M. to 10 P.M. = 12 hr × 5 days =	60 hr
	1 mall guard	5 P.M. to 10 P.M. = 5 hr × 5 days =	25 hr
	1 parking lot guard	noon to 10 P.M. = 10 hr × 5 days =	50 hr
Saturday	1 mall guard	10 A.M. to 6 P.M. =	8 hr
	1 mall guard	noon to 7 P.M. =	7 hr
	1 parking lot guard	9:30 A.M. to 6:30 P.M. =	9 hr

EXHIBIT 4.11 *(Continued)*

Sunday	1 mall guard	noon to 6 P.M.	=	6 hr
	1 mall guard	1 P.M. to 6 P.M.	=	5 hr

177 hr

Total Christmas Period   371 hr

Cost of the Security Guard Program

Monthly schedule	212 hr/mo	× $9.50/hr	=	$2,014.00/month
Halloween night	21 hr	× 9.50/hr	=	200.00
New Year's Eve	8 hr	× 9.50/hr	=	76.00
Jan. Sidewalk Sale	6 hr	× 9.50/hr	=	57.00
July Moonlight Sale	6 hr	× 9.50/hr	=	57.00
Sept. Community Bazaar	7 hr	× 9.50/hr	=	66.50
Christmas season				
Thanksgiving	52 hr	× 9.50/hr	=	494.00
December	319 hr	× 9.50/hr	=	3,030.50

Security Costs by Month

January	$ 2,014.00	monthly
	76.00	New Year's Eve and Day
	57.00	Sidewalk sale
	2,147.00	
February	2,014.00	monthly
March	2,014.00	monthly
April	2,014.00	monthly
May	2,014.00	monthly
June	2,014.00	monthly
July	2,014.00	monthly
	57.00	Sidewalk Sale
	2,071.00	
August	2,014.00	monthly
September	2,014.00	monthly
	66.50	Community Bazaar
	2,080.50	
October	2,014.00	monthly
November	2,014.00	monthly
	494.00	Thanksgiving weekend
	2,508.00	
December	2,014.00	monthly
	3,030.50	Christmas
	5,044.50	
Total	$27,892.00	

traffic the three-day weekend following Thanksgiving and the two weeks before Christmas.

(c) REGIONAL AND SUPER-REGIONAL MALLS

Regional and super-regional malls usually schedule guards 24 hours a day, or all the hours the mall is open. They also have the parking lots patrolled. If the mall has two common area maintenance budgets, a mall budget and a parking lot budget, then separate security guard budgets would be developed for each area.

Extra guards need to be scheduled for the grand opening of a community or regional mall to direct traffic in the parking lot and to patrol the mall. A security incident during a grand opening can be more devastating than at any other time, so a security schedule that is more than adequate should be developed for the grand opening. Remember, you never get a second chance to make a first impression.

(d) SECURITY GUARDS

A key decision in developing a security guard program for a shopping center is whether the mall should hire the guards as employees of the mall or contract with an outside security guard company. There are advantages to both.

In-House Staff

The first advantage to an in-house guard staff is that the property manager has greater control over the entire guard program, including selection and supervision of the guards. If the guards are employees of the mall, they know they will not be transferred to another property. This can build allegiance to their job and result in a lower turnover. The in-house guards also have a better opportunity to become familiar with the layout of the mall, the store managers, and employees. Finally, the cost per guard may be less since the profit margin of the security guard company is saved. Off-duty police officers are an excellent source of guards.

Security Guard Company

There are also distinct advantages to contracting with a security guard company. First, the company provides an expertise that the property manager may not have, and is more likely to be current on the laws of citizen's arrest, detaining a person, curfews, and other law-enforcement regulations. Hiring an outside company relieves the property manager of hiring, training, and terminating security personnel. The security company will have additional personnel to substitute for those who are ill or on vacation and can provide additional security guards during peak mall traffic periods and special events. Finally, if a guard is involved in an incident that ends in litigation, the security guard company's insurance carrier can defend the shopping center's management company and the mall. Since the property manager has required the security guard company to have insurance naming the mall and the property manager as named insured on the policy, the mall's insurance carrier is not brought into the picture, and the mall's insurance rates are not affected.

Armed or Unarmed Guards

Another security question to be decided is: Should a security guard be armed? Generally, no. Most security guards do not receive ongoing training with firearms, and few security guards are qualified to handle a situation that requires the display and possible use of a firearm.

Armed security guards in a mall can give shoppers the impression that the mall is a dangerous place. It would be more reassuring, if a situation arises that requires the use of firearms, to call in the local police, who are trained to handle emergency situations.

If the mall is in an area where guards must be armed, the property manager should work with the local police department in the selection of a security guard company. Some cities offer a parapolice program. This program allows the city to assign uniformed off-duty officers to patrol the mall. The shopping center would reimburse the city for the cost of the police patrol. The advantage to the city is that it has more officers on patrol at no additional cost to the city. The advantage to the officers is that they have an opportunity to moonlight at the approval of the police department and usually at a pay comparable to their city salary. A parapolice program costs more than contracting with a security guard company, but the police officers are professionals.

Security Guard Uniforms

Whether to outfit the security guards in either a police-type uniform or a blazer outfit is another decision for the property manager. If there is a need for a show of force, then the security guards should be in police-type uniforms. However, if the security guard's main responsibility is to serve a public relations function, then blazer uniforms may be more appropriate. Regardless of the type of uniform, it must be clean and easily identifiable.

Training the Security Guards

The property manager should develop an ongoing training program for the mall's security force. The security program is an integral part of the entire management program for the shopping center, and the security guards must believe that they are an important part of the management team. Each new guard must become familiar with the property and receive a security guard's procedure manual. Regular training sessions should be conducted. At these sessions, the property manager should review the security procedures for upcoming events and discuss how to handle specific situations. The police should be encouraged to attend these sessions. Other guest speakers that should be invited to these sessions are: fire department representatives, the mall's attorney and insurance agent or carrier, and the property manager's supervisor. The security guards should be encouraged to take an active role in these sessions and to discuss their problems and offer suggestions.

The property manager should review the equipment needed by the security force. Will a car or motorized cart be needed for parking lot patrol? Should all security guards be in radio communication with the management staff and one another? What types of flashlights, first aid kits, and other equipment will be needed?

Each guard should receive a manual from the property manager that covers every possible situation the guard might encounter. The manual should also include each guard's schedule; what happens when a guard is not relieved; areas the guard should patrol; areas that require more frequent patrols, such as restrooms; how to report vandalism and theft of the mall's property; how to assist customers with lost items, locked cars, and so on; how to handle loiterers; the mall's policy regarding skateboards, skates, and animals; the guard's responsibilities if an incident occurs in a store; areas to patrol; the procedures and requirements for using the community room and community booth; whether employees should be escorted to their cars or to on-site banks; what to do in different emergencies; responsibilities during a power failure; what happens when the fire or sprinkler alarm sounds; the location of shutoff valves; how to handle irate customers. The guards should check for burned out lights in the evening and slippery spots, especially in the exterior common areas, in the winter.

At the end of each shift, the guard should give the property manager a written report detailing the situations the guard was confronted with, how the situation was handled, and which topics should be discussed at the guards' meetings.

The guards can be assigned the responsibility to list the hours each store opens and closes. A form Irregularity in Store Opening and Closing Hours is filled out by the security guard each morning and evening and given to the mall manager or operations manager. The mall manager meets with the manager of any store that is opening too late or closing earlier.

(e) DEVELOPING A RELATIONSHIP WITH THE POLICE DEPARTMENT

The property manager should develop a working relationship with the community's public service departments, requesting the police and fire department to appoint a liaison to the mall. The police should be requested to report all incidents at the shopping center to the property manager. The department can be invited to use the shopping center after hours to practice emergencies and training. Some police departments will loan the on-site property manager a walkie-talkie for direct and immediate reporting of the incident to the police. A few regional malls have been able to locate a sheriff's or police department's substation at the mall. As a result, the sheriff or police are always cruising the parking lot and are visible within the shopping center.

Budgetary concerns should never be a factor in developing a security program. A shopping center cannot afford inadequate security.

Five

Office Building Management

§ 5.1 INTRODUCTION

The office market has become both sophisticated and competitive over the last several years, requiring a more experienced and responsive management approach. A high-rise office building is a complex entity with many interrelated systems and a large number of occupants and visitors with varying needs that must all be integrated by the skillful manager.

The fact that office buildings are vertical structures on relatively small parcels of land presents unique management responsibilities. The office building's landlord through the property manager has more maintenance responsibilities than the shopping center and multitenant industrial property owner. Emergency procedures are more involved because of the large number of people concentrated in a vertical tower. Parking and the movement of people in and out of the building often are a concern of management. The mechanical, and life safety, and energy conservation systems are highly technical.

Security in an office building centers around controlling access into and out of the building. Medical buildings present an even greater security challenge. After-hours emergency access to the building, transportation of nonambulatory patients, storage of large quantities of medications, and disposal of medical waste all mandate special consideration.

Because of the proximity of office buildings to each other, tenants can easily compare buildings. Brokers and tenants often use a comparison chart to assess their position when they are negotiating the lease. A tenant often needs to locate in a specific area, but seldom in a specific building. For a given building to be competitive, management must know which buildings are direct competition and make sure that the building measures up in terms of rental rates, maintenance, management, curb appeal, and tenant relations. If all buildings in the area provide air conditioning, and yours does not, you are likely to be at a considerable disadvantage unless there is an offsetting benefit such as a much lower rent.

Basic property management is similar for all types of properties, but each property type has its unique features. This chapter will review the subtle and unique differences in managing office buildings. Although management techniques and problem solving are similar for all types of office buildings, it is helpful to indicate the categories used as industry standards: garden office buildings, one to two stories; low-rise office buildings, three to four stories; mid-rise office buildings, five to ten stories; and high-rise office buildings, eleven or more stories. These categories will be used in this chapter when discussing management differences in each type of building.

§ 5.2   MANAGEMENT STAFFING

The basic criterion in determining whether an office building will have an on-site property manager is whether the building's income can support that cost in addition to the management fee.

Garden and low-rise office buildings are usually managed from a central office away from the project. Two questions must be addressed when managing office buildings without an on-site property manager. The first is, how many office buildings can one person manage? Several variables must be considered before answering this question. The first is the level of service offered by the property manager and the management company. Obviously, many more properties can be managed if only the minimal services of rent collection and responding to maintenance calls are provided rather than a proactive property management program designed to enhance value.

The other variables are the location of each property, the size of each building, the number of tenants in each building, unusual problems with any building, and the level of administrative support available to the property manager. A rule of thumb for the number of garden and low-rise office buildings in the 40,000- to 80,000-square-foot range, all within driving distance from the central property management office, is five to eight buildings for a high level of service and eight to twelve buildings for a medium level of service.

The second question is, How can immediate response be provided when the property manager is not available or the property is more than thirty minutes from the office? It is prudent to have an arrangement with one of the tenants in the building who can provide keys to utility rooms, respond to a maintenance emergency and, in essence, be the eyes and ears of the building. Occasionally, this tenant may open a vacant space for a prospective tenant. Caution must be exercised, however, that the duties assigned to this person do not require a real estate license.

Mid- and high-rise office buildings are usually staffed with on-site managers and administrative personnel. On-site managers should be considered for office buildings exceeding 100,000 square feet, but are not necessarily needed. When a building exceeds 150,000 square feet, it will most likely need an on-site manager. When the building exceeds 200,000 square feet, an administrative assistant is usually added to the on-site staff. The square footages discussed above are a guide and just one of several factors used to determine if a building needs and can support an on-site manager.

High-rise office buildings are usually staffed with an on-site manager, assistant manager, and secretary or administrative assistant. A tenant relations coordinator, tenant improvement construction supervisor, and a chief engineer may be added to the staff.

§ 5.3   SPACE MEASUREMENT

The industry standards for measuring space in office buildings have been established by BOMA. These standards were revised in August 1980 and can be found in BOMA's annual *Experience Exchange Report*.

Measuring space in office buildings is a critical step in the overall management, operations, and leasing process. Management wants to be accurate in space measurements and, at the same time, competitive. The more the same standards are used, the easier it is to make valid comparisons between buildings and to reduce possible disagreements in the future.

There are several different measurements to be considered:

1. **Gross Building Area.**   This includes all the area between exterior walls, less elevator shafts, pipe shafts, and stairwells. This figure in most cases would be the same as the rentable area of the building.

2. **Usable Area.**   "The usable area of an office shall be computed by measuring to the finished surface of the office side of corridor and other permanent walls, to the center of partitions that separate the office from adjoining usable areas, and to the inside finished surface of the dominant portion of the permanent outer building walls."[1]

3. Rentable Area. "The rentable area of a floor shall be computed by measuring to the inside finished surface of the dominant portion of the permanent outer building walls, excluding any major vertical penetrations of the floor."[2]

In the past, a tenant that leased a full floor in a building also paid rent on what was the common area that exclusively served its premises, such as hallways, restrooms, and telephone closets. Using this same theory, owners added a "load factor" to the usable footage of tenants on multitenanted floors so that even a small space user would pay its share of those common facilities.

For example, a building may have 50,000 square feet of usable area and 7,500 square feet of common area. Instead of collecting rent on only 50,000 square feet, the owner would add a load factor of 15% (7,500 ÷ 50,000) to each occupancy. A tenant that leased 1,000 square feet usable would pay rent on 1,150 square feet, which would include its share of the common areas.

In a garden-style open corridor building, the load factor can be as low as 5% to 6% of the usable space since there are no hallways to allocate. Another possibility is a building with a large atrium court; here the true load factor can approach 30% of the usable area. Industry experience indicates that it is very difficult to bill load factors in excess of 17% to 18% regardless of the actual amounts involved.

§ 5.4 TENANT IMPROVEMENT

Tenant improvement work is an ongoing process in most office buildings. It is critical that all work be completed in a timely fashion to meet the tenant's needs and at a competitive cost.

Space planning is an important part of the construction process. Many tenants have little idea of how much space they need to operate their business or how to plan their space layout for efficient use. On the other hand, even the most sophisticated tenant is not always aware of the latest techniques in space utilization. A good space planner can be a great help in discussing "what if" options for the leasing personnel. The final space plan makes for an easy transition to working drawings for the actual construction.

[1] Building Owners and Managers Association International, *Standard Method for Measuring Floor Area in Office Buildings* (1980).

[2] Ibid.

There are several factors to consider when interviewing and selecting a space planner. Foremost, the landlord needs to know how many
millions of square feet the space planner has planned and whether he or
she understands the leasing business. All references should be checked.

The space planner's first question should be, What is the landlord's
tenant improvement budget? The landlord's space planner is hired to
lay out the prospective tenant premises and not to provide design services to the tenant. A good space planner will work within the landlord's
budget. If the tenant asks for a relight (a glass wall used to allow light
to enter an area), the space planner will explain that a relight costs five
times the cost of studs, drywall, and paint, and the additional cost will
be a tenant expense.

A good space planner will be motivated to keep tenant improvement costs down. After the tenant has signed the lease, the space planner can offer design services to the tenant. At this point, any extras
beyond what the landlord agreed to provide is a cost to the tenant. A
professional space planner is a valuable member of the building's marketing and leasing team. Ideally, most managers would have an on-site
construction coordinator ready to contract the build-out. For most
buildings, however, this is not practical. In the absence of a building
construction coordinator, there are two choices for the use of outside
contractors.

For minor tenant improvements, use unit prices. The property manager generally knows what kind of work will be provided to tenants,
and contractors can provide specific prices for these items in advance.
A contractor may agree to charge $120 for a two-by-four-foot light fix-
ture, partition walls at $26 per linear foot, floor tile at $1.06 per foot,
and carpeting at $18 per square yard. From this listing, the property
manager can calculate the cost of the improvements while negotiating
the lease.

The alternative is to bid the work for each job. This will generally
assure the best price, but quite often this approach can delay the completion of the job. When bidding the job, contractors need to have complete
plans. Contractors should be screened and selected on the basis of experience with office buildings, reputation, financial stability, and reliabil-
ity in finishing the work on time. For a realistic bid, the process must be
completely open and honest. If contractors are used to establish each
other's prices, they will soon lose interest in providing costly bids that
will not be accepted.

All contracts should be written and include an outside finish date
with a penalty if the date is not met. Payment should be on a progress
basis, and a 10% retention should be held to cover contingencies and
get past the lien dates. Labor and material lien releases should be obtained before the contractor is paid. All work should carry a warranty,
which in most areas lasts one year.

If possible, the building's contractor should finish its work before the tenant is allowed to start its work. Otherwise the tenant's work could hold up the landlord's contractor, and then a dispute will arise over when the work was completed and when the rental period is to start.

Seldom will the property manager allow a tenant to perform or contract for construction in the building. The primary reason is to ensure the quality of the construction and the integrity of the building and its mechanical systems. An unqualified contractor, or one who isn't familiar with the building, can disturb the HVAC and electrical systems. On the other hand, exceptions need to be made for sophisticated tenants with special needs or wants.

It is the exception to allow the tenant to perform or contract for improvements. However, the tenant may negotiate this right, or it may become evident that the work will be expedited by allowing the tenant to contract the improvements. Major tenants may require the right to perform their own improvements. An owner of a small office building may allow the tenants to contract nonstructural improvements. Medical tenants may be allowed to contract for the installation of their expensive medical equipment. The property manager should place restrictions and requirements on the tenant and its contractor. The plans should be reviewed and approved by the property manager or building owner's representative. The contractor should be licensed, bonded, and required to have insurance, naming the building owner and property management company as additional insured or named insured.

Core drilling is not allowed during the building's regular hours. Parking, unloading, use of the building's elevator, and the need for union employees should be discussed with the contractor. A consent to alteration agreement is signed by the tenant before the work is commenced.

If the tenant is contracting for improvements, the landlord should be protected from liens. Each state has methods of protecting the building owner, and the property manager should apply these methods whenever tenants are contracting work on the premises.

§ 5.5 MOVE-INS AND MOVE-OUTS

Relocation is a major disruption for a business and a major frustration for its employees. If handled properly, the actual move in or out of the office building can be a smooth transition. If not, the disturbance can cause problems for everyone and sour the manager-tenant relationship. If the process is not controlled, parking will be tied up and the elevators commandeered by the movers. The building's rules and regulations should address move-ins and move-outs, giving the building manager control over the hours that the move can be accomplished and what facilities the tenant will use in the process. The tenant is required to request a specific time for moving. Based on other building activities, the manager will then prepare a convenient schedule for everyone involved.

If the building doesn't have a freight elevator, a specific elevator will be assigned and padding blankets installed. The common areas in the building may need special covering placed over the carpeting and tile flooring. Temporary storage of furniture in the common areas is prohibited. If the building doesn't have a loading dock, an area in the parking lot may need to be roped off for the moving trucks. The moving company is required to submit a certificate of insurance that includes the building's owner and the property management company as additional insured or named insured.

If the move occurs on a weekend or in the evening, the elevator company should be notified and requested to have a maintenance person on call in case the elevator breaks down. If a major tenant is moving, a member of the building staff should be available during the entire move. A move into an area of 30,000 square feet or more can take an entire weekend. Building personnel should be assigned shifts, and coffee and light refreshments should be provided.

§ 5.6   ESCALATION CHARGES

Typically, the cost to operate the building, including maintenance, management, utilities, taxes, and insurance, are billed to the tenants. There are several different methods of billing the tenants for their share of the building's operating expenses. The two most common escalation methods are the base year approach and the operating stop. Two other methods, the triple net and gross leases, are seldom used to pass on all or none of the costs of operation to the tenants. Each of these escalation or bill-back methods is discussed in Chapter 8, Lease Administration.

§ 5.7   BUILDING MAINTENANCE

The office building owner assumes more maintenance responsibilities than does the shopping center or industrial property owner. Typically, the building owner will provide janitorial service five nights a week. Electricity, plumbing, HVAC, general maintenance, and light bulb replacement are also the building owner's responsibility. The tenant is generally responsible for the care and maintenance of the carpeting and window covering.

In small buildings, the maintenance services are usually contracted because the building cannot support an on-site maintenance person.

An alternative is for the property management company to establish a maintenance company with roving personnel. A second alternative is to have a maintenance person, possibly a retiree, work a few hours a day policing the parking lot and handling minor maintenance problems. A third approach is to have the janitorial company provide light maintenance services. One last approach is to contract the work by job assignment.

Mid- and high-rise office buildings have several on-site maintenance employees. A day porter is responsible for keeping the common areas clean during the building's normal operating hours and possibly handling minor maintenance. One or several building engineers will handle the majority of the building's maintenance. Elevator maintenance, fire sprinkler inspections, and major plumbing and electrical maintenance will be contracted. HVAC maintenance can be handled in several ways. The maintenance staff may be responsible for first echelon maintenance with the balance of the maintenance contracted, or the entire HVAC maintenance may be either contracted or handled by the on-site staff.

§ 5.8 SECURITY

Security has become a concern in recent years in all types of buildings, including office buildings. An office building can be an easy target for a thief, who can enter a suite under the guise of doing business with the tenant and observe opportunities to make a return visit for illegal activities. Employees often leave purses and garments with wallets, money, or other valuables unattended, making them easy pickings for an alert thief. With the complex and costly office equipment used in most business, offices are targets for the burglar who, once inside, generally has easy access to most areas through the drop-ceiling construction.

(a) SECURITY PERSONNEL

Garden and low-rise buildings in the suburbs seldom need security guards on site. A private security company can be employed to drive by the property several times a night at random times. Janitors can be utilized to watch for problems. The exterior doors can be locked at a specified hour. Access after that is by a coded card that registers the individual in and out of the building. The employees in the building are instructed to report suspicious people in or near the building.

Mid- and high-rise buildings will have either a security guard in the lobby 24 hours a day, or starting around 5:00 P.M. until the building opens the next day and through the weekends and holidays. People entering or leaving the building after 5:00 P.M. and before 7:00 A.M. and on weekends and holidays must sign in and out at the lobby desk and indicate the tenant they are visiting. Employees show their building identification card. Additional security can be provided by having the security guard call the tenants to verify the appointment before allowing the visitor to go beyond the lobby. The elevator can be programmed so the visitor has access to only one floor. To minimize theft of business equipment, a tenant should have a pass to remove equipment from the building. Many buildings with 24-hour lobby guards will not have tenant directories. The guard provides directory service.

Additional information on security is provided in Chapter 10, Developing Emergency Procedures.

(b)   KEY CONTROL

Key control is critical to the security of the office building. A master key system is a must, but precautions must be taken to be sure that these keys do not get into the wrong hands.

The key system of the building should be designed and recorded by a qualified locksmith. Generally, there is a grand master key for all locks in the building. From that grand master, submaster keys can be made for janitor closets, telephone rooms, meter rooms, and individual floors. Each tenant's suite key is coded and marked "do not duplicate." Master keys should be numbered and issued only to individuals who need them and have signed out for them. This list should be as limited as possible, keeping in mind the operating efficiency of the building.

When a tenant moves out, the lock cylinder should be changed to assure security for the next occupant. This is easily performed by keeping four or five cylinders that have been set up for the system and rotating them throughout the building. If a tenant fires an employee and wants the locks changed, it should be done by the building's locksmith at the tenant's cost. This is the only way to preserve the original lock system in the building.

When a master key is lost or stolen, the building should be rekeyed as soon as possible. In the meantime, a security guard may need to be stationed in the building. If a security officer or janitor lost the keys, that contractor should pay for the cost to rekey the building.

Rekeying a building can be expensive, but with expensive high-tech business machines in office buildings and drugs in medical buildings, it usually is the prudent choice when master keys are missing.

§ 5.9   TENANT-RETENTION PROGRAM

Most employees spend more time in their work environment than any other place except their home. The property manager can develop a tenant-retention program that makes the office building a pleasant, enjoyable, and sometimes fun place to work. When the tenant's employees are happy with their workplace, the tenant is less likely to move out. Also, brokers regularly canvass every office building, and the property manager can counter their activities by developing a tenant-retention program. A tenant-retention program consists of improvements to the building, enhancements to the building's tenant mix, added amenities to the building, and services to the tenant's employees.

Improvement to the building includes modernizing the elevators and mechanical systems and maintaining the common areas in good condition. The building's tenant mix can be enriched by adding tenants that either provide a service to the other tenants or prestige to the building. A deli, card shop, hair salon, health club, bank, title insurance company, escrow company, real estate office, or other retail service provides conveniences to the existing tenants and their employees. A prestigious law firm or medical practice in a medical building will also enhance the building's image. A lunchroom with vending machines, a conference room, and outdoor patio areas are just a few examples of amenities that can be incorporated into a building.

Several services can be offered to tenants to help "deinstitutionalize" a building. A food drive or toy collection can build community spirit, while a series of luncheon speakers can provide education and entertainment. Speakers are easily obtained: Bankers and stockbrokers can discuss investment opportunities, specialty retailers can discuss new products or fashions, and community organizations such as a crisis clinic or YMCA/YWCA can discuss their programs. An annual tenants' appreciation picnic sponsored by the building and its service contractors is an enjoyable way to promote goodwill among the tenants.

A communications program can be developed with little time and money. A newsletter—monthly for mid- and high-rise buildings and quarterly for smaller buildings—can inform the tenants' employees of new services in the building, new tenants, upcoming practice evacuations, and community and educational events sponsored by the building. Tenants are requested to submit information about activities of their firm or their employees. A bulletin board can be placed in the building's lunchroom or lounge to post the newsletter. Service and retail announcements can be posted on a glass-enclosed display case in the elevator.

§ 5.10 RETAIL TENANTS IN AN OFFICE BUILDING

Retail tenants can provide services to the building's tenants, pay percentage rent, establish an identity for the building, and become an amenity to be promoted in the building's marketing and leasing program.

A prospective retail or service tenant must be analyzed more carefully than an office user to ensure compatibility with the other tenants and with the building. A merchant who sells inferior merchandise or provides poor service will harm the building's reputation and annoy its tenants.

The office building lease must include provisions found in shopping center leases such as hours of operation, percentage rent, sales reporting, sales audit, and a very restrictive use clause. Operational issues that must be considered are trash removal, deliveries, pest control, janitorial service, after-hours entry, signage, supplementary HVAC, and overstandard utility usage.

A restaurant, health spa, deli, card and gift shop, and most other retailers will be an asset to an office building. The manager who understands the impact these tenants will have on the building's operations and addresses that in the lease will have a better relationship with tenants and a smoother building operation.

§ 5.11 TENANT RELATIONS

The management of an office building doesn't have as direct an impact on the success of a tenant's business as the management of a shopping center has on its tenants. However, the property manager still must be sensitive to the needs of the office tenants. It is easy for the relationship between the manager and the tenant to be damaged during the interval between the signing of the lease and the day the tenant moves in.

The property manager should meet with the tenant soon after the lease is executed to give him or her a copy of the building handbook and emergency procedures. It is a good idea to review these booklets with the tenant.

Once the space is complete and the tenant has moved in, the manager should pay a visit to welcome the new occupant and check that everything is in order. If necessary, a punch list should be prepared and the work completed at the earliest possible time. Delayed response gives the impression of poor management, which can last for the entire lease term. Some property owners will have the manager send a floral arrangement when a tenant opens for business.

Follow-up monthly visits can be a big boost to the relationship. Just a quick visit to see if there are any problems will demonstrate the property manager's concern and facilitate communication. Again, quick response to any problems brought up during these visits will improve the relationship. Taking each tenant out to lunch periodically is an excellent opportunity to develop good rapport. If the manager is unable to visit the tenants on a regular basis, a questionnaire from time to time can be helpful in bringing out problems and demonstrating that management does care.

§ 5.12   PARKING MANAGEMENT

Office building parking will vary from free, open parking for most suburban office buildings to parking for a charge in garages of downtown office buildings and some suburban buildings.

The basic parking policy of all office buildings is to allow convenient parking for tenants' customers and visitors and to eliminate unauthorized parking. This can be achieved by providing twenty-minute and two-hour visitors' parking in stalls close to the building's entrance. Preventing unauthorized parking in a suburban office building's free lot can be difficult. An inexpensive approach is to provide all the employees of the tenants in the building with parking stickers for their car's rear bumper. A more effective but more costly approach is to control employee parking with a card gate. Either approach must be accompanied by signs at the entrance to the lot warning of unauthorized parking.

Most downtown office buildings and some suburban office buildings provide paid parking. Most owners will contract with a parking garage operator to manage the building's parking. The owner receives a percentage of the income, and the operator pays all the expenses from its share of the income. The owner's percentage will vary from 60% to 85%, depending upon potential income. For example, the owner's percentage may start at 60% and increase 5% for every additional $50,000 of income above a fixed base income level. Another approach is to pay the operator a management fee in lieu of a percentage of the income. A third approach is for the building's owner to operate the parking garage.

Paid and permit parking can be controlled by either parking attendants or a card system. Lots that have all-day in and out paid parking generally must be staffed. If employees pay to park, they are generally assigned to a specific area but not to a specific space. This approach allows for more paid parking and reduces the problem of one person parking in the assigned space of another.

When parking is sold on an unassigned basis, 120% of the parking stalls can be sold since all of the building's employees are not in the building at the same time. On any one day, some will be on vacation, ill, or have business out of the building.

If the parking is for tenants only, a card system can be very cost-effective compared with the cost of one or two shifts of attendants each day to cover normal business hours. Typically overnight parking is prohibited, and most free lots are legally posted so that the property manager can tow abandoned or illegally parked cars.

If an office building does not have adequate parking for its employees and visitors, leasing nearby parking can be explored. A church, lodge, or theater might not use its parking lot on weekdays, or a nearby shopping center might have abundant parking.

Parking lot security is discussed in Chapter 10.

§ 5.13   BUILDING STORAGE

As office rents become more expensive, tenants are becoming more cost conscious about how they use their space. It seldom makes sense for a tenant to pay office building rates for dead storage, yet businesses need a place to keep old records. Basements, attics, and dead corners of the building and parking garage are great locations for storage areas in any building. Storage rates can range from 25% to 60% of base rents, with higher rates charged for the convenience of having the storage space in the same building as the tenant's office. The build-out can be as simple as cubicles divided by a two-by-four inch stud open wall with a heavy mesh screen separating the units. Each unit is provided with lights and a door, and the tenant uses its own padlock. Storage can add income and value to the building while offering a convenience to the tenants.

§ 5.14   CONFERENCE ROOMS

A building conference room that is available to the occupants can be an excellent leasing tool. Many occupants do not want to pay monthly rent and costs on a room that is seldom used. However, they are quite willing to pay for the use of the room on an as-needed basis, or it can be factored into the overall rental rate for the building and offered as a service of the building.

Scheduling of the room is coordinated by the management office. The room should be fully equipped with conference tables, chairs, easel, blackboard, plug-in phone, coffee area, and a podium.

Not all buildings benefit by having a conference room for their occupants. If the room is not used regularly or is not perceived as a positive leasing tool, the space should be converted to rentable area.

§ 5.15   LOST AND FOUND

Losing personal items in office buildings is common. A lost-and-found policy should be established and conveyed to the occupants. Generally, the building office is the drop-off and pickup point. Some method of identifying missing property should be established and a record kept of what is found and who claimed it. In large buildings this activity may be handled by security, and in small buildings the management office or the maintenance personnel may handle lost and found.

The tenant kit or handbook should include a section outlining the building's lost and found procedures.

§ 5.16 MEDICAL BUILDINGS

Medical office buildings (MOB) are more expensive to build and operate than traditional office buildings. The physical structure has more complex systems such as gas and air, shielding for X-ray equipment, heavier sound proofing, and considerably more plumbing. Spaces are often divided into small cubicles for use as examining rooms. Remodeling is generally quite extensive and expensive. Heating and air-conditioning are also critical in the medical environment.

Since doctors have smaller suites than office tenants, there are usually more tenants in a medical building than in a similar-sized office building. The demands of doctors are greater than that of office tenants. As a rule of thumb, an on-site manager is needed if the building is in excess of 100,000 square feet.

Operating expenses are greater in a medical building. Janitorial expenses will usually cost 25% to 50% more than in an office building. This is due to the large number of small offices, greater number of sinks and restrooms, and the high level of janitorial service required by doctors. Utility costs are appreciably higher as well.

Special care must be provided for the removal of medical waste. A company specializing in the pickup of medical waste should be contracted. Medical waste cannot be dumped into the building's trash bins, and special containers are needed for the disposal of medical waste.

Doctors need access to the building 24 hours a day. If the building doesn't have a security guard, a card control or similar access system must be provided. The interior signage needs to be easily read. Patients with poor eyesight need large, well-defined directories showing names and suite numbers.

Medical buildings are classified as either an on-campus MOB (part of a hospital campus) or off-campus MOB (freestanding building). An off-campus building may have a tunnel connecting the building to the hospital.

One of the advantages to the MOB is that the tenant turnover is very low. Once doctors are established and happy in a building, they seldom relocate.

§ 5.17   PROFESSIONAL ASSOCIATIONS

Two professional associations provide education and information to the office building industry. Building Owners and Managers Association (BOMA) is dedicated primarily to office buildings and has chapters in major cities throughout the United States. It awards the Real Property Administrator (RPA) designation and presents classes in various aspects of office building operations. It also lobbies on behalf of building owners.

The Institute of Real Estate Management (IREM) has been a leader in office building management for many years. It awards the Certified Property Manager designation (CPM) and the Accredited Management Organization (AMO) designation. IREM sponsors classes in office building management as well as other classes in the areas of commercial and residential property management.

The services offered by BOMA and IREM are reviewed in Chapter 1, Introduction.

§ 5.18   REFERENCE MATERIALS

An outstanding service that BOMA and IREM provide to the office building industry is their annual operating expense reports. BOMA publishes the *Experience Exchange Report,* and IREM publishes the *Income/Expense Analysis, Office Buildings, Downtown and Suburban.*

The BOMA *Experience Exchange Report* is a compilation of information on office buildings of all types throughout the United States. The report compares buildings by size, age, location, and specific characteristics. Income and expenses are broken down into meaningful categories and then compared on the basis of the highest cost, the lowest cost, and the median for that item. Costs are also stated on the basis of cents per square foot.

The Institute of Real Estate Management's *Income/Expense Analysis* is an annual publication analyzing office buildings' income and expenses in every metropolitan area and suburban area. Operating expenses and vacancy trends are analyzed in chart and graph formats.

It is always helpful and enlightening to be able to compare buildings that have similar characteristics. This is a benefit when setting the budget for a proposed or new building, preparing the operating budgets of an existing building, and evaluating expenses at year's end. These reports are helpful in evaluating whether or not the building's property tax assessment is correct and in appealing the assessment.

Both BOMA and IREM publish several informative publications. BOMA has produced a two-volume *Management Notes.* This publication, edited by Jack Gringorten, RPA, covers in a concise form over 300 areas of concern to office building management. *Trends* is a five-year income and expense trends profile for office buildings. *Office Tenant Moves and Changes* reviews the space needs of tenants, what they look for in a building, and why they relocate. *Office Building Lease Manual* presents alternative approaches for lease clauses. *Leasing Concepts: A Guide to Leasing Office Space*, written by Ron Simpson, CPM, RPA, explores conducting a market survey, measuring office space, and analyzing lease documents.

IREM has published three office building publications: *Forms for Office Building Management* by Bodie Beard, Jr., CPM, and Cher Zucker, CPM; *Managing the Office Building*, written by several CPM members with office building expertise; and *Office Building Leasing* by Duane Roberts, CPM.

The Urban Land Institute has published the *Office Development Handbook*.

Six

Industrial Property Management

§ 6.1 INTRODUCTION

Industrial properties can be more complex than they appear on the surface. Years ago, industrial buildings were located in old or poor parts of town. They were dingy, with little concern for aesthetics. Today the industrial building is often located in a master planned development with strict design, sign, and maintenance controls.

Industrial properties run the gamut from a 1,000-square-foot warehouse area for the local painter to store materials, to incubator buildings with many smaller spaces for start-up business and small operators, to multitenanted industrial parks encompassing hundreds of acres, to large single-tenant buildings.

The industrial industry has identified four types of properties: industrial areas, industrial parks, planned industrial districts, and planned employment centers. Evolution of the industrial industry can be seen in the definition of these four types of industrial properties. The Urban Land Institute's *Industrial Development Handbook* identifies and defines these property types as follows:

> In older, heavily urbanized areas, large concentrations of freestanding factories, warehouses, and supply yards are frequently found intermixed with commercial and service establishments. These industrial areas are

226

characterized by multilevel masonry construction and a high level of site coverage.[1]

Properties in these areas are usually triple net leases with limited management requirements.

The next phase in the evolution of industrial properties was the industrial park. Industrial parks were the first assemblage of individual buildings in a planned development. The industrial park has also been known as the business park, the office park, the research park, and research and development park.

> The phrase business park or office park has been introduced in part to indicate a variety of industrial and related service activities, but also to deemphasize the industrial character of many of the occupants. Whatever the name, the presumption is that the industrial park is a project which has been planned and developed as an optimal environment for industrial occupants.[2]

The next stage in the evolution was the master planned development with restrictions on the design, use, and occupancy of the industrial buildings.

> A planned industrial district may be further described as a suitably located tract of land subdivided and promoted for industrial use by a sponsoring managerial organization. In this sense, industrial district connotes a restricted use of improved land over which there is a proprietor who devotes himself to the area's planning and development.[3]

The final stage in the evolution of industrial properties is the planned employment center. The planned employment center includes a variety of office and service uses to serve the industrial businesses in the master planned area and the community at large.

> The planned employment center is a multiuse district to provide for employment needs of urban areas. It should be self-sufficient to the degree that basic employee requirements are provided within its boundaries and carefully designed to provide an optimal environment for a wide range of commercial and industrial needs. It should be fully integrated with the larger community of which it is a part.[4]

---

[1] Urban Land Institute, *Industrial Development Handbook*, (1975).

[2] *Id.*

[3] *Id.*

[4] *Id.*

§ 6.2   MANAGEMENT RESPONSIBILITIES

The typical industrial tenant is more concerned with the physical needs of the space than with aesthetics, even though the appearance of the buildings may have been a strong part of the initial attraction. The industrial tenant will focus on such features as location, labor pool, prevailing wages, zoning of the building, availability of common carriers, loading facilities, floor load capacities, clear span areas within the buildings, utility needs, and other physical requirements. The effective manager will work to meet these needs while maintaining the project in such a way as to present a pleasing appearance to existing tenants, prospective tenants, and the surrounding neighborhood.

The management of industrial properties ranges from limited management services for a single-tenant building with a triple net lease to very intense management services for the multiuse planned industrial development. The management responsibilities for a building with a triple net tenant consist primarily of collecting rent, monitoring the tenant's lease requirements, insuring the building, paying real estate taxes, and maintaining the building and improvements. A long-term triple net lease (see § 6.5), with General Motors, Boeing, or a government agency would require limited property management services.

At the other end of the spectrum of industrial management services is the multiuse planned industrial development. This development, occupied by industrial, office, and retail tenants, is highly management intensive. These projects are staffed with an on-site manager, administrative support person, and possibly maintenance personnel and a construction supervisor. Their responsibilities include lease administration, common area maintenance, limited building maintenance, tenant improvement construction, a tenant-retention program, development of emergency procedures, marketing and public relations, and coordination of leasing activities with the brokerage community.

§ 6.3   INSURANCE

The insurance requirements for industrial tenants will vary, depending on whether the building is single-tenant or multitenant. Most single-tenant buildings are leased on a triple net basis. The tenant is required to obtain an insurance policy with specific, minimum limits of coverage, and the landlord is named insured. Tenants in multitenant buildings will reimburse the landlord for their pro rata cost of the insurance.

While most owners today require at least $1 million in liability coverage by the tenant, there are dangerous industrial uses that warrant a higher limit. An insurance agent can be a valuable resource in setting the proper limits for a tenant with a risky use.

§ 6.4 TAXES

Tenants commonly pay their pro rata share of real estate taxes on the premises. On a single-user building, it is not unusual for the bill to go directly to the tenant although many owners prefer to pay the bills and collect from the tenant to be sure the taxes are paid on time. In multiple occupancy buildings, the landlord pays the bill, allocates it per the leases, and generally collects it with the budget estimates outlined in § 6.5.

§ 6.5 MAINTENANCE

The single-user industrial building is quite often leased to the tenant on an absolutely net basis, known as a triple net lease, with the tenant being fully responsible for repair or replacement of all parts of the building. Even in this situation, some standards should be set, such as quarterly air-conditioning service, periodic painting of the exterior, and annual roof inspection. An inspection should be conducted regularly to be sure the work is being performed.

Maintenance responsibility for buildings with triple net leases falls solely on the tenants. The property manager must periodically visit the properties to ensure that the tenant is fulfilling the lease responsibilities. A thorough inspection of the property should be conducted within six months of the lease expiration, and the tenant should be informed of all maintenance needs. When the tenant vacates, the property manager conducts a final inspection or walk-through with the tenant. The security deposit is not released until all maintenance is completed.

Maintenance responsibility for multitenant buildings is usually divided between the landlord and the tenants. The tenant's lease must be carefully reviewed to identify areas of responsibility. The tenant is usually responsible for the interior and mechanical equipment maintenance. The landlord is usually responsible for the maintenance of the roof, common areas, and the structural components detailed in the lease.

When the property is a planned industrial development with many different uses, the maintenance responsibility will vary depending upon the building and the users. This is evidenced in an industrial development that includes incubator space, office users, retail tenants, and large industrial users. In a park with a combination of uses, the maintenance responsibilities will vary depending upon the needs of the tenants, which are reflected in the maintenance clause of their lease.

Basically, the different users are responsible for the maintenance of the interior of their premises, including janitorial services, although in some situations the landlord is responsible for providing janitorial services. It is prudent for the property manager to assume responsibility for maintenance of the HVAC units and to require tenants to reimburse the landlord for this expense. The property manager will develop maintenance specifications based on the type of equipment and the tenants' use. This will ensure that the units are in good condition when tenants vacate. Tenants are billed quarterly or semiannually for their pro rata cost of the HVAC maintenance.

Common area maintenance for industrial properties is handled much like it is in shopping centers; that is, the property manager maintains the common area and bills the tenants for the cost. The property manager develops an annual budget, bills the tenants monthly for their pro rata share, and adjusts the billing to the actual expenses at the end of the budgeted period. Depending upon the lease, roof and structural maintenance are either an expense of the landlord or are included in the common area maintenance expense.

§ 6.6   TENANT SERVICES

The maintenance management program should help tenants with their maintenance responsibilities. The property manager interviews and evaluates several service contractors such as janitorial, window washing, and carpet cleaning and provides a list to the tenants. The list should include at least three contractors for each area of maintenance with no preference.

A key-making machine on the premises enables the manager to provide keys at a charge to the tenants.

Because they have a mix of industrial, service, office, and retail tenants, multitenant industrial developments provide an opportunity to bring these businesses together to promote themselves within the development. The manager of a 500,000-square-foot multitenant industrial development in the Northwest conducts an annual trade fair at which tenants display their products and services and the landlord provides refreshments and music. This event gives tenants additional business opportunities and creates an esprit de corps within the development. A monthly or quarterly open house during the lunch period at the on-site management office gives the management staff a chance to develop rapport with the tenants and to meet their employees.

§ 6.7   CONSTRUCTION MANAGEMENT

Large industrial developments, especially those with incubator space, will have considerable ongoing tenant improvement construction. The property manager should develop a construction management program to meet the improvement requirements of new tenants and the expansion and remodeling needs of existing tenants.

The first step in developing a construction management program is to obtain the "as built" plans for the development. The next step is to compile a list of the general contractor and all subcontractors who have worked on the project. Space planners are interviewed and one is selected to work with prospective tenants. The space planner will prepare the working drawings for construction of tenant improvements. Several general contractors should be interviewed and at least three selected to bid on tenant improvements. Contractors must provide evidence of worker's compensation and liability insurance and include the landlord and property management company as named insured on their insurance policy.

Each general contractor is requested to bid each job. If the work doesn't require extensive remodeling or build-outs, the property manager may use construction unit pricing. Under unit pricing, the property manager acquires bids that are good for a year on specific construction activities, such as installing an electrical outlet or building a stud wall, and contracting the work based on the unit price. This method is often used when a tenant renews and the landlord is making minor improvements to the premises. Unit pricing eliminates the need to bid small jobs. The property manager or the maintenance supervisor conducts a final walk-through with the contractor and the tenant before the tenant moves into the space.

A construction management program will facilitate the marketing and leasing program, meet the existing tenants' construction needs, and provide a construction supervision or coordination fee for the property management company.

§ 6.8 EXTERIOR SIGNAGE

The control of exterior signs is as important in industrial properties as it is in all other types of commercial properties. The property owner should establish reasonable sign criteria for the property in conjunction with the municipal authorities and require strict adherence. The sign criteria should be included as an exhibit in the lease.

§ 6.9 EXTERIOR STORAGE

Control of exterior storage is critical to the operation of industrial properties. It is not unusual to discover delivery pallets, 55-gallon drums, or even truck trailers being stored outside the tenants' premises. These items are unsightly, often take up valuable parking space, can become a fire hazard. and may contain hazardous materials. The best way to control storage is to include the development's rules and regulations on storage in the lease as part of the overall rules and regulations for the property.

§ 6.10   SECURITY

A security audit and an ongoing security program are integral parts of a property's emergency procedure plan. Most industrial properties have few security problems because of their suburban location, limited tenant activity in the evening, and open-air common areas. Even with these advantages, the manager cannot assume that the property will never have security problems. The manager must conduct a security audit and take preventive measures to minimize or eliminate problems.

Since there are usually no interior common areas, security problems would most likely occur in the parking lot or in the tenant's premises. Parking lot security starts with good lighting to eliminate areas where people can hide. Administrative and maintenance personnel must be constantly alert for loiterers, cars cruising, and anything that appears suspicious. Tenants should be reminded to report suspicious people on or near the development to the management office or the police. In the evenings, a drive-by security patrol can check for unlocked doors, abandoned cars, and loiterers. If a security problem exists, the property manager can hire on-site guards, erect a fence around the project with limited or guarded access, and install surveillance equipment. The police should be encouraged to drive through the development and to meet with tenants to review security procedures for their premises.

§ 6.11   ENVIRONMENTAL CONCERNS

The industrial tenant that manufactures or processes chemicals on the premises may have a potential for polluting the ground, air, or water in the area. The manager must understand how the property is to be used, what environmental concerns that use may present, and how the landlord is to be protected from damage, both during the lease term and after.

§ 6.12   EVALUATING THE NEEDS OF INDUSTRIAL TENANTS

Industrial tenants have a wide variety of space needs ranging from incubator space of under 1,000 square feet with one or two offices to hundreds of thousands of square feet for manufacturing. The property manager needs to assess which space requirements the building can meet.

The first consideration to meeting tenants' needs is zoning. Most municipalities have several zoning classifications ranging from light industrial to heavy industrial. The next consideration is the size and configuration of the building. Outside storage and parking are concerns for trucking companies and central warehouses. The type of construction and the availability of a fire sprinkler system may determine whether a company can obtain insurance for its manufacturing or operations. The utilities capacity is a concern of many large users and heavy manufacturing companies. The amount of floor area, column spacing, floor load capacities, and ceiling heights will determine if a company can lay out its equipment and supplies. The ratio of warehouse space to office space will eliminate some users. However, it usually is relatively easy to build more office space in the warehouse area. Truck loading facilities, rail spur, and access to the airport, freeway, and shipping ports are essential to many firms. The property manager should try to match the building's features to specific users.

§ 6.13   SELF-SERVICE STORAGE/MINIWAREHOUSES

"A self-storage facility is a rental property consisting of individual units of space. For each unit, which has its own door, the tenant normally provides the lock, keeps the key, and handles the goods to be stored."[5]

Miniwarehouses or self-storage facilities were first developed in the 1960s to meet the storage needs of businesses and residents. The concept is to provide storage space at a cost less than expensive office space or less than renting a larger apartment or purchasing a larger home.

Miniwarehouse or self-service storage facilities are developed on industrial-zoned properties. Because of the flexibility of laying out the buildings, they often can accommodate odd-shaped parcels, be built under freeways, or used as a buffer between heavier industrial uses and office or residential areas.

Even though miniwarehouses are less than thirty years old, significant changes in their development have occurred. Early ministorage facilities were managed much like apartment buildings. The project included a small apartment, and a live-in manager was hired to manage and lease both day and night. However, no one can work twenty-four hours a day, seven days a week, and problems can occur when a relief person used the manager's home. Today it is much more common to have a small day office for leasing and management activities. After-hours activity is either not permitted or is controlled by an electronic system that is activated by a plastic entry card.

[5] R.E. Cornwell and B. Victor, *Self-Service Storage*, p. 1(1983).

The main fear in ministorage leasing is break-ins. A minimal system of security is a drive-by patrol four to five times a night. Obviously, a patient burglar will watch the routine and take advantage of the time between visits. An electronic sensing system is the most effective, especially when connected to a direct-dial system that alerts a central station or the police. This system can be tied to the card-operated entry system to allow for late-hour entry, or the entire system can be closed at a given hour and secured by the system. It is unwise to use security dogs as protection because of the physical harm they can inflict.

Retail and ministorage have proven to be a good combination in some circumstances. If the store is located on a busy street, retail can be a strong income and traffic generator on the front of the property, while storage facilities occupy the less expensive back areas. Shopping centers have used deep lot space for ministorage where retail space would not likely be successful.

§ 6.14   INDUSTRIAL ORGANIZATIONS

Four prominent organizations service the industrial real estate industry. The Society of Industrial and Office Realtors (SIOR), located in Washington, D.C., is an affiliate of the National Association of Realtors. Its membership consists primarily of industrial brokers. Most metropolitan areas have a SIOR chapter.

The National Association of Industrial & Office Parks (NAIOP) focuses its activities on multitenant industrial parks and low-rise or garden office parks. This organization consists of developers, brokers, and related professionals and has local chapters. NAIOP's headquarters are located at 1215 Jefferson Davis Highway, Arlington, VA 22202. The American Industrial Real Estate Association (AIR) is an organization of developers, brokers, and related professionals. The association has developed different forms of industrial leases. It is located at Sheraton Grande Office Center, 345 South Figueroa, Suite M-1, Los Angeles, CA 90011. Each organization conducts seminars and addresses concerns of the industry. The Urban Land Institute (ULI), a real estate research institute, has many publications and studies on industrial real estate.

§ 6.15   INDUSTRIAL PUBLICATIONS

The industrial real estate industry has published several excellent books on developing, marketing, and managing industrial properties. Three leading publications are *Industrial Development Handbook*, published by the Urban Land Institute; *Parking For Industrial and Office Parks*, by the National Association of Industrial and Office Parks; and

Self-Service Storage, formerly *The Miniwarehouse*, by Richard E. Cornwell, CPM®, and Buzz Victor, published by the Institute of Real Estate Management.

§ 6.16   CONCLUSION

At first glance, industrial properties do not appear to be very management intensive. However, with the evolution of industrial properties from freestanding masonry buildings with triple net tenants to multi-tenanted developments with multiple uses, industrial property management now entails many of the management responsibilities of office and retail properties.

Seven

Marketing and Leasing

§ 7.1 INTRODUCTION

Leasing space is the critical activity that validates development and management efforts. The success of a commercial development or investment is dependent upon a successful leasing program. Five major factors contribute to a successful leasing program: (1) the building's location, (2) the building's design and features, (3) the owner's understanding of the market, (4) the market conditions, and (5) the development and implementation of an effective leasing program. If any one of these factors is missing, the leasing program will suffer.

The success of these five factors is ultimately apparent in the building's value. Value is created in commercial properties by capitalizing the net operating income (NOI) (see Chapter 3). The components of the NOI are the building's income and expenses. The NOI can be increased by increasing the income or by reducing the expenses, the former providing far greater opportunity for increasing value. Increasing the occupancy and maintaining rent at market rates will have a greater impact on the NOI than will reducing expenses. Once a building's maintenance management program is implemented, an energy audit completed, and an energy-saving program put into place, there are limited opportunities to lower operating expenses. Leasing opportunities that significantly impact the NOI are always present. Maintaining a higher occupancy than the average for the area, maintaining the rental rates at market, and reducing tenant turnover increase the building's income and value.

This chapter will review the elements in developing and implementing an effective marketing and leasing program.

Everyone on the leasing team, especially the owner, must understand the building's position in the market. The economies of each signed lease—the "deal"—must be understood, and this chapter will discuss how to establish the rental rate.

The most important element in the leasing program is the person responsible for leasing. This chapter will discuss the three options for developing a leasing team. Remember, obtaining the cooperation of the brokerage community is a crucial element in a successful leasing program.

Every business is not a potential tenant for a commercial building because each business has its unique space and location requirements, and some tenants have cotenancy requirements. An analysis of the building's market and potential tenant mix is necessary to target an appropriate market for it.

Once the owner and the property manager have determined who can most effectively lease the building, established the building's market rate, and identified potential uses, the leasing team is ready to develop and implement a program to contact potential tenants. After prospects have been located, their financial ability must be evaluated to determine if they can fulfill their lease obligations and if their use is suitable for the building.

If the tenant is a match for the building, a lease is negotiated that includes the rental terms and lease clauses which establish the rights and obligations of the landlord and the tenants. The control the landlord has over the operation of the property is established in the rights and obligations of the lessor and lessee. Each lease clause has a specific purpose, and the property manager or leasing agent must understand the impact each clause has on the operations of the property and the property's NOI. The property manager or leasing agent needs to know which lease concessions can be given to a prospective tenant to make the deal, since an inflexible stand on all clauses will result in deals lost.

An opportunity to make a significant impact on the property's NOI can be enhanced by developing and leasing pads/outlots. This opportunity is most often found in shopping centers, but it can occur in office and industrial sites as well.

The last factor in an effective leasing and marketing program is keeping the building full, consequently the leasing effort should continue even when the building is 100% occupied. Unexpected move-outs or opportunities to replace a tenant with one who is willing to pay higher rents can happen at any time.

Lease renewals, a component of keeping the building fully occupied and the most inexpensive deals in the market, are also discussed in this chapter.

The leasing team must be able to identify which spaces, if any, are difficult to lease and adjust the leasing program to compensate for these deficiencies.

The marketing and leasing program will receive most of the property owner's attention. An ineffective leasing and marketing program will soon be evident to the property owner and result in a change in leasing agents and possible property managers.

§ 7.2   THE MARKET SURVEY

The greatest effect the property manager has on the value of a property is to influence the income side of the income-expense equation. Opportunities exist to improve the value of property by reducing operating expenses, but more significant opportunities exist to increase the property's income.

An essential element in maximizing the property's income is maintaining the building's rental rates at their market value. To do this, the property manager must be knowledgeable about market conditions. This information can be gathered through a market survey. Trends can be identified when the surveys are conducted on a regular basis.

Market surveys are also used in managing and financing the property and in the acquisition process. The surveys entail projecting rates, concessions, and lease-up or a building's absorption rate—all of which are essential to developing the income components of a budget. Market surveys are needed when developing or refinancing a building. They also are needed to satisfy the due diligence requirement when analyzing a building for purchase.

Accurate information and a correct analysis of the information are essential to meeting the objectives of the market survey.

(a)   DETERMINING THE MARKET

Determining the boundary of the market is not difficult when the property manager is active in the area, but when the manager is new to the area, a more detailed analysis is necessary.

It is impossible to place a mileage ring around the property to determine its market area. The boundaries are formed by man-made barriers such as freeways, change of property use, or location of competing buildings. Natural barriers such as a river will also shape a market area. A rule of thumb for determining market area does not take into consideration the many variables mentioned.

The size of the market is another variable in defining the boundary of a market. For instance, the market for a Class A office building in a city's central business district (CBD) may be a mile or two in each direction, while the market for a regional mall in the same city may encompass the entire county. The boundaries of the shopping center market start with the center's trade area. This is the area in which most customers live.

When determining a neighborhood shopping center's market rates, all shopping centers anchored by one or more major tenants and located in the shopping center's trade area would be surveyed. It would not be necessary to survey the small unanchored strip centers or the enclosed malls because they would not be direct competition to the neighborhood center. If there are not sufficient competing centers to provide a valid comparison, the manager would then survey neighborhood centers outside the subject center's trade area.

Office buildings are classified as Class A, B, or C buildings and are located downtown, in a secondary business district, or in the suburbs. To establish the boundaries of the area to be surveyed, the property manager must first identify the classification of the subject office building and then determine which buildings are competition.

The method used in determining the area to survey for industrial properties is similar to the method used for office building surveys. Suburban buildings do not compete directly with downtown office buildings since most tenants choose between buildings in one particular area.

(b) CONDUCTING THE SURVEY

The only effective means for gathering market information is contacting leasing agents and property managers in the marketplace and inquiring about their "asking" and "deal-making" rates, the concessions they make, and their vacancies. Some leasing agents are reluctant to spend time conducting a market survey because they believe that their ongoing activities already keep them current on market activity. However, these individual activities do not give a comprehensive picture of the market. Even though a broker can be current on the activities of one segment of the market, such as high-rise office buildings in the central business district, general assumptions should not be applied to other segments of the market or other markets.

Conducting the market survey is not a difficult or time-consuming activity. Depending on the size of the market, the initial survey can take between two and three days. Subsequent surveys will take between one and two days. The initial survey takes approximately twice as long because the boundaries of the market must be defined, competing properties within the boundaries must be identified, and the person responsible for leasing the properties must be located.

The best way to locate competing properties is to drive the area within the boundaries of the market area and inspect the competing buildings using a market survey form. Competing properties are marked on a map and updated for subsequent surveys. While inspecting the properties, the manager will find the name and phone number of the leasing agent either on the directory of the office building or mall or on a sign on the property.

The property manager needs to develop a market survey form to record the rental information and features of the subject properties and the competition. The information on the survey form will vary according to property type. Exhibits 7.1, 7.2, and 7.3 are market survey forms for shopping centers, office buildings, and industrial properties, respectively. They request information on location, building features, condition of the property, deal-making rates, tenant charges, concessions, and vacancies. With the form in hand, and the market area identified, the property manager is prepared to conduct the survey.

Each competing property must be visited to understand how it compares with the subject property. The building's leasing agent can provide the rental data, but only a visual inspection will disclose the building's features and the condition of the property. Office building features such as life safety systems, energy conservation features, and security programs may not be observed during a property inspection. These features are obtained by contacting the property manager or leasing agent.

Once the building's features and property conditions are noted, the manager then schedules an appointment with the on-site manager to review the property's rental information. Those properties without an on-site manager will either indicate a contact person on a For Lease sign on the property or list the manager on the building's directory. If this information is not readily available, inquire with one of the tenants.

Although the property manager could acquire the information for the market survey by posing as a prospective tenant, most property managers and leasing agents are willing to share their information with one another. One way to elicit market information from a competitor is to share specific rental information on one's own property. The manager should be prepared to discuss briefly the size of the building, its location, the rental information, and vacancies. He should explain the asking rate and deal-making rate and the concessions he or she typically gives. For instance: "My building is asking $19.50 per square foot, but we will make a deal at $18.50 with one month free rent for each year of the lease." It is essential to obtain the deal-making rates. If only the asking rates are requested, the survey data will be distorted and the conclusion will be incorrect.

Free rent, overstandard improvements, moving allowance, and other concessions affect the face rate that is charged. Face rate is the rent paid without deduction for concessions. For instance, a rental rate at $18 per square foot for five years with six months free rent has a face rate of $18 and an effective rate of $16.20 per square foot. The effective rate takes into account the free rent and other concessions.

EXHIBIT 7.1

Market Survey—Shopping Centers

Center	Age	Center Data				Majors			Deal-making		Rental Info							Condition						
		Number Shops	Sq.Ft.	PK Lot	Majors		Vacancy	Asking Rts	Rts	%	Tax	Ins	CAM	CPI	HVAC	Other	P/L	Bldg	Area	Access	Tenants	Comments		

EXHIBIT 7.2

Market Survey—Office Buildings

Building Data				Rental Information								Building Services							
Office Bldg	Age	Stories	Sq.Ft.	Vacancy	Asking Rental	Deal-making Rental	Escal	CPI	Other	Parking	On-Site Mgmt-Maint.	Janitorial	Secur	Elev	HVAC/HR	Life Safety	Other		

Office Building	Parking		Bldg Condition		Community Services					Comments
	Open	Covered	Interior	Exterior	Transp	Restaurants	Shopping	Other	

EXHIBIT 7.3

Market Survey—Industrial Properties

| Property | Property Date | | | | Majors | | Rental Info | | | | | | | | |
	Zoning	Age	Sq.Ft.	No. of Bldgs	Major Tenants	Vacancy	Asking Rates	Deal-making Rates	Tax	Ins	CAM	CPI	HVAC	Other

| Parking Lot | Condition | | | | Features | | | | | | | | |
	Bldg	Area	Access	Type Const	Sprinklers	Util	Ceiling Heights	% Ofc Space	Truck Loading Facilities	Rail Spur	HVAC	Misc

243

Tenant charges also affect the rental rate. Are the office building escalation charges established from a base year? If so, what is the base year? Is a stop clause used? If so, what is the dollar amount of the expense stop? Base year and stop clauses are discussed in Chapter 8, Lease Administration. If the property is a shopping center, what are the charges for common area maintenance, real estate taxes, insurance and merchants' association or marketing . . . or promotional fund dues? Does the industrial property have a base year escalation charge or triple net pass-through?

The last information to obtain is the vacancy rate or the amount of vacant square footage. For some properties, this information can be obtained by walking the property. For others, such as office buildings, the information must be provided by the property manager or leasing agent.

(c) FREQUENCY OF SURVEY

The frequency of the market survey depends on several variables. A market survey is essential when drafting the property's annual management plan and when projecting the lease-up or absorption of a new building. Lenders frequently require a survey when financing a project to estimate the building's income. A survey is also needed when estimating income for the budget; when assuming a new management account; and when establishing or adjusting market rental rates. Whatever the variables, the market survey must be conducted as often as necessary to remain current with the market. Usually a quarterly or semiannual survey will suffice.

There are additional sources of information that can be consulted in developing a market survey. Most major commercial brokerage firms produce a quarterly or annual market survey that they release to the newspapers and industry journals. The leading commercial brokerage firms often hold an annual breakfast or luncheon meeting to report on the market in their area. Many BOMA chapters produce a quarterly office building market survey, and some IREM chapters hold market survey miniseminars. The real estate or business section of local business magazines and newspapers frequently report on the real estate market.

After the market information is obtained and the information placed on the market survey form, the property manager can compare the subject property with the competition, determine the property's position in the market, establish market rates and concessions, and project the property's lease-up.

(d) INACCURATE SURVEYS

Accurate market information is essential for projecting lease-up, vacancies, and building income—key components of the leasing program.

Any error in the market survey will result in inaccurate rental rates and concessions.

If the rental rates obtained during the survey do not accurately reflect the market rates, and the conclusions drawn from the survey are inaccurate, the recommended rates may be above market. This can affect the property's competitive position and obstruct leasing activity. Brokers immediately recognize when a building's rates are above market and will be reluctant to bring deals to the property owner. They will consider that the manager or the owner are not deal makers.

Inaccurate survey conclusions can also cause the recommended rates to be lower than market. As a result, the property will have less income and, consequently, a reduced net operating income and value. Whether the recommended rates are too high or too low, the results are the same—the property's NOI and value are reduced.

The credibility of the property manager is at stake. The relationship between the manager and the owner can be jeopardized if the building's rental rates are not maintained at their market rates at all times.

(e) EVALUATING THE MARKET SURVEY

Properly evaluated, the market survey will clarify the position of the subject property in the market and rank the property within its specific classification. The survey will compare building features and indicate areas in which the subject building excels and those in which it is deficient. This information can be used to identify areas of the building that need better maintenance or capital improvements. These improvements may be necessary to maintain or upgrade the building's position in the market.

In evaluating the information from the market survey, it is important to recognize that there isn't just one market rate for a classification of properties, but a range of rates. For instance, the Class A office space in a major city's CBD may range from $24 to $30 per square foot.

The variance in the range will depend on several factors. One factor is the building's location. A Class A building adjacent to a rapid transit station may command a higher rate than a building several blocks away. Another variable is location within the building. A space with a view will command higher rents than one without a view. A corner location in a mall will rent for considerably more than an in-line location with less exposure and foot traffic.

The size of the space is a third variable. Small spaces will rent for more per square foot than larger spaces when everything else is equal. In a shopping center, deep spaces usually lease for less per square foot than shallow spaces.

Other variables include: an office building with a prestigious address, a shopping center with a strong major tenant, an office building with a unique design, the cost of the pass-through expenses to the tenants, the building's immediate neighborhood, the quality of the building's management, the condition of the property, the services the tenants receive, and the features or amenities of the building.

When determining the subject property's position in the market range of rental rates, all of these variables are compared with the competitions'. The Institute of Real Estate Management recommends using a grid chart that assigns a number rating to the subject property in comparison with the competition.

Another method calls for the property manager to rate each building based on a visit to the buildings and general knowledge of the area. Even though evaluating buildings is more of an art than a science, an accurate analysis of the market and the market rates for each building are essential for the property manager to establish the building's position in the market and its rental rates and concessions.

(f) USING MARKET SURVEY INFORMATION

Market survey information must be shared with the property owner as soon as possible to determine the building's rental rates and concessions. Rental rates must be adjusted to reflect current market conditions and to maintain the competitiveness of the building.

Although property owners are usually aware of market conditions, they may have a misconception of their property's position in the range of market rates. They inevitably err on the high side and perceive their building's rates as higher than justified. The market survey will keep the owner aware of the property's correct position in the market range of rates.

Ideally the property manager would arrange for a meeting with the owner to review the survey and establish the rental rates and concessions. If the owner is out of the area, the survey can either be included with a monthly management report or sent as a separate report. Exhibit 7.4 illustrates a market survey format suitable for either purpose. The property manager should include recommended rental rates and concessions. An owner who is aware of market conditions and deals being made in the market is in a better position to evaluate the deals the manager presents.

The market survey can also be used to promote the property management company. The survey and a brief summary can be sent to potential clients. This gives the manager an opportunity to request a meeting to discuss market conditions.

The survey can be used as background for an article on market conditions written for one of the local newspapers or business journals. In addition, the property manager can be a resource person on a panel discussion held by BOMA or IREM, or other real estate organizations.

EXHIBIT 7.4

Commercial Market Survey Format

1. Cover page
2. Table of contents
3. Recommendations and conclusions

   Based on the analysis of the subject property and comparable properties, make recommendations for the subject property and timing of recommended actions. Make a recommendation for the optimum market rentals for the property, compare with current rents, and show the gross potential monthly income and increases. Include in the conclusions the status of the overall vacancy factor in the market, including inventory levels and absorption rates. Summarize anticipated results of the actions recommended to be taken at the property (i.e., move-outs and existing tenants, vacancy factor, "return to full occupancy" timing). Include a summary of the marketing and promotional program, listing possible alterations or plans of action needed to maintain high occupancy levels. Discuss the property's future upside potential and recommend future property sale.

4. Assignment and purpose of survey

   State the area that the market survey constitutes, the subject property's name and address, the individual or company that requested the survey (if applicable), and the general purpose and reasoning for preparing this survey.

5. Trade area analysis

   Starting with a demographic report from a service such as Urban Decisions, determine the characteristics of the surrounding population as to age, family makeup, income levels, and home ownership. Plot the competition on a map and determine the trade area for the shopping center. Obtain traffic counts in the area and evaluate the center's traffic as compared with other locations.

6. Subject property

   Prepare an objective analysis of the subject property, including major tenants, overall tenant mix, ingress, egress, visibility, management, parking ratios, amenities, landscaping, security, maintenance, sales comparisons, and compatibility with population in trade area.

7. Analysis of comparables

   Compare subject property with all other competitive properties. Compare properties using the grid evaluating each property in relationship to subject property.

8. Commercial market survey analysis

   In narrative form, compare the subject property with the competition, making recommendations about property tenant mix, rental levels, probably lease terms, physical changes or improvements, management considerations, and advertising and promotional recommendations.

9. Attach all supporting materials such as demographic reports, traffic maps, area maps, photos, newspaper articles, zoning maps, zoning decisions, an/or other supporting materials.

The information can also be shared with appraisers and investment salespeople who might in turn refer their clients to the manager. In house, the survey makes an excellent topic for discussion at leasing meetings.

§ 7.3   PRO FORMA RATE VS. MARKET RATE

The correct rental rate is a critical component in the marketing and leasing plan. Leasing agents are reluctant to work on a property whose rental rate is above the market rate because they have little chance of making a deal. The property manager must work with the property owner in establishing the building's market rental rates or pro forma rate.

The pro forma rental rate is derived from the income projection in the property's pro forma. The pro forma is the financial analysis of a property for a specific time period, such as one year or five years, and includes projections for income, the vacancy factor, operating expenses, and debt service (loan payment). A pro forma is prepared for new developments, for refinancing properties, and for the sale or purchase of a property. If the pro forma is being developed for a new or remodel project, it will include an anticipated lease-up, which is a projection of different occupancy levels during different periods of the pro forma until the building reaches a stabilized occupancy.

No commercial property is ever leased at the pro forma rate simply because it is the pro forma rate. Space is leased only at market rate. When a developer's or owner's pro forma rate is the same as the market rate, it is either a coincidence or the result of a thorough analysis of market conditions.

When pro forma rates have no relationship to market rates, value is robbed from the property by a longer lease-up time and higher vacancy rate, resulting in less income. A pro forma rate that is below the market rate will result in a faster lease-up and a higher occupancy, but the building's overall income during the initial lease-up in subsequent years will be less because of the lower rental rates, and the building's value will be correspondingly less. When the property owner's rental rates are not at market, the error is usually on the high side of the market rental rate.

Frequently the developer or the owner becomes blinded to market conditions because of emotional involvement with the property or a lack of understanding of the market conditions. Sometimes the property must produce a certain income level to be financed or to achieve a desired sale price, and the pro forma rate is selected solely to achieve this income "on paper." This is known as "backing into the rental rates."

The manager has the responsibility to keep the owner aware of the market conditions and the property's market rental rate. This responsibility is especially important when rates are experiencing a rapid decline or increase. An example of a rapid change in market rates occurred in the oil-producing states in 1986 when the price of a barrel of oil dropped from above $30 to $10. In Anchorage, the rates for Class B office space and neighborhood strip center space dropped 30% to 50% in less than nine months. During the same period, Class A office space and enclosed mall space dropped 10% to 15%. The market rates in Anchorage continued to drop through 1988. The prudent manager surveyed this market every two to three months and communicated any market changes to the owner. When leasing agents or property managers did not keep current with market conditions, their buildings were not competitive and suffered from less leasing activity, a higher vacancy rate, and lower income.

It is important to note that rental rates for different property types do not increase or decrease at the same rate. Even within a property type, the market rental rates for the different classifications of property do not change at the same rate. For example, in a soft office market, Class A office space may experience a small drop in its market rates, while Class B office space will probably experience a greater reduction in rates. This is often the result of tenants in Class B space upgrading to Class A space at the same or slightly higher rates. Since rental rates do not change at the same rate for all property types, no rule of thumb for determining the percent of increase or decrease in market rates can be applied to each property type or each classification of property.

Occasionally a property owner who has experienced slow leasing activity in a building for an extended period may respond by slashing rental rates below market and adding concessions not required in the market. This panic is usually the result of the property owner's having established a rental rate higher than the market rate for an extended period and then overreacting by lowering rates below what is necessary to be competitive.

The manager has several opportunities to keep the owner current on market conditions. The best opportunity is by reviewing the market survey with the property owner. The monthly management report is another means to communicate market conditions to the property owner. A statement on the market conditions and leasing activities in the monthly management report, along with copies of articles on the market conditions, will provide the property owner with a regular review and understanding of the market. The monthly management report is thoroughly reviewed in Chapter 11, Reports to Owners.

Few issues are more important to a property owner than the building's leasing activity. The property manager can provide the owner with the necessary information to analyze the market and arrive at a realistic market rental rate. Combining market information with an effective marketing and leasing program will enable the property to achieve and maintain its highest value.

§ 7.4   BREAKEVEN ANALYSIS

How will a property manager, leasing agent, or property owner know if a proposed lease is a good deal or a bad deal? The economics of a lease are determined when a breakeven analysis is performed. When a deal is presented to the property owner, an analysis should be included showing the proposed lease profit or loss. The manager can determine the breakeven rental rate for the property and then compare it with the proposal.

The breakeven analysis amortizes the income, commission, and tenant improvements over the life of the lease and includes the building's operating expenses. These figures are then converted to a dollar per square foot per year amount to arrive at the dollar per square foot profit or loss before and after debt service. Depreciation and amortization of the loan and time value of money are not considered.

The following is an example of a breakeven analysis: A lease is proposed for 2,000 square feet of space in an office building for five years, with three months' free rent—one year and nine months at $15 per square foot, two years at $17 per square foot, and the fifth year at $19 per square foot. The landlord contribution towards tenant improvements (TI) is $15,000. The building has an operating expense stop clause of $5 per square foot. The lease commission is 5% of the base rental income over the term of the lease, payable one half on lease execution and one half when the tenant takes occupancy and commences paying base rent.

Terms:
  Space: 2,000 sq. ft.
  Rent: 3 months free, 1 year 9 months at $15/sq. ft.,
                  2 years at $17/sq. ft., and 1 year at $19/sq. ft.
  TI: $15,000
  Stop expense: $5/sq. ft.
  Commission: 5% of gross income

1. Determine rent over 5 years, average annual rent, and average annual rent per square foot.

   Rent:
   Year 1
       Three months free   = $ 0
       Nine months (2,000 sq. ft. × $15/sq. ft.   =   30,000
         ÷ 12 mo. = $2,500/mo. × 9mo.)   =   22,500

Year 2	2,000 sq. ft. × $15	=	30,000
Year 3	2,000 sq. ft. × $17	=	34,000
Year 4	2,000 sq. ft. × $17	=	34,000
Year 5	2,000 sq. ft. × $19	=	38,000
			$158,500

$158,500 ÷ 5 years   = $31,700 (avg. annual rent)

$31,700 ÷ 2,000 sq. ft. = $15.85/sq. ft. (avg. annual rent/sq. ft.)

2. Determine owner's nonreimbursable operating expenses. The lease states that the owners will pay the first $5 per square foot of operating expenses over the life of the lease. All increases in operating expenses will be paid by the tenant.

3. Determine base commission, annual commission averaged over five years, and the commission per square foot per year.

Gross income	$158,500
Commission rate	× .05
Commission	$ 7,925
Divided by five years	÷ 5
Avg. annual commission	$ 1,585
Divided by 2,000 sq. ft.	÷ 2,000
Commission/sq. ft./yr.	$ .79

4. Determine tenant improvement cost per square foot per year.

TI	$ 15,000
Divided by five years	÷ 5
TI cost/yr.	$ 3,000
Divided by sq. ft.	÷ 2,000
Cost/sq. ft./yr.	$ 1.50

5. Determine debt service.

Obtain annual debt service from the owner and divide this amount by the square footage of the rentable or usable area of the building, depending upon how the building is being leased. Assuming the debt service in this example is $400,000/year, and the rentable area of the building is 55,000 square feet, compute the following:

$$\frac{\text{Debt service}}{\text{Rentable sq. ft.}} \quad \frac{\$400,000}{55,000} = 7.27 \text{ debt service/sq. ft.}$$

	Annual Rate/Sq. Ft.
Base income	$15.85/sq. ft.
Less: Operating expenses	(5.00)
Lease commission	(.79)
Tenant improvements	(1.50)
Profit (or loss) before debt service	$ 8.56
Less: Debt service	(7.27)
Net profit (or loss)	$ 1.29/sq. ft.

Breakeven Analysis

The profit of $1.29 per square foot times the 2,000 square feet provides a total dollar profit of $2,580 per year or $12,900 for five years.

Armed with this information, the property manager can determine whether this is a good or bad deal. Each time a lease is presented to the owner, a breakeven analysis should accompany the deal. If the net amount is a loss, the property manager then compares the loss with the cost of not making this deal. The cost of not making the deal is the cost of additional lost rent added to the breakeven analysis that is projected for the next deal. The next deal is a best estimate of how long the space will remain vacant, how much rent can be collected, and how much tenant improvements will cost. During a soft market, the owner is sometimes better off accepting either a low net profit or even a small loss than gambling on finding another tenant for the space at a higher rate. Giving four months' free rent may be better than waiting for a more lucrative deal. If there is no backup prospective tenant and another deal is unlikely in the next few months, giving free rent is losing nothing since the space would be vacant and nonproductive anyway. The phrase "it is better to collect rent than dust" was common during the soft office building market of the mid-1980s. This phrase suggests that it is often better to accept a lease with a net loss than to allow the space to sit vacant for an extended period and incur a greater loss.

§ 7.5 THE LEASING TEAM

An effective leasing program must have a team that understands market conditions, has common objectives, and exhibits a willingness to work together.

The property owner selects and monitors the leasing team. If the property is held under a joint venture partnership with more than one general partner, an owner's representative must be selected among the partners. The balance of the team includes a leasing agent, who may or may not be the property manager, and administrative support persons. The advertising agency is included initially while the leasing package is being developed and continues if an ongoing public relations program is implemented.

Competition is keen in leasing space, and the leasing team must work as a cohesive unit with one objective—to lease the property at market rates as quickly as possible.

(a) WHO SHOULD LEASE THE PROPERTY?

One of the owner's most critical decisions is who should lease the property. In making this decision the owner must recognize that the choice will vary according to the circumstances. The owner first needs to clarify the leasing objectives, which are to lease the property as quickly as possible at the best rental rate to the best tenants. The property owner then needs to ask, What is the best way to achieve my leasing objectives? Who is best qualified to accomplish these objectives? Should the leasing be the responsibility of a leasing broker, an in-house leasing agent who is the employee of the owner, or the property manager? Each of these alternatives—the leasing broker, the in-house leasing agent, and the property manager—has advantages and disadvantages depending on the leasing situation.

Leasing Broker

The leasing broker working for a local or national commercial brokerage firm can offer the services of an organization geared solely to leasing or leasing and selling commercial property. The organization will have several people actively involved in commercial leasing who share ideas and regularly brainstorm leasing situations.

Since the leasing broker has one responsibility, leasing space, the total focus of his or her working day will be on leasing. The leasing broker will develop contacts with other leasing brokers in the community and will cobroker many deals. Unless a leasing broker is the exclusive agent for a major project such as a high-rise office building or a regional mall, the broker will be leasing several properties simultaneously. Even when the leasing agent has an exclusive on a major building, he or she may be leasing other properties. The broker is always in the "market" and is aware of tenant movements and new tenants in the area, and may develop a clientele who will call the broker when they need space. The broker may become a tenant's exclusive broker for locating space.

On larger projects, the leasing broker may develop a team to lease a project. For instance, in a regional mall, three or four leasing brokers will divide the leasing responsibilities, basing their leasing assignments on categories of tenants. One broker will work with the restaurant and specialty food tenants; another broker will be responsible for the gifts, speciality, and service stores; while a third broker will be responsible for the fashion stores.

A seasoned leasing broker may employ an inexperienced leasing broker, sometimes referred to as a "runner," to canvass the area.

Using a leasing broker offers a further advantage. Since the broker is active in the market, he or she may know more about the types of deals that are being made in the market. The leasing broker also has negotiating experience and the support of an entire organization experienced in leasing commercial properties.

There are some concerns, however, that must be addressed when using a leasing broker. Leasing brokers work for commission only. If a 50,000-square-foot office building has only two vacancies totaling 1,800 square feet, will the broker spend adequate time and effort leasing the space? Along this line, when deals are slow at one property, will the broker give attention to more promising properties and neglect the difficult ones? In both of these situations, the property owner may end up with an exclusive leasing agreement, a broker's sign on the property, and little else.

Many brokers are reluctant to go to the property owner and suggest the leasing agreement be terminated or not renewed. There are several reasons for this: First, the broker may be concerned that the relationship with the property owner will be severed if he or she gives up on leasing a property. Second, since one rule of real estate is, "The one who controls the property gets paid," even though the broker may not be actively working the property, if another broker brings in a tenant, the broker with the exclusive will receive a cobroker's commission. Even though these motives may be understandable in the eyes of the broker, most property owners would prefer that the broker terminate the leasing agreement rather than let an unsuccessful leasing situation continue. Owners will respect brokers who consider the good of the project as their number one priority.

In-House Leasing Agent

The in-house leasing agent is an employee of the property owner and is usually paid a salary with an incentive bonus based on leasing results. This person will devote 100% of his or her time and effort to the owner's properties. The in-house leasing agent is able to become completely familiar with the owner's property and to spend full time working (leasing) the property. If the owner has properties at which leasing is slow, the in-house leasing agent can afford to continue to work the property because he or she has a base salary to cover the lean periods when few leases are being made. The in-house leasing agent also has the same opportunity to network in the leasing market as does the outside broker.

The disadvantage of in-house agents is that they may not work as hard to make a deal because they have a base salary available and may rely too heavily on outside brokers to bring in deals. In addition, frequently the in-house agent is working *alone* and can't benefit from the creative synergy that results when several leasing brokers work together. Because of a lack of support staff, the in-house leasing agent may not be able to use his or her time effectively.

Property Manager as Leasing Agent

The property manager as leasing agent also has distinct advantages and disadvantages. One obvious advantage is that the property manager is more familiar with the area, the property, the tenants, and the goals of the owner. The property manager is either on site or visits the property regularly and is motivated to devote time to leasing even when only one or two vacancies exist. If the property manager has been conducting market surveys regularly, he or she knows the market better than anyone else. One disadvantage of using the property manager to lease space is that the manager may not have sufficient time or expertise. And because the manager may not be active in the leasing market, he or she may be unaware of new tenants coming into the area or tenants who are considering expanding or relocating. The property manager's leasing time can be diluted by pressing management responsibilities. Further, prospective tenants often prefer to work with a broker who represents several properties.

Deciding whether to use a leasing broker or a property manager to handle lease renewals is sometimes difficult. A leasing broker may be more familiar with the market and better able to obtain the best deal, but the leasing commission, especially if it is for a small space, may not be worth the time spent negotiating the renewal. Another disadvantage is that the leasing broker is not familiar with the tenant's contributions to the property and may approach the negotiations in an impersonal manner that offends the tenant.

The property manager offers the advantage of knowing tenants' backgrounds and concerns. If the renewal rate is a significant increase over the existing rate, the property manager can provide information on market rates prior to negotiating the renewal, thereby avoiding an unpleasant shock when the higher rate is discussed. On the other hand, the property manager may have too much sympathy for the tenant and not negotiate a market rate deal.

None of the advantages or disadvantages apply to all brokers, all in-house leasing agents, or all property managers, nor do they apply to every leasing situation. However, the property owner must consider these factors when evaluating who should lease the property. Remember, the objectives are to lease the space as quickly as possible to the best tenants at the market rate. If the property manager believes someone else can best accomplish this objective, he or she should state this to the owner and recommend the best leasing broker for the property.

(b) WORKING WITH THE BROKERAGE COMMUNITY

When leasing is handled by the property manager or an in-house leasing agent, the brokerage community should become part of the leasing and marketing plan.

Many tenants will appoint a broker as their leasing representative for locating space and negotiating the lease. Brokers more often represent office and industrial tenants than shopping center tenants for two reasons. First, most office and industrial space users lease larger spaces than do small shop users in shopping centers. Seldom does a retailer's space exceed 2,500 square feet, while office and industrial tenants requirements range from a few thousand square feet to in excess of one hundred thousand square feet. Hence, the commission to be earned representing an office or industrial user is usually much greater than the commission earned representing a retail user. Usually a retail broker must lease more retail spaces to equal the commission earned by an office or industrial broker. In addition, the opportunity to represent a large or major user is greater when representing office and industrial users.

Second, many of the small shop tenants are independent (mom and pop) tenants who are not familiar with the services of a broker. Many of these tenants look for space on their own and either hire an attorney or negotiate the lease themselves.

The property manager must recognize that brokers have tremendous influence over the tenants they represent. In some situations, they can even influence which buildings the tenant will visit and, of course, they have a major influence over which building the tenant selects. Alienating a broker or the brokerage community will result in some prospective tenants not being shown your property and lost deals. The property manager should emphasize that the broker's role is important throughout the lease negotiations.

The property manager can communicate in many ways to the brokerage community that broker cooperation is encouraged. First, the For Lease sign on the property should state, "Broker Cooperation Welcome." Personal contact with the brokers is the best method to communicate information concerning available space. Regularly taking brokers to breakfast or lunch is an excellent way to develop a working relationship. Membership in professional organizations provides another opportunity to meet with brokers. Some areas have multiple listing services for commercial properties, and ads in this service should be considered.

The property manager should inform the broker that he or she is more than willing to share property operating information. Escalation charges and common area costs, operating expenses, and vacancy factors are a few items that may be helpful to brokers when they are listing a property for sale or comparing lease proposals. If the property management company doesn't have a large leasing staff or leasing capacity, it may team up with a brokerage firm for joint proposals to manage and lease a property. This can result in cross-referrals.

Next, the property manager can arrange to make presentations to leasing agents at brokerage firms that have weekly sales and leasing meetings. Either the brokerage firm will specialize in leasing one type of property, such as office buildings, or it will have several divisions with each division specializing in a property type. When making a presentation to a brokerage firm with several divisions, the manager should request a meeting with the division that leases the property type he or she is representing. The manager should provide marketing materials, brochures, plot plans, photos, and aerials as handouts.

Continuous follow-up with the brokers is necessary to keep properties in front of the brokerage community. The property manager can develop a mailing to brokers listing on one side all of the properties to be leased and a collage of photos on the reverse side. The one-page mailer can be preprinted in large quantity on card stock, with the collage on one side and the other side left blank. For each broker's mailing, the list of properties with vacancies can be added to the blank side and reproduced by a quick print process. Commercial brokers should receive these mailings at least quarterly and as often as monthly.

A list of brokers can be developed by contacting the local board of realtors and requesting a list of its commercial brokers; by reviewing the multiple listing books and noting the brokers with commercial buildings for sale or lease; by developing a list from the commercial For Lease signs on buildings; by reviewing the membership list of the real estate professional organization; and by checking the Yellow Pages. Many areas will have an organization for commercial brokers, which is an excellent source for a commercial broker's mailing list. Every commercial broker has an operating network, and no broker, regardless of experience or size of the company, should be overlooked.

The broker wants to believe the property manager as the landlord's representative is a deal maker not a deal breaker. A property manager who is not flexible in negotiating the lease terms and lease clauses will be perceived as a deal breaker. The property manager doesn't have to give in on every point but should be willing to compromise when appropriate. For instance, national tenants will request several changes to the lease, and the property manager must be willing, able, and available to review the lease with the broker and negotiate many of the tenant's concerns.

Once the deal is executed, the broker's next concern is payment of the commission. Most brokers earn a commission, not a salary with a regular paycheck, and the property manager should see that the broker is paid on time per the commission agreement. If a commission payment—for example, the second half—could be paid a little early, the broker will be even more grateful.

Another means of showing appreciation for brokerage cooperation is to give Christmas gifts to brokers who brought tenants to the property. A small gift can be presented to brokers who cooperated in one or two deals and a larger gift to those who cooperated in several leases or a major lease. Gifts can be wine, fruit, or cheese assortments, which are packaged in several sizes.

A broker's open house at a new development or a remodeled property is another means to present the property to the brokerage community. Refreshments and possibly musical entertainment can be part of the event as well as a supply of materials on other properties that might be of interest to the broker.

An open house for the business community is another means to market a property. The property manager should be careful not to mix guests from the brokerage community and the business community so that the brokers will not solicit the business community for other properties.

When the broker does register a tenant and negotiations commence, the property manager should coordinate with the broker, providing information early in the negotiations. Information such as tenant charges, construction schedules, and other items that the broker must know to analyze and compare the property with other properties being considered are essential for the broker to present a proposal. The property manager should respond quickly to the broker's questions. The old saying, "Time is money," is a fitting statement for someone whose income is earned from commissions.

After a lease is executed, give the broker recognition in the community. Some major developers will annually place a half-page or full-page ad in the newspaper expressing appreciation to those brokers who have brought in leases. A list of leases executed and the names of the leasing agents can also be given to local newspapers and business journals as public relations articles about the property and for recognition for the brokers.

A major concern of the broker is that his or her position in the deal will be protected. All brokers can tell stories about how they were shut out of a commission by a landlord or another leasing agent. Since most brokers act as independent contractors whose income is from commissions, creating and protecting this income is of great interest to them. The broker wants to be protected in the deal; a written commission agreement will provide this protection. Equally important, the property manager must assure the broker that he or she will be paid a commission if the broker brings the property manager a tenant, follows the manager's requirements for registering tenants, and a lease is executed.

It is obvious that the cooperation of the leasing brokers is an essential element in a marketing and leasing plan, and the property manager should consider the broker as an additional marketing tool.

(c) LEASING AGREEMENT

The leasing agreement sets forth the understanding between the property owner and the leasing broker. Several items must be negotiated in the agreement.

The first term discussed is the commission rate. The agreement must state how the commission will be calculated—a percentage of the rents, a fixed fee, a dollar per square foot, or any formula agreed upon by the owner and broker. It also should state how the commission will be shared on a co-broker deal.

The payment schedule is the next concern. Will the commission be paid entirely when the lease is executed or will it be divided over time?

The agreement should state whether a commission is paid when the tenant renews, expands, or exercises an option. Brokers often believe that they should be paid each time a tenant renews and expands because they introduced the tenant to the property. However, many property owners refuse to pay a commission on renewals and expansions because they paid the broker for bringing the tenant to the building, and any changes to the tenants occupancy are negotiated by the owner or property manager.

The property owner and broker now need to negotiate the length of the agreement. A broker will need a year or two to market a proposed building and six months to one year for an existing building. An agreement must be reached on who pays for the marketing materials, publicity, signs, and brochures. The owner will want a right to cancel the agreement if the broker's marketing and leasing program is ineffective. The agreement will state that the broker is an independent contractor and not an employee of the owner.

The property owner will want to be held harmless and indemnified for gross negligence and misconduct of the broker. The broker will want to be held harmless for any inaccurate information provided by the owner. The agreement should state that neither party will discriminate based on race, color, creed, nationality, gender, age, or handicap. There will be other clauses generic to all contracts.

A sample leasing agreement is shown in Exhibit 7.5.

(d) LEASING COMMISSIONS

Commissions are the driving force behind all leasing activities, mainly because the leasing agent's livelihood comes solely from commission income. Therefore, structuring the commission schedule is one of the

EXHIBIT 7.5

Exclusive Leasing Commission Agreement

THIS EXCLUSIVE LEASING COMMISSION AGREEMENT (hereinafter referred to as the "Agreement") is made and entered into this _____ day of _____, 19 , by and between _____ (hereinafter referred to as "Landlord"), and _____ (hereinafter referred to as the "Broker").

W I T N E S S E T H:

WHEREAS, Landlord is the owner of _____
_____
_____

WHEREAS, Landlord desires to delegate certain leasing responsibilities to Broker subject to the terms and conditions of this Agreement, and Broker agrees to accept such responsibilities and to perform them according to the terms and conditions contained herein; and

WHEREAS, pursuant to this Agreement, Broker is or may be engaged in certain negotiations between Landlord and certain prospective tenants (hereinafter collectively referred to as the "Prospective Tenant") for one or more leases covering space in the Project; and

WHEREAS, such negotiations have not been concluded; and

WHEREAS, Landlord and Broker desire to set forth the terms and conditions which must be fulfilled prior to any commission due from Landlord being deemed to have been earned by Broker; and

WHEREAS, Landlord and Broker desire to confirm and reduce to writing their entire understanding and agreement with respect to said negotiations, commissions, and fees;

NOW, THEREFORE, in consideration of the mutual terms, covenants, and agreements herein contained, together with other good and valuable consideration, the receipt and sufficiency of which is hereby acknowledged, the parties hereto hereby agree as follows:

I. RATE OF COMMISSION AND TIME OF PAYMENT

Lease Commission Calculation. In the event, prior to the Termination Date of this Agreement as defined below or earlier termination, the Broker delivers to Landlord written leases, executed and acknowledged by the Prospective Tenant and acceptable to Landlord as evidenced by its execution thereof (hereinafter referred to as a "Lease"), Landlord will pay to Broker one (1) leasing commission based upon the following formula:

_____
_____
_____
_____
_____
_____
_____

II. LIMITATIONS ON COMMISSIONS

A.   Exclusions. In computing the rental upon which the aforesaid commission is based, the following shall be excluded and no commission shall be earned thereon:

(1) Increase in Rent. Increase(s) in rent pursuant to any escalation provision of said Lease whereby the Prospective Tenant is obligated to pay an increased rental based upon any escalator provision or index, or pay a share of Landlord's costs over the term of the Lease, including, but not limited to, taxes, assessments, insurance premiums, common area maintenance charges, and/or other expenses.

(2) Subletting by Landlord from Tenant. Rental upon any portion of the demised premises payable or credited by Landlord

EXHIBIT 7.5 *(Continued)*

to Prospective Tenant by reason of Landlord's retaining, as subtenant or otherwise, any portion of the demised premises.

(3) <u>Percentage Rent</u>. Percentage rentals.

(4) <u>Tenant's Extras</u>. Rentals or any compensation payable by the Prospective Tenant for parking, leasehold improvements, decorations, or Tenant's extras furnished or paid for by Landlord, or utilities or equipment charges where such equipment charges are identified as such in the Lease or where the cost for the same is a part of the rent charged the Prospective Tenant under the Lease.

(5) <u>Security Deposits</u>. Any security deposits, and repayments or replenishments thereof.

(6) <u>Termination Payments</u>. Any payment made or to be made by Tenant in connection with a termination or cancellation of the Lease.

B.   <u>Exclusions Based on Renewal and Additional Space</u>. No commission shall be earned or paid to Broker as a result of any renewal or extension of the Lease between Landlord and the Prospective Tenant, whether or not such renewal, or extension, is the result of an option for renewal, or extension contained in the Lease. No such commission shall be earned or paid as a result of the exercise of an option by or other right of the Prospective Tenant for additional space.

C.   <u>Exclusions Based on Cancellation</u>. If the Lease shall provide that the Lease may be cancelled by either party at any time prior to the commencement of the term thereof, then in the event that the Lease shall in fact be so cancelled, no commission shall be deemed due or earned by Broker, and Broker shall credit against future commissions earned by Broker pursuant to this Agreement any sums which may have been theretofore paid or advanced by Landlord, to Broker with respect to said Lease.

III.   <u>REGISTRATION</u>.

Landlord agrees that it shall pay any commissions earned by Broker pursuant to the requirements of Sections I.A and I.C above, if within ninety (90) days following termination of this Agreement by either Landlord or Broker, the Project or any portion thereof is leased to any person or entity to whom Broker has submitted the Project and with whom Broker has entered into substantial negotiations for the Project prior to the expiration of the term or termination of the Agreement, the identity of whom has been provided to and approved by Landlord. Broker agrees to submit a list to Landlord of all persons or entities satisfying the foregoing conditions of submittal and substantial negotiation not later than fifteen (15) days following the expiration of the term or termination of the Agreement. Landlord shall have an additional fifteen (15) days from its receipt of said list to approve it.

IV.   <u>NO COMMISSION IF LEASE NOT EXECUTED</u>.

If, for any reason whatsoever, including, but not limited to, the acts, omissions, negligence or the willful default of Landlord, its agents, employees, or representatives, any Lease shall not be entered into between Landlord and a Prospective Tenant, then no commission, shall be deemed to be due or earned, nor shall the same be paid to Broker by Landlord, and Landlord is and shall be relieved from liability for the payment of any and all commissions, claims, or charges whatsoever. It is expressly agreed that Landlord shall have the unqualified right, in its sole and absolute discretion, to refuse to enter into the Lease for any reason whatsoever without Landlord incurring any obligation to Broker for the payment of a commission, or otherwise. It is further agreed that for any commission to be deemed due or earned, Broker must satisfy the requirements set forth in Section I.A and III above.

V.   <u>INDEMNITY</u>.

Broker warrants and represents to Landlord that Broker is a licensed broker in good standing under the laws of the State of _____. Broker's Real Estate License No. in _____, is _____.

EXHIBIT 7.5 *(Continued)*

Broker shall indemnify Landlord, its partners (collectively referred to as "indemnitees") and the agents, servants, and employees of each of said Indemnitee, from any and all claims, demands, losses, causes of action, arbitrations, attorney's fees, expert witness fees and costs of defense to the extent that they are based upon any negligent, reckless or intentional wrongful act or failure to act by Broker, its agents, servants or employees, including, but not limited to, representations, concealments, nondisclosures, claims for personal injury, sickness, disease or death, or injury to or destruction of tangible property, related to or arising out of performance of the services of this Agreement to be performed by Broker.

VI.   ASSIGNMENT AND BINDING EFFECT.

This Agreement shall be binding upon and inure to the benefit of the heirs, administrators, executors, personal representatives and assigns of the respective parties hereto, provided, that this Agreement is a contract for provision of personal services by Broker pursuant to the delegations contained herein, and may not be assigned or tranferred, nor may the rights, obligations, and duties of the Broker herein contained, be delegated to any other party or individual, without the prior written approval of Landlord, which approval may be withheld or conditioned as Landlord may deem appropriate.

VII.   TERM; TERMINATION.

A.   Commencement Date and Termination Date. The term of this Agreement shall commence as of _____, which shall be the "Commencement Date." It shall continue until midnight, Seattle, Washington, time on _____ unless sooner terminated pursuant to the terms hereof, which shall be the "Termination Date" of this Agreement.

B.   Termination. It is understood and agreed that this Agreement may be terminaed by Landlord or Broker on not less than thirty (30) days written notice. In the event of such termination, Broker shall receive from Landlord any commissions earned and which are then due and payable, according to the terms of Section I above.

VIII.   EXCLUSIVE LEASING.

The Broker and Landlord agree that until the Termination Date, or earlier termination of this Agreement, the Broker shall be the exclusive Leasing Agent with respect to Leases covering all or any part of the Project.

IX.   INDEPENDENT CONTRACTOR RELATIONSHIP.

A.   Independent Contractor. It is understood and agreed that Broker's relationship to the Landlord is that of an independent contractor and not an employee and that Landlord will not be held responsible for the collection and payment of taxes or contributions of any nature on behalf of the Broker.

B.   Representations and Concessions. The Broker, its agents, employees, or affiliates, shall make no representations, misrepresentations, warranties, concessions, or agreements pertaining to the Lease or the Project without the prior written approval of Landlord, and Landlord shall not be responsbile for any representations, misrepresentations, warranties, concessions, or agreements, which Landlord does not expressly so approve and authorize.

X.   BROKER'S WARRANTIES.

Broker agrees to abide by all laws, ethical practices, standards, and regulations promulgated by the State of Washington Real Estate Commission, or equivalent thereto, as now exists or may be established from time to time. Broker further warrants and represents that it will devote sufficient time and services to secure Prospective Tenants for the Project in order to accomplish the purposes of Broker and Landlord. Broker further warrants not to make any representations, misrepresentations, concessions or agreements regarding any Lease with a Prospective Tenant, the Project, or any other Prospective Tenant, which has not been approved expressly by Landlord.

EXHIBIT 7.5 *(Continued)*

XI.   LEASING AGREEMENT.

Broker agrees and acknowledges that is is subject to all terms and conditions of the Leasing Agreement, in addition to the terms and conditions set forth herein.

XII. ENTIRE AGREEMENT AND ATTORNEY'S FEES.

This Agreement contains the entire agreement of the parties respecting the delegation to Broker by Landlord, and no representations, promises, or agreements, oral or otherwise, between the parties not embodied herein shall be of any force or effect. In the event that at any time during the term of this Agreement either Landlord or Broker shall institute any action or proceeding against the other relating to the provisions of this Agreement, or any default hereunder, then, and in that event, the unsuccessful party in such action or proceeding agrees to reimburse the prevailing party for the reasonable costs, expenses, attorneys' fees and disbursements incurred therein by the prevailing party.

XIII. NO DISCRIMINATION.

It is understood that Landlord does not discriminate against any tenant or Prospective Tenant including, but not limited to, discrimination by reason of race, color, creed, national origin, handicap, religion, sex, or age.

XIV. BROKER'S EXPENSES.

A.   Broker will be responsible for all its expenses.

B.   Broker will, at Broker's expense pay for a Project brochure which was developed by Broker and Landlord.

XV.   NOTICES

All notices and communications required under this Agreement shall be mailed certified mail, return receipt requested, or shall be delivered personally to the addresses set forth below:

Landlord:

_____
_____

To: _____
_____
_____

And to: _____
_____
_____

Broker:

_____
_____

The foregoing addresses may be changed by giving written notice to the other party. All notices shall be deemed delivered when personally served or when actually received through the mails as evidenced by the return receipt, whichever first occurs.

XVI. MISCELLANEOUS.

A.   Time. Time is of the essence of this Agreement.

B.   Law. This Agreement shall be interpreted under, and governed by, the laws of the State of Washington.

EXHIBIT 7.5 *(Continued)*

C.   No Third Party Rights. Nothing herein shall create, or give rise to, any rights, claims, benefits, or preferences in any person, corporation, partnership, or other entity whatsoever.

D.   Survival. The provisions of this Agreement shall survive the execution and delivery of any Lease.

E.   Captions. The captions of this Agreement are for convenience and reference only and in no way define, limit, or describe the scope or intent of this Agreement, nor in any way affect this Agreement.

F.   Amendment and Waiver. No agreement hereafter made shall be effective to change, modify, or discharge this Agreement or constitute a waiver of any of the provisions hereof, in whole or in part, unless such agreement is in writing and signed by the party against whom the enforcement of the change, modification, or discharge or waiver is sought.

IN WITNESS WHEREOF, the parties have entered into this Agreement as of the day and year first above written.

LANDLORD:

_____
_____

By: _____
_____
_____

By: _____
    Its: _____
_____
_____

By: _____
    Its: _____
_____
_____

Broker:

_____
_____
_____

NOTARY

STATE OF WASHINGTON)
                     : ss.
COUNTY OF KING   )

I certify that I know or have satisfactory evidence that _____ signed this instrument, on oath stated that he/she was authorized to execute the instrument, and acknowledged it as the _____ of _____ to be the free and voluntary act of such party for the uses and purposes mentioned in the instrument.

DATED: _____,

_____
Notary Public in and for the
State of Washington, residing
at _____. My
commission expires _____

most critical elements in a marketing and leasing program. The commission schedule must be carefully thought out to provide the proper incentives to the leasing agent and to be a fair expense of the project.

Commissions are negotiable; there are no standard commission rates. The rate of commission is dependent upon several factors: the size of the space being leased, the length of the lease, the gross or net income the landlord earned during part or all of the lease term, the expertise of the property manager or leasing agent, the condition of the market, the difficulty of the leasing assignment, the property management or leasing company's cost of doing business, and what the property owner is willing to pay.

Frequently there is a difference of opinion between the property owner and the person responsible for leasing over what is a fair compensation for marketing the property and negotiating the leases. The difference of opinion is usually resolved after carefully negotiating the terms of the leasing agreement. Items that are negotiated are: amount of the commission, incentive commissions, and the timing of the payment of the commission. Other business terms are also negotiated as shown in Exhibit 7.5.

Commissions may be calculated according to different formulas. They can be based on a percentage of the gross or net rents. This method requires first determining which income will be used to calculate the commission. When the commission is based on the gross income, a percentage rate is applied to all the income and tenant charges the tenant will pay during a specific period of the lease. For instance, for a commission for a three-year lease with an industrial tenant who pays base rent and the real estate taxes and insurance on the building, the property owner would calculate the base rent collected during the three years and add to this amount the tenant's estimated reimbursement for real estate taxes and insurance for calculating the commission. If the commission is paid annually, the property owner would calculate the actual reimbursement of the tenant charges for determining the commission. Another method is calculating the commission as a percentage of the base rent only (known as *net income*).

Next, determine what period of time during the lease term is used to calculate the commission. For instance, the agreement may state that the income during the entire lease term is used to calculate the commission. If the lease term is for fifty years, possibly only the income during the first ten years is used to calculate the commission. Finally, determine which percentage rate will be used and whether it will be a fixed or a sliding percentage rate for the term of the lease the commission is being paid.

An example of a commission based on a percentage of the income is shown in Table 7.1. A lease for 2,000 square feet of space in an office building for five years at $15 per square feet for three years and $17 per

TABLE 7.1

Calculation of Commission Based on Percentage of Income

Lease Year	Space (Sq. Ft.)	Rental Rate	Annual Income
1	2,000	$15	$ 30,000
2	2,000	15	30,000
3	2,000	15	30,000
4	2,000	17	34,000
5	2,000	17	34,000
		Total Base Income	$158,000

Total Base Income	$158,000
Percentage Rate (5%)	× .05
Commission	$ 7,900

square feet for two years. The commission is based on 5% of the base rent received during the entire term of the lease.

A shopping center space of 1,400 square feet is leased for four years at a base rent of $16.50 per square foot. Table 7.2 shows a commission calculated on the base rent as follows: 6% the first year, 5% the second year, 4% the third year, and 3% the fourth year.

Another method for calculating commissions is based on a dollar per square foot leased. The shopping center industry first adopted this method in the late 1970s. Some developers believed that a conflict could arise over the length of the lease if the commission were based on the income over the term of the lease. The developers preferred shorter leases, ranging from three to five years. This enabled them to roll the leases over, increase the rents, and improve other terms more frequently than they could with longer term leases. If commissions were based on a percentage of the income over the life of the lease, the

TABLE 7.2

Calculation of Commission Based on Base Rent

Lease Year	Space (Sq. Ft.)		Rental Rate	Base Income	Commission Rate (%)		Commission
1	1,400	×	$16.50	$23,100	× .06	=	$1,386
2	1,400	×	16.50	23,100	× .05	=	1,155
3	1,400	×	16.50	23,100	× .04	=	924
4	1,400	×	16.50	23,100	× .03	=	693
					Total commission		$4,158

leasing agent might be encouraged to negotiate longer term leases because the commission would be greater. These developers negotiated a fixed dollar per square foot for leases beyond a certain length, say, three years. If the lease term were less than this, the commission would be pro rated.

Examples of commissions based on a fixed dollar per square foot:

Example 1

Lease terms: A shopping center lease on 2,000 square feet for four years at $15 per square foot

Commission terms: $3 per square foot on leases of three years or longer and pro rata for less than three years.

Formula: Space square footage × commission rate
      = commission, or

      2,000-sq.-ft. space × $3/sq. ft. commission rate
      = $6,000 commission

Example 2

Lease term: A lease on an industrial space of 5,000 square feet for two years at $12 per square foot

Commission terms: $3.50 per square foot on leases three years or longer and prorated for less than three years

Formula: Space square footage × commission rate
      = commission, or

      5,000-sq.-ft. space × $2.35 prorated (.67 × $3.50)
      commission rate = $11,750 commission

Commissions can be negotiated as a fixed amount for a specific space. For example, a commission of $10,000 will be paid for a sublease of 4,000 square feet for 2½ years at a rate in excess of $11 per square foot.

A commission may be paid based on an hourly basis to negotiate a lease. For example, a property owner has a prospective tenant and hires a property manager or leasing agent to negotiate the terms and pays the broker $200 per hour.

How commissions are to be paid is another negotiable item. One method is to pay the commission in its entirety when the lease is executed. Most landlords do not favor this method because the tenant may never move into the space.

Another method is to pay one half when the lease is executed and one half when the tenant opens for business. Some property owners will extend the second half commission to the time the tenant opens for business and commences to pay base rent. This extension is to encourage the leasing agent to give as little free rent as possible. If the tenant is financially weak, the owner may wish to delay paying a portion of the commission until the tenant has paid a few month's rent. For instance, the commission may be paid in thirds: at the time of lease execution, when the tenant opens for business and commences paying base rent, and when the twelfth monthly rent payment is received. Commissions may be paid monthly during the term of the lease. When the tenant pays its monthly rent, a commission is paid for that portion of the income from that lease. The commission on a five-year lease is paid at a rate of one sixtieth each month. When this is the agreement, the property owner may be willing to pay the entire commission on a discounted basis when the tenant moves in.

Commissions for a pad or ground lease could be based on a percentage of the gross or net income, an amount per square foot of building or pad area, the first year's rent or a fixed amount, or any other method left up to the imagination of the property owner and the property manager or leasing agent.

Incentive Commissions

Incentive commissions are offered by the property owner when the leasing market is soft or as an incentive to achieve a specific leasing goal. They can be an effective method of obtaining either the attention of the brokerage community or the additional effort of the exclusive leasing agent. A simple incentive is a commission and a half or a double commission.

In a soft market, a property owner may offer a double commission for making a deal on the property. Some owners will offer an expensive gift, a car, or a trip to the Caribbean or Hawaii if a leasing agent or property manager leases a minimum amount of space. A word of caution: All states require commissions to be paid to the broker, not the real estate salesperson or leasing agent. Most property managers and leasing agents are not brokers but associate brokers or real estate salespeople. When a commission is paid to the broker, it is shared with the person making the lease based on a formula the brokerage firm has agreed on. If an expensive gift is all or part of the commission, it must be given to the broker, not the leasing agent. The broker and the leasing agent then decide who will receive the gift.

Most incentive commissions are additional monies paid to the broker and can be based on a number of situations—for example, leasing a particular space that has been vacant for a long time. On a new development, incentive commissions can be based on a percentage of the space leased by the grand opening of the building or a specific period of time after the grand opening. For instance, an additional $1 per square foot can be paid on all spaces leased if the office building is 75% leased at grand opening, and an additional 50¢ per square foot on all spaces leased if the office building is 90% leased one year after the grand opening.

Incentive commissions can also be based on an average rental rate. For example, an additional 2% commission can be paid on all space leased within twelve months of the date the new building receiving its certificate of occupancy if the average rental rate exceeds $30 per square foot and 80% of the building is leased.

Renewals

Renewals are another source of commission income. Renewal commissions can be determined any number of ways, including a fixed dollar amount, a percentage of the commission for a new lease, the same commission as for a new lease, or an hourly rate. Lease renewals may be one of the responsibilities of the management company and compensation is included in the management fee. The management fee may include lease renewals, with the property manager being responsible for the renewals, or it may be an additional fee to the property management company.

Options

Most property owners prefer not to pay a commission when a tenant exercises an option. If the commission on the original terms of the lease were based on a dollar per square foot, an agreed upon fixed dollar amount, or an hourly basis, there would be no additional commission if the tenant exercised an option. If the commission were based on a percentage of the gross or net income, the option period would become an issue to negotiate. The property owner would probably maintain that the commission paid on the original term of the lease completed the agreement between the owner and the leasing agent. The leasing agent would argue that another commission is due because the option was included in the lease negotiations. This is yet another issue to negotiate in the commission agreement or management agreement.

If the commission agreement excludes payment on options, and the property manager receives a commission on renewals, the question is, Should the leasing agent or the property manager be paid a commission when the tenant exercises an option right? Most property owners will argue that if the terms of the option were prenegotiated, and the tenant only has to notify the owner or manager in writing that the option will be exercised, a commission has not been earned by the manager. The manager will reason that if the option states that the rental rate must be negotiated or is adjusted to market rate, then the rental rate must be negotiated, and this is similar to negotiating a lease renewal.

Should a commission be reimbursed to the property owner if the tenant does not fulfill the terms of the lease? This is an issue that should be addressed in the leasing agreement. This situation usually arises when a tenant files bankruptcy or vacates without notice before the lease expires. The leasing agent or property manager presents a prospective tenant to the property owner who has the responsibility of deciding whether or not to accept the tenant. If the tenant files bankruptcy and stops paying rent, or vacates the premises and stops paying rent during the first year of the lease, the property manager or leasing agent would be prudent to maintain a good relationship with the property owner and either refuse the portion of the commission yet to be paid or find a replacement tenant at no additional fee to the owner.

Commissions have traditionally been paid by the property owner, but more and more tenants are hiring and paying brokers to find them space and to negotiate on their behalf. Commissions can be a major expense of the property owner and a major source of income for the property manager and leasing agent. All the terms of the commission agreement are negotiable, and care must be exercised when negotiating the terms, especially the commission amount and payment schedule. The property owner must always remember that commissions are the driving force behind leasing deals, and these deals create the value of a building.

(e) LEASING MEETINGS AND REPORTS

There is no issue more important to a property owner than leasing. Value is created by the income stream, and the income stream starts with leasing. A property owner who is not aware of the activities of the leasing and marketing program can easily become discouraged with the leasing team and may eventually change leasing personnel.

Regular leasing meetings and reports can accomplish several objectives:

1. Keep the property owner informed of the leasing team's activities
2. Keep the property owner aware of changes in the market rental rates
3. Enable the property owner and leasing team to adjust the property's rental rates and concessions to reflect changes in the market
4. Review the marketing and leasing activities since the previous leasing meeting
5. Review the prospects listed in the leasing report
6. Review proposals and counterproposals

A leasing report is provided by the leasing personnel at the beginning of the meting. The report needs to be tailored to the property.

The leasing prospect report in Exhibit 7.6 outlines the state of each prospect. A supplementary report may be included to show: the amount of space available, leases out for signature, spaces occupied and vacant, tenant move-in and move-out during the past month, the amount of tenant improvements, the commission paid and budgeted to date, and the average rent per square foot achieved to date. A map or floor plan of the property is color coded for spaces leased, occupied, leases out for signature, and leases in serious negotiations.

Meetings should not be held too often or be too lengthy to avoid taking up the leasing personnel's valuable leasing time. Yet, if the meetings are held too infrequently, communication breaks down. A one- to two-hour meeting every three to four weeks is usually sufficient to accomplish the objectives. During these meetings the property owner or representative will be able to judge whether or not the leasing personnel are motivated to continue to lease the property and whether they are devoting sufficient time to marketing and leasing the property.

If the property owner is an absentee owner or asset manager who visits the property only two to four times a year, the property manager needs to include a thorough leasing report in the monthly management report. In addition, the property manager and leasing personnel should call the owner or asset manager at least monthly to review the leasing status of the property. (Exhibit 7.6)

§ 7.6   LEASING PACKAGE

The leasing package is helpful for both brokers and prospective tenants. Brokers use it to keep current on the property. Prospective tenants most often become aware of a property either by driving the area and visiting the property or by receiving a leasing package.

There are three approaches to presenting a prospective tenant with a leasing package. The first approach is to provide sufficient but limited information to pique the prospect's interest. If the prospect shows continued interest, then the full leasing package is provided. This approach is used when the leasing package is too expensive to be mailed to thousands of prospects. The other approach is to provide the entire package to each prospect. A hybrid approach is to send the complete package to those prospects who have a high probability of leasing space, with all other prospects receiving the limited package.

All materials should be professionally prepared to reflect the quality of operation. An expensive four-color brochure is not required, but all materials should be complete, attractive, and easily understood.

The leasing package is designed to present the property in its best light and to answer as many questions as possible. An incomplete leasing package can misinform the prospect.

EXHIBIT 7.6

Leasing Prospects Report

PROJECT NAME: College Plaza

MONTH: March/1988

DATE PREPARED: March 30, 1988

PREPARED BY: Joan Jones

Suite #	Usable Sq.Ft.	Date Shown Space	Prospective Tenant (Company)	Type of Business	Name of Contact	Current Location	Phone #	* Source	Term yrs	Rent Quoted	TI Work (est.)	Free Rent	Broker Comm.	Status/Remarks
A-12	1,400	3-23	Anita Cross	Health Fd	Anita	Highland St.	786-5321	C	5	$12.00	?	?	$4200	4
A-14	1,400	3-23	Little Nickel Ads	Ads	Sandy	6th Avenue	881-4646	A	5	$12.00	?	?	$4200	4
B-2	1,500	2-3	Crystal Jewelers	Jewelry	George	None	985-3568	A	7	$13.50	$2,000	2 mos	$4500	0
B-4	2,800	2-15	Cards Galore	Cards/Gifts	Mary	West Mall	773-7766	C	10	$11.75	0	1 mo	$8400	1
B-6	1,400	1-6	Tanning/Toning	Tone/Tan	Karen	Main St	898-6868	B	3	$12.00	0	1 mo	$4200	2
B-10	2,800	12-10	Pizza/Pizza/Pizza	Restaurant	Mario	Broadway	689-6896	D	10	$11.75	0	2 mos	$8400	3
A-16	1,800	2-15	Sandwich Shop	"	Jim	None	785-1234	E	7	$12.00	0	1 mo	$5400	6

STATUS LEGEND

0 - Lease Completed
1 - Lease Out For Signatures
2 - Lease Under Negotiations
3 - General Terms Discussion
4 - Preliminary Project Talks
5 - Problem in Talks
6 - Dead Deal

* SOURCE LEGEND
(How prospect found out about Building)

A. Drive-by
B. Newspaper Advertising
C. Cold Call by Property Staff
D. Direct Mailing
E. Broker
F. Other

Page ____ of ____

A discussion of items to include in a shopping center, office building, and industrial leasing package follows.

(a) THE LEASING PACKAGE: SHOPPING CENTERS

The leasing package for a retail tenant should include general information of interest to all retailers but should also be tailored to the specific retailer. There must be a balance between sending too much material, which will likely go unread, and sending too little information, which keeps the prospect from reaching any conclusions. The basic leasing package should contain a transmittal letter, a list of tenants, a plot plan, an area map, an aerial photograph of the site, if available, a demographic profile of the trade area, comments on the shopping center's sales and, if available, a merchants' association or marketing/promotional fund activity calendar.

Transmittal Letter

The letter of transmittal is a critical part of the leasing package. Neither leasing agents, especially for large chains who receive a great number of leasing packages, nor prospective tenants have the time to read long complicated packages. Therefore, the letter should be brief, professionally prepared, and addressed to an individual by name, telling the benefits of leasing space in the shopping center. Letters can be easily personalized through computer technology to address the specific features of the location and the specific requirements of the tenant. For example, a cover letter sent to ice cream parlors could mention the number of schools within walking distance of the shopping center. A letter sent to auto supply stores could emphasize the large percentage of blue-collar workers in the area.

Tenant List

Prospective tenants are most often interested in the center's existing and future tenants. Some merchants follow other merchants into new locations, as their past experience tells them they will do well next to a given merchant. It is helpful to list the merchant's trade name as well as what is sold: for example, "Lucky Market, a discount grocer."

It is also very important that the list of tenants not imply that a tenant has signed a lease for the subject center when the tenant is only in the negotiating stages. Should those negotiations fail, the leasing agent is open to possible liability from a tenant who was counting on a specific tenant for cross-traffic. Prudent owners will not reveal the name of a tenant if the lease has not been executed.

Plot Plan

The plot plan should either be prepared specifically for leasing or modified for inclusion in the leasing package. The engineering plot plan may
suffice, but it is not attractive. It is more helpful to show trees and
automobiles as well as tenants' names in the locations they occupy. A
prospect may want to be next to the dress store or, conversely, may not
want to be next to the pet store or the record shop. A disclaimer stating
that the landlord does not guarantee the information, and that the information is subject to change, may protect the landlord from a lawsuit
if the layout of the center changes, a tenant is replaced, or a major tenant moves out.

Map of the Area

The area map should show freeways and major roads. Important items
should be clearly labeled for quick identification by the reader. If the
location is not in an area readily known to many retailers, an area map
is helpful in orienting the reader.

Aerial Photograph

Sophisticated retailers are most interested in the immediate trade area.
An aerial photograph very quickly tells the retailers the housing density
in the area, the road patterns, and the shopping center's proximity to
its competition. These photographs can be obtained rather inexpen-
sively from companies that specialize in aerial photography. Many are
shelf items.

Demographics

Complete demographic packages can be obtained from any one of several companies specializing in demographic information. The demographic company is informed of the shopping center's cross streets and
the area of demographic interest, such as a two- or four-mile radius. The
information is usually prepared and delivered within forty-eight hours.
This provides the prospect with a quick look at the area to help decide if
the population in the area represents the store's customer base.

Center's Sale

An experienced tenant views any retail location on the basis of its probable sales potential. Rent is a function of sales. For this reason, it is important to show the tenant a strong sales potential, if it really exists. Care
must be taken to keep the confidentiality of an individual merchant's

sales, unless that merchant gives specific approval to reveal them. However, general indications can be given, such as: the shopping center sales are averaging $225 per square foot; sales are up 11% for the most recent twelve-month period; the fashion merchants are averaging sales of $260 per square foot; the market share of the shopping center is increasing steadily; the supermarket is number one in its division.

Any positive sales information is of interest to the knowledgeable merchant. Comparing a center's merchant sales with those in the *Dollars and Cents of Shopping Centers* will provide the basis for a meaningful evaluation.

Traffic Counts

Traffic passing the shopping center is very important. Absolutely accurate car counts are not required for any center, but traffic volume can be reported relative to other locations in town and by comparing current traffic counts with past counts. Traffic counts are measured on the basis of average daily automobile traffic passing the center. These figures are generally available from city, county, or state traffic agencies for little or no cost.

It is important to compare the automobile traffic counts on the shopping center's street with other streets in the area, as their relative counts are significant, but it is also important to measure the increase or decrease in traffic counts because it may affect the shopping center's location. At times the street with the second-best traffic count may be a better location because of less congestion at peak hours. It is possible that the automobile traffic on a street travels too fast to be of help to the shopping center. If traffic is one way and in the direction of work, many retailers, such as liquor stores, prefer homebound traffic. Many regional shopping centers have car counters built in at each entrance to provide daily traffic counts into the mall. Multiplying this number by the average number of persons in the car will provide daily customer traffic counts.

Merchants' Association or Marketing/Promotional Fund's Calendar of Events

While some major tenants do not want any involvement with a merchants' association or marketing/promotional fund, it is still a positive aspect to any shopping center to have a coordinated advertising and promotion program. A professionally prepared calendar of events will show the prospect that there is a concern for the tenants' success and that there is a coordinated, ongoing effort to generate traffic, which should translate into higher sales for everyone. Photographs of successful merchandising, sales, or promotional events can create interest in a prospective tenant.

(b) THE LEASING PACKAGE: OFFICE BUILDINGS AND INDUSTRIAL PROPERTIES

Leasing packages for office buildings and industrial properties are very similar. Following is a review of information that can be included for either of these properties.

Brochure

Brochures can be a simple one-page, two-color handout or an elaborate, multicolor presentation. They may include a photo or rendering of the building, a location map, list of the building's features, and the leasing agent's name and phone number.

Building Photo

Color photos of the exterior and interior features of the building are of great assistance to an out-of-town company or prospects who must convince their headquarters of their building selection.

View Photo

Views are a desirable feature of an office building, especially water views. Photos taken from several floors will give different view perspectives. If the building is proposed or under construction, aerial photos are useful.

Floor Plan

A large floor plan showing common areas and window modules is used for office buildings. A plan showing office and warehouse space is used for industrial properties.

Transportation

A map indicating public transportation routes, freeways, and major arterials is useful for prospective tenants of both industrial and office properties. The industrial user may need additional information on air, water, and bus transportation.

Employment

The cost and availability of skilled and unskilled, union and nonunion labor are a major concern to industrial users and major service office users.

Housing

The cost of rental housing and the price of homes is a concern of some businesses.

Building Services

A list of tenants in the building who provide a service to other tenants, such as a stockbroker, restaurant, post office, or escrow company, is a helpful part of the leasing package.

Building Features

Special features, such as life safety, common area, and covered parking, are excellent selling points.

List of Tenants

Fortune 500 companies, well-known law firms, restaurants, and health clubs can add prestige to the building. Their names should be included in the leasing package.

Any information that will convey the message of service and quality and distinguish the building from the competition should be included in the leasing package.

§ 7.7 MEASURING TENANT SPACE

The method of measuring space in a building will have an impact on the building in many ways. Since rent is usually calculated on a dollar-per-square-foot basis, a tenant's rent is determined by multiplying this rate times the number of square feet leased. If a building is being measured by a method that is confusing or uncommon in the area, the building may develop a reputation for charging more for space than is common in the industry.

The property manager should contact other property managers, leasing agents, and property owners to investigate the accepted methods of measuring space in the geographic area in which the building is located. Managers who wish to pioneer a new method for measuring space in an area should proceed with caution, for the marketability of the building may be affected.

The only recognized standard for measuring office space is the one established in the 1970s and revised in the early 1980s by BOMA and the American National Standard (Exhibit 7.7). However, there are regional differences that vary from this method, and some property owners prefer to use their own method.

EXHIBIT 7.7

Standards for Measuring Office Space

American National Standard Z65.1-1980

Usable Area

The Usable Area of an office shall be computed by measuring to the finished surface of the office side of corridor and other permanent walls, to the center of partitions that separate the office from adjoining Usable Areas, and to the inside finished surface of the dominant portion of the permanent outer building walls.

No deductions shall be made for columns and projections necessary to the building.

The Usable Area of a floor shall be equal to the sum of all Usable Areas on that floor.

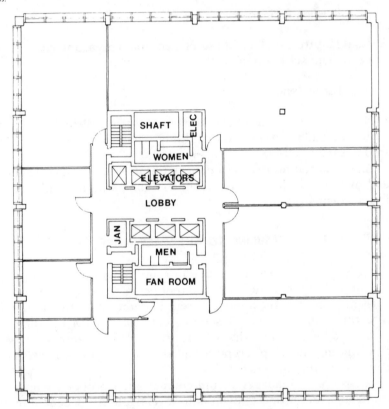

*Note: Assumes glass line as illustrated is the dominant portion. See illustrations "A" through "D".

> **Page six of a ten page document.** *To avoid misinterpretation, this page should not be used without the complete document.*

Reprinted with permission of Building Owners and Managers Association (BOMA) International, Washington, DC.

EXHIBIT 7.7 *(Continued)*

Rentable Area

American National Standard Z65.1-1980

The Rentable Area of a floor shall be computed by measuring to the inside finished surface of the dominant portion of the permanent outer building walls, excluding any major vertical penetrations of the floor.

No deductions shall be made for columns and projections necessary to the building.

The Rentable Area of an office on the floor shall be computed by multiplying the Usable Area of that office by the quotient of the division of the Rentable Area of the floor by the Usable Area of the floor resulting in the "R/U Ratio" described herein.

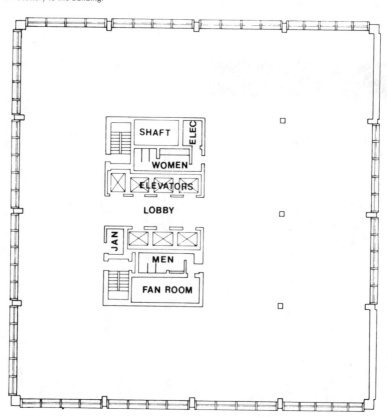

*Note: Assumes glass line as illustrated is the dominant portion. See illustrations "A" through "D".

> **Page seven of a ten page document.** *To avoid misinterpretation, this page should not be used without the complete document.*

Reprinted with permission of Building Owners and Managers Association (BOMA) International, Washington, DC.

EXHIBIT 7.7 *(Continued)*

Construction Area

American National Standard Z65.1-1980

The Construction Area of a floor shall be computed by measuring to the outside finished surface of permanent outer building walls. The Construction Area of a building shall be the sum of the Construction Area of all enclosed floors of the building, including basements, mechanical equipment floors, penthouses, and the like.

Store Area

The number of square feet in a ground floor Store Area shall be computed by measuring from the building line in the case of street frontages, and from the inner surface of other outer building walls and from the inner surface of corridor and other permanent partitons and to the center of partitions that separate the premises from adjoining rentable areas.

No deduction shall be made for vestibules inside the building line or for columns or projections necessary to the building.

No addition should be made for bay windows extending outside the building line.

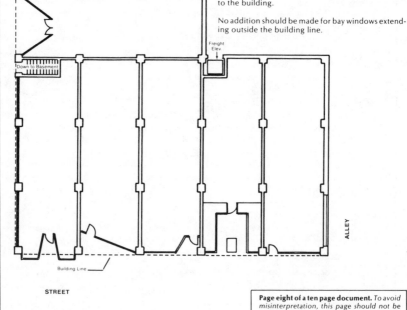

Page eight of a ten page document. To avoid misinterpretation, this page should not be used without the complete document.

Reprinted with permission of Building Owners and Managers Association (BOMA) International, Washington, DC.

Usable and rentable square footage, two commonly used methods to measure office building space, can be misleading to a tenant. Usable square footage is the space the tenant has within the demised premises. It is measured from the center of the demising walls (the walls between tenants) and from the inside surface of the dominant exterior wall and common area walls. The square footage is approximately the amount of square footage the tenant occupies. The slight difference is in the square footage lost by measuring to the center of the stud in the demising wall. For many years space was measured in this way. Tenants understood this measurement and knew that if they leased 1,000 square feet they had approximately 1,000 square feet to use; hence the term *usable square footage*. A 1,000-square-foot space at $20 per square foot rented for $20,000 annually.

New buildings usually must be leased at a higher rental rate than older buildings because of the increased costs of land, materials, and labor. In the late 1970s, some developers, wanting to have their rental rates sound competitive, switched to a rentable method of measuring space. For example, a developer needs a rent of $22,000 for 1,000 square feet of space but might not want to quote a rate of $22 per square foot when existing buildings are leasing for $20. The additional rent may be difficult to achieve in a soft leasing market. So the developer added on a "load factor" to the 1,000 square feet of usable area. The load factor is the percentage of the square footage of the common area on the tenant's floor and, in some cases, of the common areas in the building's entrance lobby. If the common area was 1,500 square feet and the tenant occupied 1,000 square feet on a 15,000-square-foot floor, the tenant is occupying 7.41% of the usable space on the floor (15,000 sq. ft. – 1,500 sq. ft. = 13,500 sq. ft. of usable area; 1,000 sq. ft. ÷ 13,500 sq. ft. = 7.41%); 7.41% of the 1,500 square feet of common area is 111 square feet of common area that will be added to the tenant's usable space of 1,000 square feet, giving the tenant 1,111 rentable square feet.

The developer must get $19.80 per square foot on 1,111 square feet to achieve $22,000. This space of 1,111 square feet rentable, which includes 1,000 square feet usable and 111 square feet of common area, generates $22,000 of income when it is leased at $19.80. The $19.80 rentable rate appears to be more competitive than the $22 usable rate.

Another method of determining the load factor is to measure all common areas, including the building's lobby, and divide this number by the square footage of usable area to arrive at a percentage load factor.

Some owners believe they are generating additional rent by leasing a building on a rentable basis instead of a usable basis, but it is difficult to believe that tenants would be fooled by the different methods of quoting rent per square foot. A building can only achieve market rents, regardless of how space is calculated. Tenants know that they need a certain amount of usable space; when leasing agents are comparing rents for several buildings, they will determine the monthly or annual rental cost for the amount of the space actually occupied regardless of how the landlord measures the space.

Developers are conscious of the tenant's concerns regarding the cost of space and are responding by attempting to minimize inefficient common areas and decrease the load factor. The exception to this is buildings that have a special common area feature such as a spacious and elegant lobby or atrium to create a prestigious ambience.

Neither the shopping center industry nor the industrial building industry has adopted a standard method of measuring space, so the property manager will need to conduct a survey of how space is measured in the area. While measuring usable space from the center of the demising walls to either the interior surface or exterior surface of outer walls is a common method, few property owners would go so far as to measure to the outside of the overhang in front of the building, known as the drip line. This aggressive method could earn a landlord a shady reputation when tenants realize that the landlord did not explain that rent is being paid on the sidewalk or the area under the building's overhang.

Whatever method is used for measuring space, the person responsible for leasing should explain the method to the prospective tenant to avoid any misunderstandings or ill will.

§ 7.8   PROSPECTING FOR TENANTS

Prospecting for commercial tenants is one of those never-ending responsibilities that takes the leasing agent down many paths, quite often with uncertain results. However, most leasing agents indicate that in spite of the uncertainties, they are most successful when they are actively prospecting, no matter the particular activity.

(a)   PROSPECTING TECHNIQUES

Following is a review of prospecting techniques for shopping centers, office and medical buildings, and industrial properties.

The Leasing Sign

It is generally agreed that one of the most effective leasing tools is a sign on the property. The sign should be in good condition and professionally designed and fabricated to reflect well on the project. It should be easily read from the street, with the leasing agent's name and phone number in large print, the name of the developer, particularly if the developer is known for quality projects, major tenants and, where applicable, an indication of broker cooperation. Some leasing agents like to indicate the square footage of space available, but that can limit the inquiries, and quite often tenants are not sure of their space needs.

Direct Mail

A direct-mail program to selected prospects can be very effective. The mailer should be professionally prepared and typeset and should have all necessary information without being too cluttered. An 8½-by-11-inch sheet folded three ways can be sent out without an envelope or placed in an envelope with a letter. The mailing can be targeted to a specific use or to tenants in a specific area. Even those who are not in the market for space become aware of the project and may discuss it with someone who does have an interest. Those who do extensive direct mailings indicate a better response if the mailing includes a postage-paid response card. An overall response of 1% to 2% is considered good in direct-mail campaigns.

Cold Canvass

Calling on tenants in their place of business can be very time consuming, but it is still considered to be a very productive prospecting activity. The leasing agent can canvass for specific uses or for overall knowledge of an area and can find prospects for other properties as an additional benefit. For each canvassing trip, a goal of a specific number of calls should be determined. Business cards and information sheets should be handed out freely. It is wise not to try to accomplish too much in the first visit. If the decision maker is not in, the astute leasing agent will speak with the manager, clerk, or receptionist; leave the information; and request that the information be passed on to the decision maker.

Telephone Canvass

From the point of view of time, the telephone can be a very effective leasing tool because it allows one to contact many prospects in a single day. As in canvassing, specific goals are necessary. The purpose of the call is to find out if the business owner is in the market for additional space and to obtain permission to send a brochure or schedule a follow-up visit.

Billboards

Larger centers, specialty centers, and major commercial projects with a large trade area can often benefit from a "coming soon" billboard campaign. It is difficult to measure the impact of billboards, but there are many situations where they can be a useful marketing tool.

Project Signs

New projects will often have a large project sign with a color rendering, with the names of the developer, leasing agent, architect, general contractor, and lender. The leasing agent's phone number is placed strategically on the sign.

Trade Journal Ads

Every profession has a trade organization with a trade journal. Advertising property in a trade journal—for example, advertising a shopping center in *Women's Wear Daily* or a restaurant pad in *Restaurant News*—is an effective way to reach a specific category of tenants.

Classified Ads

It is generally agreed that in most major cities classified ads for the renting of commercial space do not work well. Quite often they are effective in smaller cities, but heavy reliance should not be placed on this source for tenant prospects.

Display Ads

These larger box-shaped ads are used to announce the grand opening or remodeling of major buildings, major lease-up activities, or major tenants who have just executed leases in the building.

Ads in Business Magazines

Ads in the weekly business newspaper or business magazine in the community are a direct way to reach businesses.

Radio and TV Advertising

These sources are almost never used for leasing. If the shopping center is using radio or TV for merchants' association or marketing/promotional fund advertising, it may make sense to add a "space available" trailer, but as a primary source it is not effective in most markets.

Publicity

Publicity has a credibility well beyond that of advertising. The leasing agent should develop a publicity program to cover the entire leasing effort. A creative leasing agent can find many legitimate opportunities for publicity. These include: unique building features, energy-saving features, design features, ground breaking, placing of the corner store, topping off, signing of well-known tenants, signing of anchor tenants, impressive levels of lease-up, naming a building or center manager, assigning a new store manager, and the grand opening. A public relations agency can assure maximum coverage of the property's news. If public relations are handled in-house, a rapport with the media should be developed.

Civic and Business Meetings

Being active in local civic and business organizations offers another means of broadcasting the leasing message and of meeting prospective tenants. These meetings offer an opportunity to tell your story and to listen to what others are doing in the business and civic areas.

Open House

Hosting an open house for the brokerage community and another for the business community to show off a new or remodeled building is a means to bring prospects to the site. Events for an open house include ground breaking, topping off, grand opening, and remodeling.

Employment Ads

Employment ads can indicate which companies are expanding and in need of additional space.

Business Directories

Business and trade associations such as the chamber of commerce, the local economic development council, and the downtown business association have directories that are excellent leasing leads.

Community Charitable Events

Encouraging a community organization such as the metropolitan cultural arts association to hold a benefit black-tie party at the mall or on one of the top floors of an office building will bring community and business leaders to the property and generate excellent publicity for the building.

Monitoring Government Contracts

When the government awards a contract to a manufacturer, the Boeing Company for example, the manufacturer and its suppliers may need additional office or industrial space.

Government's Space Requirements

The General Services Administration sends out mailers for its space requirements. Property owners can be included on the mailing list by contacting the local GSA office. State and local municipalities may have similar mailings for their space needs.

Model Office

Furnishing a model office and inviting brokers to tour the building can help them market the unique features of the building.

Developing Contacts at a Hospital

Medical buildings and office buildings with medical space should be marketed to hospital administrators. Hospitals are encouraging doctors to affiliate with them, and these doctors often need medical office space.

Medical Building Mailing List

The mailing list of the county's medical society is usually available for purchase.

Medical Journal Ads

Another means of direct contact with the medical profession is to advertise in local and regional medical journals. In the Seattle area, the local journal is the King County Medical Society *Bulletin*, and the regional journal is the *Western Journal of Medicine*. The best position for the ads would be the back cover or inside cover pages.

Luncheon for Medical Business Manager

Host a luncheon for the business managers of medical practices to present a new medical building.

Networking

The buzz word in the early 1980s was networking. Networking is simply developing and sharing contacts. It is important to stay active with real estate and business organizations and to have a finger on the pulse of the market.

Brokers' Tours

Scheduling a tour of the building with individual brokerage companies is an excellent opportunity to develop a rapport with a brokerage company and to discuss the building with small groups of leasing agents.

Managers and Leasing Agents of Other Projects

It is worthwhile to build a network with managers and leasing agents of competitive projects. Sharing can produce valuable information on prospective tenants for everyone.

Suppliers

Suppliers of goods or services often have a vested interest in new tenants who could be their new customers. For example, a supplier of restaurant equipment would suggest prospects who would be interested in purchasing equipment from that supplier. A manufacturer of ice cream could be helpful in locating an operator who would then provide another retail outlet for the ice cream. Suppliers can suggest many uses, such as laundromats, dry cleaners, and gift stores.

Building Tenants

Existing tenants are a good source of new tenants. Keep tenants aware of vacancies, as they may be in need of expansion space or know of prospects who would be interested in the building. Remember, the competition is canvassing your building's tenants and so should you.

(b)   SOURCES OF RETAIL PROSPECTS

There are several useful prospecting resources for leasing shopping centers and retail properties.

1.   The Yellow Pages.   The telephone directory in every city has a list of retailers by category.

2.   Polk's Directory and Contacts Influential.   These companies and other mailing list suppliers will, for a fee, provide a list of retailers by category in almost any area. For example, a list of all men's wear stores in a given city, county, zip code, or state can be purchased from this resource.

3. Annual Franchise Handbook Directory. Not only does this source list hundreds of franchise opportunities, but the franchisor provides the novice merchant with business backup and a plan. While all franchise opportunities are not top-notch, the responsible franchisor can be of great help to the leasing agent in providing recognized businesses to inexperienced operators.

4. ICSC Leasing Opportunities (Annual). This annual publication lists retailers nationwide that have specific expansion plans for the coming year. This is one of the best sources of tenants because the retailers are definitely interested in expanding. The publication provides such information as required size, location, and type of center desired.

5. Directory of Leading Chain Stores (Semiannual). This directory lists all leading chain stores in the country with five or more locations. The tenants are listed by category and by state. Information includes the company name, address and phone, the number of stores, area of activity, and the names of responsible parties in that company.

6. The Book on Value Retailing. This book lists the off-price and outlet discount tenants throughout the country, showing their existing locations and providing information on contacting those merchants. These tenants are now going into more traditional centers, making them likely prospects for leasing all types of centers.

7. Retail Tenant Directory. This directory, published by the *National Mall Monitor*, lists tenants in the major centers in the United States plus many tenants in smaller shopping centers.

8. Retail Lease Trac. A new publication that publishes tenant prospects by areas of the country, by size, category, and needs.

9. Deal Maker's Weekly and Retail Leasing Reporter. These two biweekly publications list tenants around the country who are actively seeking space. They also cover what is happening in various chains, areas of the country, and segments of the business.

10. Shopping Center Digest. This publication covers many of the same areas of the previously mentioned publications but concentrates on centers of 500,000 square feet or more.

11. Factory Outlet World. This publication lists outlet centers and outlet tenants by category.

12. Chamber of Commerce. Prospective tenants sometimes stop by the chamber office to see what's going on, and they will note any leasing opportunities that are registered at the chamber.

13. Redevelopment Agencies. One of the most active sources of tenants today is the redevelopment agency. Its function is to market the benefits of its area to create interest.

14. Other Shopping Centers. The leasing agent should regularly visit other shopping centers and shopping areas with an eye to new tenants, new uses, and new ideas.

15. Monitoring Tenants' Ads. Advertisements on radio and television or in the magazines and newspapers provides a viable list of desirable tenants. Those who advertise warrant special attention in leasing efforts.

16. Classified Ads. Read the classified ads for retailers looking for managers or additional help because they could be in the market for expansion space.

17. Local and Area Directories and Newsletters. Many local directories and newsletters supply excellent information. A call to the leasing leaders in your area should turn up specific publications for a given area.

18. Shopping Center Conventions. The International Council of Shopping Centers' (ICSC) annual convention in May includes a leasing mall. During this three-day event, developers, brokers, and retailers rent booths to display their products. It is not necessary to have a booth to attend, however. The leasing agent can make many contacts with retailers by visiting their booths and scheduling meetings with them during the convention.

19. Deal-Making Sessions and Idea Exchanges. ICSC conducts a deal-making session in the fall similar to the leasing mall activity during its May convention. These trade shows are an excellent place to talk with many tenants in a short period of time. Idea exchanges are two-day conferences attended by brokers, developers, managers, and retailers held in every region of the country.

20. Shopping Center Trade Journals. The following journals are good sources of prospects:

- *Shopping Centers Today*, published monthly by the International Council of Shopping Centers, contains news of the industry, feature stories about retailers, and advertisements.
- *Shopping Center World* is published by Communication Channels and includes information and advertisements related to retailers.
- *Chain Store Age Executive* is published by Lebhar-Friedman, Inc. and carries in-depth information on retailers and the latest trends in retailing.
- *National Mall Monitor* focuses on malls but contains general information on shopping centers as well as retailer's ads and news.

Techniques for prospecting are limited only by the property manager's and leasing agent's imagination.

§ 7.9 APPRAISING PROSPECTIVE TENANTS

Proper evaluation of prospective tenants is almost as important as setting the rents at the right levels. If qualifications are too restrictive, some excellent tenant prospects will be lost. On the other hand, if care is not taken, the property manager will be faced with rent collection problems and needless evictions. In very tough leasing markets when tenants are hard to come by, financial requirements can often be relaxed and a chance taken on a weak tenant.

In all properties the leasing agent should ascertain if the prospect has a good history of paying bills and sufficient capital to fulfill the lease obligations. A credit check should be made on the entity that will sign the lease. It is not uncommon for individuals to present themselves as tenant prospects, produce an excellent credit history and financial statement, and then ask that the lease be in the name of a corporation that has poor credit or no credit history at all.

It is not necessary that a tenant prospect have a perfect credit history, but it is a disadvantage if the tenant is burdened with many delinquent accounts. Some tenants pay their bills promptly even in the worst of times, and some pay their bills late even in the best of times. There are no hard and fast rules to determine a good or bad credit report, but it is essential to review each credit and financial report.

A financial statement is always helpful. It should be a signed statement and reasonably current. The building owner is looking for the tenant to have sufficient capital to meet the lease obligations even in difficult times. It is always reassuring to see ownership of real estate on the financial statement since a tenant is less likely to leave without notice if he or she owns property. It must also be remembered, however, that the home is often protected against claims of creditors.

Liquidity commensurate with the obligation being undertaken and a reasonable debt-to-equity ratio is another plus factor. It is not productive to set a minimum net worth. It is better to evaluate each prospect in light of the space being leased, the history of the tenant, the probable investment by the landlord, the risk involved, and the condition of the building in the marketplace.

In offices and industrial spaces, the use of the space is seldom the reason a tenant is turned down. Sometimes a prospective tenant may want to employ too many people in the space or will generate too much noise but, generally, office and industrial tenants are evaluated with emphasis on their financial statement rather than on their use.

In shopping centers, the property manager not only will review a tenant's financial statement and credit checks, but also will look at the tenant as a merchant and analyze how the business fits the shopping center's intended tenant mix. In most uses, these considerations are equal to the financial considerations. While property managers should not discriminate in commercial properties based on a tenant's race, color, creed, national origin, age, or gender, a tenant can be turned down if its use does not fit the tenant mix.

The tenant's ability as a merchant must be evaluated. What are the tenant's current sales? Does the tenant have a good reputation in the community? It can be harmful to the other merchants if a tenant does not maintain the center's hours, sells shoddy merchandise, offers misleading sales, has an unreasonable return policy, or has rude help. On the other hand, the well-respected, high-volume merchant is highly desirable and is often granted concessions because he or she will attract other good merchants and create traffic for the center.

Sales in shopping centers are stated, for comparison purposes, in sales per square foot. By using *The Dollars and Cents of Shopping Centers* as a guide, the property manager can evaluate how a tenant measures up to similar merchants in the area. If, for instance, a prospective boutique tenant plans to generate sales of $80 per square foot, and *Dollars and Cents* indicates that an independent women's shop will generally gross about $100 per square foot, this prospect is probably not a successful operator and will generate less traffic than a typical women's shop. If the rent is more than 15% of its sales, the tenant may have problems paying the rent. While the lease may still make sense, the situation requires clarification. The manager needs to know the sales trend for the merchant, the merchandise line, and the industry's performance as a whole.

Each tenant's merchandise must be viewed in light of the type of customers it will attract to the center. An auto parts store does not fit into a fashion center because it draws the wrong type of customer and will not generate traffic for the other merchants. The appearance of the store is another factor in evaluating a prospect. Is the tenant's present store attractive, well stocked, modern, inviting, and clean? If the prospect falls short in any of these areas, it may create a poor image for the center.

Does the merchant advertise? Many small tenants mistakenly assume that the center will provide their traffic and they will not have to advertise. Retail tenants should expect to spend 3% to 4% of their projected gross sales on advertising.

In evaluating retail tenants it is necessary to talk with them about their business plan, their philosophy, and how they work with other tenants and center management. Making inquiries of other merchants, suppliers, and former landlords can provide valuable information.

If a merchant is opening his or her first store, the property manager might want to locate a similar shop and visit it to be able to discuss likes and dislikes and suggestions for adapting to the prospect's new operation. A business plan with an operating budget and sales projection is essential in evaluating a first-time operator. The new merchants needs to be aware that most retail businesses do not generate a profit during its first year of operations.

The appraising process is more of an art than a science. The final decision will be based on many factors, including the financial strength of the tenant, the tenant's ability as a merchant, how much the landlord has to spend on improvements, how crucial it is to have that particular use, how many vacancies are available on this property, and how many vacancies are available in the general marketing area. The goal is to obtain the best possible merchant under the existing circumstances, thus minimizing the risks of tenant failure and maximizing the potential for percentage rent.

§ 7.10   TENANT MIX

Tenant mix is the synergism created by the right grouping of tenants. Webster defines synergism as "the simultaneous action of separate agencies which, together, have greater total effect than the sum of their individual effect." In other words, with the right mix, the whole is greater than the sum of its parts.

In a shopping center, the strength of the synergism created by several merchants in close proximity is dependent upon which merchants are grouped together. The correct tenant mix in a shopping center will maximize each tenant's sales potential and the center's percentage rent potential. For instance, regional malls are tenanted primarily by fashion department stores and fashion and gift shops. A neighborhood center anchored by a supermarket and drugstore will be occupied primarily by service and food tenants who service the customer's daily needs.

Another aspect of tenant mix is the placement of tenants. Some businesses will thrive in a space with high traffic and high visibility. For instance, a jewelry store is an ideal center court tenant in a mall. A pharmacy should be on the ground floor of a medical building and have street-level exposure.

When a leasing plan is developed, the leasing team compiles a list of ideal tenants and assigns each a location in the building. When negotiating a lease with these tenants, the agent attempts to sell them on a particular location. The leasing agent's success depends primarily upon the strength of the negotiating parties. Seldom is every tenant located on the first proposed leasing plan, but this plan is the starting place for locating tenants.

(a)   SHOPPING CENTERS

Once the property manager has completed an in-depth market survey, the elements of the shopping center's tenant mix start to form. The purpose of the tenant mix is to provide the broadest range of goods and services consistent with the customers within the trade area and within the center itself.

Each type of shopping center will have a different tenant mix because it is meeting or serving different customer needs and different trade areas. A neighborhood shopping center anchored by a supermarket and drugstore provides the daily household needs for its customers and must fit the neighborhood. You would not place a gourmet supermarket in a low- or middle-income neighborhood, nor would you place a discount drugstore in an affluent suburb. If the market and drugstore are properly selected for the trade area and the other stores are consistent with these anchors, the tenant mix will be compatible with the purpose of the center and the trade area.

Restaurants are usually a good draw to a shopping center, but again, they must be in keeping with the residents in the trade area. Fast-food restaurants might be very successful in younger markets but are not likely to do as well in the affluent, older market. A community of retired persons is not likely to support a pizza parlor or a jeans shop; a small college town is not likely to support a guild jeweler or a Gucci store.

Typical tenants for a neighborhood shopping center include cleaners, laundromat, shoe repair, florist, bank, savings and loan, real estate office, card and gift shop, travel agent, video rental, fast food, restaurant, delicatessen, pizza, books, ice cream, yogurt, hobby shop, liquor store, records, film developer, health spa, hardware, variety store and, to a very small degree, fashion.

The community center generally has a fashion focus in addition to the service tenants found in the neighborhood center. It is usually anchored by two or three major tenants, including a junior department store or discount fashion store, and draws from a wider trade area than a neighborhood center. Because of the fashion draw of the community center, it is not unusual to see several men's and women's apparel, jewelry, and shoe stores in this type of center. Community centers also provide for the daily needs of its trade area, so supermarkets, drugstores, variety stores, and home improvement stores are additional anchors.

The regional and super-regional centers are heavily fashion oriented because of the fashion orientation of the anchors—the department stores. You would probably find Saks or Neiman Marcus as an anchor in a regional center serving a high-income area and Sears or Ward in a middle-income area. The emphasis in regional and superregional centers is on fashion, with upwards of 20% of the square footage of the small shops leased to fashion stores.

Food is always a good draw, and because of the traffic generated, small specialty shops can do very well. Generally, supermarkets are not compatible with mall tenants. If a supermarket is part of a very large center, it is generally located on the perimeter of the parking lot rather than on the mall.

The festival or theme center is oriented to the tourist and, to a lesser degree, to nearby workers. The center itself is a draw, and the merchandise is more "one of a kind" than in traditional shops. For example, music box shops, teddy bear shops, or kite shops will not usually survive in a neighborhood or community center but will thrive in a specialty center. Restaurants are the traditional anchors for festival or theme centers. Some smaller theme centers specialize in very specific uses such as restaurants only, automobile service and support, home decorating and furnishings. A very large trade area is usually required to support these types of centers.

Discount, outlet, and off-price centers are now referred to as "value centers" and have tenants selling in all three areas. It is important to maintain the value image, but it is also difficult to ensure that merchants will actually sell at a discount. "Fashion for less" is the main attraction of this type of center, with other merchandise lines filling out the balance of the mix. Restaurants, again, are an important part of the tenant mix, as are linens, shoes, jewelry, children's wear, and gifts.

Sources like *Sales and Marketing Management* magazine, *Dollars and Cents of Shopping Centers,* and other trade publications reveal how customers generally spend their money. This information can be measured against what is actually being spent in the area, and why, to determine the probable market support available for new retail ventures in the area. This is not a science, as many factors must be evaluated, but such an exercise can help the leasing agent or owner direct the leasing effort to uses that have the greatest probability of success.

(b) OFFICE AND MEDICAL BUILDINGS

The tenant mix is not as critical to the success of an office or medical building as it is to the success of a shopping center. However, office building tenants can enhance or impair the reputation of the building and its marketing and leasing program.

In marketing the building, the property manager can use the presence of respected and established tenants to great advantage. For example, an office building tenanted primarily by Fortune 500 companies will provide a reputation of success and prosperity to the building, as will a building with leading law firms. An office building located in the state capital may have several government agencies as tenants, lending a sense of stability and strength to the tenant mix. A building's tenant mix may include services to the business community. A restaurant, bank, escrow office, stockbroker, printer, health club, business club, and gift shop are amenities that should be marketed as additional services in the building.

A building's tenant mix will be reflected in its population level. A building with mostly professional offices usually has a low population count, while one tenanted mostly with service companies will have a high density. In a heavily populated building, everything from paper supplies to elevators will receive greater use. This is a consideration in estimating the operating expenses for a building.

The tenant mix or tenant profile of a medical building can be a positive feature in marketing and leasing. A pharmacist is a convenience to physicians and their patients. A coffee shop is a convenience to the doctors and their staff. A general practitioner may use specialists such as cardiologists or obstetricians for consultation and referral. Medical groups such as radiology labs and physical therapy departments are draws for other doctors to locate in the building. All of these services should be used in marketing and leasing the building.

(c) INDUSTRIAL PARKS

The industrial park is least affected by the tenant mix but, like the office building, it does benefit from prestigious tenants and supporting uses within the park. Larger industrial parks will develop pads or outlots for restaurants and market space to tenants that will provide services to other tenants in the park. If an industrial park is near a major manufacturer or can attract a major manufacturer, this tenant may attract its suppliers to locate in the park.

Planned industrial developments will include areas for businesses that service the employees of the industrial tenants. The Irvine Industrial Park in southern California includes fast-food facilities, full-service restaurants, a medical facility, business services, hotels, and retail facilities. Smaller industrial parks frequently develop a similar tenant mix on a smaller scale. Supporting uses within or adjacent to an industrial park provide important services to the park's tenants and their employees.

The tenant mix in an industrial park or area should be one of the features in the marketing materials for the project.

§ 7.11 NEGOTIATING THE LEASE

The last steps in a successful marketing and leasing program are negotiating the lease, executing the lease, and delivering it to the landlord and tenant. Since the lease is the document that sets forth the rights and obligations of each party, it will affect the landlord's operation of the property as well as the NOI and the value of the property.

The lease must be carefully negotiated. Each clause has a specific purpose, and negotiated revisions must be carefully prepared to determine their impact on the property, operations, income, and value both on a short- and long-term basis. Obviously, the property manager must have a working knowledge of the lease and know the purpose of each clause.

With this understanding, property managers will know when they can give lease clause concessions. The market conditions, the need for the tenant, and the tenant itself will determine whether or not lease clause concessions must be granted. In soft markets and in properties with high vacancies, lease clause concessions will be given that otherwise wouldn't be necessary to make the deal.

A very desirable tenant, a major tenant, and national tenants will require lease clause concessions. The independent and local tenant is seldom in a strong negotiating position to command lease clause concessions. Disputes are more likely to occur with small independent tenants than with national ones, so the landlord should maintain more protection in the lease with these smaller tenants. A landlord is seldom sued by a national tenant, but it is not uncommon for a mom-and-pop retail tenant to sue the landlord when its business fails. The suit is usually based on alleged false representation.

It is important to assess the relative negotiating positions of all parties before starting the negotiations. Do you need the tenant more than he or she needs you? What alternative locations are available and what are their features? The market survey discussed in this chapter will provide information about the relative strength of your building in the market. All of these factors will determine the strengths and weaknesses of your negotiating position.

Many major tenants require that their lease form be used, but most other tenants will accept the landlord's lease. The property manager must protect the landlord's interest without obstructing the deal. Following is a review of lease clauses for shopping centers, office buildings, and industrial properties along with generic lease clauses.

(a) COMMON COMMERCIAL LEASE CLAUSES

There are many business issues common to all commercial leases. These issues should be considered for every leasing situation and handled in accordance with the type of building, the nature of the tenants, and probability of that particular issue becoming a problem.

The Parties

For novice tenants, it is best to use the designations *landlord* and *tenant* rather than *lessor* and *lessee*. With the words *landlord* and *tenant* there is no doubt as to the identity or responsibilities of the parties. It is also very important to know exactly who the tenant is. Is it a corporation, partnership, married couple, individual, or association? Knowing who is involved in negotiating will often make a difference in how the negotiations are handled. It should be noted that in most states a minor can

Use Clause

Rather than relying on broad terms such as *general office* or *storage*, the lease should indicate the specific use to which the space will be put. This applies to all properties.

Entry by Landlord

The landlord must retain the right to enter the premises at all reasonable times to inspect it or to provide essential services.

Fire and Extended Coverage Insurance

When the tenant is required to provide fire and extended coverage insurance, the lease should define the levels of coverage, that is, full replacement or 90% replacement; require that the landlord be named as additional or named insured; require that the landlord be notified ten to twenty days prior to any cancellation; and require that any proceeds be payable jointly to the landlord and the tenant for the purposes of rebuilding. The lease should also allow the landlord to provide coverage if the tenant does not and to be reimbursed by the tenant for the cost.

Security Deposits

Generally, a security deposit is not required from a nationally recognized, creditworthy tenant, but a deposit roughly equivalent to one month's rent should be required from independent and noncredit tenants. It is used to repair damage caused by the tenant and to offset any unpaid obligations and should not be considered the last month's rent. When the security deposit is considered the last month's rent, there are no funds to offset the tenant's defaults. Furthermore, if the rent has increased during the term of the lease, the security deposit may not be sufficient for a full month's rent. Obviously, larger deposits are appropriate when there are credit problems or large front-end investments are required on the landlord's part. Unless otherwise required by law, avoid paying interest on deposits, and retain the right to commingle those funds with the landlord's operating funds.

Reconstruction

Most leases will require that the landlord reconstruct the premises within so many days after a fire or other disaster if a certain percentage of the building is left standing. It is important that this percentage be the same for all tenants and that the landlord allow sufficient time for rebuilding, including insurance and fire department investigations and approvals.

Landlord Work and Tenant Improvements

If no work is to be performed by the landlord, the lease should indicate that the tenant is accepting the premises in "as is" condition. If the landlord is providing improvements, the specifics should be carefully spelled out. The lease or construction exhibit should then indicate that anything not specifically included as landlord work is to be supplied and paid for by the tenant.

Lease Term

The actual lease term should be carefully indicated, usually in words and numbers—"three (3) years"—along with the beginning and ending dates. If the building is under construction or being remodeled and specific dates are unknown, the lease will indicate that the term will commence under specific conditions. Once those conditions have been met, a letter of understanding or a lease amendment should be completed, signed by the parties, and attached to the lease. This will prevent disputes as to when rent commences and the lease expires.

Base Rents

The minimum monthly rent should be clearly indicated as to amounts and due dates. If free rent is to be given as a concession, the number of months of free rent must be stated. It is also critical to address bill-back items and utilities during periods of free rent, as the tenant generally assumes that "free rent" means occupying the premises at no cost.

Holdover

Quite often when the lease ends, the new rental will be substantially higher than the former rate, and the tenant may ignore the landlord's attempts to renew the lease, hoping to keep the rent low. The holdover clause provides that at the expiration of the lease any holdover is automatically on a month-to-month basis under all of the terms of the original lease and that the rent during the holdover period will be from $1\frac{1}{2}$ to 4 times the rent due during the last month of the lease term. The greater the rent during the holdover, the more of an incentive for the tenant to renew or vacate.

Hazardous Substances

The damage caused to the environment and the cost of cleanup for hazardous substances became an important issue in the early 1980s. This clause addresses the storage and disposal of hazardous substances. It assigns liability for cleanup costs, fines, and annual penalties to the tenant and requires the tenant to indemnify the landlord from costs, penalties, and charges imposed upon the landlord, including attorney's fees as a result of the tenant's illegal use, disposal, and sale of hazardous substances.

(b) SHOPPING CENTER LEASE CLAUSES

The relationship between landlord and tenant in a shopping center is complex. Because of the synergism between the tenants and the need for the public to accept the shopping center, it is critical to establish operating standards and a mechanism for enforcement. On the other hand, if the lease is too sophisticated or complicated, the small, inexperienced, but desirable prospect may be frightened away. The lease that is required for a department store in a superregional mall would be totally unacceptable for a card and gift shop in a strip center. A review of clauses unique or critical to the shopping center lease follows.

Percentage Rents

Percentage rental clauses are unique to retail and service tenants. A poorly drafted percentage rental clause can be the source of considerable disagreement between landlord and tenant. The actual percentage rates to be used are fully negotiable; *Dollars and Cents of Shopping Centers* and the December issue of *Buildings Magazine* provide excellent guidance in establishing percentage rates.

Once the rate is agreed upon, reporting and payment must be negotiated. Major tenants almost always report sales and pay percentage rent annually. National chains and independent tenants should report and pay monthly but have an annual adjustment to even out discrepancies between very high and very low sales months.

Percentages are applicable to gross sales, less sales taxes, returns, and allowances. An experienced tenant may ask to exclude sales to employees, lottery tickets, or small items such as newspapers or cigarettes carried more for customer convenience than profit. The landlord must carefully evaluate the impact of these requests on the ultimate rents from that prospect. Sales to employees at a discount not to exceed a percentage of the stores sales, say 2%, are excluded when determining percentage rent owing.

Sales Audits

With a percentage rent clause in the lease, the landlord must retain the right to audit the tenant. A typical audit clause will allow the landlord to audit the tenant's sales up to three years or more after submission. If an error of more than 2% is found, the tenant pays for the audit. Improper reporting is often considered to be a default of the lease.

Store Hours

This clause requires the tenant to remain open during specific stated times. The early leases allowed the Merchants' Association to set the hours. Seldom could the merchants agree on the hours. Next, the tenants were required to maintain the same hours as the majors. This became impractical when supermarkets remained opened 18 to 24 hours each day. Now the landlord either reserves the right to set the hours or the lease will pre-set the hours, such as, Mondays thru Fridays 10 to 9, Saturday 10 to 6 and Sundays to 5. When all or most of the tenants remain open the same hours there is a higher probability their sales will exceed their breakpoint and they will pay percentage rent.

Radius Restriction

When a lease has a percentage rent clause, the landlord will often place a radius restriction on the tenant to avoid dilution of the sales and percentage rental income. The actual radius will depend on the type of center. A neighborhood center will generally have a radius restriction of two to four miles (approximately the trade area of the center), and a regional or superregional mall may have a radius of five to fifteen miles.

The radius restriction is meant to prevent the tenant from opening a similar store within the specified area. Should the tenant open another store in that designated area, it would be a default of the lease. The lease may provide a penalty either of adding the sales from both locations to compute percentage rents due or of increasing the base rent by, say, 50% should the tenant violate the radius restriction.

Common Area Costs

The common area clause needs careful attention. Most shopping centers bill the tenants for their pro rata share of all common area operating costs. The landlord should list everything that is likely to be needed for operating the common areas, repairs, and replacement, and should add a catchall such as "and anything else necessary for the legal and safe operation of the common areas."

In addition to the actual costs, the landlord is entitled to a fee for the administration and supervision of the common area repairs and maintenance. This fee is generally between 10% and 15% of the actual costs. Major tenants will try to eliminate the supervision fee or reduce it to closer to 5%. Be wary of pioneering a tenant charge, especially a major charge such as a management fee, in a soft market. Some landlords are requiring tenants to pay their share of the management cost of the center instead of a common area maintenance supervision fee, and some centers require tenants to pay their share of both.

Common Area Billings

Billings for common area costs can be monthly, quarterly, or even annually based on actual costs, but all of these methods have problems. The most equitable approach is to prepare an annual budget at the beginning of the year, estimating all bill-back items, and have the tenant pay one-twelfth each month, with an adjustment at the end of the year based on actual costs.

Building Maintenance

The lease must clearly spell out what areas are landlord responsibilities and what areas the tenant must maintain. Generally, the tenant is responsible for the store's interior, all windows, doors, and glass, and all systems serving the store exclusively. In the past, landlords maintained at their cost the roof and structural portions of the building. In modern leases, landlords still maintain the roof and structural portions, but the cost is billed back to the tenants as part of the common area costs. These two items in particular should be spelled out carefully, as there is considerable room for misunderstanding.

Real Estate Taxes

In the 1950s and 1960s, the landlord would pay the taxes in the first year of a lease, and the tenant would pay any future increases. This is known as billing the tenant on a base year formula. Since the early 1970s, the tenant pays the full pro rata share of all taxes on the premises. Before this clause is written, the landlord should understand how the property will be taxed and then determine how the tenants will be billed for taxes. Pad tenants, for instance, generally have more valuable real estate and their tax bills are higher than in-line tenants. The taxes for the pad tenants, in most cases, should be segregated rather than averaged into the taxes for the entire center. On the other hand, very large supermarkets are generally assessed at a lower rate per square foot and will want their own parcel tax assessment to realize that economy. Taxes can be billed separately once or twice a year, but it is more expeditious for the landlord and tenant either to combine them with the common area cost estimates or create a separate estimated line item expense and bill the tenants one-twelfth of the estimate each month. Major tenants will reimburse the landlord only when the taxes are due.

Tenant Insurance

It is important for tenants to be properly insured for both their benefit and that of the landlord. The modern lease will require tenants to carry liability insurance in reasonable amounts. Today $1 million liability coverage appears to be acceptable. Tenant's insurance requirements includes fire and extended coverage on tenant improvements; stock and fixtures for either full replacement value or 80% to 90% of value; boiler insurance for pressure vessels (if appropriate); and plate glass insurance. In all cases the landlord is to be named insured and is to receive ten to twenty days advance notice of tenants' cancellation of the policy. Tenants provide the landlord with a certificate of insurance as evidence of such coverage. Major tenants and some pad tenants may provide full fire and extended coverage on their entire premises plus the aforementioned coverages. Most major tenants will self-insure for plate glass loss.

Landlord Insurance

Generally the landlord will provide a basic fire and extended coverage policy along with a liability policy on the shopping center and then bill the tenants their pro rata share of the premium. If the premium covers rental value insurance, some tenants will try to negotiate that out of the lease. Also, some major tenants will try to negotiate limits on liability coverage.

HVAC Maintenance

Besides requiring tenants to maintain their demised premises, the landlord should single out the HVAC system for special attention.

Some landlords require the tenant to perform routine maintenance on the HVAC and provide the landlord with evidence of a contract for such service. A disadvantage to this method is that several HVAC maintenance contractors will be walking the roofs and possibly leaving their materials there, which can cause roof problems. An alternative is for the landlord to maintain all HVAC units and bill the tenants for their pro rata cost.

This often results in time-consuming problems for the center owner with no compensation. Another alternative is for the lease to allow the landlord to contract for the HVAC maintenance and have the contractor bill the tenant quarterly in advance.

Use Clause

A shopping center is like a department store in which each department is owned and operated by a different owner. To assure the best tenant mix and avoid unnecessary overlap, the landlord must carefully define the merchandise or services that may be sold from each store. The use should be defined as narrowly as possible. The use clause should not say "shoe store," but should specify men's or women's shoes. Avoid "and accessories" or a clause that allows for merchandise as "sold in tenant's other locations," since that tenant may not have any restrictions there.

Merchants' Association and Marketing/Promotional Fund

The tenant is required to become a member and pay dues to the merchants' association or marketing/promotional fund. Minimum dues are stated, and the association or fund has the right to increase the dues annually.

Advertising

The tenant is requested to spend a percentage, usually 2% of sales, on advertising. This clause may also require the tenant to advertise in the shopping center tabloid.

Cancellation Based on Sales

It is not unusual today for merchants to ask for the right to cancel the lease based on their failure to reach a given sales level. This right should not be easily given but may be a consideration to attract stronger tenants that a landlord may need for the shopping center. If that is the case, the sales level should be a reasonable one that is attainable under the existing circumstances. The right to cancel should be a one-time rather than an ongoing right and should be a mutual right of both landlord and tenant. If there will be any unamortized tenant improvements or leasing commissions at the time of cancellation, the tenant should be obligated to pay those as a condition of the cancellation. The tenant should provide the landlord with four to six months' advance notice in exercising the cancellation right.

Options

With the exception of major tenants and tenants requiring a large investment in fixtures, such as a restaurant, there is little reason to grant options to renew. The only reason, other than the above, is if the landlord definitely wants the tenant, and the tenant is adamant about having an option. In that case, the option should never be longer than the initial term.

The tenant should be required to give at least 180 days' advance written notice in exercising the option. The lease should require that the option is null and void if the tenant is in default, that the option will not apply to assignees or subtenants, and that the tenant will have achieved a specific minimum sales volume to exercise the option. Options favor the tenant with little or no offsetting benefits to the landlord.

Relocation

The astute owner is always looking for opportunities to improve the center. To maintain flexibility in that regard, the landlord will have a relocation clause. Most major tenants and national tenants will resist such a clause, but this right is generally not too difficult to obtain from smaller tenants. The clause requires the tenant to move to another location within the center at the landlord's request as long as it is approximately the same size, similar location and the landlord pays all of the reasonable costs for the move.

Parking Control

Parking is a critical element of the success of shopping centers. One parking stall near the center can provide eight to twelve customers per day with convenient parking. Because of this, the lease will provide that the tenant and the tenant's employees will park only in designated employee parking areas. If the requirement is violated after sufficient notice, the tenant, not the employee, will pay a fine of $10 to $25 for each offense.

Sign Control

Sign control is a critical element in the esthetic appeal of shopping centers. The signs must be attractive and readable, but the landlord must avoid oversize signs, blinking or rotating signs, or signs that are in questionable taste. The landlord should have an architect prepare sign criteria for the center that conform to city sign restrictions; these criteria should be an addendum to the lease so there is no doubt of their importance. Additionally, the lease prohibits the tenant from putting up window signs that have not been approved by the landlord.

Exclusives

Supermarkets and drugstores will demand, and receive, exclusives. Other than major tenants that a center must have, landlords should avoid granting exclusives. If a restaurant is absolutely necessary in the shopping center, and the operator demands an exclusive, the landlord may have to relent. The exclusive should apply only if the lease has not been assigned or sublet and should be worded that "landlord will not lease space to any tenant whose primary business is _____."

Cotenancy

This is a clause a landlord wants to avoid. A tenant with a cotenancy clause has the right to cancel the lease if a particular tenant vacates. For instance, a drugstore may have the right to cancel the lease if the supermarket closes. A variation on this clause is for the tenant's rent to convert from a minimum rent versus percentage rent to percentage rent only if a particular tenant vacates. Either approach can be deadly to the shopping center.

Guarantees

Tenants who want to use a corporation to sign the lease should be required to guarantee the lease personally if the corporation does not have a strong financial net worth. The personal guarantee could extend for the entire term of the lease or for the first few years of the lease, providing the tenant has never been in default. A lease guarantee should be signed as a document separate from the lease itself.

"Favored Nation" Clause

This clause gives the tenant all of the concessions that the other tenants have and is another clause to avoid.

Maintenance Reserves

This clause allows the landlord to charge for future major maintenance. For instance, the parking lot may need to be resurfaced in three years and the landlord bills each tenant his pro rata cost monthly for the next thirty-six months. Major tenants will not pay a maintenance reserve but will pay their pro rate obligation as the expense is incurred.

(c) OFFICE BUILDING LEASE CLAUSES

The following clauses are either unique to office buildings or are of particular concern to the operations of an office building.

Use

The most common error in describing a tenant's use in an office building is to state, "Tenant may use the premises for general business purposes." This gives the tenant an endless number of uses. A tenant in 800 square feet with this use clause could convert from an insurance agency of five people to an answering service of twenty people. A small building may not be able to accommodate the additional employees in terms of parking and use of other building services. The description of the tenant's use should always be very specific and very restrictive, so that the landlord maintains control over the building.

Escalation

Escalation clauses state which expenses are passed on to the tenants. A common approach is to state, "The building's operating expenses will include, but not be limited to, the following. . . ." All of the typical operating expenses are then listed. Since the late 1970s, the following have been included as escalatable expenses by many owners: management fee, amortization of the cost to replace capital improvement in the common areas, expenses to upgrade the life safety features, and expenses to upgrade energy conservation features. Some property owners include a reserve for future maintenance such as roof or parking lot repairs. The escalation clause will also state how escalation charges are determined, such as base year or expense stop clause, how the tenant's pro rata share is calculated, and the frequency of escalation payments.

Triple Net or Fully Net Lease

In rare cases, an office building lease may be a triple net lease, which requires the tenant to pay for real estate taxes, insurance, and maintenance. This type of lease is usually used in a single-tenant building.

HVAC Hours

If the lease does not state the hours during which the building will provide heating, ventilating, and air-conditioning, a tenant can demand HVAC at any time of the day or night or during the weekend. For example, an accounting firm may work late into the night and on weekends during the tax season, January through April, and need HVAC service during those hours. If the lease does not state the hours for HVAC, the property owner would probably be required to provide this service after hours at the expense of the escalation cost paid by all the tenants. Typical hours for HVAC service would be 7:00 A.M. to 5:00 P.M., Monday through Friday; 8:00 A.M. to 2:00 P.M., Saturday; and no service on Sunday or holidays. These hours will change slightly depending on the area of the country and the building's tenant profile.

To accommodate the need of an accounting firm that will work long hours and weekends during tax season, the lease can provide for after-hours (after the building's stated hours of service) HVAC for a charge. The charge is based on the cost of energy, the use of the equipment, and the cost of a building maintenance person or engineer if one is required to be on duty. The after-hours HVAC income is credited to the escalation expenses. The amount of the charge is not stated in the lease because it will vary.

Janitorial Services

The lease should state the frequency of janitorial service and stipulate that the landlord will determine the janitorial specifications and the days the service will be provided.

Maintenance of Carpeting and Window Covering

Most leases will assign the maintenance of the tenant's carpeting and window covering to the tenant. The landlord will provide vacuuming and spot cleaning of the carpeting, but major cleaning of these items is at the tenant's expense.

Overstandard Utilities

The landlord must have the right to charge the tenant for the consumption of utilities in excess of the standard amount consumed by an office tenant.

Landlord's Right to Recapture Premises

This clause came about in the early 1980s. In the mid-1970s, the office building market was soft in most areas of the country, so tenants could negotiate long-term leases on very favorable terms. When the office market firmed up in the early 1980s, and rents more than doubled, some tenants sublet or assigned part or all of their space at a considerably higher rent than they were paying, realizing a substantial profit. Naturally, most landlords object to tenants earning a profit on their space because the landlord assumed the original risk in developing or purchasing the project and sustained the losses during the soft market. The landlord's right to recapture gives the landlord the right to take back space that the tenant wants to sublet or assign.

Another approach is to allow the tenant the right to sublet or assign the space provided that the increased rent is paid to the landlord. An alternative is for the landlord and the tenant to share the increase.

Estoppels

An estoppel is a summary of the business terms of the lease, including rent, expiration dates, options, rent payment status, and security deposit. The lease requires the tenant to sign an estoppel at the landlord's request. Estoppels are required by lenders and purchasers to ensure the accuracy of the landlord's information regarding the tenant's lease obligations.

Alterations

To maintain the integrity of the building's mechanical, electrical, and structural systems, the landlord usually reserves the right to perform all tenant alterations. If a major tenant insists on performing its own alterations, the landlord must place stringent requirements on the tenant and the contractor doing the work. These include requiring the contractor to have insurance, to obtain all necessary building permits, and possibly to use union labor. The clause also designates when construction may occur, when the elevators may be used, how materials may be delivered to the premises, and, of course, the landlord's right to approve all plans.

Title to Improvements

This clause states that the landlord has title to the tenant's improvements, which remain with the premises when the tenant vacates.

Taxes on Overstandard Improvements

If the building tax assessment is increased because of a tenant's overstandard improvements, that tenant pays the increase in taxes.

Acceptance of Keys

This clause prevents tenants from claiming they are relieved of all lease obligation because they returned the keys and vacated the premises prior to the lease expiration.

Building Rules and Regulations

The building's rules and regulations are a part of the lease, and the landlord reserves the right to change these rules. A sophisticated tenant will require the landlord to be reasonable in changing the rules and regulations and to give adequate notice before they go into effect.

Sample rules and regulations are shown in Exhibit 7.7. A few rules that deserve special mention are listed below.

1. Any coffee machines or similar devices must be on a timer, or the electrical outlet must be on a timer. This is to avoid a fire started by an electrical coffeemaker left on after the office is closed.
2. Tenant will not use the premises for lodging.
3. Animals will not be kept on the premises.
4. Tenant will not use the building's photo, logo, or name in tenant's advertising without the landlord's approval.
5. Tenant will not canvass or solicit in the building.
6. Landlord will designate time and manner the tenant will move all freight, furniture, and supplies in and out of the building.
7. Tenant will not place equipment of unusual size or weight on the premises.
8. Tenant will not install additional locks or change the keying to the premises without prior approval.
9. Tenant will not install window coverings without prior approval of landlord.

Medical Waste

Medical waste can be classified as hazardous materials. The lease must outline how medical waste will be disposed of and stipulate that the tenant will be liable for any damages or fines resulting from the use of hazardous materials. (See Exhibit 7.8.)

(d) INDUSTRIAL BUILDING LEASE CLAUSES

Many of the clauses in shopping center and office building leases are used in the industrial lease.

Use Clause

The use clause in every commercial lease, including the industrial lease, should be very specific about the type of business that must be conducted. Possibly no other clause in the lease conveys as many rights

EXHIBIT 7.8

600 BROADWAY MEDICAL CENTER RULES AND REGULATIONS

1. Lessee shall not prepare any food or do any cooking (except for microwave cooking) or install any vending machines or permit delivery of food or beverages to Premises without the written approval of the Lessor.

2. No common area shall be blocked by the Lessee and shall be used only for ingress and egress to and from the demised Premises or the Building.

3. No signs, advertisements or notices shall be attached to, or placed on, the exterior or interior of the Building, or the parking areas or sidewalks without prior written approval of Lessor.

4. No animal or bird of any kind shall be brought into, or kept in or about, the demised Premises or the Building. No bicycle shall be brought into the Building except in the garage or at an authorized bike rack.

5. Lessee shall lower window coverings and turn off all lights prior to leaving for the day.

6. Lessee, or Lessee's agents, shall not bring or store in the Building or demised Premises, any kerosene, gasoline, combustible, inflammable or explosive substance.

7. No additional locks, bolts or mail slots shall be placed on the doors, windows or walls without the Lessor's prior written approval.

8. All carrying or removal of equipment, furniture or bulky matter must take place during the hours which the Lessor, or its agents, may determine, and Lessor will assign which elevator that the Lessee may use.

9. Lessor shall have the right to prohibit Lessee's use of the Building name or photo in its advertisement which in the opinion of the Lessor tends to impair the reputation of the Building.

10. Lessor reserves the right to exclude from the Building, between the hours of 6:00 p.m. and 8:00 a.m. on all days and all the hours of Saturday, Sunday and legal holidays, all persons who do not present a Building pass issued by Lessee.

11. All persons entering or exiting the Building after 6:00 p.m. Monday through Friday and on all hours of Saturday, Sunday and Holidays shall, at Lessor's request, be required to present the appropriate pass and sign in and out.

12. Temporary notices are not to be Scotch taped, thumbtacked, nailed or glued, etc., to entry doors.

13. Lessee's contractor, while in the Building or Premises or Lessee's parking area, if any, shall be subject to the Rules and Regulations of the Building, and will also be subject to direction from the Lessor or its agents, but will not be an agent or contractor of the Lessor or its agents. Lessee's contractor shall be licensed by the State, insured and bonded at the amount requested by Lessor.

14. If the demised Premises or any part of the Building becomes infested with vermin as a result of the use or neglect on the part of the Lessee, the Lessee shall reimburse Lessor for the extermination expense.

15. If, as a result of any governmental rule or regulation or law, Lessor imposes a curtailment of services or a reduction of energy usage, the Lessee shall comply and shall be liable for any surcharges imposed upon Lessor for non-compliance.

16. Lessee shall install and maintain, at Lessee's expense, fire extinguishers, per local governmental regulations or law, next to any duplicating machine or similar heat producing equipment.

17. Lessee shall install and maintain, at Lessee's expense, any life safety equipment required by governmental rules, regulations or laws to be kept in its Premises.

18. Lessee and Lessee's agents and employees shall park only in those areas designated by Lessor or Lessor's agents. Lessee shall pay a fine to Lessor of Ten Dollars ($10.00) per violation for each parking violation of Lessee, Lessee's employees, agents, invitees or licensees.

19. No air conditioning or heater shall be used without the prior approval of the Lessor.

EXHIBIT 7.8 *(Continued)*

20. No canvassing or soliciting shall be allowed in the Building.

21. All Lessee's requests for service must be in writing and sent to the Lessor's Building office. Lessee shall report all burnt out lights, leaking faucets, plugged drains and electrical problems to the Building Management.

22. Lessee will not use the Building for lodging, sleeping or cooking, or conduct mechanical or manufacturing operations.

23. Lessee shall not conduct, in or about the Building, any auction, public or private, without the prior written approval of Lessor.

24. Lessee shall not use any machines in the Building, other than standard office machines such as typewriters, calculators, copying machines and similar machines, without the prior written approval of Lessor. All office equipment and any other devices of any electrical or mechanical nature shall be placed by Lessee in the Premises in settings approved by Lessor so as to absorb or prevent any vibrations or odors within the Building.

25. Lessee shall use the common areas of the Building only as a means of ingress and egress, and Lessee shall permit no loitering by any persons upon the common area or elsewhere within the Building.

26. Lessor will furnish Lessee, free of charge, two (2) keys to the Lessee's entry door. Lessor shall make a reasonable charge for any additional keys. Lessee shall not have any such keys copied. Lessee, upon the termination of its Lease, shall deliver to Lessor all keys to doors in the Building.

27. Lessor reserves the right to restrict the amount of directory space utilized by Lessee.

28. Lessor shall provide Lessee electricity and HVAC for normal operations Monday through Friday 7:00 a.m. to 9:00 p.m. and Saturday 7:00 a.m. to 5:00 p.m. Any additional usage required by Lessee must be arranged with Lessor, or its agents, and shall be subject to additional charge.

29. Lessee shall not contract or initiate any improvements beyond original Leasehold improvements without written consent of Lessor (this includes concrete and core drilling).

30. If Lessee desires a music sound system, Lessee must use the system provided by the Lessor and a separate charge will be assessed for the service.

31. If Lessee wishes to maintain a coffee machine, or like device, in the Premises, a timer must be connected to the outlet into which said machine is connected to prevent the possibility of coffee pots being left on and presenting possible fire hazards.

32. Lessee shall provide adequate security for storage of all drugs used in its practice.

33. Lessee shall comply with all governmental rules and regulations regarding biological or disposable waste and shall cause the removal the said waste from the Building in a manner acceptable to Lessor.

34. Lessee shall report all theft of property or other crime to the Police Department and Building Management. Lessee shall report all slip and fall accidens or other potential liability claims to Building Management.

35. Lessee shall not make or permit to be made any unseemly or disturbing noises, sounds or vibrations or disturb or interfere with occupants of the Building or neighboring buildings or premises, whether by the use of any musical instrument, radio, stereo, unusual noise, or in any other way.

36. Lessee shall not install any antenna or other device on the roof or exterior of the Building without Lessor's prior written approval.

LESSOR: _____

LESSEE: _____

to the tenant as the use clause. The property owner will lose considerable control over the property with poorly written use clauses.

Maintenance

The industrial lease usually provides the tenant with more direct maintenance responsibility than do leases for other types of properties. The lease must be specific regarding each party's maintenance responsibility and who will perform the maintenance. The landlord usually assumes responsibility for performing major maintenance tasks and requires the tenant to reimburse the cost.

Insurance

The lease will state the required type of insurance coverage and the minimum amount of coverage the tenant must carry, including the landlord as named insured on the policy. The lease will also state that if the tenant's business causes the landlord's insurance premium to increase, the tenant will pay the increase.

Storage

Many industrial parks will not allow storage outside the building. The lease might state that toxic materials cannot be stored on the premises.

Signage

If the industrial park has sign criteria, the tenant will be required to submit a request for sign approval to the landlord's agent and to adhere to the park's sign criteria.

Alterations and Additions

This clause states that the tenant either cannot make alterations or additions without the landlord's prior written approval or can make nonstructural alterations and additions if a certain cost is not exceeded.

§ 7.12   LEASE NET-NESS

Net-ness is a lease term used to describe building expenses that are paid by the tenant. Leases are either gross, single net, double net, triple net, or modified net.

In a *gross lease,* the tenant pays base rent and is not billed for any tenant charges. In theory, these charges are included in the gross rent.

In a *single net lease,* the tenant pays base rent and real estate taxes.

In a *double net lease* (net, net lease), the tenant pays base rent, real estate taxes, and building insurance.

In a *triple net lease* (net, net, net lease), the tenant pays base rent, real estate taxes, building insurance, and maintenance. This lease is also referred to as a *fully net lease.*

A useful mnemonic device is the name TIM: T = taxes, TI = taxes and insurance, TIM = taxes, insurance, and maintenance.

The property manager should be careful how lease terms are used. Some people will refer to a lease as a "net lease" and mean the tenant pays base rent, taxes, insurance, and maintenance, while others will use the textbook definition of a net lease to mean the tenant pays only base rent and taxes. When someone refers to the *net-ness* of a lease, that term should be clarified during lease negotiation or sale of a property to avoid future problems and possible litigation. Imagine an agent entering into a lease with a tenant, using the term *net lease* to mean triple net rather than single net.

A modified net lease doesn't fit the definition of any of the net leases. If a lease required the tenant to pay full pro rata insurance and maintenance but had a cap on real estate taxes, this lease would not be a triple net lease but a modified net lease.

Different geographic areas have different terms for exceptions to a triple net lease, such as special net or industrial net lease. It is important to read such leases carefully and inquire about the definition of the terms.

Building expenses can be paid directly by tenants or paid by the landlord and billed back to tenants for reimbursement. In multitenant buildings, the landlord will pay the real estate taxes and insurance and bill the tenants for reimbursement. Most tenants are either billed one-twelfth of the cost of these expenses monthly, based on an estimate and adjusted to actual costs, or they are billed for the entire expense thirty days before the expenses are due. Major tenants in a shopping center or industrial park prefer to reimburse the landlord just prior to the date the expenses must be paid.

The lease for a single-tenant building may require the tenant to purchase insurance coverage and pay the insurance premium directly to the insurance carrier. An example of this is a freestanding K Mart store or an industrial building occupied solely by Boeing Aircraft. In this case, the lease will state the type and minimum amount of insurance coverage and require that the property owner be an additional named insured on the tenant's insurance policy.

Maintenance on single-tenant buildings is usually contracted and paid directly by the tenant to the contractors. On a multitenant building, the landlord may perform various levels of maintenance and bill the tenants for reimbursement. The tenants contract for the maintenance in their premises in industrial properties, shopping centers, and some garden office buildings. The landlord assumes this responsibility in mid- to high-rise office and medical buildings and most garden office and medical buildings.

Regardless of the net-ness of a lease, each expense item, especially maintenance items for which the tenant is responsible, should be carefully explained in the lease. Items such as the roof, utility lines, and structural repair of the building should be specifically mentioned.

§ 7.13   LEASE CLAUSES THAT IMPACT NET OPERATING INCOME

Every clause in a commercial lease has an impact on the property's net operating income and value. Income and expense clauses have a direct impact, whereas clauses concerning the operations of the property can have an indirect impact on the bottom line. When negotiating a commercial lease, the property manager should measure the financial impact on the property before changing or deleting any of these clauses.

The income and tenant reimbursement clauses have immediate and direct effect on the property. Of these clauses the base rent clause has the greatest effect and is the center of most lease negotiations. When negotiating this clause, the property manager has to work from a position of strength, as determined by market conditions, the property's position in the market, and the property's break-even analysis. Understanding present market conditions and market trends will assist in negotiating rent step-ups. A key question is: Will demand increase or will the market soften over the next few years? Analyzing future trends are part of the management plan and market survey.

Another clause that affects base rent is the consumer price index (CPI) clause, which adjusts the base rent upward as indicated by increases in the index. Negotiating an annual CPI clause will keep the income stream current with inflation. Tenants whose rent was adjusted based on the CPI in the late 1970s and early 1980s, when inflation was in the double digits, will frequently request a cap, or ceiling, on the CPI. If a tenant prevails in obtaining a cap, then the property manager should negotiate a floor on the CPI. A floor is a minimum amount the CPI will increase. For example, a lease may call for an annual CPI increase with a cap of 6% and a floor of 3%. The CPI may be adjusted annually, every two or three years, or at any agreed-upon interval.

Another income source is percentage rent. The percentage rent clause is intended to preserve the value of the income stream from a tenant. In theory, as inflation increases, the tenant's sales increase, and the tenant pays percentage or overage rent. The overage represents the percentage rent paid above or over the base rent. Another rationale for charging percentage rent is that the developer or property owner has created a unique retail environment in which each tenant benefits from the synergism of the tenant mix. The tenant's sales in the shopping center should be higher than if the tenant were in a freestanding building. The owner, therefore, wants a share of the tenant's success in this unique environment.

Percentage rates for each category of use are not specific numbers, but a range. For instance, a women's ready-to-wear store has a range from 4% to 6%. The property manager must know the correct percentage rate and negotiate for the highest point on the range. *Dollars and Cents of Shopping Centers,* published by the Urban Land Institute, is the most complete resource, listing percentage ranges for every category of tenant in different classifications of shopping centers.

Other income components are the direct operating expense reimbursements. These include real estate taxes, insurance, and maintenance. In an office building, these components are combined with the tenant's escalation charge. In industrial properties and shopping centers, they are billed to the tenant separately. Although these clauses may be treated as additional income, they have the effect of reducing the property owner's operating expenses.

The real estate tax clause should include all property assessments such as street improvements and stoplights, known as LID (local improvement district). The insurance clause should allow the landlord to determine the type of coverage and the limits of coverage, although the tenant may attempt to negotiate a cap on these expenses. For instance, a shopping center tenant may offer to pay the pro rata share of real estate taxes on its premises not exceeding $1,000 annually. The property manager needs to know the cost of these items for each space and obtain full reimbursement from the tenants. When this is not possible, the property manager should know the cost of the negotiated cap.

Maintenance reimbursements are included in the escalation expenses for office tenants, common area maintenance costs for shopping center tenants, and maintenance bill-backs for industrial tenants. These clauses should include all operating expenses. They may also include the cost to install or upgrade life safety equipment and energy conservation features. Reserves for future maintenance and replacement or for capital improvements in common areas are two additional items found in maintenance pass-through clauses in some leases. Most tenants will accept paying full reimbursement of the operating expenses but may wish to negotiate reserves and replacement of capital improvements in the common areas.

Several lease clauses have an indirect effect on the property's current or future net operating income and value. The late charge provision, for example, is not intended as a source of additional income, but is an incentive to encourage the tenants to pay rent on time. The holdover clause, in which the tenant's rent increases significantly, is a motivator for the tenant either to renew before the lease expires or vacate at lease expiration. The insurance clause is intended to reduce the property owner's liability by requiring the tenant to have specific insurance coverage with minimum limits and to include the property owner as named insured on the policy.

A tenant who assumes direct maintenance responsibilities reduces the owner's operating expenses. Direct maintenance is more commonly found in industrial and shopping center leases. On the other hand, the lease must give the landlord the right to construct the tenant improvements or to approve the plans and construction procedures when the tenant performs its own improvements.

The assignment provision can improve the security of the income stream either by allowing an assignment to a financially stronger tenant (the assignee), or by having two tenants (the assignor and the assignee) responsible for fulfilling the lease provisions. This is accomplished by allowing the assignment without release. The assignor, the tenant assigning the lease, is not released from the lease obligation. If the assignee, the tenant assuming the lease, defaults, the assignor is responsible for fulfilling the lease terms.

The security deposit, in some situations, is the only source of income to offset part or all of the cost of a tenant's default. The amount of the security deposit is determined by market conditions and by the strength of the tenant. A tenant with an AAA credit rating seldom pays a security deposit, while a financially weak tenant may be required to pay two or three months' security deposit. A one-month deposit is most common.

The right to charge tenants for overstandard utilities or other services minimizes operating expenses either for the property owner or the other tenants by lowering escalation costs when the building's operating expenses are reduced.

Several clauses are pertinent to shopping center leases and to leases with retail tenants in an office building or industrial property. The first is the sales report clause, which stipulates the frequency of the sales report; percentage rent payment; which terms, if any, are excluded from calculating percentage rent; and the owner's right to audit the tenant's sales. Other clauses that affect percentage rent are the radius clause and hours of operation.

The tenant's inclusion in the merchants' association or marketing/promotional fund and the advertising clause requires the tenant to participate in the promotions and advertising of the property. These activities should increase the tenant's sales and the property's percentage rent.

The exclusive clause and the "favored nation" clause should be avoided. The exclusive clause gives the tenant an exclusive right to sell a particular product or provide a particular service. A tenant's exclusive will prevent leasing to a similar use. The lost income and property value from these clauses can be considerable.

The "favored nation" clause, which derives from the favored nation trade advantages that one country gives another, provides the tenant with all the concessions that other tenants were granted. For instance, if one tenant has a cap on real estate taxes and another doesn't pay common area maintenance charges, the tenant with the "favored nation" clause is granted these same privileges.

The property manager has an opportunity to improve the property's net operating income and value by carefully structuring and negotiating the commercial lease, paying particular attention to the clauses that affect the income stream and the operating expenses of the building.

§ 7.14 NEGOTIATING WITH MAJOR RETAIL TENANTS

Most of the negotiating strategies used with small mom-and-pop tenants are not appropriate with major tenants because the property needs the major tenant more than the tenant needs the property.

Major retail tenants have a clear understanding of who their customers are, what environments work best for them, what economics they can live with, and the store's best size and configuration for their operation. They are very concerned about the developer's ability to develop the project in the first place and then how it will be managed when it is operating. The more experienced and respected the developer is, the more likely a major tenant will be to consider a lease. When a major tenant commits to a new store, it will devote considerable time and expense to analysis and negotiations. The tenant wants reasonable assurance that the project will be completed.

Major retail tenants may want to buy their own parcel and tie it into the center for parking and maintenance. The potential danger to the center owner under these circumstances is that the major tenant may close the store, eliminating the major source of traffic to the center. The developer should try to obtain the right to purchase the building should the major tenant close.

The major tenant will most likely negotiate a break-even deal with the developer. Usually the rent is determined by calculating the land cost plus the improvement cost times the loan constant. The formula can vary, but the point is that major tenant deals are not profitable at the outset of the lease. Major tenants know they create the traffic; their presence in the shopping center helps in obtaining financing; and they are often the deciding factor in the initial plans to build a shopping center.

Most major retail tenants will report and pay percentage rent annually, but they will usually step down the percentage rate. For example, a supermarket might pay 1.5% of the first $8 million in sales over the breakpoint, 1% of the next $4 million, and .75% above that.

Major retail tenants will often accept responsibility for full maintenance, although some will still expect the landlord to pay the cost of roof and structural maintenance.

Often major tenants will contribute to common area costs but exclude some items such as security, trash removal, and administrative or supervisory fee. They quite often will try to negotiate a cap on their pro rata share of the expenses to protect themselves from a landlord who does not watch costs.

Major retail tenants will most likely pay their full share of property taxes and will insure their own building for fire and extended coverage. However, many major tenants ask that any expense they incur for common areas, taxes, and insurance be deducted from percentage rent owned. If such a deduction must be granted, every effort should be made to make it noncumulative, meaning that each year stands on its own. If they are allowed to accumulate these costs in the first years, when there are no percentage rents, the amounts they can recapture later may effectively eliminate any chance of the landlord's ever collecting any percentage rents. Usually the developer can negotiate a lease that does not have caps on common area maintenance expenses and does not allow for recapture of reimbursements from percentage rents.

Major retail tenants have varying attitudes about joining merchants' associations. A few will not join; others will join but pay dues at a much lower rate per square foot than the small shops; and some will not join but will cooperate and contribute to individual events. Inasmuch as the major tenant is the main draw of the shopping center and often advertises very heavily, it is not difficult to understand a reluctance to join a merchants' association or a marketing/promotional fund.

Major retail tenants are not likely to sign an operating covenant that requires them to keep the store open and operating during the term of the lease. Major tenants want the flexibility of being able to close a store if their business plan indicates it should be done. The best defense for the landlord is to obtain the right to cancel the lease and regain possession of the store if the tenant closes. While it may appear to be drastic action, it is much better for the landlord to have possession of a vacant store and be prospecting for a suitable replacement tenant than having a 40,000-square-foot supermarket sit empty or be subleased to an auto supply or fabric store.

Generally, major retail tenants want an initial term of twenty to thirty years, usually at a fixed rental, but the landlord may be able to obtain rental increases at five- to ten-year intervals. These increases are negotiated in advance and are not tied to the consumer price index. Additionally, the major tenant will ask for six to eight renewal options in five-year increments.

Major tenants do not provide a security deposit and will generally have considerable control over any proposed change in the plot plan and design of the shopping center after it has been approved. They may even restrict other uses in the shopping center or within a certain distance from their premises. These uses usually include office and medical uses, bowling alleys, health clubs, theaters, and other uses that require long-term parking.

Even though the major tenant is almost always in a stronger negotiating position than the landlord, the landlord does not need to acquiesce to every request.

§ 7.15 PAD OR OUTLOT LEASING

Property managers can generate additional income and create additional value in their property by creating pad sites also known as outlots. A pad is a separate parcel that usually accommodates a single tenant's building, such as a bank or a fast-food restaurant. A pad can be sold, leased, or leased with a build-to-suit building.

The pad tenant has excellent visibility from the street, convenient access for its customers and, in many cases, drive-through window service. The pad tenant can also create an identity for itself. A pad location usually generates more business than an in-line location. Rent for a pad building is considerably higher than rent for the same square footage in the main building.

Many owners prefer to lease their pads to generate a long-term income stream, and many tenants prefer leasing rather than purchasing the pad to avoid the initial cost of the purchase. These tenants either cannot obtain the financing, do not have the funds to purchase the pad, or prefer to invest the funds in their business rather than in real estate. A ground lease is a form of financing the use of the land.

The property owner may prefer to lease the pad to a tenant who finances and builds the building. Another option is for the owner to build the tenant's building, or pay for the cost of the building, and lease the pad and building to the tenant. The latter is known as a build-to-suit lease.

There is a greater risk in the build-to-suit lease because the owner is investing additional funds to build the tenant's specialized building. The owner may obtain financing to build the tenant's building and charge a rent that is higher than the payment on the loan plus the rent on the ground lease. However, if a tenant defaults on a build-to-suit lease, the owner has a mortgage payment but no income from the building. After gaining possession of the premises the owner must attempt to re-lease the building. A building designed for a specific use might attract a limited number of tenants if the original tenant defaults. This is seldom a problem if the build-to-suit tenant is financially strong.

Because of the added risks of the build-to-suit lease, property owners usually prefer a straight ground lease. They limit build-to-suit leases to AAA-credit tenants.

Most pads are created on shopping center sites where excess land is available, but office building and industrial sites may also have opportunities to create pads. The property owner or manager should check for restrictions before creating a pad. These may be found in tenants' leases.

The major tenant in a shopping center may prohibit pads altogether or in a certain area. The concern is that the pad may block the tenant's visibility and disrupt customer parking. In rare cases, even a small tenant may have a pad restriction that must be honored. If the site plan exhibit attached to the tenant's lease doesn't indicate future pad sites or give the landlord the right to alter the site plan, the landlord may be prohibited from adding a pad building. If this situation exists, it should be corrected at the tenant's lease renewal.

Other documents to check for restrictions are the covenants, conditions and restrictions, the reciprocal easement agreement, and the common area maintenance agreement. These documents are discussed in Chapter 4 on shopping center management.

Because adding a pad changes the parking ratio of a property, the municipality's parking requirements might restrict pad leasing. Also, most states require that the pad be a separate parcel for it to be ground leased. The property manager might have to parcel or short plat the pad and should check with the municipality's building department for this procedure.

Before the oil shortage, service stations were major users of pads. Now most pads hold restaurants and financial institutions. Other pad users are automobile quick lubes, doughnut or ice cream shops, florists, and film-developing services.

Some pads are used for additional small shops. For example, a 5,000-square-foot building divided into five 1,000-square-foot shops may be built on the pad. Care must be exercised in creating such a building, for it could limit the visibility of the rest of the shopping center. Some shopping centers have so many large pad buildings that the main portion of the shopping center is not visible from the street, considerably decreasing the value and marketability of these spaces.

When a pad is leased, the property owner usually brings the utilities to the property line of the pad. The tenant is responsible for extending the utilities to the building.

Pad leases, also referred to as ground leases and build-to-suit leases, are for a long term because the tenant needs time to amortize its improvement costs, which are substantial. The typical term is between twenty and thirty years. Multiple options are common. The option right can be contingent upon the tenant's paying percentage rent for two years prior to the option. Obviously this would not apply to a tenant that did not pay percentage rent, such as a bank. The rent during the initial term is usually an escalating rent. The rental increases are either based on an agreed-upon figure every few years or a consumer price index increase.

The ground lease or build-to-suit lease is long and complicated, so legal advice should be obtained when negotiating this document. This type of lease is usually a triple net lease.

In marketing the pad, the property manager should develop many of the leasing materials described in the section on the leasing package. The most likely users are restaurant franchisers and franchisees, banks, and savings and loans. The property manager should contact these users by direct mail and follow up with a phone call. The *Annual Franchize Handbook* is a good source for potential users.

The property manager should be knowledgeable about the process of creating a pad to take advantage of the opportunity to increase the property's cash flow and value.

§ 7.16 LEASE RENEWALS

It is a misconception in the commercial real estate field that lease renewals are automatic and require little effort. Shopping center tenants, if their volume is good, are reluctant to move, but office tenants generally have no specific need to be in one building or another. A tenant's investment in improvements may keep it in a building; however, if the market is soft, another landlord may offer that tenant a turnkey lease. In turnkey leases the landlord pays for all the tenant's improvements. All the tenant needs to do is turn the key in the lock, open the door, and the tenant is ready to do business.

The existing tenant should be treated throughout the lease term as though the lease were about to expire. All too often the tenant is ignored until the lease is up for renewal, then the property manager reappears like a long lost friend.

Leases for small tenants should be renewed at least six months before expiration. Major tenants' renewal should be completed at least a year before expiration. When evaluating a shopping center tenant whose lease is expiring in a year, the property manager should ask: Are the tenant's sales satisfactory? Is the tenant still important to the mix of the center? Is there a better use or operator for that space? Would it be better to split that space to allow for expansion of an adjacent more productive tenant? In offices and industrial spaces, the property manager is more concerned about rental payment history and any history of problems. Again, look at adjacent uses to see if a more valuable, usually a larger, tenant has expansion needs.

Several months before a lease expires, a decision should be made about whether a tenant should be retained and under what terms. The tenant should be contacted to discuss its position on renewing. Is the tenant thinking of moving? Is the tenant concerned about market rents? Are tenant improvements needed, or is the space in fairly good shape? Does the market favor the tenant? Does the tenant have employees that may not move if the location were changed? Is there a major expense to move a computer network or fixtures? Does the tenant rely heavily on other tenants in the building?

Generally, owners try to negotiate market rents on a renewal even if it is necessary to offer tenant improvements or other concessions. It is too easy to allow a tenant's lease to slide well below market rents, and then when the attempt is made to bring the rents up to market at a subsequent renewal the percentage increase is so high that the tenant focuses on the percentage increase rather than the market rent. Additionally, the loss in property value due to below-market rents is approximately ten times the loss in income. In other words, giving away one dollar in rent is really giving away approximately ten dollars in value. So all leasing decisions should be evaluated in terms of how the deal affects the value of the property.

Negotiation with the tenant will take considerable time. Lease decisions in commercial properties are very important to the tenant and often require a substantial commitment. For these reasons, tenants should not be rushed. Rather, the manager should keep in touch with them and encourage them to do the same. The manager should let the tenant know that he or she cares about the business and is understanding about the rental increases. The tenant may have no alternative but to renew, especially if the space is correctly priced, but the new rent may still represent a substantial increase. If the manager takes an arrogant position, the tenant may move at considerable expense as a matter of pride.

The renewal lease should be finalized at least sixty days and preferably up to six months before expiration. As soon as the landlord and tenant are in agreement, an extension or new lease should be drawn up and delivered to the tenant. If the documents are not returned in a reasonable time, the tenant should be called. If in the last sixty days before the lease expires the lease has not been signed, the manager should begin showing the space to other prospects. Realizing it could lose the space, the tenant might decide to finalize negotiations and sign the lease. With rare exception, the tenant should sign the lease first. Then the landlord reviews the document, signs it, and returns a copy to the tenant as quickly as possible. It is a nice touch to hand deliver the lease or transmit it to the tenant with a cover letter indicating pleasure that the tenant has decided to remain and promising to do all possible to accommodate the tenant.

A renewal is often the most cost-effective deal that can be made in a building. There is no vacancy factor during the time between tenants, tenant improvements are usually considerably lower, free rent is often less or nonexistent, and the lease commission is often substantially reduced. A 1988 study revealed that a new tenant cost an office building $1.69 per square foot per year in free rent, leasing commissions, and tenant improvements. The renewal lease cost the building .87¢ per square foot.

§ 7.17 LEASING WHEN NO VACANCIES EXIST

Every property owner wants to have a fully leased property producing the maximum income. A fully occupied property, however, is not the end of the leasing effort, but the beginning of a fine-tuning process that can add substantially to the value of the building.

It is a rare building that does not have older leases at under market rents, tenants who have too much or too little space, underutilized space that can be converted to leasable area, or open space that can be converted to rent-producing storage. For these reasons, the property manager should continue leasing activities even when there are no vacancies. A leasing sign, in good taste, should always be on the property. When prospects inquire about space, they should not be told "We have nothing available." Rather the manager should discuss their needs to see if they might be potential replacement tenants. Regular visits with existing tenants will reveal their needs or potential business failures and early move-outs. On the other hand, any tenant who wants to increase or decrease its space is a potential opportunity to improve the income and value of the property.

The following cases are good examples of leasing opportunities when no vacancies exist.

- A small office building 100% leased had a conference room of 500 square feet that was rented out approximately ten times a year at $100 per day. The space was converted to an office at no cost and rented at $13.20 per foot per year. A net gain of $5,600 was realized. At a cap rate of 10%, an additional building value of $56,000 was created.

- The same building has six small enclosed areas under the stairwells. All were empty and dirty. They were cleaned, painted white, and offered as storage to tenants in the building at $30 each, totaling $180 per month. The added value to the building was in excess of $20,000 with an investment of less than $500.

- Another small office building had a hallway 10 feet wide by 30 feet long that was no longer in use. An enterprising young man was told that he could rent the hallway for a snack bar at $10.80

per foot, with an allowance of $1,800 to install the plumbing. The added value to the building was more than $30,000 for a space that appeared to have no value.

- A 5,000-square-foot apparel shop owner was not doing well and could not pay the rent. After some negotiations, the landlord split the store in half. The tenant was paying 70¢ per square foot per month, and the rent was increased to $1 on the new 2,500-square-foot store, saving the tenant $100 a month in rent while reducing tenant charges, utilities, and inventory needs. The other half of the space was leased at $1.30 per square foot. The added value to the center was in excess of $250,000 for an investment of approximately $48,000. The center now has two strong tenants instead of one weak tenant.

- A 2,000-square-foot recliner store was doing poorly but did not want to leave the center. Reducing the footage would not reduce its sales but would cut overhead. After some negotiations, the store was divided almost in half, leaving a 1,100-square-foot recliner store and another store of 900 feet in a prime location in the center. The recliner store's rent increased from $10.20 per square foot per year to $13.20, and the new space was leased for $15.60. Total value added to the center was in excess of $80,000 for an investment of under $3,000. The center ultimately gained two stronger merchants.

There are hundreds of stories in the industry of abandoned elevator shafts being refinished as one-person offices or tobacco stands; storerooms being refinished into office space; breezeways being closed in for rentable space; basements and attics being converted to leasable area or storage; three-story atriums being split into separate floors and leased; kiosks and carts added to the mall; and shallow shops built in front of blank walls on a mall.

Opportunities to improve the income of the property are endless, and the property manager should not stop leasing activities when the property is full.

§ 7.18   TENANT BUY-OUTS

One of the great opportunities in leasing is a tenant buy-out. Retailers, in particular, are downsizing their space needs, and many older retailers are not able to compete in today's market. If they occupy space at below-market rates, it may make sense to buy them out and re-lease their space, especially if the property may be sold or refinanced in the near future. There are endless approaches to the terms of the buy-out of an existing tenant. One approach is to see if the tenant might pay to have the lease cancelled. Two other common approaches are:

1. Tenant's Benefit. Estimate the profit that the tenant is taking from the store, multiply that by the years left in the lease, and suggest that the tenant can have the same profit without risk if the landlord buys out the lease. Obviously, the landlord has to be able to recapture that cost when the space is re-leased.

2. Landlord's Benefit. Consider the income from the existing tenant. For example, compare the tenants 5,000 square feet at $6 per square foot with the current market value of the space split into two stores at $11.60 per square foot. The difference is $28,000 in rent or $280,000 in value if the increased income is capitalized at 10%. If the cost of the division is $50,000, the owner could spend up to $230,000 buying out the tenant and still break even. Obviously, the offer would start substantially below that point and would consider other benefits and drawbacks of making the change. A buy-out is accomplished with a much greater comfort level if the replacement tenants are in hand before the deal is negotiated.

If a buy-out is negotiated without a tenant in hand, it is safer to make the buy-out conditional on getting a suitable replacement, with a time limit for the tenant's benefit. The market can easily change midstream, and the anticipated profit quickly becomes a painful loss. If a buy-out seems to make sense, but the owner does not have the cash, the tenant might still accept the offer and take the monies over an extended period of time at a reasonable interest rate or a slightly higher price.

Buy-outs, store splits, and recapture of underutilized spaces can be very complicated. This type of deal generally takes considerable up-front selling and requires a great deal of time to finalize. Once an agreement has been reached, it should immediately be documented and signed by the parties. It is too easy for tenants to back out of a verbal arrangement.

§ 7.19 BUILDINGS WITH BUILT-IN LEASING PROBLEMS

The process of developing a marketing and leasing plan includes analyzing the space to lease and all the physical aspects of the property. This analysis is required to determine the marketability of the property and to identify space that will be difficult to lease. When this analysis is applied to a proposed building, it can result in a redesign of the building, thus preventing the creation of space that is difficult to lease. The analysis is necessary in an existing building to identify difficult-to-lease spaces, to determine their market rental rate, and to decide what could be done to correct the problem.

Spaces that are difficult to lease will have a negative impact on the property, its cash flow, and its value. The tenant mix is affected because fewer uses are available for difficult spaces. Limiting the selection of tenants weakens the synergism that results from a good tenant mix. Spaces that remain vacant for an extended period are eventually presented to secondary tenants that add little or nothing to the tenant mix. If the property is a shopping center, this will result in less traffic to the center, fewer sales, and a reduction in percentage rent.

Following is a list of potential leasing problems for shopping centers, office buildings, and industrial properties. Properties with built-in problems give the tenant leverage in negotiating lease terms. The building will not be competitive in the marketplace if the property manager is unaware of these problems or unwilling to compensate for them.

(a) SHOPPING CENTERS

Vacancies and a weak tenant mix affect shoppers, prospective tenants, and existing tenants. The property manager or leasing agent may be subconsciously affected by the situation and not work as enthusiastically on the leasing effort. This only perpetuates the problem. These shopping centers will usually have additional operating expenses such as cleaning and utility costs and possibly an incentive commission.

Built-in leasing problems in shopping centers can be caused by changes in the tenant's space requirements or by design problems. Tenants' space requirements are based on the size of their premises, their location, or the major tenants in the shopping center.

Tenant's Space Requirements

In the mid to late 1970s, many retailers downsized their space to reduce their occupancy cost. They soon discovered that they could produce the same or greater sales in smaller spaces by operating more efficiently. Retailers found they didn't need a large back room or mezzanine area for storage and an administrative office. They learned to display more merchandise and use their space more effectively. For example, many clothing stores now merchandise their entire cube rather than just the floor area. Dresses and blouses are hung from the walls and even displayed on the ceilings. Fixtures are used to merchandise clothes as well as hold them. Coordinated outfits are displayed on the end of fixtures and on platforms extended above them.

Other retailers have adopted similar merchandising strategy. The result of the merchants' desire to lower their occupancy costs has resulted in many users downsizing their space requirements. For example, a women's shoe store in the mid-1970s was 3,000 to 5,000 square feet. Ten years later these stores were 1,500 to 2,800 square feet. Men's shoe stores were 2,500 to 3,000 square feet in the 1970s but 800 to 1,800 square feet in the 1980s.

Most retailers have downsized their space since the mid-1970s. Regional shopping centers with large spaces or many spaces beyond 3,000 square feet will now find fewer prospective tenants. The same is true for neighborhood and community centers with spaces larger than 1,800 square feet.

Not all shopping center tenants are downsizing, however. One noticeable exception is the supermarket. The typical grocery store has grown from a 20,000-square-foot store to a superstore of 40,000 to 50,000 square feet, even 70,000 square feet. These superstores expanded their traditional merchandise line to include a fresh fish market, deli, salad bar, prepared foods, wine shop, flower shop, video rentals, and camera and TV department. In the early 1980s, the megasized supermarkets, known as hypermarkets entered the United States. These stores, popular in Europe, range in size from 70,000 to 100,000 square feet or more.

How has this evolutionary growth affected the shopping center? The older centers anchored with a 20,000- to 30,000-square-foot market are susceptible to losing the supermarket to a new center a short distance away. When this happens, the supermarket frequently re-leased the space to a fabric store, an auto supply, or a furniture store. The shopping center traffic could be reduced by up to 80% which would hurt other merchants' sales and possibly start an exodus from the shopping center.

Another result of supermarkets expanding their lines of merchandise is that they now compete directly with many of the small retailers in the shopping center. The superstores and hypermarkets eliminate many of the traditional mom-and-pop uses in the center.

Tenant's Location

Tenants sometimes change or expand their location criteria. Service tenants who would not consider a regional center location in the past now locate in these centers, creating additional competition for the neighborhood center. In the 1950s, 1960s, and early 1970s, fashion retailers located in neighborhood centers. Today neighborhood centers are tenanted primarily by service and food merchants.

Design Concerns

Design problems can lead to built-in leasing problems. They often occur in older centers where tenants' requirements have changed or the center's design and layout are outdated. In some cases, though, developers create built-in design problems when they bow down to the density god. This occurs when they try to build the maximum gross leasable area to maximize the pro forma income and to obtain what appears on paper to be an efficient land utilization and a lower land cost per gross leasable area (GLA). When the developer builds more GLA than the market can absorb, spaces can remain vacant for years and may have to be leased at a lower rate than anticipated. Maximizing the GLA on a site can also result in spaces that are poorly configured or poorly located. An alternative is to phase in the development or build less gross leasable area.

Following are some typical design problems in shopping centers.

Spaces Too Deep. Since most retailers have downsized, they seek spaces with shallow depth. Centers with depths beyond 75 feet find fewer and fewer potential tenants.

Spaces Too Large. Spaces in neighborhood shopping centers greater than 1,800 square feet have fewer potential uses, and spaces beyond 3,000 square feet have limited uses.

Spaces Too Narrow. Tenants want as much frontage and as little depth as possible. Space in excess of 1,000 square feet with widths of less than 15 feet are difficult to lease.

L- and T-Shaped Spaces. Spaces that are L- or T-shaped, with the wider area in the rear, have limited appeal.

Minimalls. When W.T. Grant's, a national 50,000-square-foot variety store, closed all its stores in the early 1970s, some owners converted these stores to minimalls. They created a mall down the middle of the space and developed small shops on both sides of the mall. The owners were able to increase the rent on the space from the $2 to $3 per square foot that Grant's usually paid to $8 to $15 per square foot from the small shops. Most of the minimalls failed because the small shops could not attract sufficient traffic to generate adequate sales.

Unanchored Wings of a Mall. Expanding a mall by developing a wing of small shops without an anchor tenant can be deadly. Without a major draw, this area of the mall has little traffic, poor sales, high tenant turnover, and high vacancies.

Spaces with Poor Visibility. Most small shop tenants need good visibility. A neighborhood center with too many pad buildings in front of the shopping center may block the visibility of the small, in-line shops. A shopping center that fronts on a major street might also have shops on the side of the center, along a poorly traveled street.

Unanchored Malls. Enclosed malls with small shops and no anchor tenant have neither a major draw nor visibility. The small shops collectively are not strong enough to draw shoppers into the mall. The mall eliminates storefront visibility from the street.

Mall with No Anchor on Second Level.   Two-level malls with an anchor tenant, such as a junior department store or a major discounter on the first level but with no anchor tenant on the second level, will find a great disparity in traffic between the first and second levels. The second level is slow to lease and has a high turnover of tenants.

Side Hallways on Mall.   Many malls have secondary exits to the parking lot with hallways that are usually tenanted with small shops. These areas receive little traffic, so many tenants find them undesirable.

U-Shaped Centers.   Neighborhood and community shopping centers that are U-shaped with the anchor tenants on the ends find little draw to the small shops in the inside area of the center.

Anchor Tenants Grouped Together.   A shopping center design that groups the anchor tenants together instead of at each end of the center leaves the smaller shops clustered away from the anchors where they will receive little traffic.

Malls Too Wide.   The mall area between stores should range from 30 to 40 feet. When the width is beyond 40 feet, the customer does not easily notice the stores on both sides of the mall.

Pie-Shaped Spaces.   Spaces in the middle of an L-shaped strip of shops are pie-shaped. They are large spaces with little frontage and wide rear areas, which is not a desirable configuration.

Second-Level Office Space.   Shopping centers with a second level for office space often have incompatible uses. The office space usually becomes less desirable, Class B space. The office employees who park all day may take away valuable customer parking. Quite often the office space suffers from a high turnover of tenants and a high vacancy rate.

Inadequate Parking.   Seldom does a shopping center have inadequate parking, although there are exceptions. A neighborhood center with a large multiscreen theater may have inadequate parking on weekends. A regional center may have inadequate parking during special events and peak shopping days during the Christmas season.

Possible solutions include finding an office building or industrial building where the parking space is not used or has limited use during nights and weekends and negotiate the right to use the lots during these periods. The shopping center owner may offer to maintain the parking lot, including resurfacing it; allow the office building the use of the shopping center lot during the weekdays; or pay for the use of the parking lot. The lot can be used for employee or restaurant valet parking.

Obsolescence.   In a shopping center, obsolescence can be seen in outdated store fronts, shopping center design, lighting, landscaping, or signage.

Ideally, the property manager is consulted during the design phase of the shopping center. If problems exist, however, the first step in solving them is to recognize the problem. This is usually evidenced in existing shopping centers by several vacancies, poor traffic in certain areas of the shopping center, high tenant turnover, and low rental rates. Although a reduction in rental rates is usually unavoidable, the property manager may be able to minimize or prevent the reduction by being creative with these problem spaces. The following suggestions might be helpful in dealing with some typical problems.

- Large spaces can be divided into several roughly equal-sized small shops. A 4,000-square-foot space with a 50-foot frontage and 80-foot depth can be divided into three 1,633-square-foot spaces with 17-foot frontage and 80-foot depth. However, if the spaces are divided too narrowly, they will be as undesirable as the one larger space.

- A large space with great depth could be divided into an L- or T-shaped space with smaller adjacent spaces. The L or T shape could be leased to a large user such as a hardware store, an auto supply store, or a spa, and the one or two small spaces in the front would be ideal for any number of uses.

- A drastic way to reduce space, in some cases the only way, is to cut off the final 25 or 50 linear feet of a space that is deeper than 125 feet. A new back wall is created at a depth of, say, 80 feet, and the rear area is used or leased as storage space. This is one of the least desirable solutions to deep spaces.

- Some malls with dead ends or unanchored wings have been successful in creating a food court at the end of this area. The food court may be strong enough to draw sufficient traffic to support the small shops in this wing. Just as converting the old W.T. Grant's stores to minimalls was not suitable for all shopping centers, creating a food court is not always the answer for dead ends or unanchored wings.

- Another possible solution is to change the tenant mix for an area of the shopping center. The areas with poor visibility or poor traffic can be marketed to destination users—tenants that draw their own traffic and don't feed off other tenant's traffic, such as service, office, and governmental tenants.

- Spaces that are unmarketable may be donated for a public use such as a library, a senior citizens meeting room, or to the chamber of commerce. These spaces can be converted to a community room or leased to temporary tenants. See Chapter 4 on shopping center management for more information on merchandising vacant spaces and temporary tenants.

- Along these same lines, consider converting a large vacancy into a weekend swap meet, public market, or arts and crafts fair. To keep a positive image for the shopping center, use careful judgment in allowing these uses.

- A directory to lead customers to a low traffic area is often helpful. A pylon sign near the street with the tenants listed is another possible solution, but limit the listing to a few names or none will be noticed.

- Additional promotion and advertising may bring more traffic to a weak area of the shopping center. Kiosks in the center of the mall and wall shops built against blank walls will reduce the illusion that a mall is too wide.

Whether a shopping center has one difficult space to lease or several, the property manager must analyze each space for its marketability and devise ways to improve the rental value of a center with built-in leasing problems.

(b) OFFICE BUILDINGS

Location

The two features of an office building that are first noticed are its location and its exterior appearance. Two questions might be asked regarding location: Is the building pioneering a location? Is the building located in the central business district (CBD), the downtown core area for office buildings, or on the fringe of the business district? Although office building development may be moving in that direction, a building that is located on the outskirts of the CBD may be two or three years ahead of the movement. During this period, leasing may be slow, and unbudgeted lease concessions will be necessary to make deals.

Location can present a problem when a business district shifts to another area of the city. An example of this is the mid-Wilshire area in Los Angeles. In the 1960s, this area was one of the city's premiere office building areas; but by the mid-1970s, the area lost its luster when other newer business areas were developed. However, with the office building boom in the early 1980s, renovation of some of the buildings in mid-Wilshire was profitable, and the area began to regain its former popularity.

An office building that pioneers a suburban area can be a problem because initially there may be low demand for office space. Another concern with location is the usage in the immediate area. Are they compatible uses? Is the area run down? What is the building's location in relation to public transportation, shopping, restaurants? With more women in the work force, are day care facilities available in the area?

Access

Access to a building can be a negative feature if travel time cuts into productive work time. The more time salespeople spend driving on the freeway and streets to their office building, the less time they have to make sales calls. A medical building that is off the main thoroughfares and some distance from the hospitals reduces the time the doctors can spend with their patients.

Building's Appearance

The other noticeable feature of an office building is its appearance. Is the building in harmony with its surroundings? Is it a low-rise building that looks cheap because the developers cut corners to save a few dollars? Is the architectural style inappropriate? Employing an architect to analyze the building's design and make recommendations is one way to alleviate or correct this problem for some buildings.

Parking

Availability of parking is a major concern of tenants. Proximity of parking is another time concern. Does the building have adequate parking? How much time is lost finding a parking space and walking to the building? Is the parking adjacent to the building? Is parking free, as it is in most suburban areas, or is there a charge? If the building has a garage, is the garage designed properly? Are the drive lanes too narrow so that large cars scrape the side of the walls on the ramps? Is the garage safe? Is the lighting adequate in all parts of the garage?

Lobby

A prospective tenant's first impression when entering the building is of the lobby. Before entering the premises, the prospect will form a positive or negative opinion about the building's exterior and common areas that will influence his or her thinking about the actual space being shown.

Improving the lobby can compensate for other negative features in the building.

Elevators

Are there sufficient elevators to service the building's tenant mix? What is the appearance of the elevator cabs? Do the elevator doors close too quickly or too slowly?

Corridors

Are the corridors well lighted? Are the walls scraped or scored? Is the wall treatment in good condition? What is the condition of the carpet? Are the corridors too narrow or too wide, too long, poorly lighted, or dingy?

Bay Depth

A major problem can arise with poor floor layouts. The ideal bay depth (the area between the corridor wall and the curtain wall) depends on the size and type of tenant. Floors with bay depth greater than 35 feet can create space planning problems for small tenants. Floors with bay depth greater than 45 feet may create problems for larger tenants. Some larger tenants or tenants with open landscaping prefer a larger bay depth.

Mullion Spacing

Five-foot mullion spacing will provide partition walls on 10- and 15-foot widths, and the office width will be this dimension minus a few inches for the stud partition walls. A 4-foot mullion creates office width of 8 and 12 feet minus a few inches for the stud walls.

Windows and Views

When a prospective tenant is shown space, one of the first things the tenant does is to look out the windows. The view is an important feature to many tenants. To save costs, was the size of the windows reduced? Are the windows less than half of the curtain wall? Natural lighting is important to many tenants.

Operating Features

Other considerations include: Does the building have state-of-the-art life safety, wiring, HVAC, power, and communication features?

Security

Security problems can be a detriment to leasing. Is the security problem outside the building or throughout the area? Is the building a repeated target of vandalism and theft? If the building has a restaurant on the top or middle floor, is there direct access to it without stopping at other floors? Can designated floors be locked off after hours?

HVAC

Another major concern of all tenants is comfort. Are the HVAC zones too large and do tenants share a zone? In this case, often one tenant will be comfortable and the other too cold or too hot. Is there a noise problem with the equipment or the movement of air?

Maintenance Program

A poor maintenance management program will be evident in the appearance of the building, in its operations, and in tenant dissatisfaction with poor response to maintenance needs.

Restrooms

Restrooms are a good indicator of the quality of the building. Are the fixtures and the lighting in good condition? Do the restrooms have adequate facilities?

Operating Expenses

Several economic factors can be classified as built-in leasing problems. First are the operating expenses of the building. All or a portion of these expenses are passed through to the tenants in some form of escalation charge. Are these costs higher than they are for competing buildings? Should they be higher or lower? The manager must also review the building's energy costs to determine if it is energy-efficient.

Real estate taxes are another major expense. Is the building correctly assessed? In the mid-1980s, insurance costs increased up to fivefold and are now a major building operating expense. Has the insurance program been analyzed and does the building have a risk management program?

Load Factor

Another economic impact on the tenants is the building load factor. What percentage of the building is common area? If the building is leasing on a rentable basis and has a high load factor, tenants will be paying for a greater share of nonusable space than tenants in competing buildings.

Building Management

What are the property management services? Is the building professionally managed? Slow response to tenant's problems will create a poor management image.

Architecture

Did the architect create such an unusual design that only a limited number of tenants find it appealing? Avant-garde or any other uncommon design can narrow the leasing market.

Many built-in leasing difficulties are curable, some are partially curable, and a few, such as outside influences on a building, are incurable. The property manager needs to recognize these problems, correct them, and adjust the market rate to be competitive.

(c) INDUSTRIAL PROPERTIES

No group of tenants has such diverse requirements as industrial users. The space and facility requirements will vary to such an extent that almost any industrial property will meet the needs of some tenant. An impossible building for one tenant will be the ideal building for another.

Following are some typical built-in leasing problems for industrial properties.

Zoning

The most limiting factor for marketing industrial buildings is the zoning of the property. Most municipalities break industrial zoning into several use classifications, from high-tech to heavy industrial. The property's zoning and the allowable uses within that zoning classification must be determined. If a specific use is not allowed, can the property be rezoned, a variance obtained, or a conditional use permit granted?

Location

Next, the location must be considered. Is the property near major freeways, airports, seaports, or manufacturers? A property that is not strategically located may present leasing problems.

Site

The site is another major consideration. Industrial firms usually remain in one location for a long time because they have made a major investment to adapt a site and building to their specific needs. What types of users can and cannot be accommodated by the site? Are there expansion opportunities?

Labor Market

The labor market is a major concern of large industrial users. The cost and availability of skilled and unskilled labor and the cost of the labor are considerations in selecting a location.

Housing Cost

Housing costs relate to the availability of labor. Areas with high housing costs, such as Orange County, California, will have less unskilled labor.

Educational Institutions

Institutions of higher learning in the area are a source of skilled technical and management personnel, which will be a positive feature for high-tech users.

Floor Plan

A building's features will be a plus for some users and a minus for others. The floor plan must be analyzed to determine how the building is divided between office and warehouse space, column spacing, ceiling heights, and floor load capacity.

Construction

The type of construction—concrete, concrete block, metal, or other materials—is another factor in finding appropriate tenants.

Fire Sprinkler System

Is the building sprinklered? What is the building's utility capacity?

Environmental Concerns

Environmental concerns are a major issue for some industrial users. Are toxic materials allowed on the site? What type of floor drains, sewer systems, and disposal facilities are available?

HVAC

Is the HVAC system adequate for the needs of the employees in the office and warehouse areas?

Restrictions

Does the industrial park have covenants, conditions, and restrictions? If so, what are they? Will they impact the operations of any users?

All these features must be analyzed to determine if the building has built-in leasing problems and to select appropriate users.

§ 7.20 CONCLUSION

Today, institutions are the major owners of larger commercial properties, either through joint ventures with developers or by outright purchase. In either case, institutions are purchasing properties with one goal in mind—to achieve a yield on their investment. Yield is created through cash flow and increased value.

An institution's asset managers will emphasize marketing and leasing over building operation. From their viewpoint, good building operations are a given. When the property manager meets with the asset manager, they are not concerned with negotiating a sweeping contract, but with discussing market conditions, lease rental rates, current prospects, marketing activities, and anticipated vacancies.

Clearly, no other factor has a greater impact on the property's NOI and value than its marketing and leasing program. A property with an effective marketing and leasing program will be able to maintain its rent at market rates and enjoy maximum occupancy.

Eight

Lease Administration

§ 8.1 INTRODUCTION

L ease administration, the paperwork of property management, is one of the most critical elements of a successful management program. It starts before any space is leased. The lease document must be drafted properly to meet the objectives of the owner and the needs of the property. While lease provisions that address rental rates and operating expenses have a direct effect on a property's value, provisions that address operations, especially lease restrictions, have an indirect but significant effect as well. A poor lease administration program may result in errors in tenant billing, violations of lease restrictions, dissatisfied tenants, and an unhappy property owner.

§ 8.2 LEASE FORMS

The property management company that services multiple owners will have several different lease forms to administer because institutional owners and developers often prefer to use their own lease forms. Many private owners will use the management company's or the brokerage firm's lease forms. The major differences in administering the different leases are how escalation and common area maintenance are billed to the tenants; what items are included in the operating expense billbacks; how monetary defaults are handled; and how late charges are billed.

When the property management company prepares the lease, a system must be developed to ensure that the proper lease is used for each property. Since a property owner's lease is pro-landlord, numerous clauses will be negotiated with the tenant. A lease with a local business may have three to five lease changes, while a lease with a national tenant such as Kinney Shoes or IBM could have as many as fifty changes. These are made on the lease form either by crossing out sentences and adding new ones at the bottom of the page or by attaching an addendum to the lease.

The word processor has facilitated the preparation of lease forms by allowing changes to be made directly in the text. Although this approach provides a clean form, it can cause problems in administering the lease because the person summarizing the lease can't readily see the exceptions to the building's standard lease. But when a preprinted form is used, with corrections made directly on the form, the person need only look for the blank lines that were filled in and typed items that were deleted or added to the printed form.

When a lease is prepared by word processing, the entire document must be read carefully. Changing one word in a paragraph or section can change the meaning of an entire section. It is easy to miss a word or misinterpret an intent when reading a twelve- to thirty-page commercial lease and such mistakes can be very costly to the owner and the management company. In addition, a preprinted lease with corrections typed in can be summarized in five to ten minutes, while carefully reading an entire lease will take much longer.

All in all, it is more efficient to use a preprinted lease form. If a word processor is used the lease corrections should be underlined.

§ 8.3 LEASE PREPARATION

Preparing the lease correctly is one of the most important functions in lease administration. It is best to have at least two persons in the office become proficient in lease preparation. They should be fully trained in preparing leases and have a working knowledge of their provisions.

When several different forms are used, a sample of each should be kept on file. The sample would have all blanks filled in and would include the landlord's signature block, notary and guarantee pages, and all exhibits.

After the lease is prepared, it should be thoroughly reviewed by the leasing agent. One caution: a productive agent may not necessarily be a good administrator and may not have time for routine paperwork. If this is the case, it may be best to have a second knowledgeable person review the prepared lease.

Usually five or six copies of the lease are prepared. Two are needed by the property management company, one is for the tenant, and one for the landlord. Sometimes the lender on the property will request a copy. The fifth or sixth copy is kept in the management office when the rest of the copies are sent to the tenant for signatures. This copy is needed in case the other leases are lost and to make sure the tenant did not make unauthorized changes in the signed copies of the lease.

When the lease is signed by the tenant and returned to the property management company, it should be thoroughly reviewed before it is sent to the landlord for execution. Each page should be checked to be sure that corrections and additions have been initialed; that the tenant did not add items not agreed upon; that the lease is properly signed; that the guarantee, if required, is signed; and that the lease is officially notarized. A deal that is favorable to the landlord can be negated by a lease drafted with errors.

§ 8.4   EXECUTED LEASE NOTIFICATION

When a lease is executed, the property manager, accounting department, and the administrative assistant must be notified. An executed lease notification form simplifies this process (see Exhibit 8.1).

From information on the form, the accounting department records the tenant's security deposit and first month's rent. Authorization to pay the commission is recorded. If the tenant is to receive reimbursement for its tenant improvement (TI) expenditures, the form will tell the accounting department how much of the TI allowance to pay the tenant and what the tenant must do to receive the allowance. When the requirements are met, the property manager provides written notice to the accounting department to release the funds to the tenant.

The form notifies the property manager or administrative assistant to set up the tenant's file, add the tenant to the project data book, send a welcome letter, and schedule a meeting with the tenant.

§ 8.5   LEASE SUMMARIES

Each lease is summarized so that the salient points can be readily available, providing the property manager and the accounting department with an abbreviated view of the lease. The information needed for the day-to-day administration of the lease includes lease terms, tenant information, rental information, and bill-back items. Commercial property management software programs have a lease summary report. Although

EXHIBIT 8.1

Executed Lease Notification

Project ID: _____ _____
                                        (center)   (no.)
Tenant: _____
Tenant trade name: _____
Space #: _____   Sq. Ft.: _____
Lease commencement date: _____   Lease expiration date: _____

Security deposit:

    Date received: _____   Amount: $_____
         Comments: _____

Rent: Rent commencement: _____

    Date received: _____   Amount: $_____

Commission:

    Pay to: _____
    Commission rate: _____
    Commission total: $_____
    Commission payment schedule:
      ____ First half   Authorized by: _____
      ____ Second half   Authorized by: _____
      ____ Full   Authorized by: _____
                   Date: _____

- -

TI Allowance: Amount (If applicable): $_____
____ Open for business   ____ Estoppel rec'd
____ Cert. of occupancy   ____ Cert. of insurance rec'd
____ Waiver of lien   ____ Other
                                    _____

All requirements met, release TI funds: $_____

Authorized by: _____ _____
                                                                            (Date)

these reports differ in form and layout, they all contain the same basic information (see Exhibit 8.2).

The property manager, the administrative assistant, or the book-keeper is assigned the responsibility of summarizing leases. One person should summarize all leases for a building to enable that person to become familiar with the property's standard lease form. Many firms prefer to have the bookkeeper summarize the lease since he or she will administer the tenant's billings and record the rental payments.

The top third of the lease summary form includes the tenant's address, phone number, and trade name; the manager's home phone number and address; the phone number and address of the tenant's headquarters; and the lease commencement and expiration dates and options. The middle section of the form notes the monthly and annual rent and rent step-ups. The lower portion provides space to indicate how the tenant is billed for escalation, common area maintenance, taxes, insurance, and other items. A second page is provided for additional information.

An error in summarizing a lease—for example, missing a CPI increase—can result in incorrect billings, so it is prudent to have a second person, such as the controller or property manager, check the income section of the lease summary by comparing rental increases and the escalation, and common area maintenance clauses to the lease summary. Reviewing the lease summary also familiarizes the property manager with each tenant's lease terms.

§ 8.6 LEASE RESTRICTIONS

In a soft leasing market, it is not uncommon to give lease concessions to some tenants. Major tenants, such as the anchor in a shopping center or a large user of space in an office building, will inevitably negotiate concessions. If the concessions place restrictions on leasing or developing the property, they need to be summarized on a lease restriction report and distributed to the property manager, the leasing agent, and the owner. Violating a restriction can be very costly to the owner and management company. Restrictions should be reported by type, the most common of which are as follows:

(a) OPTION TO RENEW

An option to renew a lease is a right for the tenant and an obligation for the landlord. The tenant has the right, but not the obligation, to renew its lease, while the landlord has an obligation to accept the tenant's decision.

The property manager should look for restrictions placed on the tenant's option to renew. For instance, the option may be valid only if the

EXHIBIT 8.2

Lease Summary

PROJECT: _____

PREPARED BY: _____

DATE: _____

TENANT NAME: _____   LEASE DATE: _____

TRADE NAME: _____   LEASE COMMENCEMENT DATE: _____

ADDRESS: _____   LEASE TERMINATION DATE: _____

_____   GROSS LEASABLE AREA: _____

STORE MANAGER: _____   NET LEASABLE AREA: _____

HOME PHONE: _____   SECURITY DEPOSIT: _____

TERMS:

MONTHLY BASE RENTS (NOTE ANY OPTIONS):   PER NET LEASEABLE AREA (MONTHLY)

$_____ EFFECTIVE FOR THE PERIOD _____ TO _____ _____ SQ. FT.
                      MO. DAY YR.   MO. DAY YR.

$_____ EFFECTIVE FOR THE PERIOD _____ TO _____ _____ SQ. FT.

$_____ EFFECTIVE FOR THE PERIOD _____ TO _____ _____ SQ. FT.

PERCENTAGE RENT RATE (PRR) _____ PRR PAID _____ ON A

SALES BREAKPOINT OF $ _____ ($ _____ PER SQ. FT.) BASE _____
                                                  MO.   QTR.   ANNUAL

OPERATING EXPENSES;   TENANT EXPENSES   LANDLORD

% OF EXPENSES _____ %
BASED ON _____ TOTAL
OR _____ OCCUPIED SPACE

	BILLED DIRECT TO TENANT	REIMBURSE LANDLORD	BASE YEAR	INCREASE ABOVE BASE YEAR	PAID BY LANDLORD
C/A MAINTENANCE MONTHLY RESERVE $					
PROPERTY TAXES					
FIRE INSURANCE					
LIABILITY INSURANCE					
OTHER INSURANCE					
OVERHEAD ALLOWANCE					
EXECUTIVE MANAGEMENT TOTAL STRUCTURAL MAINTENANCE					
HVAC					
OTHER					

MERCHANTS ASSOCIATION CLAUSE:

_____

_____

OTHER PERTINENT DATA:

_____

_____

tenant has not defaulted at any time during the lease or if the rent was paid by a certain date each month. A retail tenant's option may be contingent upon payment of percentage rent during the last two years of the lease. To renew, the tenant usually must notify the landlord within a predetermined period—for example, not less than 120 days or more than 180 days prior to the expiration date.

(b) FIRST RIGHT OF REFUSAL

A first right of refusal gives the tenant the priority right to lease additional space. This lease restriction is most often found in office buildings. For example, a tenant leases 10,000 square feet on the fifth floor and has the first right to lease the additional 5,000 square feet on that floor. When the landlord has a prospect for a vacant space on the fifth floor, the tenant is notified and has a fixed period, usually two to ten business days, to exercise its priority right to lease the space.

When a building has one or more tenants with first right of refusal, the property manager should indicate on a site or floor plan which tenants have first right of refusal and what space is encumbered by this restriction.

(c) RIGHT TO CANCEL

A right to cancel is seldom given, but when it is, it is usually given to a retail tenant. A retailer may lease space in a weak shopping center and require the right to cancel its lease if the business is not profitable. A right to cancel should be tied to a sales volume, and the tenant must have sufficient time to achieve this volume. The right should be a one-time right that can be exercised during a short, fixed period. For instance, a tenant may have the right to cancel the lease during the January immediately following the second calendar year of the lease if the tenant's sales did not exceed $400,000 during that year.

(d) EXCLUSIVES

An exclusive gives a tenant the sole and exclusive right to sell a particular product or provide a particular service. Each exclusive should be listed on a summary sheet using the exact wording from the lease.

(e) USE RESTRICTIONS

An anchor tenant in a shopping center may place use restrictions on the balance of the property. The restriction may prohibit specific uses of the property or within a specified distance from the tenant's premises. For example, a supermarket's lease may restrict bowling alleys, dance halls, skating rinks, schools, theaters, or adult book stores from the center. The lease may continue to state that medical, dental or other offices cannot be within 150 feet of either supermarket entrance. The anchor tenant is concerned that prime parking will be taken for long-term use by office employees or customers of entertainment tenants.

(f) PARKING REQUIREMENTS

Major tenants in a shopping center want to be certain that there will always be sufficient parking for their customers. They may negotiate a lease provision that requires the landlord to provide a minimum number of parking stalls. The lease may state that the shopping center will have a parking ratio of at least five stalls per 1,000 square feet of gross leasable area or that the center will never have fewer than 665 parking stalls.

§ 8.7 DEFERRED CONDITIONS

The deferred conditions report, or tickler file, is a system that helps the property manager and accounting personnel keep track of important dates and conditions in the lease. These include: lease expiration date, options, fixed rent increases, CPI increases, rights of cancellation, dates when the tenants are obligated to take additional space, and any other future obligation or right of the tenant or landlord. If the landlord is required to repaint the premises after the third year of the lease, this would be included on the deferred conditions report.

This report can be computerized or recorded manually. A computerized report would list the deferred conditions by month and property for the next twelve months or whatever time is desired.

In a manual system, three-by-five-inch cards are prepared for each month of the next two years. Beyond two years, cards are prepared for months when something is to happen. Upcoming events are entered on the appropriate cards. Expiration dates for tenants' insurance certificates should be listed sixty days prior to expiration. Negotiated rent increases should be filed thirty days before the effective date and CPI rent adjustments ninety days before the effective date. Lease expirations should be shown six months in advance for all tenants except major tenants, whose expiration cards should be filed one to two years early.

The computerized deferred conditions report or the tickler card file should be reviewed on the first of every month.

§ 8.8   RENTAL RECORDS

To be sure that nothing is overlooked, attach a checklist to the lease like the one shown in Exhibit 8.3. The lease should not be filed until all items have been completed. One staff person should set up each new lease and follow a specific procedure to become familiar with the leases and to see that each is filed at the earliest possible date. Because there are many reasons to refer to a new lease, it will be more efficient for all parties if the lease is processed quickly.

The tenant should be properly entered into the tenant roster. If the tenants are listed by space rather than alphabetically, all spaces are accounted for, and the roster need not be reorganized when tenants change. It is also suggested that the tenant be listed on all documents, other than the lease, by the name most familiar to the property manager, operations manager, and accounting personnel. In a shopping center this is generally the store's trade name.

Since property owners often require different information on the tenant rosters, the manager should determine the purpose of the roster and design a format to accommodate the needs of both the owner and the management company. Too much information serves no real purpose and must be duplicated elsewhere for proper lease administration. All rosters must show the date of preparation. Many property management software programs include a lease summary and roster reports (Exhibit 8.4).

The next step is to set up the tenant's lease information in the accounting records. Each tenant should have a manual or computerized ledger card, noted with both the tenant's corporate and trade names for the purpose of identifying checks.

The ledger card (see Exhibit 8.5) should indicate commencement and ending dates of the lease, rental increases, the amount of security or last month's rent deposit, current common area (CCA) billings, and any percentage rent requirements. Every item of income—base rent, percentage rent, taxes, CCA and utility payments,—should be posted and recorded separately so that an audit trail is established and future questions can be answered.

The delinquency report (see Exhibit 8.6) is generally prepared some time after the fifth of the month and is updated as monies are received. It is seldom prepared before the fifth since commercial tenants mail their rental payments to the property management company then. At month's end, a final report is generally included as part of the owner's monthly report.

A separate log should be maintained on the status of deposits (see Exhibit 8.7). Again, to ensure ease of administration and completeness, the log should show who is assigned to each space in the building, and the amount and type of any deposits (security or last month's rents).

EXHIBIT 8.3

Lease Status Checklist

Tenant: _____

	Date	
	Lessor	Lessee
1. Lease prepared	_____	_____
2. Leases sent to lessee	_____	_____
3. Properly signed	_____	_____
4. Initialed changes	_____	_____
5. Guaranty signed	_____	_____
6. Lease notarized	_____	_____
7. Financial statement	_____	_____
8. Corporate resolution	_____	_____
9. Security deposit	_____	_____

Comments:

_____
_____
_____
_____

The person who negotiates a lease is responsible for its proper preparation. The lease status checklist form lists the items that must be provided by the lessor or the lessee. The date is indicated when each item is completed. This form ensures that each lease is properly prepared.

EXECUTED LEASE DISTRIBUTION

	Date
1. Fully executed lease	_____
2. Copy to tenant	_____
3. Copy to landlord	_____
4. Copy to building manager	_____
5. Copy to management company file	_____
6. Copy to lender	_____
7. Copy of construction exhibit to contractor	_____
8. Other: _____	_____

The executed lease distribution form is used to keep track of who received copies of the executed lease. The date the lease is executed is recorded on the top line and the date is recorded after each party receives a lessee copy.

EXHIBIT 8.4

Tenant Roster

Bldg. Neighborhood Center

Tenant	Suite #	Type of Store	Sq. Ft.	Rent Year	Rent $/Sq. Ft.	Rent Month	Security Deposit	Term Years	Lease Date	Commencement	Termination Date	Percent Rent	Special Notes	CAC
Friendly Market	A-1	Supermarket	42,000	147,000	3.50	12,250	None	30	4-15-77	2-1-78	1-31-08	1½	Options	Cap.
Kathy's Kards	A-2	Cards & gifts	2,000	19,000	9.50	1,583.33	1583.33	5	2-1-78	3-1-78	3-31-83	6		Yes
Today's Styles	A-3	Hair styling	1,500	14,625	9.75	1,218.75	2437.50	5	1-15-78	4-15-78	4-14-83	7½		Yes
White Cleaners	A-4	Dry cleaners	1,600	15,600	9.75	1,300	1300.00	5	1-8-78	4-1-78	3-31-83	7		Yes
Advance T.V. & Radio	A-5	TV, radio, stereo	2,000	19,000	9.50	1,583.33	1583.33	5	1-20-78	4-1-78	3-31-83	4		Yes
Vacant	A-6		700	7,700	11.00	641.66								
King's Hardware	A-7	Hardware	5,000	43,750	8.75	3,645.83	3645.83	10	10-10-77	2-1-78	1-31-88	4		Yes
Pizza Plus	A-8	Pizza rest.	3,200	29,600	9.25	2,466.66	2466.66	15	9-12-77	4-1-78	3-31-94	5	CPI 6&10 yr.	Yes
Fast Sell Realty	A-9	Real est. office	1,500	17,250	11.50	1,437.50	2875.00	5	4-3-80	5-1-80	4-30-85	—	+10% 3rd yr.	Yes
Goodies Ice Cream	A-10	Ice cream parlor	1,700	16,150	9.50	1,345.83	1345.83	10	2-1-78	4-15-78	4-14-88	5	CPI 6th yr.	Yes
Fancy's Fabric	A-11	Fabric	3,400	31,450	9.25	2,620.83	2620.83	5	4-10-78	6-15-78	6-14-83	5		Yes
Slim & Trim Figure Salon	A-12	Figure salon	3,200	30,080	9.40	2,506.66	2506.66	5	4-5-78	6-1-78	5-31-83	7		Yes
Family Discount Shoes	A-13	Family shoes	2,600	26,000	10.00	2,166.66	2166.66	5	9-20-78	11-1-78	10-31-83	6		Yes
Speedy's Bikes	A-14	Bike sales/service	1,600	16,400	10.25	1,366.66	1366.66	5	10-6-78	11-15-78	11-14-83	5		Yes
Discount Drugs	A-15	Drugs & sundries	22,000	79,200	3.60	6,600	None	30	5-3-77	2-15-78	2-14-08	3-2-1	Options	Yes
Dine 'n' Dash	P-1	Family restaurant	3,600	57,600	16.00	4,800	9600.00	20	6-12-77	5-10-78	5-9-98	5	Options	Yes
Home Town Bank	P-2	Bank	2,400	48,000	20.00	4,000	8000.00	20	10-3-77	6-20-78	6-19-98	—	Option	Yes

350

EXHIBIT 8.5

Tenant Ledger Card

| | | | | | Mo. Rental | Deposit | Bldg. No. | Unit No. |

Lesee: _____

Rent Starts __/__/__ Occupancy __/__/__

Lease Term __/__/__ Option __/__/__

Address: _____

Bill To: _____

Contact: _____

Contact: _____ Phone _____

% of Gross _____

| | CAMS Yes__ No__ | TAX ESCAL Yes__ No__ | MTC ESCAL Yes__ No__ | Other Charges Explain: Yes__ No__ |

Date	Unit No.	Name	Charges	Total Amount Received	Balance Due	In Payment Of					
						Rent	Deposits	CAMS	Tax Escal	Utilities	Reimb	Misc

EXHIBIT 8.6

Delinquency Report

Bldg __Neighborhood Center__

Date __4-10-81__

Tenant	Total Due	RENTS					COMMON AREA		TAXES		GENERAL BILL BACKS					Comments
		Current Month	30 Days	60 Days	90 Days or More	Percentage Rent	Current	Previous	Current	Previous	Insurance	Utilities	HVAC	MA	Misc	
Advance T.V.	1769.33	1583.33					25		77		26		15	33		
Speedy's Bike	3017.32	1366.66	1366.66				28	28	61	61	22		30	54		
Dine 'n' Dash	215.00														215.	1980 CAM Adj.
TOTALS	5001.65	2949.99	1366.66				63	28	138	61	48		45	87	215	

352

EXHIBIT 8.7

HVAC Cost Allocation

Location	Tenant	Footage	Percent Service	Filter Charge
A		4,200	.0824	3 ea.
B		9,088	.1784	3 ea.
C-1		2,394	.0470	2 ea.
C-2		1,235	.0242	1 ea.
C-3		1,200	.0236	1 ea.
C-4-5-6		4,001	.0785	3 ea.
C-7		1,840	.0342	2 ea.
C-8		1,000	.0196	1 ea.
C-9		1,415	.0278	1 ea.
D-1		2,847	.0559	2 ea.
D-2		2,400	.0471	2 ea.
D-3		1,699	.0334	2 ea.
D-4		1,238	.0243	1 ea.
D-5		1,500	.0294	1 ea.
D-6		1,931	.0379	2 ea.
D-7		1,400	.0275	1 ea.
D-8		1,400	.0275	1 ea.
D-9		3,360	.0660	3 ea.
D-10		3,000	.0589	2 ea.
D-11		3,893	.0764	3 ea.
Total		50,951		

Each tenant's pro rata percentage of the total GLA.
Based on number of filters per store.

Any changes should be recorded in the log to prevent future misunderstandings.

§ 8.9 LEASE FILE

A standard procedure should be established for filing each tenant's lease and correspondence. This allows easy access of information for anyone in the property management company.

Two files should be maintained for each tenant, a vault file and a working copy. The vault, or "gold" file is a signed original that is placed in a fireproof cabinet. It is not used for day-to-day operations. The working copy of the lease does not need to be an original. When the building has an on-site manager, the working file is kept in his or her office; otherwise it is kept at the main office.

The file label should identify the tenant by trade name, property, and space number. It helps to color code folders to reduce the chances of misfiling. Within the folder, the lease and all amendments can be kept in an envelope on one side and all correspondence kept on the other side. This makes the basic agreement easy to find.

The lease and amendments should be filed chronologically, with the last document executed placed on top, making it readily apparent that changes have been made to the original agreement. It is also helpful to rubber-stamp an "amended" note on the original document. When a lease file is removed, a "lease out" card should be signed and dated by the person removing it and placed in the file.

§ 8.10   TENANTS' INSURANCE CERTIFICATES

The commercial lease requires the tenant to maintain specific types of insurance coverage with stated minimum limits of coverage. The tenant is also required to provide the landlord with evidence of the coverage, and the insurance policy must include the landlord as additional insured or named insured.

The property management company is responsible for monitoring the tenants' lease obligations. The property manager, or an administrative assistant, requests a certificate of insurance from the tenant and makes sure that each certificate states the proper type and amount of coverage and that the landlord's name is correctly stated as additional or named insured.

A follow-up system similar to the deferred conditions report can be developed to list each tenant's insurance expiration date sixty days in advance. The property manager's assistant sends a notice reminding the tenant of the insurance expiration date and requesting a new certificate for the renewed insurance. Keeping track of tenants' insurance can be even more time-consuming and difficult than collecting rent.

§ 8.11   TENANTS' SALES REPORTS

Every tenant that has a percentage rent clause in its lease is obligated to submit a sales report to the landlord. The property manager determines when each tenant's sales report is due. Most tenants submit these reports monthly; a few national tenants report quarterly; and almost all major tenants report annually.

The tenants' sales figures are entered into the computer each month to produce an overall sales report. From this report the property manager analyzes each tenant, each category of tenant, and the entire shopping center. When a few tenants' sales are missing, the analysis of the entire center is affected. The most objective means of collecting sales reports is by phone calls and periodic visits.

§ 8.12   OPERATING EXPENSE BILL-BACK ITEMS

Tenant bill-backs should be timely, fair, and accurate. A series of inaccurate bills to tenants will destroy their confidence in the property manager and landlord. Slow billings can hurt a property's cash flow, and failure to collect monies due can reduce the value of the property as well.

There are four basic methods for billing operating expenses: tenants can be billed on a pro rata share, or on a base year, a stop expense, or a triple net basis. Some tenants will negotiate exceptions to the standard method of charging for the building's operating expenses.

There are countless exceptions to the four basic methods of charging for common area maintenance or escalation expenses. Specific operating expense items may be deleted from a tenant's charges. For instance, a supermarket may negotiate security costs out of its charges. A cap or ceiling on billable operating expenses may be negotiated, such as a 3% limit on annual increases in office building escalation charges. In some cases, a cap is placed on specific operating expense items. An industrial park tenant may pay its pro rata share of taxes and insurance but negotiate a 4% cap on all other operating expenses. Another method is for the retail tenant, usually a major one, to negotiate a pro rata share of common area maintenance expenses not to exceed .25% to 1% of sales.

These negotiated exceptions are time consuming to administer. A separate operating expense budget, or budgets, must be developed to determine the correct amount to bill each tenant with exceptions.

(a)   SHOPPING CENTER BILL-BACK EXPENSES

In a shopping center, common areas are those areas where the tenants and their customers have common use, or all areas other than where tenants have exclusive use (their premises). Common area maintenance (CAM) is a means to bill tenants for the expenses associated with those areas.

Modern shopping center leases typically call for tenants to pay a portion of the center's operating costs, taxes, insurance, and maintenance. These are referred to as *net items, bill back items, pass-through items,* or *tenant charges.* These terms are synonymous. With any change in occupancy or new tenant, there is a potential for error in the billing or, even worse, a failure to bill altogether.

It is not unusual for a center to have two or three different formulas for the distribution of the various charges. For instance, taxes for the entire center may be allocated to each parcel, but insurance may be allocated on only a portion of the center because major tenants often insure their own buildings. For these reasons, it is very important to have a complete understanding of all individual lease terms as well as the center's operational characteristics.

Calculating Tenants' Common Area Maintenance Costs

Even though the concept of common area maintenance charges is to bill the tenants for the cost of maintaining the common area, the property manager can bill the tenants for only those expenses allowed in the lease. In summarizing the tenant's lease, the manager determines which charges are billable, how the tenant's share is calculated, and how the tenant will reimburse these expenses. The tenants pay a pro rata share of the CAM expenses based on a formula whereby the square footage of their premises is the numerator and the square footage of the shopping center is the denominator.

Common area maintenance billings would be easy to ascertain if all tenants paid on the same basis, with no exceptions to the above formula, but this is seldom the case. One common exception in calculating the tenant's share of the expenses is to use the leased square footage of the shopping center rather than the leasable square footage as the denominator. The leasable square footage includes all the occupied and vacant spaces in the denominator, but the leased square footage uses only those spaces actually rented to determine the denominator, a figure that can change every month as the center's occupancy changes.

Some landlords take the position that tenants should pay the total cost to maintain the common area since they and their customers are the only ones using the facilities. Otherwise, some of this cost is allocated to vacant spaces and paid by the landlord. The tenants, on the other hand, do not believe they should be penalized for the landlord's inability to lease the vacancies. If a tenant occupies 2,000 square feet and the gross leasable area is 100,000 square feet, the tenant's share of the CAM expenses based on the leasable square feet would be 2%. If the same tenant's lease required paying a pro rata share of CAM expenses of the leased square footage, and the center had 20,000 square feet vacant, the tenant would pay 2.5% of the CAM budget (calculated using the 80,000 square feet occupied as the denominator and tenant's 2,000 square feet as the numerator).

The leased square footage is used when the landlord is attempting to pass on all expenses, but most sophisticated tenants will not accept leased square footage as the denominator. The great majority of leases in shopping centers use leasable square footage to determine each tenant's share of CAM expenses.

Another exception to each tenant paying its pro rata share of common area maintenance occurs when one or several major tenants exercise their right to maintain a portion of the common area. The major tenant is concerned that a poorly maintained common area will have an adverse impact on its sales. For example, if a supermarket with its own building and land and a reciprocal easement agreement making the landlord responsible for maintaining the common area is not satisfied with the level of maintenance, it may exercise its right to maintain either the entire common area or just the part on the land it owns.

A further exception is the major tenant that occupies, for example, 28% of the leasable area of the center but negotiates only a 25% share of the common area maintenance costs. The center owner must either pay the 3% difference or, if the lease permits, pass that cost along to the remaining tenants. It is also not uncommon for a fast-food tenant to be required to pay a premium on common area costs to cover increased common area expenses due to the nature of operations. This premium is generally stated as a higher percentage (for example, the fast-food operator who occupies 2.5% of the center but, by agreement, actually pays 3.5% of the costs). The excess amount should be credited against the expense balance of the other tenants as they are presumably paying the higher maintenance costs within their allocations.

Major tenants create another exception when the terms of their lease do not require them to pay a particular expense. Most use their own lease form when entering into an agreement with the landlord. For example, if a supermarket's lease form does not require the tenant to pay for security, and the shopping center's guards are a common area maintenance expense, the property manager would bill the supermarket for its pro rata share of the CAM expenses without security expense. This becomes an unreimbursed expense that the landlord absorbs. It is not added to the other tenant's CAM costs.

Individual and Central HVAC

Another situation that creates an exception to the simple pro rata share of the CAM billings is when the landlord is responsible for maintaining all but the major tenants' HVAC units as part of the CAM budget. In this case, the property manager would remove HVAC maintenance from the CAM budget and establish a separate tenant charge for it. Only those tenants whose HVAC units are maintained by the landlord would be billed for this expense. If the landlord maintains the HVAC units on 30,000 square feet of tenant space, then a tenant in a 2,000-square-foot space would pay 6.66% of the landlord's HVAC maintenance costs. If tenants do not have the same number or size of HVAC units, each would be billed for the cost to maintain its unit.

There are two choices in billing tenants for HVAC when the shopping center has a central plant. It can be set up as a profit center and the tenants billed an agreed-upon rate to include a profit. The owner would be responsible for repairs, replacements, and the basic costs of operating the system. If this approach is taken, the cost to the tenant should not exceed the cost if the tenants owned and operated their own HVAC units.

The second approach is to include the cost to operate the HVAC central plant as part of the common area bill-backs. The tenants would receive HVAC service at the actual cost of the service and, of course, share in the cost of all repairs, replacements, and day-to-day operations.

In either case, a model like the one in Exhibit 8.8 should be established to determine which expenses are in each billing and how each tenant (or space) is to be billed, including any negotiated exceptions or limits.

EXHIBIT 8.8

Security Deposit Log

Space	Use	Prepaid Rent	Date	Security Deposit	Date
1	Dress Shop	First mo $1825.00	5/18/83	$1825.00	5/18/83
2	Savings & Loan	First mo $1900.00	6/3/84	-0-	-0-
3	Barber Shop	First & last mo $3200.00	7/15/84	$1600.00	7/15/84
4	Supermarket	-0-		-0-	
5	Variety Store	-0-		-0-	
6	Restaurant	First mo $2100.00	8/1/82	original deposit returned	8/7/88
7	Pet Store	First mo $1560.00	3/7/82	$1560.00	3/7/82
8	Mens Wear	First mo $1750.00	5/3/82	$1750.00	5/3/82
9	Ice Cream	First mo $1320.00	5/16/82	-0-	
10	Kinney Shoe	-0-		-0-	
11	Card & Gift	-0-		1900.00*	4/3/83
12	Fish & Chips	First mo $1620.00	4/16/83	$1620.00	4/16/83
13	T V Sales	-0-		$2320.00	8/8/84
14	Beauty Supply	First & last mo $2700.00	3/3/84	$2700.00	3/3/84
15	Vacant				
16	Delicatessen	First mo $985.00	2/2/85	$1000.00	2/2/85
17	Radio Shack	-0-		-0-	
18	Bank	-0-		-0-	

*Returned per lease agreement 5/1/84

Enclosed Malls

An enclosed mall has two CAM budgets: a parking lot budget paid by all the tenants pro rata, and an enclosed mall budget paid only by those tenants in the mall. A shopping center of 500,000 square feet has 450,000 square feet of tenant space in the mall and 50,000 square feet in buildings adjacent to the parking lot. The denominator for the enclosed mall CAM budget is 450,000 square feet, and the denominator for the parking lot CAM budget is 500,000 square feet. A tenant on the mall with 5,000 square feet would pay 1.11% of the mall CAM budget and 1% of the parking lot CAM budget. The theory behind the two formulas is that only those tenants that receive the benefits of the enclosed mall common area should be responsible for its expenses.

Major tenants, such as department stores, are usually able to negotiate an important exception in their lease. Instead of paying pro rata shares of all enclosed mall CAM expenses, the tenant pays its full pro rata share of parking lot expenses but either pays none of the enclosed mall CAM costs or pays only a nominal contribution toward them. Although most landlords and property managers don't agree, the major tenant's reasoning for not paying its pro rata share of the enclosed mall CAM expenses is that it receives no benefit from the mall since it has entrances from the parking lot. However, because their customers use the parking facilities, major tenants are willing to pay their pro rata share of the parking lot maintenance.

When a major tenant is not required to contribute to the expenses of the mall CAM budget, the leases of the small shops must state that the denominator for these expenses will exclude the square footage of the major tenants. The cost of the mall CAM expense is then paid entirely by the small shops. If the small shops' leases do not exclude the square footage of the major tenants in the denominator, the landlord would not be reimbursed for the major tenants' pro rata share of the mall CAM expenses. In the example mentioned earlier, if two major tenants occupied 300,000 feet and they did not pay mall CAM costs, the denominator for the mall CAM budget would be 150,000 square feet. The tenant with 5,000 square feet would pay 3.33% of the mall CAM expenses instead of 1.11% in the earlier example. If the major tenant makes a nominal contribution to the mall CAM budget, this amount is credited against the actual expenses before calculating each tenant's CAM share.

Capital Improvements

The shopping center lease may include roof maintenance, exterior painting, replacement of existing capital improvement, and common area energy conservation improvement in the CAM expenses. Some leases allow reserves for future replacements. If the parking lot will need a major resurfacing at a cost of $50,000 in five years, the property manager could include in the CAM budget a $10,000 reserve for each of the next five years. The manager may establish a reserve amount less than $10,000 per year if the reserve fund interest is credited towards the $50,000 needed in five years. When the maintenance is completed, the funds are available and the tenants would not be billed for a major expense all in one year.

The amount to reserve can be set by determining first which maintenance or capital improvement items are allowed in the lease, then establishing how much of an expense will be incurred and when. Major tenants seldom will contribute to a reserve but will pay their pro rata share of the expense when it is incurred and if it is allowed in their lease. In this case the amount to reserve would be determined by subtracting the major tenants' pro rata share. If the major tenants are responsible for 75% of the CAM expense, the landlord would need to reserve $12,500 of the $50,000 parking lot resurfacing costs. The small tenants would be billed for their portion of the reserve over five years. When the work is completed, the major tenants would contribute their share of the expense, $37,500.

Administrative Fees

The typical shopping center tenant's lease will state that the landlord may add a 10% to 15% administrative fee to the CAM budget. If the CAM budget is $20,000 and the administrative fee is 10%, the total CAM budget is $22,000. Most major tenants will either pay no administrative fee or a nominal one. As a result, the other tenants are paying shares of a CAM budget that include a higher administrative fee.

All operating costs of a shopping center are not CAM expenses, and the property manager must be careful to include only those that are allowed in the lease. The tenants' leases provide them with the right to audit the CAM expenses.

CAM Billing Policies

When shopping centers were first developed, tenants were billed for their pro rata share of CAM expenses the month after the expenses were actually incurred. In the 1960s, the industry began billing tenants based on an estimated budget. The property manager would develop an annual budget, and the tenant would be billed one twelfth of the budget each month. This eliminated the need to calculate and bill each tenant monthly for its share of the CAM expenses.

Some major tenants still require the landlord to bill them monthly based on actual cost. In this situation, the property manager should request that the major tenant accept an estimated monthly bill once it has confidence in the management company's billing procedures.

When the CAM charges are billed on a monthly estimate, the current budget is adjusted to the actual expenses the following year. The typical lease states that the landlord will adjust the CAM billing by March 1. If the estimate is less than the actual cost, the tenant receives a bill for the difference. If the estimate exceeds the actual expenses, the tenant receives a refund or a credit on the next payment. The advantage of crediting the tenant's account is that the landlord keeps the overpayment and thus receives the next rental payment early. The disadvantage is that even when the landlord notifies the tenant of its credit, the tenant is likely to continue paying the full estimated amount. It usually takes several months to correct the credit the tenant received.

The advantage of sending the tenants a refund, in the event of an overpayment based on estimated expenses, is that there is no adjustment to the tenant's accounts and no continual reconciliation until the account is even. In addition, there are positive public relations to sending a tenant a check from the landlord because CAM expenses were under budget. Another consideration in refunding the credit is that the money belongs to the tenant since the tenant overpaid the CAM expenses.

Some tenants may have the right to recapture their CAM expenses from their percentage rent. If a tenant has this right, it would deduct from percentage rent owed the amount paid towards the CAM charges. This tenant's right is a rare exception today although this was common in many leases entered in the 1950s and 1960s.

The landlord's right to be reimbursed for CAM expenses has a significant impact on the cash flow and the value of the shopping center. The property manager should be current with the trends in the shopping center industry regarding current practices with respect to CAM expenses and methods of billing tenants.

Taxes

Pro Rata Allocation.   Most shopping centers have one real property tax bill for the entire center. The landlord pays the taxes and bills the tenants for their pro rata share based on the total leasable area of the center. For example, in a shopping center of 100,000 square feet of leasable area, a tenant occupying 2,500 square feet is responsible for 2.5% of the tax bill.

Exceptions exist, however, to having one tax bill covering the entire shopping center. The property manager must be aware of these exceptions to be sure all taxes are properly allocated and that the landlord is being properly reimbursed. It is not uncommon for major or out-lot (pad) tenants to have their parcels segregated and billed separately for taxes. Before starting any allocations, the property manager should obtain an assessor's map (see Exhibit 8.9) to determine how the center is segregated for tax purposes and reconcile that map to the leases. A property tax record (see Exhibit 8.10) can then be prepared to allocate the costs properly.

It is also not uncommon for a major tenant to have its building footprint, but not its share of the common areas, segregated for taxes. In such a case, the taxes on the land and common area improvements of the balance of the center would be allocated over the gross leasable area that would *include the footage* of the major tenant. Another approach is for the major tenant parcel, including its parking, to be separately taxed. Failure to recognize this distinction could result in an unfair charge to the rest of the tenants and an undercharge of taxes to the major tenant. In a mall, the taxes on the enclosed structure are allocated only to the mall tenants, while taxes on the parking lot are allocated to all tenants. Because of these variations, the potential for misallocation is great.

Base Year Allocation.   Another variation on tax billings is the base year tax approach. The theory of the base year billing is that the landlord

EXHIBIT 8.9

Assessors Map

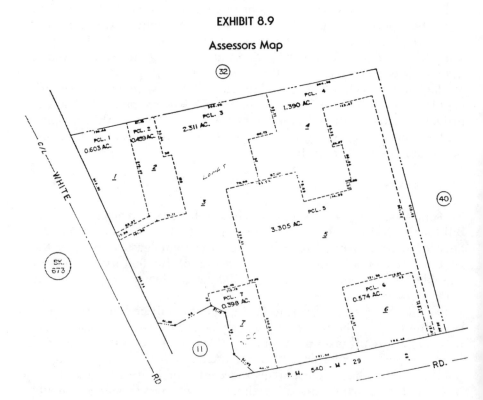

EXHIBIT 8.9 *(Continued)*
Plot Plan

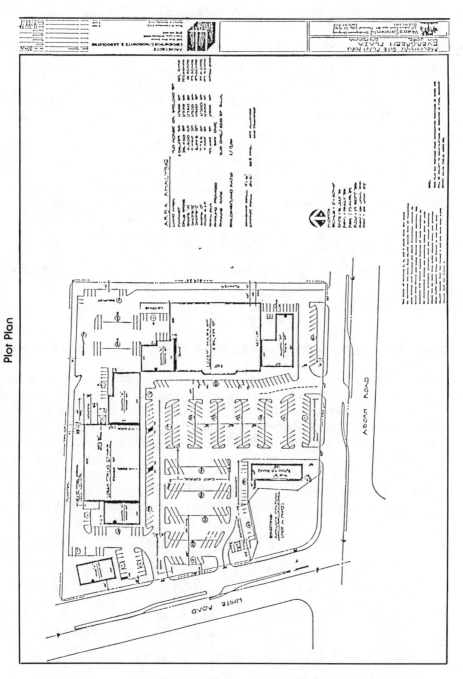

EXHIBIT 8.10

Property Tax Record

PARCEL #02-177-639   CURRENT TAX $83,726.22

Space	Tenant	Footage	%	Notes	Total Due
A-1	Hair Express	1,200	1.39	Pro Rata	$ 1,163.79
A-2	Markets Inc.	27,200	31.48	Pro Rata	$26,357.01
A-3	Drug Emporium	13,300	15.39	Base Year 84/85 $9,633.20	$ 3,252.33
B-1	Family Fashion	2,230	2.58	Pro Rata	$ 2,160.14
B-2	Laundromat	1,830	2.12	Pro Rata	$ 1,775.00
B-3	Vacant	1,770	2.05	—	-0-
B-4	Wileys	3,620	4.19	Pro Rata	$ 3,508.13
B-9	Discount Hardware	33,600	38.89	Taxes not to exceed .60 cents per square foot	$20,160.00
B-10	Hobbies House	1,650	1.91	Pro Rata	$ 1,599.17
	Totals	86,400	100%		$59,975.47

Total Center 86,400 feet

sets the rents knowing what the taxes are the year the tenant takes occupancy.

The tenant's base year is stated in the lease. The base year is netotiable but is usually the year the tenant takes occupancy of the leased premises. If the taxes on the premises were $800 during the base year, the landlord pays $800, and the tenant pays the annual increase above $800. For example, a lease is negotiated today. The current taxes on the premises are $1,120. For this example, assume a 5% per year increase in taxes. The amount each party would pay on a five-year lease is shown in Table 8.1. If and when a new lease is signed, the new base rent would reflect the current taxes on the new commencement date. The full pro rata bill-back is

TABLE 8.1

Five-Year Allocation of Taxes Using Base Year Approach

	Taxes	Landlord Pays	Tenant Pays
Year 1	$1,120.00	$1,120.00	-0-
Year 2	$1,176.00	$1,120.00	$ 56.00
Year 3	$1,234.80	$1,120.00	$114.80
Year 4	$1,296.54	$1,120.00	$176.54
Year 5	$1,361.37	$1,120.00	$241.37

much more common, but it is still possible to find base year formulas in older leases and, from time to time, in current negotiations.

Insurance

The landlord is responsible for providing and billing back insurance on the common areas and on the buildings. The landlord's insurance does not cover the tenants' improvements, stock, or fixtures.

Because major and many pad or out-lot tenants are required to provide fire and extended coverage insurance for their own premises, liability insurance is generally billed with the common area maintenance costs. When this situation exists, a different denominator is used for allocating common area insurance and building insurance. These distinctions are quite important both when purchasing the insurance coverage and when allocating the costs.

Modern commercial leases will allow the landlord to bill the tenants on a full pro rata basis. Insurance has also been subject to base year considerations in leases. The theory is the same as that used for taxes in the previous example. The insurance premium in effect at the commencement of the lease will be paid by the landlord throughout the lease term. Should the premium decline, there is usually not a reduction in rent to reflect that decrease. Increases in premiums over the base year are shared pro rata by the tenants.

To illustrate, the landlord's premium was $2,470 during the tenant's base year, the premium decreased the next year and then increased 3% per year thereafter. The allocation is shown in Table 8.2.

Most landlords will include rental interruption insurance premiums as part of the bill-backs under the insurance clause. National chain and major tenants generally will negotiate this out of the lease, believing that the landlord should pay for the protection of the income stream, not the tenant who will be out of business during the interruption. The tenant also will argue that it has its own income stream to protect.

TABLE 8.2

Five-Year Allocation of Insurance Costs Using Base Year Approach

	Premium	Landlord Cost	Tenant Cost
Year 1	$2,470.00	$2,470.00	-0-
Year 2	$2,100.00	$2,100.00	-0-*
Year 3	$2,163.00	$2,163.00	-0-
Year 4	$2,228.00	$2,228.00	-0-
Year 5	$2,295.00	$2,295.00	-0-

*In an unusual situation like this, the tenant receives no rental reduction unless specifically negotiated.

The property manager must be alert to coverage limits set by tenants that may impact the ability of the landlord to fully recover the premiums. If both parties agree that the tenant will reimburse the landlord for a pro rata share of premiums for $1 million liability coverage, but the owner elects to carry $5 million in coverage, the owner will be liable for the premiums above the agreed amounts.

Utilities

If at all possible, management should avoid billing back utilities to tenants. If there is no choice because of the excess cost of retrofitting meters for each space, the next best choice is submetering to prevent any argument about each tenant's usage. It is difficult to allocate electricity cost between a 1,200-square-foot store open eight hours a day, six days a week, and a 2,300-square-foot diner open fourteen hours a day, seven days a week. Consider also the problems in allocating water costs to five different tenants ranging in size from 900 square feet to 4,000 square feet and in use from a laundromat to a variety store.

Tenants such as supermarkets and restaurants may want to control the lighting around their premises because their business hours extend beyond those of the shopping center. For example, if a supermarket is open twenty-four hours a day, the electricity to the light poles in the parking lot in front of it may be connected to the supermarket's electrical meter. In this situation, the property manager should remove the electricity cost from the CAM budget, create a separate billing for it, and bill all the tenants except the supermarket for their pro rata share of the CAM electricity expense.

Another difficulty in allocating utility costs occurs when a tenant has excessive usage. This situation can be resolved in several ways. The first is to bill the tenants whose use is excessive an overstandard utility charge and then credit this charge to the common area maintenance budget. A consultant or utility company representative should determine the amount of overstandard utilities consumed by the tenant. A second solution would be to remove the utility expense from the common area maintenance budget and have a separate meter for the tenant with excessive usage. This tenant is billed on its actual usage, and the other tenants are billed a pro rata share of the master-meter utility cost. The denominator for calculating these pro rata utility shares would be the square footage of all the tenants except the one with the separate meter.

A procedure for billing tenants their cost of a master-metered utility is as follows: Check to see which spaces are being served by which meter or system. This can be done by reviewing the original plans or, if necessary, by physically checking each space.

Every tenant's usage must be determined because a pro rata square footage allocation is seldom an equitable approach to utility distribution.

The local utility company generally will be of help in determining probable usage by each type of tenant in a shopping center, giving special consideration to minimum billings and peak demands. Again, a model such
as the water use allocation form shown in Exhibit 8.11 should be prepared and monitored.

A profit is created when the landlord purchases the utility at a bulk
or wholesale rate and bills the tenants at a higher rate. In many jurisdictions, however, rate structures are such that the owner cannot buy
utilities in bulk at a lesser fee and sell them to tenants at a markup.
Most leases provide that if the landlord sells utilities to the tenant, the
price will not exceed what the tenant would pay to buy the utilities
directly.

A few years ago, a major regional center elected to sell electricity
although its management was not knowledgeable in meter reading and
rates structures. After the first year, management realized that it had
used the wrong billing rate the previous year, causing the center to lose
in excess of $50,000.

(b)   OFFICE BUILDING BILL-BACK EXPENSES

Office building tenants are usually billed for their share of the operating expense, also known as escalation expense, on a base year expense
or stop expense method.

EXHIBIT 8.11

Water Usage Allocation

Meter   # 01-227
Account # 727-01-343

Space	Tenant	Allocation Basis*	
		Minimum	% Usage
C-1	Delicatessen	$26.00	22
C-2	Shoe store	12.00	4
C-3	Yogurt	18.00	22
C-4	Dentist	16.00	14
C-5	Cleaners	18.00	18
C-6	Card shop	12.00	4
C-7	Gift store	12.00	4
C-8	Beauty supply	14.00	8
C-9	Video rental	12.00	4

*Allocation per analysis with River City Water Department consistent with
water billing rates if each tenant were separately metered.

Until around 1980 most office building tenants were billed on the base year method. The tenant would pay its pro rata share of the increase above the operating expenses in the year it took occupancy (its base year). If a tenant occupied 5,000 square feet in a 100,000-square-foot building, and the operating expenses increased from $600,000 in its base year to $650,000, the tenant would pay $2,500 in escalation expenses. The tenant occupies 5% of the building, so this percentage is multiplied by the $50,000 increase in operating expenses.

If during the tenant's third year of occupancy the expenses increased to $689,000, the tenant's share of escalation would be $4,450 (5% of the $89,000 increase above the $600,000 base year).

In a soft leasing market, the tenant may be able to negotiate the base year later in the lease. For instance, the tenant occupies its premises in 1990 but negotiates its base year to be 1992. The tenant would start paying escalation expenses in 1993. If the market is strong, the landlord may negotiate the base year to precede the year the tenant occupies its premises. In this situation, the tenant pays escalation charges during the first year of its occupancy.

In the late 1970s, several developers changed the method of billing escalation charges to a stop expense method. The landlord would pay the operating expenses to a predetermined dollar amount per square foot and the tenants would pay everything above that amount. A tenant with 7,500 square feet in a building with a $6 stop and operating expenses of $6.65 would pay $4,875 in escalation charges. The tenant is paying $ .65 per square foot on 7,500 square feet. In theory, if all the tenants have the same stop, the landlord will always know the share of the operating expenses. In practice, many tenants will negotiate a high stop expense when their lease renews.

Exceptions to a building's standard method of billing escalation charges are similar to those reviewed in the preceding section on common area billings. An office building tenant may have a cap on its share of the increase in operating expenses or one on specific expenses such as maintenance. The tenant will rationalize that the landlord has little or no control over the cost of insurance, taxes, and utilities but has direct control over maintenance expenses.

For many years, office building escalation charges were billed in the year after the expenses were incurred. If a tenant's base year was 1985, the tenant would pay the 1986 increase in 1987. In the late 1970s, most new office buildings started to bill escalation charges based on the methods shopping centers had used for years. Toward the end of 1985, the property manager would estimate the building's operating expenses for 1986 and bill the tenants commencing January 1986 on a one-twelfth basis monthly. In early 1987, the estimated bills would be reconciled to the actual expenses.

(c) INDUSTRIAL PROPERTY BILL-BACK EXPENSES

Industrial properties are usually billed on a base year or triple net method. The base year method is similar to the one used for office buildings. The triple net method allows the landlord to bill all operating expenses to the tenant or tenants on a pro rata basis. The three net charges are taxes, insurance, and maintenance. When a tenant pays operating expenses on a triple net basis, there are no exceptions to any of the charges.

(d) BILL-BACK POLICY

The property manager should bill tenants for only those items that the lease allows to be included in common area maintenance or escalation charges. Some landlords attempt to include in the bill-back charges items that are not allowed in the lease. However, it is often more prudent not to include a nominal expense in the tenants' charges if the item is questionable. If the expense is more than nominal, a decision to bill would require a thorough review.

There can be many exceptions to billing each tenant its pro rata share of CAM expenses. The leases must be carefully summarized to determine each tenant's expense obligation, and all billings must be accurate. If the management company continually sends out improper billings, it will lose its credibility with the tenants.

§ 8.13 CONCLUSION

It is easy for property managers to devote all of their time to responsibilities that directly enhance the value of the property. Although the excitement of finalizing a lease is unmatched in property management, a deal can be negated by a poor lease administration program.

Nine

Maintenance Management

§ 9.1 WHY MAINTAIN THE PROPERTY

The physical condition of a property has a major impact on its net operating income and value as well as on the surrounding community. The property can control the property manager if the maintenance program consists simply of crisis intervention. This chapter will discuss in detail the process of developing and implementing a maintenance management program that will allow the property manager to maintain control over the appearance and operations of a property. A well-conceived program will include preventive maintenance services, routine maintenance, and a plan for emergencies.

A good maintenance management program will enhance the leasing effort and improve tenant relations. A prospect will not be impressed with the building if told, for example, that the peeling fascia boards will be painted shortly. Tenants occupy their spaces upwards of fifty to seventy hours a week. Every defect, every item of deferred maintenance, and every day spent waiting for service convinces the tenant that the manager or owner either does not care or is unable to cope with the property's needs. A sound maintenance program is an obligation to the tenants. The tenant has little or no say about common area standards in commercial properties, so it is up to the management to set reasonable standards and see that they are met.

A good maintenance management program will also preserve the building's physical life. A well-maintained building will generally command higher rents and therefore maximize the value of the asset.

The longer the physical life of the property is maintained, the longer the building has potential for economic life. A well-conceived maintenance management program should reduce the cost and frequency of major repairs and stabilize the day-to-day operating expenses.

Pride of ownership is an excellent reason for maintaining the property at high standards. Commercial properties are often very visible and important parts of the community. A well-maintained commercial property is an asset to the community. City officials, civic leaders, and the public often take great pride in the condition of the commercial properties in their areas.

The most compelling reason for a good maintenance management program is safety. Certainly no owner or manager wants to shoulder the ethical or legal responsibility for a customer or tenant being injured on the property.

§ 9.2 ESTABLISHING MAINTENANCE NEEDS

Input for developing a maintenance management program comes from many sources. The manufacturers of the various materials and operating systems recommend maintenance schedules to retain warranties and to preserve their products. Even though an item may be many years old, most manufacturers will provide information and guidance.

Governmental agencies and regulations play a big part in maintenance management. States mandate elevator maintenance standards and require regular inspection of the equipment to be sure standards are met. Most jurisdictions today require fire sprinkler systems and extinguishers to be inspected and tested regularly to be sure they will be operable when needed. Fire departments and building inspectors make routine inspections in many cities to help prevent problems before they arise.

The public may lodge complaints in commercial buildings, especially if the property manager is on site. Because they serve as another set of eyes and ears, the public should be thanked for bringing these items to the property manager's attention.

Tenants' requests for service fall into two general categories: (1) routine maintenance on equipment such as air-conditioners, sump pumps, door openers, elevators, and escalators, and requests for janitorial service; and (2) repairs or breakdowns. Tenant requests should be handled with courtesy and enthusiasm. The building owner is much better off when a tenant registers a complaint about a broken system than if the tenant ignores the problem. Many repairs start out as small problems but can develop into major repairs if they are ignored. For example, a tenant notices moisture on a wall but, thinking it was not important, says nothing. By the time the problem becomes obvious, dry rot has corroded an eight-foot section of wall and exterior siding. The replacement cost was substantial although the initial repair would have cost less than $50.

It is a good idea to meet with each tenant upon taking over the management of a property. During this visit, the tenant should be questioned about the effectiveness of current maintenance and asked for suggestions to improve the service. When the management account is up and running, it is a good idea to maintain an open line of communication with the tenants by inquiring about how well ongoing maintenance services are being performed.

In shopping centers and in industrial properties where interior maintenance is a tenant's responsibility, the owner or manager should still check periodically to be sure the maintenance is being performed; if it is not, the tenant should be prompted to fulfill his or her lease obligations. Ultimately, when these spaces are no longer leased, any deferred maintenance may become the owner's responsibility.

Finally, the tenant's lease may set standards for maintenance such as frequency of janitorial service and window washing. In shopping centers, major tenants' leases often set forth standards of maintenance for the common area. It is not unusual, for example, for a major supermarket to require a shopping center to be swept a minimum of three times per week. These standards are a definite obligation and should not be ignored or minimized.

The property management industry has over a dozen publications with excellent articles on maintenance. *The Journal of Property Management,* the bimonthly magazine of the Institute of Real Estate Management, has an operating techniques and products section that discusses a specific maintenance concern each issue. *Buildings* and *Building Maintenance* are monthly magazines devoted primarily to maintenance. *Grounds Maintenance* is a magazine for the professional landscaper. Many trade associations provide magazines, booklets, and other educational materials on maintenance.

§ 9.3   INSPECTIONS

Inspections are the heart of a maintenance management program and are undertaken for three reasons. First, inspecting the property is the quickest way to become familiar with a new management account. The initial inspection will determine the condition of the property, including an inventory of personal property, and provide a comparison with competing properties. Second, inspections identify current and future maintenance needs. For instance, an inspection may identify a need to restripe a parking lot in six months. Third, property inspection is one of the preliminary steps in developing an operating budget and establishing capital improvement expenditures.

The property manager does not conduct a structural or mechanical inspection. However, managers are trained to conduct a visual inspection of property and to identify first-echelon maintenance. Consultants are hired to conduct inspections for major structural, mechanical, and maintenance problems. Some maintenance agreements, such as the elevator and HVAC agreements, include regular inspections.

Inspections should be a routine element in the property's maintenance management program. Several factors will determine the frequency of inspections. First is the property's condition and age. A property in poor condition will need to be inspected more frequently than a property maintained in good condition. Older buildings have a greater need for repairs.

The type of property is another factor to consider. A regional mall will have considerably more traffic and thus more wear and tear, especially in common areas, than a garden office building. If the property is located in an area with a high incidence of vandalism, it will need to be inspected more frequently. The distance of the property from the manager's office is another factor. An on-site manager can inspect the property more frequently than a manager who is located hundreds of miles away. The last, and frequently determining factor is the time available to the property manager. The manager with a large portfolio of properties has less time for inspections than does the manager with fewer properties. An ideal inspection frequency is monthly, although all properties do not need inspections this often.

When the property manager, especially an on-site manager, is the only one who conducts the inspections, items may be overlooked because the manager is too familiar with the property. Thus, while the property manager should have the primary responsibility for and conduct the majority of inspections, he or she should alternate inspections with the maintenance personnel and clerical and administrative staff. If the leasing is in-house, the leasing agent should be encouraged to conduct an inspection. Property managers can annually inspect each other's properties. Each person has a different perspective and will see things the others miss. The clerical staff may be more attentive to cleanliness, while the leasing agent looks at merchandising features, and the maintenance people look for wear and tear to the property.

Inspection forms are provided in this chapter. Exhibit 9.1 is a two-page shopping center exterior form designed for the exterior common areas; Exhibit 9.2 is a four-page shopping center interior form, developed for the enclosed mall's common area; and Exhibit 9.3 is an office building form.

The first set of forms provides a column for the inspector to comment on each item to be inspected. When a separate comment is noted for

EXHIBIT 9.1

Inspection Report

SHOPPING CENTERS

PROJECT: _____ DATE: _____

ADDRESS: _____ INSPECTED BY: _____

EXTERIOR

	STATUS	ACTION	EST. COST
I. SURROUNDING AREA 1. Neighborhood			
2. Access to Project			
3. Street Condition			
4.			
5. Comments:			
II. SIGNAGE 1. Pylon Signs			
2. Entry Signs			
3. Parking Lot Signs			
4. Tenant Signs			
5.			
6. Comments:			
III. PARKING LOT 1. Driveways			
2. Parking Stalls			
3. Striping			
4. Parking Bumpers			
5. Drainage			
6. Concrete Curbing			
7.			
8. Comments:			
IV. LIGHTING 1. Pole Mounted			
2. Wall Mounted			
3.			
4. Comments:			
V. LANDSCAPING 1. General Appearance			
2. Ground Cover			
3. Trees			
4. Shrubs			
5. Sprinklers			
6. Curbing			
7.			
8. Comments:			
VI. OTHER ITEMS 1. Walls & Fences			
2. Sidewalk & Ramps			
3. Bike Rack			
4. Newspaper Rack			
5. Trash Bins			
6. Loading Docks			
7. Electrical Cabinet			

Reprinted with permission of the Institute of Real Estate Management (IREM), Chicago, Ill.

EXHIBIT 9.1 *(Continued)*

	STATUS	ACTION	EST. COST
8. Meters			
9. Sprinklers (Bldg.)			
10.			
11. Comments:			
VII. BUILDING EXTERIOR			
1. Walls			
2. Stucco			
3. Wood Siding			
4. Wood Beams & Trim			
5. Columns/Posts			
6. Store Fronts			
7. Doors			
8.			
9. Comments:			
VII. ROOFS			
1. Soffit/Overhang			
2. Main Roof			
3. Flashing			
4. Drains/Gutters			
5. Mansand/Decorative			
6.			
7. Comments:			
IX. VACANCIES			
1. Store Fronts			
2. Doors			
3. Door Hardware			
4. Flooring			
5. Walls			
6. Base			
7. Ceilings			
8. Sprinklers			
9. Thermostats			
10. H.V.A.C. Vents			
11. Restrooms			
12. Comments:			
X. MISCELLANEOUS			
1.			
2.			
3.			

XI. GENERAL COMMENTS:
1. Total cost of work needed: _____

_____

2. Capital expenditure anticipated: _____

_____

3. Special problem: _____

_____

4. Comments: _____

_____

EXHIBIT 9.2

Inspection Report

SHOPPING CENTERS

PROJECT: _____ DATE: _____

ADDRESS: _____ INSPECTED BY: _____

INTERIOR

ITEMS	STATUS	ACTION	EST. COST
I. ENTRANCES			
1. Glass			
2. Doors			
3. Door Hardware			
4. Sign (Entry)			
5. Sign (Doors)			
6.			
7. Comments:			
II. VESTIBULE			
1. Glass			
2. Door			
3. Flooring			
4. Walls			
5. Furniture			
6. Lighting			
7.			
8. Comments:			
III. MALL			
1. Carpet			
2. Wood Flooring			
3. Tile			
4. Stairs			
5. Elevator			
6. Escalator			
7. Benches			
8. Walls			
9. Columns			
10. Hand Railings			
11. Fountains/Pools			
12. Drinking Fountains			
13. Telephones			
14. Sand Urns			
15. Trash Bins			
16. Fire Extinguisher			
17. H.V.A.C.			
18. Hose Cabinet			
19. Return Air Vent			
20. Light Fixture			
21. Banners			
22. Windows			
23. Skylights			
24. Ceiling			
25. Fire Detector			
26.			
27.			
28. Comments:			

Reprinted with permission of the Institute of Real Estate Management (IREM), Chicago, Ill.

ITEMS	STATUS	ACTION	EST. COST
IV. LANDSCAPING			
1. Planters			
2. Sprinkler			
3. Hose Bibs			
4. Ground Cover			
5. Color			
6. Shrubs			
7. Trees			
8.			
9. Comments:			
V. RESTROOMS (MEN)			
1. Doors			
2. Door Hardware			
3. Floors			
4. Base			
5. Walls			
6. Ceilings			
7. Partitions			
8. Watercloset			
9. Paper Dispenser			
10. Urinal			
11. Counter			
12. Sinks			
13. Mirror			
14. Soap Dispenser			
15. H.V.A.C. Vent			
16. Fire Detector			
17.			
18. Comments:			
VI. RESTROOM (WOMEN)			
1. Doors			
2. Door Hardware			
3. Floors			
4. Base			
5. Walls			
6. Ceilings			
7. Partitions			
8. Watercloset			
9. Paper Dispenser			
10. Vending Machine			
11. Counter			
12. Sinks			
13. Mirror			
14. Soap Dispenser			
15. H.V.A.C. Vent			
16. Fire Detector			
17.			
18. Comments:			

EXHIBIT 9.2 *(Continued)*

ITEMS	STATUS	ACTION	EST. COST
VII. CORRIDORS			
1. Doors			
2. Door Hardware			
3. Floors			
4. Base			
5. Walls			
6. Ceiling			
7. Lighting			
8. Signs			
9. Ventilation			
10. Vents			
11. Fire Detector			
12.			
13. Comments:			
VIII. ELECTRICAL ROOMS			
1. Doors			
2. Door Hardware			
3. Floors			
4. Base			
5. Walls			
6. Ceiling			
7. Lighting			
8. Signs			
9. Ventilation			
10. Vents			
11. Electrical Panels			
12. Fire Detector			
13.			
14. Comments:			
IX. STORAGE ROOM			
1. Doors			
2. Door Hardware			
3. Floors			
4. Base			
5. Walls			
6. Ceiling			
7. Lighting			
8. Signs			
9. Ventilation			
10. Vents			
11. Lockers			
12. Cabinets			
13. Fire Detector			
14.			
15. Comments:			

EXHIBIT 9.2 *(Continued)*

ITEMS	STATUS	ACTION	EST. COST
X. VACANCIES			
1. Storefront			
2. Doors			
3. Door Hardware			
4. Flooring			
5. Base			
6. Wall			
7. Ceiling			
8. Sprinkler			
9. Thermostat			
10. H.V.A.C. Vents			
11. Restroom			
12. Fire Detector			
13.			
14. Comments:			
XI. OCCUPIER STORE			
1. Storefront			
2. Door			
3. Signs			
4.			
5. Comments			
XII. MISC.			
1.			
2.			
3.			

XIII. GENERAL COMMENTS

1. Total cost of work needed: _____

_____

_____

2. Capital expenditure anticipated: _____

_____

_____

3. Special problem: _____

_____

_____

4. Comments: _____

_____

_____

EXHIBIT 9.3

Office Building Inspection Report (Partial)

PROJECT _____ DATE _____

ADDRESS _____ INSPECTED BY _____

INTERIOR

ITEMS LOBBY	FLOOR	STATUS	ACTION	EST. COST
1. Carpeting				
2. Ceiling				
3. Directory				
4. Doors				
5. Entry Floor (Vestibule)				
6. Furniture				
7. Glass				
8. Kick Plates				
9. Landscaping				
10. Lighting Fixtures				
11. Locks				
12. Mail Box				
13. Mail Slot				
14. Pulls				
15. Push Plates				
16. Signs				
17. Walls				
18.				

19. COMMENTS:

STAIRWAYS				
1. Ceilings				
2. Doors				
3. Electric Lights				
4. Emergency Lights				
5. Gates				
6. Handrails				
7. Life Safety Equipment				
8. Risers				
9. Treads				
10. Wall Numbers				
11. Walls				
12.				

13. COMMENTS:

CORRIDORS/ELEVATOR LOBBY				
1. Ashtrays				
2. Carpeting				
3. Ceilings				
4. Directory				
5. Doors				
6. Fire Extinguishers				
7. Fire Hose Cabinets				
8. Hardware				
9. Janitorial Room				
10. Life Safety Equipment				
11. Lighting Fixtures				
12. Required Signs				
13. Safety Code Violations				
14. Walls				
15.				

16. COMMENTS:

Adapted from *Property Management* by Robert C. Kyle and Ann M. Kennehan (Chicago, IL: Real Estate Education Co., 1979).

EXHIBIT 9.3 *(Continued)*

ITEMS ELEVATORS Passenger & Freight	FLOOR	STATUS	ACTION	EST. COST
1. Cab Ceiling				
2. Cab Lighting				
3. Cab Ventilation				
4. Cab Walls				
5. Carpeting				
6. Control Panels				
7. Corridor Door Fronts				
8. Emergency Switches				
9. Floor Indicator				
10. Floor Numbers on Door				
11. Lobby Door Fronts				
12. Permit Expiration Date				
13. Position Indicators				
14. Signal Buttons				
15. Signal Lanterns				
16. Telephone				
17. Telephone Cabinets				
18. Threshold Lights				
19. Walls				
20.				
21.				
22.				

23. COMMENTS:

RESTROOMS - MEN AND WOMEN				
1. Bowl				
2. Ceiling				
3. Deodorants				
4. Doors				
5. Floor				
6. Hardware on Door				
7. Lavatory				
8. Light Fixtures				
9. Locks				
10. Mirrors				
11. Seat				
12. Signs				
13. Soap Dispensers				
14. Stall Panel				
15. Switches				
16. Tank				
17. Toilet Paper Holder				
18. Towel Cabinets				
19. Trim				
20. Urinal				
21. Ventilation				
22. Vestibule				
23. Wainscote				
24. Walls				
25. Waste Receptacle				
26. Watercloset				
27.				
27.				
29.				

30. COMMENTS:

EXHIBIT 9.3 *(Continued)*

ITEMS

MECHANICAL PENTHOUSE	FLOOR	STATUS	ACTION	EST. COST
1. Carpenter Shop				
2. Heating				
3. Life Safety Equipment				
4. Paint Shop				
5. Plumber				
6. Storage Space				
7. Superintendent Office				
8. Utility Space				
9.				
10.				
11.				

11. COMMENTS:

EXTERIOR

PARKING LOT				
1. Curbs				
2. Landscaping				
3. Landscaping Boxes				
4. Landscaping Controls				
5. Light Poles				
6. Monument Signs				
7. Ramps				
8. Signs - Service, Misc.				
9. Striping				
10. Trash Area				
11.				
12.				
13.				

14. COMMENTS:

GARAGE				
1. Elevator				
2. Lighting				
3. Ramps				
4. Signs				
5. Stairs				
6. Striping				
7.				
8.				
9.				

10. COMMENTS:

GENERAL COMMENTS:

1. Total Cost of Work Needed: _____

2. Capital Expenditure Anticipated: _____

3. Special Problems: _____

4. Comments: _____

each item, the property manager can be assured that each item on the form was inspected. A statement describing required maintenance goes in the "Work Needed" column. The following column provides a place to estimate the cost of the work. Each vacancy should be inspected with the rest of the property and maintained in a broom-clean condition. The last section of the form provides space for the total cost of the work needed, capital improvement costs, special problems, and general comments.

The inspection forms are turned in to the property manager, who expedites the maintenance work. After the work is completed, the forms are kept on file to be used for reference when developing the next budget. The inspection forms also are useful in slip-and-fall suits as evidence that the property has a maintenance management program. However, if maintenance items are identified and corrective action is not taken, the form will be evidence of neglect.

§ 9.4 SCHEDULING

Once maintenance needs have been identified, the work is scheduled. Maintenance is divided into two categories: preventive and routine. According to one management text, "Preventive maintenance is a program of regular inspection and care that allows potential problems to be prevented or at least detected and solved before major repairs are required."[1]

Maintenance specifications can be developed from observation or obtained from the equipment manufacturers, service contractors, consultants, published articles, and information from trade associations. Maintenance specification manuals are provided with most equipment. Consultants may be hired to develop preventive maintenance programs for individual components of the building such as the roof.

Schedules should be included in the contractor's bid package. When reviewing the bids, the property manager must be careful to compare "apples with apples." For instance, in reviewing bids for HVAC maintenance, the manager should compare the type and frequency of filter changes, the list of items covered by each preventive maintenance inspection, and the frequency of these inspections.

Routine maintenance is ongoing maintenance. It includes a variety of maintenance tasks, from mowing the lawn to sweeping the parking lot to emptying waste receptacles. The property manager should review the routine maintenance schedule periodically with the maintenance staff to determine if the frequency and job specifications are adequate.

The two schedules, preventive and routine maintenance, are normally developed for a one-year period that coincides with the budget period.

[1] J.C. Downs, Jr., *Principles of Real Estate Management*, p. 154 (1987).

Major preventive maintenance, such as roof or parking lot maintenance, may be scheduled over a five-year period.

§ 9.5 MAINTENANCE SCHEDULING CHART

Whether the property manager has a portfolio of several properties or serves as the on-site manager for a commercial building, several preventive and routine maintenance tasks will need to be performed each month or periodically. It is easy to budget for several maintenance tasks, most of which will be performed well after the budget is developed, and then forget to perform one or two items.

To prevent this from happening, each recurring routine maintenance item should be listed on a chart that is posted in the maintenance shop. Nonroutine maintenance, such as striping the parking lot, and nonroutine preventive maintenance, such as roof or parking lot patching, can be listed on a monthly chart posted in the property management company's office and in the maintenance shop. This chart can be a magnetic board with each maintenance item placed under the month it is to be performed and removed when work is completed. Another approach is to use a large sheet of paper or acetate with a special marking pen to record each work item in the same manner described above. When the work is completed the item can be erased or removed from the chart.

§ 9.6 WORK ORDERS

Once the maintenance request has been received and recorded, a work order can be used to route the request to the maintenance personnel or contractor and to follow up on the work. A work order accomplishes four basic objectives:

1. Serves as a notice that the periodic operation is to be performed
2. Provides authorization for the expenditure of labor and materials in performance of the work
3. Furnishes a document for recording that the operation was performed
4. Provides a document for the written feedback of other information such as materials used, other work that was or may be required, etc.[2]

---

[2] J.E. Heintzelman, *The Complete Handbook of Maintenance Management*, p. 85 (1976).

When a maintenance request is received, it is written on a two-part work order form such as that shown in Exhibit 9.4. The original copy is given to the building maintenance person. If the maintenance request is radioed or phoned in to the maintenance person, he or she completes the work and calls back the status of the request. This information is then added to the work request. When the work is to be completed by a contractor, the same procedure is followed.

If the management office is on-site, the maintenance person may be able to pick up the work order. In this case, the tenant should sign the work order when the work is completed.

The second copy of the work order is placed in a tickler file. If the request was received on Monday, for example, and it is determined that the work should be completed by Tuesday, the second copy is placed in the reminder file for that day. If notification of work completion or the status of the work has not been received by Tuesday afternoon, the maintenance person is again contacted.

Sometimes the work cannot be completed until a part has been ordered. In this case, the tenant would be informed of the reason for the

EXHIBIT 9.4

Sample Work Order Form

MAINTENANCE REQUEST

TO: _____ DATE: _____

BLDG: _____

ADDRESS: _____

REQUEST: _____
_____

RETURN TO TRFMC

STATUS: _____
_____

COMPLETION DATE: _____ SIGNATURE _____

---

delay and given assurance that the request is being followed up. If the maintenance person orders the part but doesn't tell the tenant or the property manager about the delay in completing the work, the tenant will believe that the request is being ignored, and the property manager will believe that the work was completed. The follow-up system will eliminate such an occurrence.

When the work is completed, the original copy of the work order is placed in the tenant's file, and the second copy is kept with other work orders and periodically reviewed to identify maintenance problems or trends.

§ 9.7   RECORDING MAINTENANCE REQUESTS

Maintenance requests from tenants must be handled quickly and efficiently. Each maintenance call is recorded, responded to, and noted when completed.

Usually either the secretary or the property manager receives the request and records the date, the suite or location, and the problem on the maintenance request form. Some calls should always be referred to the property manager, while others can be handled by the assistant.

Logging the requests not only provides documentation, but starts the follow-up process. Retaining the log helps develop a history and pattern of maintenance needs. This list can be analyzed to identify recurring maintenance problems that might lead to future problems.

Two maintenance request forms are provided. The first form, found in Exhibit 9.5, is for general maintenance, and the second, found in Exhibit 9.6, is for HVAC—"hot and cold calls"—service requests. Periodically review the "hot and cold" log with the HVAC service contractor and both forms with the maintenance staff. This information is helpful when developing the property's operating budget.

§ 9.8   SERVICE REPORT CARDS

When maintenance, whether preventive or corrective, is performed on mechanical equipment, the work is recorded in the equipment's service report card. The information noted includes the problem, the maintenance performed, and date, and who performed the work. The service report card should be located near the equipment. When the equipment breaks down, the service person can quickly review the history of the equipment's problems and better identify the cause of the breakdown. This lowers repair costs and gets the equipment online more quickly.

EXHIBIT 9.5

General Maintenance Calls

Building

Date	Tenant	Suite #	Request

EXHIBIT 9.6

HVAC Calls

Building

Date	Tenant	Suite #	Request

§ 9.9   EQUIPMENT CONTROL

Equipment, whether kept on site, at the property management office, or with the roving maintenance personnel, must be accounted for and controlled. The equipment should be inventoried and marked with the company or building's name. Equipment assigned to a maintenance person should be signed out. People take better care of equipment that is assigned to them. Few things are more frustrating than to have a piece of equipment missing when it is needed, especially in an emergency.

§ 9.10   EQUIPMENT MAINTENANCE

There are three reasons for developing an equipment maintenance program: (1) safety of the users; (2) assurance of proper equipment operation; and (3) extension of the equipment's life. Manufacturers will provide recommended maintenance and cleaning procedures for the equipment.

§ 9.11   UNIT PRICING

Under unit pricing, a fixed price is obtained from contractors for specific maintenance work for a predetermined period, usually one year. The contractors agree to maintain their prices for the predetermined period, and the property manager commits to using these contractors, provided that the quality of their service is maintained.

Unit prices can be obtained on a variety of work, including shampooing carpets, sweeping parking lots, cleaning drapery, security, and extra janitorial service.

Unit prices are frequently used for tenant improvement work on items such as carpeting, light fixtures, doors and hardware, electrical and phone outlets, and interior reconstruction. When developing an operating budget, or when estimating costs for remodeling or building out office space, the property manager can obtain most estimates from the unit prices. Unit prices save the property manager the time required to bid work for each job and enable the work to be performed more efficiently and at a known cost.

§ 9.12   EMERGENCY PHONE NUMBERS

Nothing is more frustrating than to receive a call at home after business hours for emergency maintenance and not be able to contact a service contractor. Delays in responding often result in additional damage and expense. Every property manager should develop a list of all the contractors serving the building and of others, such as glass contractors, who are not used regularly but would be needed in an emergency.

Companies that do not have a twenty-four-hour answering service must provide the home phone numbers of several of their service personnel. If the contractor will not provide an after-hours phone number, the property manager should select another contractor. Remember, emergency maintenance is needed immediately.

In addition to the contractor's phone numbers, the list should include phone numbers of at least two employees of each tenant, the original construction contractor and subcontractors (if available), the utility companies, police and fire department, and all management company employees. An emergency phone list for each property should be placed in a binder and organized by property name. Each property manager, assistant, and everyone on the management company's answering service call list should have three copies—one for the office, one for home, and one for the car. This booklet is referred to as the project data book.

§ 9.13   COORDINATING AND COMMUNICATING WITH THE TENANT

In the rush to implement segments of the maintenance management program, it is easy to overlook the tenants who must continue to operate their businesses while the maintenance work is being performed. Of most concern to the tenants are HVAC service and access to the property, the common areas, and the parking lot. A shopping center tenant's visibility is important to the store's sales volume. Blocking the store's visibility with equipment when reroofing or repairing a roof, for example, can be detrimental to the tenant's business.

Tenants should be given sufficient written notice of any maintenance that may disrupt or interrupt their business. Sealing a parking lot, core drilling, and major roof or HVAC repairs will disrupt the normal operations of a building and possibly its tenants. In the written notice, the property manager informs the tenants of the nature and timing of the work, why it is required, and how it might affect their day-to-day business operations.

Some maintenance work will require special consideration to avoid disruption. A shopping center parking lot cannot be sealed in one day without closing the entire lot. This can be avoided by dividing the lot into three sections, with each sealed in one day, allowing customer parking on two thirds of the lot and continual operation of the stores. Major HVAC repairs that require shutting down the system probably should be scheduled in the evenings, on weekends, or when the building is closed. The tenants are notified of the work and informed that it should be completed before the following business day. If the work isn't completed on time, the tenants will be aware of the problem and be more understanding.

One shopping center manager in southern California scheduled parking lot resurfacing over three days and notified the tenants of the work a month in advance. The supermarket manager called to tell the manager that the week scheduled was Easter week, one of the busiest weeks of the year. The manager rescheduled the work for the following week. If the property manager hadn't notified the tenants, the supermarket owner might have sued the property owner for loss of profit during those three days.

Tenants seldom object to the timing of maintenance work, and when they do their objections are usually valid. Of course, emergency maintenance must be handled on the spot. An effective maintenance management program will minimize the emergency situations.

§ 9.14 PROPERTY MANAGER'S AVAILABILITY

When the owner of a property transfers full operational management of the property to the property manager, he or she expects the manager or the staff to be available twenty-four hours a day, seven days a week, to respond to the needs of the property.

The property management company must have a twenty-four-hour answering service. An answering machine is unable to contact the manager, so it is totally unacceptable. The answering service is provided with a list of people to call for each property. The list is prioritized with the property manager heading the list and the names of other property managers and staff assistants following. All of the staff people on the list should be familiar with the property and be provided with the emergency phone list. The property manager should also be available through a paging system so that when an emergency arises after hours the property manager can be reached immediately.

§ 9.15 SNOW REMOVAL

An effective snow removal plan must be developed and implemented to provide a safe environment and to facilitate the tenants' business activities. A property without a snow removal program will have little or no control over that aspect of the budget and will be highly susceptible to accidents ranging from minor slips and falls to major automobile accidents. If customers avoid shopping at a center or other retail property because the parking lot and sidewalks are blocked with snow or ice, the merchants' sales will slump.

There are several steps in developing an effective snow removal plan. The first is to contract with a reliable snow removal contractor. Sweeping companies and construction contractors with earth moving equipment provide snow removal service to keep their equipment and workforce busy during the off season. When accepting bids, the property manager should carefully check the contractor's references and inquire whether the contractor's equipment is owned or rented. If the equipment is rented, is there a chance that the equipment would not be available when needed? Since damage frequently occurs during snow removal, the contractor must have adequate insurance. The contract fee can be negotiated based on an hourly rate, on the amount of snowfall, or on a flat rate per snow removal.

After selecting the contractor, the property manager should inspect the parking lot with the contractor. The purpose is twofold: to identify existing damage that can be either repaired or noted, thus protecting the contractor from blame after the snow season; and to identify curbs, signs, speed bumps, and other features that would be hidden under the snow and could be inadvertently damaged during snow removal. Many of these features will need to be identified with markers. In addition, drains will need to be located and marked so they can be cleared when the snow melts, and parking lanes may need to be marked as reference points.

It is not always necessary to remove snow from the entire parking lot. Many lots have areas that are seldom used. An office building with a high vacancy will use only a portion of the parking lot. A community or superregional mall will need the entire parking lot during the Christmas season but only a portion of it in January and February. The property manager analyzes the parking needs of the property, divides the lot into sections, and determines which sections must be kept clear of snow during which months.

Snow can be piled onto the sections of the lot that are not needed for parking. However, piling snow too high around the perimeter of a shopping center can block its visibility. These piles can become dirty and unsightly. As the snow melts, debris that surfaces must be removed. If the snow cannot be piled anywhere in the parking lot, the manager must obtain permission to use nearby vacant lots.

Be careful that the chemicals and salt used on the sidewalk and parking lot do not damage these areas or the lobby of the building when they are tracked inside. Sand and hot gravel are used on the parking lot to reduce its slickness and provide traction for cars. After the thaw, the lot will need a good spring cleanup to remove sand, gravel, and debris.

The snow removal budget is based on an average or slightly above average annual snowfall. An entire season's budget can be spent in one month, but a snow removal plan can minimize the chances of this occurring. Even when the entire budget is spent in a month or two, the property manager must continue to maintain a parking lot that is safe and has adequate parking for tenants, visitors, and customers.

§ 9.16 ROOFS

Few systems in a building causes more problems than roofs. If possible, have a set of the plans and specifications for the roof. Is it tar and gravel; is it built up with a cap sheet, rubber membrane, or shake? Each type of roof requires a different approach to repairs.

Traffic should be minimized on the roof. A roof holds up quite well if no one steps on a bubble or crushes something through the membrane. Special paths built into or onto the roof can be helpful, but workers often prefer the shortest path between two points, negating that precaution.

Roof penetrations are problems in the making and should be minimized. Television antennas, exhaust fan ducts, and satellite dishes can cause numerous problems. If they must be installed, a roofing contractor should properly seal the penetration. The lease should prohibit the tenant from installing equipment on the roof without the landlord's approval.

The roof should be carefully inspected twice a year and checked from time to time in between. Inspections should be performed before winter and again in the spring. Look for splits, bubbles, low spots, new penetrations, and blocked drains. The latter are easily cleaned by roto-rooter-type services. Select a qualified, reliable maintenance company and stay with it. This is one job that does not fare well when bid out each time a leak is found.

§ 9.17 ASPHALT PARKING LOTS

The second biggest problem in property management appears to be parking lots. Many were not properly installed originally and many have deteriorated because of poor care. Water and nonuse are two big enemies of asphalt parking lots. Good drainage is essential. Small cracks should be cleaned and sealed before water flows into the substructure and destroys the surface from below. Employee parking should be concentrated in seldom-used areas to keep them from deteriorating.

Annual inspections are a must and should be supplemented with more frequent checks for potential problems. Overlays and seal coatings can solve some minor problems and extend the life of the parking lot, but when the subsurface has broken down, the only answer is to remove and replace.

§ 9.18 LANDSCAPE MAINTENANCE

Landscaping is one of the most sophisticated systems in commercial properties. An attractive, well-planned system is very expensive to install, and its maintenance should not be trusted to neophytes. What is the watering schedule for each plant? When should the plants be fertilized and sprayed for insects? When is pruning and shaping necessary? Is the contractor knowledgeable enough to spot disease or infestation? Is the sprinkler system tested regularly or is it repaired only after breakdown? These are just a few concerns of a landscape maintenance program.

§ 9.19   HEATING, VENTILATING, AND AIR CONDITIONING

The property manager must develop maintenance specifications for the HVAC system, bid the work, and be willing to pay the price for quality maintenance. Nothing annoys a tenant more than being too cold in the winter or too hot in the summer.

§ 9.20   JANITORIAL MAINTENANCE

A good janitorial program starts with good janitorial specifications and a reliable company. The key to good janitorial service is supervision. The janitors must be supervised by the janitorial company, which in turn must be supervised by the property manager. In malls and medium- to high-rise office buildings, the manager should walk the building each week with the janitorial supervisor. A monthly walk-through is usually sufficient in neighborhood centers and low-rise or garden office buildings.

Bill Steele, president of American Building Maintenance Company, insists that contractors be screened thoroughly before they are invited to submit a proposal. In screening a contractor, the property manager should visit at least two of the contractor's present accounts, which pay a similar cost per square foot, in order to determine if their quality is at a level that meets the building's requirements. A visit to the contractor's business offices can also give the manager a sense of the cleaning company's professional capability to provide training to its hourly and supervisory employees.

A contractor's proposal should include not only specifications that have been previously agreed to, but the contractor's intended staffing and work load plans. Each contractor should also include a specific management plan for the cleaning services, the name and background of the project manager if the size of the job warrants such a position, and the amount of management time that would be devoted each month to smaller projects. In addition to reviewing the terms, conditions, and the operations plan, the property manager should compare the proposed service costs with a city industry average. Twenty percent below or above that average could indicate misunderstanding, misrepresentation, or a misbid.

After evaluating all of the contractors and bids, the manager can make an intelligent buying decision. Once a contractor is selected, two weeks should be allowed to ensure that all details about the property have been shared with its management, that crew assignments and work load plans have been established, that keys and other security clearances have been arranged, and that equipment and supplies have been purchased for delivery the day before the new contractor's term begins. Whenever possible, the contractor should supply its crews with their own equipment, and require janitors to wear ID badges and uniforms. Contractors also should be asked to submit a price for restroom supplies. If it is competitive, the contractor should order all restroom paper supplies and bill the building for actual supplies used each month.

The Building Service Contractors Association International has prepared a bulletin titled *How To Select a Building Contractor*. This bulletin defines three levels of cleaning standards.

- *Prestige Cleaning.* A cleaning standard that will provide unsolicited compliments from tenants, occupants, employees, or visitors, and one that will make the cleaning complaint a rarity.
- *Adequate Cleaning.* A standard that will provide neither compliments nor serious criticism. Some tenants will complain from time to time, but not to the point of threatening to seek other office space or not pay their rent.
- *Minimal Cleaning.* A standard that results in criticism from tenants, occupants, employees, and visitors. Complaints from tenants would be common, to the degree that some may threaten to move to another building. To retain tenants, periodic special cleanups are needed on heavy work.

In many buildings, different standards will be required for different areas or tenants.

§ 9.21   ELEVATOR AND ESCALATOR MAINTENANCE

This is the area most property managers know little about. Again, specifications must be developed and bid by several reliable companies. The manager needs to be assured that the service company has an adequate supply of parts on hand and has the staff to respond to emergencies and after-hour breakdowns.

§ 9.22   CONTRACT VS. EMPLOYEES

When establishing or evaluating a maintenance program, the property manager has to decide whether to contract the maintenance work, to provide an in-house maintenance staff, or to have a combination of both. Seldom can all maintenance be handled in house, so most managers either contract all maintenance or use a combination of in-house and contract service. Quite often local circumstances such as the size of the property and its proximity to other properties in the portfolio will influence who performs the maintenance work.

Contract services have the advantage of built-in supervision and a fixed price. If one of the contracted company's employees becomes ill, the contractor must find a replacement. Likewise, if the equipment breaks down and needs repair, the contractor must deal with it, not the property manager.

Technical knowledge is one of the main reasons to use contract services. It is unlikely that an in-house maintenance person can fill all of the property's maintenance needs, which will range from air-conditioning to roof repair to landscaping. By using contract services, the property manager can hire a specialist in the area needed, receive expert attention, and be billed accordingly.

The smaller the project, the more practical it is to use contract services. A 400,000-square-foot office can support staff specialists, but a 40,000-square-foot commercial property cannot. In addition, smaller projects generally do not have a secure place to store equipment. Owning equipment also means ongoing repairs, replacements, and insurance costs.

Finally, with contract services all the responsibilities of hiring, firing, training, and payroll administration are eliminated. Many in-house jobs in commercial properties are low paying, with a very high turnover. This can cause gaps in efficiency and productivity.

On the other hand, an in-house maintenance staff has several advantages. It is generally less expensive than hiring a contractor, and additional personnel are available for emergencies. For example, the landscape staff can be deployed to clean up a spill or barricade a dangerous area is the need arises.

One of the main advantages on an in-house staff is direct control. Maintenance personnel are a critical part of the management image, and an outside contractor who has no understanding of tenant relations at a specific property can make negative or inappropriate comments that could harm the tenant-management relationship. For example, an air-conditioning contractor might tell tenants that the units were cheap and no amount of work would make them function properly. On the other hand, the property manager can instruct the in-house staff in the importance of good tenant relations. And, with a minimum of training, the in-house staff can learn to handle tenant requests that are beyond the landlord's obligations.

If the property manager handles only smaller properties, it is possible to have an in-house staff that can cover a number of locations on a roving basis. Maintenance personnel with radio-equipped trucks can handle several properties and respond to most general emergencies.

When the property manager employs the maintenance personnel directly, it is a good idea to provide uniforms and identification. The uniform gives a more professional appearance at a fairly small cost.

The property manager must also monitor the work habits and behavior of maintenance people. In almost all commercial properties, most costs are billed back to the tenants. If tenants observe workers malingering, they may be reluctant to pay common area or escalation charges when billed. Judgment should also be used in hiring relatives for contract services or as employees since this can give the impression that the manager is taking care of a relative rather than obtaining the best service for the property.

§ 9.23 THE MAINTENANCE AGREEMENT

The final step in securing a maintenance contractor is negotiating a maintenance agreement. Usually the maintenance contractor provides an agreement designed to provide maximum protection to the contractor. The property manager should realize that almost everything in the maintenance agreement is negotiable. The terms that receive the most attention are: the length of the agreement, the fee, contractor's insurance requirement, indemnification or hold harmless clause, cancellation rights, and maintenance specifications.

Maintenance agreements are usually for one year; however, some of the major service contractors, such as elevator and HVAC contractors, will offer a discount for a longer term, such as five years. The cancellation right is essential. The property manager must have the right to terminate an agreement if the contractor does not perform. Also, the indemnification and hold harmless clause must be carefully reviewed to ensure that the property owner is not assuming needless or unwise liability.

An alternative is for the property manager to provide the maintenance agreement. This agreement, which will protect the property owner and the manager, is designed for nontechnical maintenance, such as janitorial, sweeping, and snow removal. As with the contractor's agreement, it is negotiable.

A carelessly negotiated maintenance agreement not only jeopardizes the quality of maintenance, but also exposes the property to potential maintenance problems and to liabilities that can be costly.

The maintenance agreements can be summarized on a form for quick reference. A sample maintenance agreement and a summary form are shown in Exhibits 9.7 and 9.8. The summary form provides a place to list

EXHIBIT 9.7

Maintenance Agreement

THIS MAINTENANCE AGREEMENT is made this _____ day of _____,
19_____, and between _____
(hereinafter referred to as the "Owner") and _____
(hereinafter referred to as the "Contractor").

WHEREAS, the Owner is the owner in fee or ground lessee of that certain real
property situated in _____ county,
_____, as more fully set
forth in the legal description thereof attached hereto and made a part
hereof as "Exhibit A" (hereinafter referred to as the "Property") which Property
is improved for commercial purposes (hereinafter referred to as the
_____); and
               (shopping center or office building)

WHEREAS, the Owner has employed _____,
a _____, (hereinafter referred to as the "Agent")
to provide the overall management and operation of the Property constructed
thereon; and

WHEREAS, the Owner desires to employ the Contractor as an independent
contractor, and the Contractor desires to accept such employment, for the purposes of providing the services set forth herein; and

WHEREAS, the Agent shall direct the performance and activities of the Contractor hereunder and be authorized to act for and on behalf of the Owner in all
respects;

NOW, THEREFORE, in consideration of the mutual terms and conditions
herein set forth and for other good and valuable consideration and receipt of
sufficiency of which is hereby acknowledged, the parties hereto hereby agree as
follows:

1. *Incorporation of Recitals.* The foregoing recitals are incorporated herein
as if set forth at length at this point.

2. *Employment and Work.* The Owner hereby appoints and hires the Contractor, as an independent contractor and not as an employee or an agent, and the
Contractor hereby accepts such employment as an independent contractor and
agrees to furnish and properly perform the necessary services, labor, and other
activities (hereinafter collectively referred to as the "Work") at the times and in
the manner with respect to the Property as is more completely set forth in the
Specifications of Work attached hereto and made a part hereof as "Exhibit B."
The Contractor agrees to furnish, at Contractor's sole cost and expense, all
necessary labor, materials, supplies, uniforms, equipment, and other materials
required to properly perform the Work. Contractor warrants that it has a sufficient number of qualified personnel, materials, and equipment to perform the
Work in a first-class manner.

3. *Term.* This Agreement shall commence on _____, 19_____,
and shall terminate at midnight on _____, 19_____, (which period
is referred to herein as the "Term"); provided that this Agreement may be terminated at any time during the Term hereof by Owner upon not less than ten (10)

EXHIBIT 9.7 *(Continued)*

day's written notice to Contractor, or by Contractor as of the last day of any calendar month during the Term hereof upon giving not less than thirty (30) days prior written notice to Owner. In the event of such determination, all payments due hereunder shall be prorated to the date of termination.

4. *Performance.* Contractor shall perform the Work on the days and at the times as set forth in the Specifications of Work attached hereto; provided, that the hours of completion at the Work are subject to such changes as Owner may direct from time to time. The Work shall not be performed on days or at times other than set forth in the Specifications of Work without the Owner's prior written consent. Contractor shall at all times perform the Work in a first-class, professional manner and to the satisfaction of Owner.

5. *Fee.* The Owner shall pay Contractor for the Work the sum of $_____ (hereinafter referred to as the "Fee") per month, in arrears, on the last day of each month provided said sum is substantiated by the job verifications described in Exhibit "B", the Specifications of Work.

6. *Risk of Loss.* The Contractor, at its sole cost and expense, shall bear the risk of loss to all equipment used to perform the Work where such loss arises by reason of fire, theft, vandalism, negligence, or any other cause whatsoever, excluding, however, any loss directly caused by the negligence of Owner, its employees or agents. Contractor, at its sole cost and expense, shall forthwith replace or repair any lost, stolen, or damaged equipment.

7. *Maintenance of Equipment.* The Contractor at its sole cost and expense, shall maintain all of its equipment in good working and serviceable order so as to enable it to perform the Work in a first-class and professional manner and a failure in this regard shall constitute a material breach of this Agreement.

8. *Storage.* The Contractor shall neither store any supplies, equipment, or materials nor permit any equipment to be left on the Property without the prior written consent of Owner.

9. *Notices.* All notices required or desired to be given under Agreement shall be given in person or served upon the parties hereto by certified mail, postage prepaid, return receipt requested, and addressed to Owner as follows:

        c/o TRF Management Corporation
        12400 SE 38th Street
        P.O. Box 5727
        Bellevue, WA 98006-5727

and if to the Contractor

or such other place or places as may be provided in writing from time to time.

10. *Attorney's Fees.* In the event litigation is filed to enforce any of the provisions of this Agreement or by reason of a breach hereof by a party, the prevailing party shall be entitled to recover all attorney's fees as well as costs and expenses as may be granted in such litigation.

EXHIBIT 9.7 *(Continued)*

11. *Compliance with Law.* The Contractor, at its sole cost and expense, shall comply with all federal, state, and local statutes, laws, ordinances, executive orders, rules, and regulations applicable to it, the Work, its employees and to the use of its equipment and; further, the Contractor at its sole cost and expense shall procure and maintain in full force and effect any and all necessary permits and licenses and shall pay all fees or charges in connection therewith together with all worker's compensation and union benefits, if any, applicable to its employees. The Contractor, at its sole cost and expense, shall pay in a timely manner all taxes, assessments and charges of every nature whatsoever levied upon Contractor's equipment, its use or operation.

12. *Assignment.*

(a) *No Assignment by Contractor.* It is specifically understood and agreed that this Agreement is personal to the Contractor and shall not be assigned by Contractor without the prior written consent of Owner, which consent, if given, shall be subject to such conditions as may be deemed appropriate by the Owner. Any such assignment, without the Owner's permission shall, at the option of the Owner, be null and void and deemed a material breach of this Agreement.

(b) *Assignment By Owner.* The Owner may assign this Agreement without the consent or approval of the Contractor.

(c) *Binding Nature.* Upon any valid assignment of this Agreement, the terms and conditions hereof shall inure to and be binding upon the successors and assigns of the parties hereto.

13. *Use of Name.* The Contractor shall not use the name of the Owner, Agent, or any of their affiliates or the Property in any sign, advertisement, or written communication without the prior written consent of Owner or Agent as may be appropriate.

14. *No Waiver.* The failure of the Owner to seek redress for violation of, or to insist upon the strict performance of, any term, covenant, condition, provision, or agreement contained in this Agreement shall not prevent any subsequent act or failure on the part of the Contractor which would have originally constituted a violation from having all the force and effect of an original violation and the failure of the Owner to enforce any of the terms, covenants, conditions, provisions, or agreements contained in this Agreement shall not be deemed a waiver of any of said terms, covenants, conditions, provisions, or agreements. No provisions of the Agreement shall be deemed to have been waived by Owner unless such waiver shall be in writing signed by Owner.

15. *Entire Agreement.* This Agreement contains the entire agreement and understanding between the parties and recites the entire consideration given and accepted by the parties.

16. *Amendment.* Any modification, change of amendment hereafter made relating hereto shall be ineffective to change, modify, waive, amend, or discharge this Agreement in whole or in part unless such subsequent agreement is in writing and signed by the party against whom enforcement of the change, modification, amendment, waiver, or discharge is sought. All provisions of this Agreement shall remain in full force and effect throughout the term hereof.

EXHIBIT 9.7 *(Continued)*

17. *Insurance and Indemnity.*

(A) *Insurance Coverage.* The Contractor shall at its sole cost and expense maintain the following insurance covering every aspect of the work to be done and operations described in this Agreement during the entire Term:

(1) Worker's Compensation Insurance in accordance with Law and Employer's liability insurance with limits of not less than $1,000,000;

(2) Comprehensive General Liability Insurance including Broad Form Contractual Liability and Completed Operations Insurance with the following limits of liability.

(i) Coverage for personal injury to or death of one or more persons, with a single limit of not less than $1,000,000 per occurrence (which insurance shall additionally include, but shall not be limited to, coverage in the event of false arrest, libel, slander, assault, battery, and invasion of the right of privacy);

(ii) Coverage for injury to or destruction or loss of property of others with a single limit of not less than $1,000,000 per occurrence (including but not limited to theft or vandalism or malicious mischief perpetrated by any person including, without limitation, any servant, agent, representative, or employee of the Contractor);

(3) Complete Automobile Liability Insurance containing personal injury, death, and property damage coverage with a single limit of not less than $1,000,000 per occurrence;

(4) Broad form Fidelity Bond Insurance in limits of not less than $50,000 per occurrence covering all servants, employees, agents, and representatives of the Contractor.

(B) *Original Policies.* All insurance shall be written only as original policies and shall be placed only with companies of recognized repute. Each policy shall name as additional named insured the Owner and the Agent.

(C) *Delivery of Certificate of Insurance.* Said certificate of insurance shall be delivered by the Contractor to the Owner at least thirty (30) days before the commencement of the term of this Agreement, or before the Contractor first commences performance hereunder, whichever is earlier, or at such other times as the Owner may direct. Renewal policies of said insurance shall be delivered by the Contractor to the Owner at least thirty (30) days prior to the expiration date of each of such policies. Should the Contractor fail to deliver such Certificate of Insurance within the time aforesaid, the Owner may, at its option, procure such insurance and pay the premiums therefore, in which case the Contractor shall reimburse Owner for the cost thereof on the first day of the calendar month following the delivery of the bill or bills therefore, or the Owner may deduct the cost of insurance from the Contractor's fees. Each Certificate of Insurance shall name as additional named insured the Owner and the Agent.

(D) *Termination.* Each of the policies of insurance required hereunder shall provide that the same may not be terminated or modified in any material respect unless at least thirty (30) days' prior written notice by registered mail shall have been given to the Owner. The Contractor agrees to notify the Owner at least thirty (30) days prior to the expiration date if any policy of insurance is, for

EXHIBIT 9.7 *(Continued)*

any reason, not to be renewed upon precisely the same basis as the preceding policy. Each policy shall name the Owner and its agent as an additional named insured. The Contractor assumes complete responsibility for its materials and equipment and relieves each of such indemnified persons of any liability whatsoever in connection with such materials and equipment, whether arising from theft, loss, damage, or otherwise.

(E) *Indemnity.*

(i) Subject to the provisions of Section 17 (E) (ii) below, in addition to all of the foregoing, the Contractor shall completely indemnify and defend (or cause its insurance companies to completely defend) the Owner and agent (and their respective employees, agents, officers, directors, and partners) promptly and diligently, at its or their sole cost and expense, against any claim, action, loss, damage, injury, or expense (including attorney's fees) or proceeding brought, incurred, or claimed by any person against Owner and/or agent with respect to any and all of the matters referred to in this Agreement (including but not limited to liability imposed by law or by breach of any statutory duty of administrative rule or regulation, false arrest, libel, slander, death, or injury to person or destruction of or damage to property, the refusal or failure of Contractor to perform its obligations hereunder or otherwise) and the Contractor shall pay, upon the demand of any insured party, any and all attorney's fees, costs, and other charges incurred by any of the insured parties to be afforded insurance or indemnity protections pursuant to this Agreement in the event the Contractor fails to give such a complete defense.

(ii) Notwithstanding Section 17(E) (i) above, in the event of concurrent negligence of Contractor, its agents, employees, sublessee, invitees, licensees, or contractors on the one hand, and that of Owner, its partners, directors, officers, agents, employees, lessees, sublessee, licensees, invitees, or contractors (other than the Contractor) on the other hand, which concurrent negligence results in injury or damage to persons or property and relates to the construction, alteration, repair, addition to, subtraction from, improvement to, or maintenance of the Property, or any improvements thereto, Contractor's obligation to indemnify Owner as set forth in Section 17(E) (i) above shall be limited to the extent of Contractor's negligence, and that of its agents, employees, invitees, licensees or contractors, including all fees and expenses incurred by Contractor, its agents, employees, invitees, licensees and contractors, in connection with any claim, action or proceeding brought with respect to such injury or damage. Contractor hereby agrees to waive its immunity under industrial insurance.

18. *Subrogation.* Contractor agrees that in no event will any right of subrogation be asserted against any of the insured parties to be afforded insurance or indemnity protection for any damage, loss of injury, whether arising from negligence or otherwise.

19. *Hazardous Substances.*

(a) *Presence and Use of Hazardous Substances.* Subcontractor shall not, without Owner's prior written consent, keep on or around the Premises and Common Areas, for use, disposal, treatment, generation, storage or sale any substances, wastes, or materials designated as, or containing components designated as hazardous, dangerous, toxic, or harmful and/or which are subject to

EXHIBIT 9.7 *(Continued)*

regulation by any federal, state, or local law, regulation, statute, or ordinance. With respect to any such Hazardous Substance, Contractor shall.

(i)   Comply promptly, timely, and completely with all governmental requirements for reporting, keeping and submitting manifests, and obtaining and keeping current identification numbers;

(ii)   Submit to Agent true and correct copies of all reports, manifests, and identification numbers at the same time as they are required to be and/or are submitted to the appropriate governmental authorities;

(iii)   Within five (5) days of Agent's request, submit written reports to Agent regarding Contractor's use, storage, treatment, transportation, generation, disposal, or sale of Hazardous Substances and provide evidence satisfactory to Agent of Contractor's compliance with the applicable government regulations;

(iv)   Allow Agent or Agent's representative to come on the area in which Contractor is working or which is covered by this Contract at all times to check Contractor's compliance with all applicable governmental regulations regarding Hazardous Substances:

(v)   Comply with minimum levels, standards, or other performance standards or requirements which may be set forth or established for certain Hazardous Substances (if minimum standards or levels are applicable to Hazardous Substances present on the property or any part thereof, such levels or standards shall be established by an on-site inspection by the appropriate governmental authorities and shall be set forth in an addendum to this Contact); and

(vi)   Comply with all applicable governmental rules, regulations, and requirements regarding the proper and lawful use, sale, transportation, generation, treatment, and disposal of Hazardous Substances.

Any and all costs incurred by Agent or Owner and associated with Agent or Owner's inspection of the property and Agent's monitoring of Contractor's compliance with this Section, including Agent's and/or Owner's attorneys' fees and costs, shall be due and payable by Contractor upon demand by Agent and/or Owner.

(b)   *Cleanup Costs, Default and Indemnification.*

(i)   Contractor shall be fully and completely liable to Agent and Owner for any and all cleanup costs, and any and all other charges, fees, penalties (civil and criminal) imposed by any governmental authority with respect to Contractor's use, disposal, transportation, generation, and/or sale of Hazardous Substances, in or about the property.

(ii)   Contractor shall indemnify, defend, and save Agent and Owner, and their respective officers, directors, shareholders, and employees, harmless from any and all of the costs, fees, penalties, and charges assessed against or imposed upon Agent and/or Owner (as well as Agent's and/or Owner's attorneys' fees and costs) as a result of Contractor's use, disposal, transportation, generation, and/or sale of Hazardous Substances.

(iii)   Upon Contractor's default under this Section, in addition to the rights and remedies set forth elsewhere in this Contract, Agent shall be entitled to the following rights and remedies:

(A)   At Agent's option, to terminate this Contract immediately; and/or

EXHIBIT 9.7 *(Continued)*

(B) To recover any and all damages associated with the default, including, but not limited to, cleanup costs and charges, civil and criminal penalties and fees, loss of business by Agent and/or Owner and by tenants in the property, any and all damages and claims asserted by third parties, and Agent's and/or Owner's attorneys' fees and costs.

20. *Binding Nature.* This Agreement shall be binding upon the parties hereto, their successors and assigns.

21. *Law.* This Agreement shall be interpreted pursuant to the laws of the State in which the Property is located.

22. *Agent.* It is specifically understood and agreed that the Owner has employed the Agent to provide overall management and operation services with respect to the Property. The Agent has the right and authority to speak for and bind the Owner on all matters covered by this Agreement.

IN WITNESS WHEREOF, the parties hereto have caused this instrument to be executed by their duly authorized representatives the day and year first above written.

OWNER:

_____

_____

By its Agent:

By: _____

CONTRACTOR

_____

_____

_____

_____

EXHIBIT 9.8

Maintenance/Service Contracts

VENDOR		NO.	TYPE OF SERVICE	PROJECT	BILLING AMOUNT			TERM			EXPENSE CODE		MISC.
					Annual	$/S.F.	Monthly	Length	Start	End	Project # —	Acct. #	

the most frequent terms and conditions of the agreement, such as fee, expiration date, and frequency of service.

§ 9.24   CONTRACTOR'S INSURANCE

Today, to be fully protected in our litigious society, contractors must carry full insurance coverage. Most contracts require the contractor to hold the following coverage:

1. **Worker's Compensation.**   The contractor should be required to meet the state minimums.
2. **Liability Insurance.**   Generally, $1 million in coverage is adequate, but the actual limit should be commensurate with risks involved in the job.
3. **Automobile Liability.**   Almost every contractor comes onto the property in a truck or car. That vehicle should be insured for liability.
4. **Fidelity Bond.**   Any contractor who works inside tenant spaces should have a fidelity bond in a minimum amount of $50,000.
5. **False Arrests and Invasion of Privacy.**   Security companies should be requested to have these coverages.

The contractor should provide the owner with certificates of insurance to evidence each required coverage. The property owner and the management company should be named insured, and the certificate should provide for ten days' advance notice before cancellation. If appropriate, the fee manager should also be named insured on the contractor's policy. These named insured endorsements are usually issued at no additional charge in most markets and can be obtained in a matter of hours.

§ 9.25   NEGOTIATING TIPS

There are very few shortcuts in the maintenance of commercial properties. The fact that many of the expenses are passed along to the tenants emphasizes the need to receive value for the money spent. The best way to do this is to bid larger jobs. Handymen are often less expensive than contractors, but only if they are properly insured and know how to do the job at hand. Preventive maintenance, when properly done, will extend the life of the system and reduce breakdowns. Below are some more suggestions to help the manager maintain an efficient and cost-effective maintenance program.

- Always provide bidding contractors with a very specific description of what is to be done. If they want to suggest other methods, have those items quoted separately.
- Have as much included in the initial contract as possible because changes are usually much higher than comparable items included in the basic proposal.
- Consider buying parts such as ballasts, filters, or bulbs and having them installed. Quite often the cost will be considerably less than the contractor's price. On the other hand, a national janitorial contractor might sell you these items at wholesale prices.
- Combine contracts when possible. In small projects it often pays to have the landscape people sweep the lot, replace damaged signs, and remove graffiti.
- Require a twenty-four-hour-a-day, seven-day-a-week emergency number from all contractors. Problems that require immediate response can happen at all hours.
- Where possible, select contractors fairly close to the properties. This eliminates travel time and allows for quick response in an emergency.
- Find out if contractors have any talents or abilities beyond their specialty. Quite often a person on the job can handle other small tasks negating the need to bring in someone else.
- When negotiating an elevator contract, obtain a light-load credit for low occupancy. For instance, if the building is 60% occupied, a 15% credit may be obtained. The credit is a sliding discount based on occupancy.
- When negotiating a music contract for an office building, request that the tenant provide free music service in the common areas. This savings is passed on to the tenants in lower escalation costs.

§ 9.26 SOURCES OF MAINTENANCE INFORMATION

The following publications offer good sources of maintenance information:

Heintzelman, John E. *The Complete Handbook of Maintenance Management.* Englewood Cliffs, N.J.: Prentice-Hall, Inc., 1976.
Henderson, John K., William J. Hartnett, and Phil Skatkun. *The Handbook of HVAC Systems for Commercial Buildings.* Arnold, Md.: Building Owners and Managers Institute International, 1982.
Management Insights, published quarterly by American Building Maintenance Industries, San Francisco.

§ 9.27   CONCLUSION

When the property management profession was in its early stages, the property manager's responsibilities were limited to rent collection and maintenance. Through the changing needs of ownership, the competitive nature of real estate, and changes in the consumer laws, the property manager's responsibilities have expanded to include many specialties. However, maintenance is still one of the most basic and important responsibilities of the property manager. Maintenance costs are part of the expense side of the NOI equation. An effective and efficient maintenance management program will reduce expenses and minimize increases, thus enhancing the value of the property.

Ten

Emergency Procedures

§ 10.1 INTRODUCTION

Disasters and emergencies are a regular occurrence in our society. For the property manager, it is not a matter of whether an incident will occur but *when* it will happen and what kind it will be. Generally, disasters or emergencies can be classified as either natural or man-made.

The National Weather Bureau is often able to give advance warning for natural disasters such as hurricanes, tornadoes, and floods, but other catastrophes, such as earthquakes, are not as easily predicted. When Mount St. Helens erupted in May 1980, little was known about the effects of a major volcanic eruption, leaving property managers inadequately prepared in the aftermath. Now scientists can often predict when a volcano will erupt, and property managers can be ready for its effects.

Man-made emergencies usually catch the property manager unaware. Arson, vandalism, theft, random shootings, hostage taking, assaults, and medical emergencies all come without warning. Bombings may be an exception, but information prior to a bombing is often sketchy and unpredictable.

The property manager and his or her staff must be prepared to respond to any emergency. Emergency procedures can be written to address the known disaster. Such a model plan will provide a basic frame of reference for the unexpected.

This chapter will provide the property manager with information on how to develop an emergency procedures plan for a commercial building. These suggestions will need to be tailored to the specific needs and unique character of each building.

§ 10.2   DETERMINING POTENTIAL EMERGENCIES

Before preparing an emergency plan for a building, the property manager must determine likely disasters and emergencies that could occur in the building's area. For example, a property manager in California will prepare for earthquakes, not tornadoes. However, if a tornado did hit the area, the basic emergency procedures would provide a frame of reference for responding to such a disaster.

To determine likely disasters and emergencies, the area and the building must be analyzed. First, probable natural disasters must be specified. Most people already know if their area is prone to earthquakes, floods, forest fires, hurricanes, or tornadoes. The weather bureau can provide further information on the history of any natural disasters in the area.

Next the sociopolitical climate must be assessed. Is the building in a city with civil unrest, radical groups, or activists prone to picketing and unruly demonstrations? Are bombings a distinct possibility? Response to any such disturbances will become a major component in the building's emergency procedures plan.

The building itself must be evaluated for emergency potential. First, the tenant mix is reviewed. Embassies, government offices, and international corporations are all likely targets of bomb threats, picketing, or civil disturbance. Children and handicapped persons require special consideration in the building's emergency procedures.

The building's type of construction is another factor. Is it a wood frame, concrete tilt-up, or steel building? Does it have a fire sprinkler system? What are its life safety features? Is it vertical or horizontal? What is the building's size, and how many people work and visit there? In the event of a bomb threat a fifty-story office building with 5,000 employees will require a far different plan than a two-story walk-up.

Location is another factor in developing an emergency procedures plan. Is the building in an area where there is adequate police and fire protection? Does the fire department have the equipment and training to respond promptly to any type of emergency? Is the building in a congested downtown area with access to only one side of the building? What are the adjacent buildings? Can they be used if the building had to be evacuated? Could the police or fire department use an adjacent building as a command station? What is the building's proximity to police, fire, and medical assistance?

§ 10.3   DEVELOPING THE EMERGENCY TEAM

Either the on-site management team or, in the case of a commercial building without on-site personnel, the property manager and staff in the management company's central office will respond to an emergency. Additional people outside the property management staff may be called, depending on the nature and extent of the emergency.

The property manager needs to develop and train two response teams. The first team consists of the property manager and staff; the second consists of any people or government agencies that have specialized skills needed in an emergency.

The number of persons on the primary team—those who respond to every emergency—depends on the size of the building. In a high-rise office building, regional mall, or a large mixed-use development, the team will consist of the property manager and administrative support staff, maintenance, and security personnel. For a small strip center managed from the company's central office, the team will be the property manager and secretary. No matter what the size of the property, all personnel involved in the day-to-day management need to be trained to respond to any emergency.

The second team includes anyone who provides expert support services for the property management staff. Heading the list are the police and fire departments, which will be called upon for every emergency. Utility company representatives may be needed to shut off or turn on service to the building.

The building's contractors need to be ready to respond to an emergency. The janitorial firm often is called on to provide cleanup immediately after an emergency. The security company may be asked to provide additional security during and after the emergency. The HVAC and elevator contractors may be needed to shut down, repair, or start up their equipment. Specific maintenance contractors, such as electricians, plumbers, and painters, will be needed to restore the property after the emergency. Other contractors are employed as the occasion warrants. A glass company, a company that removes smoke or other odors, and an equipment rental firm are three resources that may be called when an emergency occurs.

The property manager develops a list of all companies that could play a supporting role in an emergency. The list of cooperating firms will include complete phone information—after-hours numbers are very important—and contact persons. This information is kept for easy access in the property's project data book and in the property manager's emergency procedures handbook.

The building's and management company's insurance agents and attorneys may be called upon in an emergency. Also, depending on the building, the tenants may be included on the emergency team. Mid- and high-rise buildings frequently use tenants' employees as floor captains and in other responsible positions during an emergency.

Property managers in adjacent buildings may coordinate and assist during an emergency. For example, during a building evacuation, the tenants may be moved to an adjacent building's garage, or the adjoining building may be used as a command post or staging area for police, fire department, or contractors.

Although property owners are seldom involved directly in the action taken during most emergencies, they must be considered an integral part of the team. They need to be informed immediately of the emergency and the activity of the property manager and emergency teams. If the emergency is prolonged, such as a hostage taking, or requires extensive action or restoration afterwards, the property owner will probably take an active position and possibly a leading role in evaluating the situation and making decisions.

§ 10.4   TRAINING THE EMERGENCY TEAM

All members of the emergency team, whether on site or at the central office, must be trained to respond to an emergency. When a commercial property has no on-site personnel, the property manager, support staff, and personnel responsible for the building's maintenance should walk the property to become familiar with the building and the parking lot. A map is prepared indicating the location of shutoff valves, electrical panels, and fire equipment. A copy of the map should be posted on site, possibly in a maintenance or storage room, and included in the project data book.

The staff in the central property management office will need special training for bomb threats, a building evacuation, and any other emergencies that could occur when they are not on site to direct the response. When the property management staff are not on site, they will be more dependent on members of the second emergency team for assistance.

On-site staff at a commercial property can respond to every emergency that occurs during the hours the building is staffed. Each person can be assigned a specific responsibility, depending on the emergency.

For example, when the staff of a large suburban mixed-use development in southern California received a bomb threat, they were ready to carry out their assigned responsibilities. As soon as the receptionist received the threat she immediately notified the property manager and called the police. The property manager then went to the tenant who had received the threat and conducted a search of the premises with the tenant, looking for suspicious or unfamiliar objects, such as, briefcases, or equipment. The day porters and maintenance personnel

searched their assigned common areas, the stairwells, restrooms, closets, and outside the building. The security guard prevented anyone
from entering the building. Additional security personnel were called
in to assist in keeping people away from the building. The building
engineer reserved an elevator for possible use by the police and fire
departments. The assistant property manager waited for the police department and escorted officers to the suite where the bomb threat was
received. Day porters served as runners between personnel, since using
a walkie-talkie might have triggered an explosive. The property manager's secretary documented action taken during the incident.

Each person in the above scenario had an assigned duty to carry out.
There was no panic, and business was resumed when the threat proved
false. If the property manager had elected to evacuate all or part of the
building, a different procedure would have been enacted.

Regardless of the size of the property and its staff, everyone must be
trained to carry out his or her assigned responsibilities. Training begins
by walking the building, reviewing the emergency procedures handbook, and becoming familiar with the use of the building's life safety
equipment. In addition, the property manager should invite the police
and fire departments to meet periodically with the building's staff to review specific emergency roles and to conduct practice drills in the building. The drills can be held in the evening or on weekends and should
include the entire building's staff.

Tenants' employees and visitors to the building are the primary concern of the building's management during an emergency. The tenants'
employees need to be instructed on emergency procedures. Their training starts before the tenant takes occupancy, when the property manager
meets with each office manager and reviews the tenants' handbook and
emergency procedures. The property manager or another staff member
should walk the building with the tenants' employees to show them the
stairs, the exits, and other basic features of the building. Regular training sessions can be conducted periodically for new employees. Police
and fire department representatives lend credibility to the training sessions and provide valuable information.

Special consideration needs to be given to handicapped people who
work in the building. The management office should have a list of handicapped employees, the nature of their handicap, and where they are
located in the building. This list should be given to those responding to
an emergency situation.

In multistory office buildings, employees of the tenants will become
members of the emergency team. Some municipalities require that every floor of the building have a floor captain, an assistant floor captain,
a person instructed in first aid, and a person responsible for the handicapped on that floor. These team members need additional training
and must be replaced immediately if they move out of the building. In

some buildings it is difficult to find volunteers for these positions, and the property manager must impress upon the tenants the necessity of having people fill these emergency roles.

Another group to train is the building's contractors. They, especially the janitors and the security guard(s), spend most of their time in the building when the property management staff is gone and the building is closed. These people need to know how to contact the property manager and the building's staff, what to do when an alarm goes off, and how to respond to any emergency. Since there may be a high turnover of janitorial and security personnel, their supervisor must be prepared to train new employees. If any of the maintenance personnel do not speak English the training should be in their native language.

§ 10.5   EVALUATION AFTER AN EMERGENCY

An emergency, even a false alarm, is an intense experience. Therefore, it is important for the property manager to debrief the team after the emergency and evaluate everyone's actions. This is also an opportune time to critique the building's emergency procedures. A plan that appears to be superb on paper may not work during the actual emergency.

The evaluation should be conducted as soon after the emergency as possible. The building's staff may still be on emotional overload, and simply talking about the event will help to calm people down. Police and fire department personnel and contractors can be included in the meeting, or they can meet separately with selected building staff. The evaluation should start with a review of what actually happened during the emergency. To relieve anxiety about performance, feedback on specific positive behavior should be given to each person. Participants should share suggestions for improvement. If any changes to the emergency procedures are required, they should immediately be implemented and the staff instructed on the revised procedures and practiced if appropriate.

§ 10.6   SECURITY

The security needs for buildings will vary, depending upon the type of building, the tenant mix, the community's involvement in the building, the location, and the physical characteristics of the building. In some structures, such as mid- to high-rise office buildings, a security program is designed to control ingress and egress to the building. In a regional mall, on the other hand, a security program will create a safe and pleasant shopping experience for customers. In many areas of the country, the security needs of neighborhood centers, industrial properties, and garden office buildings are handled adequately by the local police force. However, the property manager cannot assume that a commercial building in the suburbs will not need security or that a building cannot afford security. A building can never *not* afford to have adequate security.

A security program can take many forms, including on-site security guards, a drive-by security patrol, electronic devices such as closed-circuit television (CCTV), and card access control. Security can be enhanced by training maintenance personnel and tenants to be aware of suspicious people, using maintenance personnel to open and lock the building, and coordinating a program with the local police department. Lighting is one of the most important components of a good security program. The common areas, both inside and outside the building, need to be checked regularly in the evening for burned out lights, dimly lit areas, and areas that are hidden by shrubbery.

The tenants should be encouraged to report any suspicious people, loiterers, or abandoned vehicles to the property manager. The manager can schedule a meeting with the tenants and the police to review theft and shoplifting prevention. Prior to the Christmas season and periodically throughout the year, the property manager can send a security awareness letter like the one shown in Exhibit 10.1 to all tenants.

The maintenance personnel, whether employees of the property management company or contracted, should also be a part of the building's security awareness program. The more eyes and ears the building has, the more secure it will be.

When security guards are used in a building, they become the frontline defense in reducing risks. Frequently, the guard is the only person in the building after hours and must respond correctly to fire alarms, power outages, earthquakes, or trespassers. The wrong action or no action at all can cause serious fire damage, theft loss, harm to computer equipment, or even injury to the guard.

The property manager must determine whether to contract security or develop an in-house security staff. American Building Maintenance Industries lists the following advantages and disadvantages of contracting security service and developing a proprietary security force.

Advantages of Contract Security Services

1. **Selectivity.** Employer retains only those personally approved.
2. **Flexibility.** More or fewer personnel, as required.
3. **Absenteeism.** Replacement of absentees on short notice.
4. **Supervision.** Supplied at no additional cost to the client.
5. **Training.** Supplied at no additional cost to client, may be superior to in-house training program.
6. **Objectivity.** Judgment not clouded by personalities.

EXHIBIT 10.1

Security Awareness Letter

November 17, 1989   In Reply Refer To:

Dear Tenant:

The following procedures should be followed throughout the year, but more specifically, with the holiday shopping season approaching, there will be more money carried by individuals and more purses and packages left on desks in your building.

Many of our tenants have trained their office personnel to observe the following suggestions and have thereby reduced or eliminated losses of personal and company property:

1. Valuables such as women's purses should never be left unattended, even in areas where visitors seldom go, and especially in the reception room. Never leave a purse on the floor underneath the desk or on top of a file cabinet—put them out of sight.
2. In the office, after a noontime shopping spree, do not leave the packages exposed, but place them in a cabinet or drawer.
3. All visitors, including messengers and delivery personnel, should be watched while on your premises. It is better to escort them to inner offices or work areas rather than simply directing them.
4. Special care should be taken during the times most suited for pilferage—30 minutes just after opening and before closing—when there is maximum movement from work areas and offices.
5. Thorough investigation of prospective employees' backgrounds will help eliminate potential threats before loss occurs.
6. Locks should be changed after the discharge of any employees who have had keys or access to keys, as should safe combinations. If business keys are lost, change the lock. All rekeying must be done through the building office for control.
7. Personnel carrying keys to the premises should never have any identifying tags on their key rings, since loss of a key ring would enable a dishonest finder to locate and use business keys to gain illegal entry.
8. If personnel carrying keys park in garages that require leaving keys in the auto ignition, they should leave only the car keys. Duplicates can readily be made from other keys on the ring.

EXHIBIT 10.1 *(Continued)*

9. Never leave the reception area unattended with the room unlocked. Extra care should be taken regarding small items such as radios, pocket calculators, pen and desk ornaments—these are usually of special attraction. Use caution and do not leave such items unattended.
10. Checkbooks and other valuable corporate property should be kept under lock and key when not in use.
11. Avoid giving keys to outsiders for special deliveries or for early or late arrival for special purposes.
12. If your firm plans to close for a special holiday or plans an early closing on a particular day, notify the post office or building superintendent to discontinue deliveries. A stack of undelivered items outside the door is a sure tip-off that the premises are unoccupied.
13. Serial numbers of all items should be recorded to aid police in recovering property in the event of loss or theft.
14. Report immediately to the building management any strangers seen loitering in the building.
15. Should a loss of any equipment or valuables occur, and after you have reported same to the police and insurance company, please advise the building manager as well.
16. Last but certainly not least, if you have an office party, be very careful when driving. IF YOU DRINK, DON'T DRIVE. Leave the driving to someone else.

May we extend our best wishes to you for a Merry Christmas and a Happy New Year!

Sincerely,

TRF MANAGEMENT CORPORATION

Richard F. Muhlebach
President

RFM/nw

7. **Cost.** Generally 20% less than in-house, not counting administrative savings (e.g., insurance, retirement pension, social security, medical care).

8. **Quality.** May be of higher caliber than an in-house officer.

9. **Administration and Budgeting.** Brunt borne by security company.

10. **Variety of Services and Equipment.** Security company may be specialists in various criminal justice skills or provide expensive equipment unavailable to home security.

11. **Hiring and Screening Costs.** Borne by security company.

12. **Better Local Law Enforcement Contacts.** May know more law enforcement personnel.

13. **Sharing Expertise and Knowledge.** May have developed security skills, as a result of many jobs, that can be shared with a client.

Disadvantages of Contract Security Services

1. **Turnover.** Extremely high industrywide.

2. **Divided Loyalties.** Serving-two-masters quandary.

3. **Moonlighting.** Low salary for officers may force them into secondary jobs, resulting in tired and unalert personnel.

4. **Reassignment.** Some agencies send in the best men at inception of contract and then replace with others as new contracts open.

5. **Screening Standards.** May be inadequate.

6. **Insurance.** Determine liability and ensure individual officers are bonded and insured.

Advantages of Proprietary Security Forces

1. **Loyalty.** A positive quality.

2. **Incentive.** Promotion possibilities within the entire company structure.

3. **Knowledge.** Of operation, products, personnel of the company because of permanent employment.

4. **Tenure.** Can be specifically geared to the job performed.

5. **Control.** Stays inside company structure.

6. **Supervision.** Stays inside company structure.

7. **Training.** Can be specifically geared to the job performed.

8. **Company Image.** May become a status symbol.

9. **Morale.** A hoped-for state maintained by security manager.

10. **Courtesy.** Can render courtesies to VIPs because of familiarity with company personnel.
11. **Better Law Enforcement Liaison.** Security manager can informally develop law enforcement liaison with less conflict.
12. **Selection.** Company selection procedures apply.
13. **Better Communication.** More direct.

Disadvantages of Proprietary Security Forces

1. **Familiarity.** May become too familiar with personnel to be effective on job.
2. **Cost.** Expensive (salary, benefits, workmen's compensation, social security, liability insurance, work space, equipment, training).
3. **Flexibility.** Hard to replace absent personnel.
4. **Administrative Burdens.** Must develop an upper-level staff to handle these personnel.[1]

When evaluating a professional security company with properly trained guards, the following twelve points should be considered:

To Make an Informed Choice of a
Contract Security Service

1. Check the background and experience of the contractor's firm, including the specific experience of the management staff.
2. Ask for a list of past and present clients.
3. Review the evaluation process which will be applied to analyzing your needs.
4. Review the minimum personnel standards the contractor maintains.
5. Establish that the contractor has formal and periodic training of personnel.
6. Assure that the contractor has supervisory personnel in each locality where business is solicited.
7. Assure that the contractor can provide the multiple services you may need.
8. Establish the contractor's relationship with local law enforcement agencies.
9. Establish that the contractor has adequate insurance to protect you.

[1] *Mgmt. Insights,* (Spring 1983).

10. Establish that the contractor is licensed and bonded, as required by law.

11. Review the reporting procedures which are used to keep clients informed.

12. Assure yourself that you will be able to gain free information on costs of specific services.[2]

Another criterion in evaluating security guards is salary and benefits. The salary levels are one of the major determining factors in the quality of the security personnel. When negotiating a security contract, the guards' salaries and salary adjustments can be stated in the contract.

An alternative to a contract service or a proprietary security force is to contract police officers directly through the municipality. Although most communities do not offer this service, some communities have a program whereby a police officer in uniform and under the auspices of the police department is hired for security service. These officers are the best security guards available. However, the cost for this level of service can be two or three times the cost of a private guard service.

When security guards are needed, the property manager must decide whether they should be in a police-type uniform or blazer and slacks. If one of the security needs is to show a strong presence, a police-type uniform is preferred. If the building wants to project a low-profile security program, then blazer and slacks will be appropriate.

Security guards rarely need to be armed. Catching criminals is not the purpose of a security program, and in most situations the danger of arming security guards far outweighs any advantages. When an officer with a gun is needed, the police should be called. Obviously, if the guards are police officers, they will be armed.

Each security guard should submit a daily report. Even when nothing unusual appears to have happened, a daily report should be prepared by the guard and reviewed by the property manager. A sample daily security report is shown in Exhibit 10.2. Special reports for accidents, injuries, and property damage and thefts and burglaries are shown in Exhibits 10.3 and 10.4. These reports are also prepared by the security guard.

Security guards are an integral part of a building's security and risk reduction program, and they should be made to feel a part of the overall management team. One way to do this is by holding monthly meetings with the guards. The guards should be paid to attend these meetings, and refreshments should be provided. The manager uses the time to review the building's procedures, and the guards ask questions and offer suggestions. The police should be invited to attend some of these meetings.

EXHIBIT 10.2

Daily Security Report

DATE: _____

LOCATION: _____

DUTY OFFICER	ON DUTY Start	End	RECEIVING OFFICER

TIME	LOCATION	OCCURRENCES

Duty Officer (Signed) _____

Relieving Officer (Signed) _____

EXHIBIT 10.3

Accident/Injury/Property Damage Report

Building _____

Date of Occurrence _____ Time _____ A.M. _____ P.M.

Person Claiming Injury _____ Age _____

Residence _____ Phone _____

Business Address _____ Phone _____

Address or Location of Occurrence _____

Was Emergency First Aid Rendered? _____ If so, by whom? _____

Nature of Treatment _____

Ambulance or Physican Called? _____ If so, by whom? _____

Describe how Accident or Injury Occurred & Nature of Injury _____

_____

_____

_____

_____

_____

_____

Names & Addresses of Witnesses _____

_____

_____

_____

_____

Automobile Liability Insurance Information (In cases involving damage to TRF property)

Name of Insurance Co. or Agent _____

Address _____ Phone _____

Policy Number _____ Automobile License No. _____

Make & Model of Automobile _____

Driver's License No. _____

Person Claiming Injury (Signature if possible)	Reporting Officer (Print)
	Reporting Officer (Signature)

EXHIBIT 10.4

Theft/Burglary Report

BUILDING _____

DATE OF REPORT _____ TIME _____ am _____ pm _____

LOCATION _____

VICTIM _____ PHONE — HOME: _____ WORK: _____

HOME ADDRESS _____

EMPLOYER _____
                                    (Company Name & Address)

MISSING ITEMS & VALUE _____

_____

_____

TIME DISCOVERED _____ BY WHOM _____

METHOD OF ENTRY _____

FORCE USED _____

REMARKS _____

_____

_____

WAS VICTIM ADVISED TO NOTIFY POLICE   YES   NO   (Circle)

POLICE NOTIFIED   YES   NO   BY WHOM _____ TIME _____

TIME POLICE ARRIVED _____

POLICE REPORT MADE   YES   NO

_____

OFFICER TAKING REPORT (Print)   REPORTING PARTY

SHIFT & ASSIGNMENT   ADDRESS

OFFICER'S SIGNATURE   TELEPHONE

§ 10.7   EMERGENCY PROCEDURES HANDBOOK

The property manager must tailor an emergency procedures handbook for the tenants to the specific requirements of the building. An emergency procedures handbook for a high-rise will be more complex than one for a neighborhood shopping center or multitenant industrial park. Evacuation is a major concern in a multitenant building while it is usually a relatively smooth process in a one-story building.

The handbook informs the tenant of managements role in an emergency how the tenant should respond to different situations, that is, fire, bomb threat, earthquake, etc, and it provides emergency phone numbers.

The emergency procedures handbook can be part of the building's tenant information kit or booklet, or it can be a separate publication. Tenants should be encouraged to keep this booklet in a convenient place known to all of its employees and to require employees to review the booklet regularly.

§ 10.8   BOMB THREATS

The bomb threat is one of the more terrifying emergencies that can confront a building's staff and tenants. A caller reporting a bomb in a building is attempting to (1) warn the occupants of an explosive placed in the building; (2) create an atmosphere of fear and panic; (3) disrupt normal activities.

Seldom is a bomb threat real, yet every threat must be taken as a potential explosion. The property manager must assess the situation and determine whether or not the building should be evacuated. A hasty overresponse may result in greater hazard through panic than the potential danger from a blast. Evacuation for every bomb threat may encourage a deranged person to call in a bomb threat daily to a building. Such a situation will be disruptive to the tenants' business, and constant evacuation will not be taken seriously by the employees.

The property manager and staff need to plan for the potential of a bomb threat. Part of the planning should include police presentations on bomb threats. The building's staff and a representative of each tenant should attend these sessions.

When a bomb threat is received, the police are immediately called. In most municipalities, the police will decide whether or not to evacuate only when the bomb or an object that appears to be a bomb is found. Until the police take charge, the property manager is responsible and, using the information available, will have to make the most prudent decision on whether or not to evacuate.

Bomb threats are usually received over the phone, with the call placed to the building's management office or to a tenant. The building's staff or the tenant should be prepared to gather as much information as possible from and about the caller. It is important to remain calm. The recipient of the call should have a checklist to record data for the building's manager and the police.

After the bomb threat is received, a search is conducted. Common areas are assigned to the building's staff. If a tenant received the call, the property manager joins the tenant's representative in searching the suite. The common areas to search include the ground around the exterior of the building, the lobby, stairwells, restrooms, halls, and any other areas accessible to visitors or tenants.

In a high-rise office building or a regional mall, areas of the building are assigned to different members of the management and maintenance staff. The search starts at either the top or bottom of the building and works its way up or down systematically from floor to floor. All personnel should be instructed that if a suspicious device or box is found, it must not be touched or disturbed.

While the building's common areas are being inspected, the property manager inspects the targeted tenant's premises with a tenant representative who will be able to spot any item that does not belong in the suite. During the search, a staff person or security guard is assigned to prevent anyone from entering the building.

Whether to evacuate a building when a bomb threat is received is one of the most difficult decisions the property manager will face. A one- or two-story office building, an industrial park, or a nonenclosed shopping center can be evacuated with less risk of injury than can a multistory building or an enclosed mall. In some high-rise buildings with thousands of employees, it is often more prudent not to evacuate the entire building.

If a bomb is found, the police will take charge of the building. The entire building can be evacuated, or one or two floors above and below the planted bomb, or just the floor where the bomb is planted. A first aid team may be summoned to the building. Utility services such as gas may need to be shut off in the area where the bomb is located or in the entire building. The building's maintenance staff and the elevator and HVAC contractors should be notified.

The decision must be weighed against the possibility that the threat is a nuisance call that could become a daily occurrence. Other factors to consider include the information provided by the caller, the building owner's policy, and the location and height of the building.

§ 10.9 EARTHQUAKES

Earthquakes can occur not only in California but anywhere in the Western Hemisphere. "During an earthquake, the 'solid' earth moves like the deck of a ship. The actual movement of the ground, however, is seldom the direct cause of death or injury. Most casualties result from falling objects and debris because the shocks can shake, damage, or demolish buildings. Earthquakes may also trigger landslides, cause fires, and generate high ocean waves called tsunamis."[3] Injuries or deaths may be caused by falling objects such as roof parapets, brick from the exterior of buildings, flying glass, overturned furniture, and fallen power lines. Aftershocks are usually smaller than the initial quake, but they may be of sufficient magnitude to cause additional damage.

The property manager needs to inspect the building for objects that may fall or break off during an earthquake. Secure decorative features, repair cracks in the building, and secure any object that is suspended by a chain or rope. Tenants should be informed of potential dangers caused by falling items in their premises. Top-heavy shelves or filing cabinets, light fixtures, and hanging plants should be secured.

During an earthquake, people should remain in the building, move away from the windows, and seek cover under a desk or in a doorway. The elevator should not be used because power may be lost. If outdoors, people should move away from buildings and utility lines.

After an earthquake, the property manager should check for injuries, broken utility lines, and damage to the building. If no injuries or damage occurred, the property manager should still visit all tenants to reassure them that everything is under control.

§ 10.10   FIRES

A fire plan is included in every building's emergency procedures. There are six parts to a fire plan: "developing a fire disaster plan, appointing a 'fire marshall,' forming a fire brigade, providing fire safety education and training, staging periodic fire drills and emergency evacuations, and working with local or state fire officials on all aspects of fire safety."[4]

The fire plan starts with walking the building with a representative from the fire department. Next, the building staff and tenants need to be instructed on fire safety in a commercial building. The fire department spokesperson will conduct educational sessions for a building's tenants and staff upon request. Topics will include how to evacuate the building during a fire, where the fire pull stations are located, what fire equipment is required in each suite, and how to use the equipment. Floor wardens will receive additional training.

[3] Federal Emergency Management Agency, *Safety Tips for Earthquakes* (1983).

[4] Morgan, "Fire Safety: What Owners and Managers Can Do, *Mgmt. Insights* (Summer 1978).

§ 10.11   ELEVATORS

Most people feel totally helpless when they are trapped in an elevator. Whether a person is claustrophobic or not, being trapped in an elevator is a frightening experience. The building's emergency procedures should address this situation.

The elevator cab should contain a direct-dial telephone connected to an answering service, the elevator service company, or a twenty-four-hour monitored security station. A button that rings an outside alarm may not be heard in the evenings or on weekends. A telephone allows the representative of the building management to keep in constant communication to assure the people in the elevator that they are safe and that help is on the way.

It is critical that the building's staff not exceed its knowledge and abilities in attempting to assist someone in a jammed elevator. A sudden movement of the elevator during such an attempt can cause serious injury or death. Unless lives are in immediate danger, passengers should not be removed from the elevator by anyone other than the elevator service company or fire department.

§ 10.12   EVACUATION

There are many reasons to evacuate a building, including fire, bomb threats, explosions, power outages, or a major storm. Each building is unique in its design, location, construction, floor layout, number of occupants, tenant mix, and visitors or customers. Each of these variables presents unique problems in evacuating a building. Some buildings, such as a one- or two-story office building, an industrial building, or a nonenclosed shopping center, present fewer potential problems in evacuation than a multistory office building or an enclosed mall filled with shoppers.

The property manager should request the assistance of the fire department in developing an evacuation plan. If the building is a large mall or a multistory office building, tenants should be asked to volunteer to be floor wardens or floor monitors. There should be a floor warden on each floor or in each area of the mall. These volunteers are trained to conduct an orderly evacuation of their floor. They, or someone else on their floor, may be assigned the responsibility to assist the elderly or handicapped on their floor.

A list of people who may need assistance in an evacuation should be kept by the building management staff, and floor wardens should have a similar list for the employees on their floor or in their area. This list should be given to the police or fire department when they arrive on the scene. The property manager and the fire department need to plan how they will evacuate handicapped people.

Next, the property manager must develop a plan to communicate the message to evacuate to the tenants in the office building or the stores in the mall. In an office building, the message can be broadcast by the security guards over the building's emergency paging system or communicated by maintenance and administrative personnel personally visiting or calling each tenant.

The mall can be evacuated by making an announcement over the public address system, by guards requesting people to move outside the building, and by contacting each store individually. A three-call system can be used in any building. The building management calls three tenants, each one calls another three, and so on until everyone receives the message.

Several options are available when evacuating a building. The entire building can be evacuated. When this occurs, people can be evacuated through the lobby entrance, from the top of the building or, in some cases, by both means. In some high-rise buildings, the people above the floor of the fire may be instructed to go to the roof for an aerial evacuation.

A partial evacuation may be the most prudent plan. For instance, if a bomb is found on the third floor, the police may advise evacuating the employees on the first three floors to outside the building and the people on floors four through six to the seventh and eighth floors. When evacuating to the outside, waiting areas should be designated to avoid confusion. In almost all situations during an evacuation, the elevator will be returned to the ground floor and not used.

Certain stairwells may be assigned for evacuation. If only one stairwell is pressurized, that may be the assigned stairwell to use. In another situation, one stairwell may be assigned to the fire department for access to a fire, while the employees use an alternative stairwell. Alternate floors may be assigned different stairwells to allow a safe and easy evacuation.

During an evacuation, employees might go directly to their cars, creating a traffic jam and impeding access by the police, fire, or medical personnel. A traffic control plan must be part of the overall evacuation plan.

After an evacuation plan is developed the property manager should conduct practice evacuations on multistory buildings. The fire department should be requested to attend each practice, and the format of each should vary. For example, the first practice evacuation might be floor by floor and with advance notice. Before each floor is evacuated, the property manager and fire department representative should explain the dos and don'ts of evacuation and walk the employees through the evacuation. The next evacuation can be of the entire building at once without advance notice. The fire department should conduct a short evaluation following each practice. The evacuation plan should be reviewed often and practice evacuations conducted regularly.

§ 10.13   RESTORATION AFTER THE EMERGENCY

A restoration plan should be an integral part of the emergency procedures. After an emergency, the building needs to be back in operation and the tenants back in business as soon as safety will allow. A responsive restoration program will also minimize any loss of the building's reputation in the community. The property manager, a consultant, or the fire department must determine when it will be safe to reenter the building and start the restoration. Restoration can be cleanup, cosmetic improvements, structural repairs, or rebuilding. A restoration program will reduce the possibility of further damage to the building and reduce the time tenants' businesses are closed.

Items that need special attention in the restoration program include restoring utility service to the building, checking for safety hazards, and inspecting the roof and roof drains. Several contractors specializing in restoration should be interviewed and listed in the project data book. Each one should be questioned for area of expertise, size of restoration that can be handled, size of contractor's staff, equipment owned or accessible, licenses held, and insurance coverage.

If the tenants' premises are vulnerable to theft, a security guard or guards should be hired immediately. No one should be allowed into the building without proper identification, and restricted areas should be clearly defined.

§ 10.14   ON-SITE EQUIPMENT

The property manager should evaluate what equipment should be on site in case of an emergency. Not every building has the same requirements for on-site equipment. A neighborhood center would not need the extensive equipment that a high-rise office building would need. The on-site equipment selected by the property manager will be determined by the type of building, the possibility of occupants being stranded in the building, the method of evacuation, and the potential natural disasters in the area. Hand tools, especially pipe and crescent wrenches for turning off gas and water mains, and a crow bar are essential. Other equipment to consider are: ladders, flashlight with spare batteries, bullhorn, CB radio with spare batteries, water, food, rope, tape, stretcher, cots and blankets, clipboards, pens and paper, pumps, wet/dry vacuum, hard hats, marked vests, plywood, first aid kits, and the project data book.

A list of special equipment such as large pumps and generators and where they can be rented or borrowed should be kept on site and in the emergency procedures handbook.

§ 10.15   PUBLIC RELATIONS

Most emergencies will be reported by the press. The property manager needs to develop an emergency public relations program. This program is designed to provide accurate and timely information to the press, to the tenants, and to the community.

"Emergency public relations is that portion of overall crisis and disaster planning that ensures that verbal and nonverbal communications carried out during the life of an incident aid rather than hinder relief, recovery and rehabilitation. . . . Emergency public relations concerns the second reality in any emergency—that is, what people think has happened, what people perceive."[5]

The first step in developing the public relations program is to appoint a spokesperson or public relations agency to speak with the media. No one other than the assigned spokesperson should be authorized to provide information on the emergency or the building. All of the employees of the property management firm and all of the building's contractors, especially on-site security guards, maintenance, and janitorial personnel, must be told that they are forbidden to discuss the incident with anyone. The information they provide could be incomplete, inaccurate, or sensitive and could hinder a police or fire department investigation, initiate a law suit, or present the building in an unfavorable light.

Since it is rare for most people to be approached by the media for their opinions, the temptation to answer a reporter's question can be overwhelming. The company's policy must be continually reinforced with all employees and contractors.

If the property manager or another representative of the firm is the designated spokesperson, that person should receive training in handling the media. If no one in the firm is qualified to be the designated spokesperson, a public relations firm, experienced in crisis public relations, can be assigned this responsibility. A public relations firm can also be hired to assist in developing contingent public relations plans for different types of emergencies.

Next, the property manager and the owner need to discuss the manager's role in releasing information. For example, if the emergency, cleanup, or restoration extends over several days, will the property owner approve all media releases?

[5] Bernstein, Alan B., *The Emergency Public Relations Manual*, p. 13 (1986).

A plan for releasing the information must be developed. The police or fire department may establish a command post or insist that only their representatives talk to the media. Such a situation is likely if a hostage is held in a building or if an arson or assault investigation is under way. If the property manager or public relations firm is disseminating the information, it is best to provide accurate information as soon as possible.

If all the information is not available, the message should be, "We don't have all the information to comment on that question, but we are investigating and will release the information as soon as possible."

The spokesperson should cooperate with the media and with all police or fire department investigations. A story will be written or broadcast on the emergency whether or not the spokesperson is cooperative. Information unnecessarily concealed will prompt future media investigation and lead to distrust by the media and the community. When information is released, the positive action should also be included in the release. Phrases such as "quick response by the fire department" or "professionally handled by the police" develop trust in the action taken.

Tenants need to be informed after a crisis. One or several spokespersons should contact the tenants as soon as possible to explain what happened and what action the building manager is taking. If an earthquake occurs that causes no damage, the building's manager should visit with each tenant and explain that. If the emergency damaged the building or required the closing of the building, the tenants should be informed of the action taken by building management and, if known, when the building will be ready for occupancy. If tenants must retrieve materials from their suites or stores, the property manager should have them escorted into the building when it is safe.

§ 10.16 REPORTING AND DOCUMENTATION

After an emergency, it may be necessary to prepare several reports. These reports must be filed with the appropriate agencies and also kept in the management company's office.

If damage occurred to the building, an accurate account of the expenditures is necessary to receive the proper reimbursement on the insurance claim. The property manager and controller must develop a separate account where all expenditures can be charged. The property management, operations, and accounting staff need to be aware of the special account and code all invoices for the emergency to this account.

All employees should keep track of the time, especially overtime, that they spend on the emergency. The property's insurance agent should be requested to instruct the manager on which expenses are reimbursable by the insurance carrier. When in doubt, an expense should be charged to the emergency, and the insurance carrier will decide if it is a reimbursable expense.

The insurance carrier may require a narrative report on the incident. The property manager may instruct all persons involved in the emergency to write a report on their actions during the emergency. The company's attorney may advise on the type and extent of these reports. All written reports should be submitted to the manager for compilation.

Depending on the extent of the damage, the property manager, the building's maintenance superintendent or chief engineer, or even an outside consultant will need to assess the damage. Formats for all reports should be determined when the emergency procedures are developed.

§ 10.17   REFERENCE MATERIALS

There is a wealth of information available on emergency procedures. In 1989, the Institute of Real Estate Management (IREM) formed an emergency procedures committee that has formulated general guidelines for emergencies in commercial and residential properties, written articles in the *Journal of Property Management,* and developed a video and manual for sale to the public. The task force also presents a two-hour seminar on emergency procedures at IREM's annual conventions and has developed two one-day seminars for presentation by its chapters.

Almost every real estate periodical has presented articles on emergency procedures. The *Journal of Property Management* has published the majority of articles that directly or indirectly address emergency procedures.

BOMA publishes an annual *Office Building Fire Survey.* Most police and fire departments have available information on bomb threats, assaults, crimes, and fire. The federal government and many states have published booklets on several different types of emergencies and disasters.

The following is a sampling of publications on emergency procedures that will assist in developing a building's emergency handbook:

Bernstein, Alan B. *The Emergency Public Relations Manual.* Highland Park, NJ: Pase Inc., 1986.

Broder, James F. *Security Manager's Desk Reference.* Boston: Butterworth Publishers, 1984.

Coping with Children's Reactions to Earthquakes and Other Disasters, San Fernando Valley Child Guidance Clinic, 9650 Zelzah Ave., Northridge, Ca. 91325; 1983.

Department of Defense. *In Time of Emergency: A Citizens Handbook on Nuclear Attack and National Disasters.* Washington, DC: Department of Defense, Office of Civil Defense, 1968.

Emergency Broadcast System, Federal Emergency Management Agency, Washington DC 20472, 1984, (202) 287-0050.

Emergency Management Information Center: National Emergency Training Center, 16825 South Seton Ave, Emmitsburg, MD 21727, 1988, 1-800-638-1821.

Emergency Preparations Checklist, Federal Emergency Management Agency, P.O. Box 70274, Washington DC 20024, 1987.

Federal Emergency Management Agency. *Earthquakes: Safety Tips for Earthquakes.* Washington, DC: FEMA, July 1983.

────── *Reducing the Risks of Non-structural Earthquake Damage: A Practical Guide.* Washington, DC: FEMA, June 1985.

United Technology, Otis. *How to Operate Elevators Under Emergency Conditions.* Farmington, CT.

Post, Richard S., and David A. Schachtseik. *Security Managers Desk Reference.* Boston: Butterworth Publishers, 1986.

Security Officers Handbook. San Francisco: ABM Security Services, n.d.

Shopping Center Security. New York: International Council of Shopping Centers, 1976.

Teenage Behavior in Shopping Centers. New York: International Council of Shopping Centers, 1976.

Tsunami: The Great Waves in Alaska. Juneau: State of Alaska, Division of Emergency Services, 1983.

Life safety and security associations are another source of information on emergency procedures.

American Fire Sprinkler Association
1957 Whitney Avenue, No. 200
Hamden, CT 06517   (203)248-2367

Fire Equipment Manufacturers Association
1230 Keith Boulevard
Cleveland, OH 44115   (216)241-7333

The Foundation for Fire Safety
1700 N. Moore Street, No. 1508
Rosslyn, VA 22209   (804)276-9222

National Automatic Sprinkler and Fire Control Association
PO Box 1000
Patterson, NY 12563   (914)241-2400

National Fire Protection Association
Batterymarch Park
Quincy, MA 92269   (617)328-9290

Security Equipment Industry Association
2665 - 30th Street
Santa Monica, CA 90405

Society of Fire Protection Engineers
6060 Batterymarch Street
Boston, MA 02110   (617)482-0686

§ 10.18 CONCLUSION

Commercial buildings are a relatively safe environment. Most people feel safe shopping at a mall or working in a high-rise. BOMA's 1987 fire survey found that 96% of the office buildings it surveyed experienced no fires in 1986, and only one fire death was reported.

Even with this excellent record, the property manager must be prepared to respond to expected and unexpected emergencies. Each building, regardless of its size and location, should have an emergency procedures plan that provides a frame of reference for responding to a particular emergency.

Eleven

Reports
to Owners

§ 11.1 INTRODUCTION

One frequent criticism of property managers, and one that is often justified, is that they don't communicate effectively with the property owners. While the manager is working long hours, the property owner is sometimes wondering what the manager is doing for the fee being paid. Once the owner starts to question the value of the manager's service, the account is in jeopardy. When this situation occurs, it is usually the manager's fault for not communicating effectively with the owner.

The primary reason to communicate with the property owner is to keep him or her aware of the ongoing activities of the property, especially potential problems. Property owners do not like surprises, especially those that require cash. When the management company provides a comprehensive reporting program, the owner is able to make informed and timely decisions. Potential problems can be investigated, and a strategy can be developed to handle them. In addition, the owner is fully cognizant of the time and effort the property manager is devoting to the property. The expertise and accomplishments of the property manager are recognized.

Property management firms need a standardized reporting program that incorporates narrative and account reports and meetings with the owner. However, the manager must know how to modify the reports to meet the client's particular needs. Asset managers, who are often in another state, usually visit properties quarterly, and reports must be designed to take these visits into account. Many owners—especially institutional owners, who are now the major purchasers of medium to large commercial properties—require that the management firm adapt to its reporting requirements. The management company's annual management plan and the monthly management reports may need to be modified to meet the internal evaluation of the institutional owner.

In the 1980s, institutions, insurance companies, and pension funds became the major purchasers of medium to large commercial properties. This trend will continue into the 1990s. Those commercial property management firms that cannot meet the needs of the institutional owner and its advisors will have limited management opportunities. The manager needs to assess the owner's main concern or "hot button" and be responsive to the owner's needs in all written and verbal communication.

When the client uses the management company's standard reporting program, it is essential that the manager be aware of the owner's greatest concerns. These vary, depending on the client's goals, the status of the property, and the economic climate and market conditions of the area. Special emphasis, even top priority, should be given to these concerns.

If the property is experiencing financial difficulties, every income and expense component will be of interest to the property owner. In this situation, the manager would not only address each income and expense variance but would monitor the anticipated income and expenses for the remainder of the budgeted period. If the owner had a background in marketing and leasing, or the property had a high vacancy factor, special attention would be given in this area. The property owner would expect a thorough monthly analysis of the market, movement of tenants within the market, major tenants entering the market, and proposed buildings.

§ 11.2 TYPES OF REPORTS

The management firm must develop a program of reporting to the owner. There are two types of reports: written reports and presentations at formal or informal meetings.

The written reports start with the annual management plan and are followed up with monthly management reports. Special reports may be needed throughout the year to address specific issues. For instance, during a building's lease-up, the property owner may request semimonthly leasing status reports.

Meetings with the property owner usually occur quarterly. These meetings provide a unique opportunity for the property manager to develop a working rapport with the owner. The property manager can be vulnerable at these meetings if he or she is not fully aware of what is happening with the property.

(a) ANNUAL MANAGEMENT PLAN

The Institute of Real Estate Management defines the management plan as a documentation of the manner in which a property is to be run from the physical, fiscal, and operational standpoint.[1] When the property management company is awarded a management account, the property manager and the director of property management should meet with the property owner to review the ownership's needs and to develop the property's short- and long-range goals. Based on these goals, the property manager develops the management plan, which is updated annually.

The annual management plan analyzes the economic conditions of the region and of the property's neighborhood. It also discusses the short- and long-term impact of economic conditions on the property. It presents a thorough physical analysis of the property and establishes goals and objectives for the budgeted period. A thorough income and expense projection is developed providing a monthly net operating income (NOI) projection. A market and leasing strategy is prepared, and leasing projections are established. The management plan should also include a market survey (discussed in Chapter 7).

The operational plan for the property includes maintenance management, security, and emergency procedures. If the property is a shopping center, the annual calendar of promotions, merchandising events, and advertising is presented.

The performance of all retail tenants is analyzed. Their sales are compared with similar uses in the property and with national averages. Any tenant who may expand, not renew, or move out prior to the expiration of its lease is discussed. Remodeling, major maintenance, and tenant construction are reviewed with estimated costs and construction timing. Supportive information such as articles on the economy and market conditions; prospectuses of new developments; photos or videos of the property and the competition; and especially descriptions of proposed major maintenance or renovation work is also useful to the property owner.

The annual management plan includes all the financial reports that will be reviewed in the monthly management reports.

When the property owner or asset manager reads the annual management plan, he or she thoroughly understands the property and what the property can be expected to achieve. The property manager and the property owner or asset manager then have a collaborative interest in the property's management. This is the first step in developing a working relationship.

---

[1] James C. Downs, *Principles of Real Estate Management* (12th ed. 1980).

(b) MONTHLY MANAGEMENT REPORT

Progress on the goals and objectives stated in the annual management plan must be monitored, and the status of the property must be reported to the owner. This information can be communicated most effectively through the monthly management report, which consists of a narrative and financial reports.

The narrative section is a brief review of eight basic topics that give the owner a summary of the property's activities for the preceding month. This report is also used to discuss potential problems and to monitor the property's short- and long-term goals and objectives. The narrative will usually range from three to twelve pages, depending on the size and activities of the property.

Financial Analysis

The first section of the narrative reviews the financial reports. Every owner considers the financial progress of the property a top priority. This section reviews the actual income and expense compared with the budgeted income and expense for the month and year to date.

Significant variance in any income component, including base rent, percentage rent, and tenant charges, is discussed. Each operating budget, such as the owner's nonreimbursable, escalation, or common area maintenance budget, is reviewed, and any expense item that is significantly over or under budget is explained. A significant variance can be either a percentage or a dollar amount.

If the income or expenses are on budget but a future variance is anticipated, this should also be reviewed. Property owners want as much lead time as possible to address major financial variances. The budget variance report is one part of the accounting section of the monthly management report.

Operations and Maintenance

The operations section reviews maintenance problems, anticipated maintenance problems, changing contractors, personnel changes, and other operational issues. Daily operational activities are not discussed, but the property's general operations and certain specific concerns are addressed. Photos of maintenance problems or corrective maintenance help the property owner to understand the narrative. The inspection forms (see Chapter 9) are also included in the report.

Litigation Report

The litigation section keeps the property owner aware of any legal action taken by the property manager on behalf of the owner. This is usually legal action for tenant's default, which is almost always due to nonpayment of rent. Any suits filed against the property are also reviewed. These are usually slip and fall cases. Occasionally a tenant may sue the landlord.

Each case should be summarized, and the attorney's fees paid to date and anticipated fees to resolve the suit should be included in the report. This information is necessary for the owner to determine whether it would be prudent to drop the case, to settle, or to continue the legal action.

Tenants' Sales Analysis

If the property is a shopping center or other commercial property with retail tenants, a sales analysis section reviews the sales performance of the tenants (see Exhibit 11.1). Each merchant's sales for the month are compared with the same month the previous year, and the year-to-date sales are compared with the same period of the prior year. Since community and regional malls have multiple tenants in each category, the categories, (for example, restaurants or gift shops) are compared for the same two periods. Special attention is given to those categories with significant increases or decreases, with explanation for the variance.

The sales analysis provides a wealth of information and has several applications. Declining sales or consistently low sales are the first sign of a potential tenant failure. This is a clue for the property manager to investigate the viability of the tenant and possibly start marketing its space. The sales analysis is used to determine if a tenant should be offered a lease renewal. This information also indicates strengths and weaknesses in the tenant mix of the property. This information is used in developing the leasing plan and determining which uses can be marketed to potential tenants.

Delinquencies

The delinquencies or arrearage section includes a brief statement about each tenant in arrears, the amount of each tenant's arrearage, and the action the property manager is taking or the tenant's payment plan. Property owners scrutinize this section closely.

Promotions and Advertising

If the property is a shopping center, a section on promotions and advertising reviews each promotional and merchandising event along with the media advertising of the merchants' association or marketing fund/promotional fund. The impact that these events had on the center's traffic

EXHIBIT 11.1

Tenant Sales Analysis

CENTER: _____

MONTH, YEAR _____

MONTH: _____

MERCHANT	AREA	MONTHLY SALES COMPARISON					YEAR-TO-DATE COMPARISON					BREAK-POINT	OVERAGE POTENTIAL EVALUATION					
		MONTH ___ 19 ___	MONTH ___ 19 ___	% CHANGE	$/S.F.	$/S.F.	CURRENT YEAR	PREVIOUS YEAR	% CHANGE	$/S.F.	$/S.F.		CURRENT MONTH			YEAR-TO-DATE		
													SALES	SALES	% CHANGE	SALES	SALES	% CHANGE
Remaining merchants report yearly.																		

and sales is reviewed. Specific remarks from the merchants are helpful. Copies of the print ads and photos of the events give the owner visual evidence of specific activities.

All advertising and promotional activities that are part of the marketing and leasing program are reviewed in this section of the report. For instance, clippings from the local newspapers on businesses that have moved into the property are included with this report. If the property manager held an open house for the tenants, this would be mentioned and an announcement flier along with photos of the event would be included in this report.

Construction

If the property is being remodeled or expanded, a construction or remodeling section discusses the progress of the work along with the cost to date and anticipated final cost compared with the budget. This section includes any tenant-improvement construction in progress. The progress of each space's construction activity and the expected completed cost are also reviewed.

Leasing Report

The leasing section is one of the most important and frequently read sections of the monthly report. It starts with a short summary of the market conditions followed by a listing of likely prospects who are negotiating for space in the building, their use, and square footage. Spaces under construction also can be listed if a construction section isn't included.

The section ends with a list of vacant spaces, their square footage, and the deal-making monthly and annual rents for the vacancies, plus a list of prospective tenants for each vacancy and the percentage probability of finalizing a lease with each prospect. This section also discusses which tenants' leases are expiring within the next twelve months and the strategy to either renew or replace the tenant. A list of tenants who have options that can be exercised within the next twelve months, and a statement of whether they will exercise their option are included.

Additional Information

The maintenance inspection report along with copies of articles pertinent to the leasing market, and the economy of the area, are included at the end of the narrative section. This information provides a broad picture of the area.

Accounting Reports

The narrative sections are followed by the financial reports. These may include:

1. Balance Sheet. This is a statement of financial condition at a given date, usually the last day of each month.

2. Income Statement. This is a statement of all income, expenses, and profit or loss for the month and year to date.

3. Budget vs. Actual. This report compares actual income and expense with the budgeted income and expense for the month and year to date. Dollar and percentage variances are provided for each line item.

4. Expenditure Journal. A list by account number of each bill paid, expense incurred or paid, a brief description of the services, and the vendor.

5. Open Accounts Receivable (Delinquency Report). This is also referred to as the arrearage report or A/R aged summary. Each delinquent tenant is listed along with the amount of arrearage for each income category.

6. Open Accounts Payable. This report lists invoices that have not been paid but have been incurred. Information includes vendor, invoice number, description, invoice date, invoice amount, and the general ledger account distributions of the invoice.

7. Future Rent Analysis. This report lists each tenant's space number, name, square footage, and the commencement and expiration date of each tenant's lease. It lists the base rent for each tenant for the month of the report. It also indicates any rent step-ups and future annual rents for a given period such as five years. Vacant spaces are listed and the lost rent due to vacancies is calculated.

8. Deferred Conditions. This report shows on a monthly basis, for the next twelve months or longer, any changes to the tenant's lease such as rent step-ups, consumer price index adjustments, lease expirations, and option dates.

9. Rent Roll. This report lists each tenant along with its space number, square footage, commencement and expiration date of the lease, rent and tenant charges, and miscellaneous information. The report may be integrated into the future rent analysis.

10. Tenant's Sales Analysis. An analysis of each tenant's sales for the current month and year to date compared with the same periods the previous year. This report groups tenants by category and analyzes each category in the same number.

11. Miscellaneous. Other reports as required by state real estate law. These may include itemization of cash transactions for the month and security deposit schedule.

§ 11.3   MEETINGS WITH THE OWNER

The most effective means of communication is to meet with the property owner. Absentee asset managers usually visit the properties quarterly or semiannually.

If the owner is local and the property is in a lease-up situation or has leasing problems, the property manager should meet monthly to review the leasing progress. If there are other important activities, such as major remodeling, the manager should meet frequently with the owner. At a minimum, the manager should meet at least quarterly with a local owner to review the status of the property.

A premeeting with the property manager, staff, and director of property management should be held two or three days before the meeting with the owner. At this meeting, the property manager should thoroughly review the financial, leasing, and operational status of the property. The property manager and his or her supervisor should role play questions the owner might ask. A thorough inspection of the property should be made immediately preceding the premeeting. A follow-up inspection the day before the owner arrives will prevent any last-minute maintenance problems or embarrassment such as graffiti when walking the property with the owner.

At the end of the premeeting, the property manager should develop an agenda for the meeting with the owner. The meeting should be attended by the manager, the leasing agent, the management firm's controller, and the director of property management. The property manager should have available the annual management plan, the most current monthly management report, lease summaries, maintenance contract summaries, plot plat or floor plans indicating vacancies, and any other information that might be discussed.

Most owners and asset managers find frequent phone calls from the property manager helpful in keeping current with the status of the property. The property manager should never believe that phone calls are an intrusion on the owner's or asset manager's time. The manager should prepare for the phone meeting as he or she would for a face-to-face meeting.

All asset managers have regular reports to prepare, and most owners report to their investors. Direct communication enables the owner's representatives to fulfill their reporting responsibilities.

§ 11.4   COMMUNICATING AS A PUBLIC RELATIONS STRATEGY

A planned and effective communications program is one of the best means to promote the property management company to its clients. Property managers seldom receive compliments but are sure to hear from the owner when something goes wrong or leasing is slow. A communications program gives managers a chance to promote their expertise and the services of the management company. Regular communication helps the owner to develop an appreciation of what is involved in managing a commercial property and gives the manager a chance to develop a rapport with the owner. When the owner develops confidence in the property manager and his or her staff, the opportunity exists for additional business with the owner or business referrals.

§ 11.5   CONCLUSION

An extensive and thorough reporting program is the only way most property owners and asset managers can monitor the status of the property. These reports contain the information needed to make the critical decisions that impact the property's value. The reporting program also serves as an internal discipline that forces the manager to analyze the property annually and to review its status each month. The property manager should know more about the property than anyone else, even the owner. This fact will be evident to the owner through effective reporting.

Index